Coast to Coast,
# Howard Stern's
Outrageous #1 *New York Times* Bestseller Scores!
## <u>Private Parts</u>

"Forget *SeinLanguage*. Put down that copy of *The Bridges of Madison County*. Howard Stern's PRIVATE PARTS is the most entertaining read to come down the pike since you discovered your sister's diary in her underwear drawer."
> —Fred Shuster, *L.A. Daily News*

"Breasts, behinds, insults, and a lot of kvetching from the self-described sweetest radio personality on the planet. . . . PRIVATE PARTS catches the voice that . . . agitated the FCC . . . Stern socks it to currently protected species."
> —Walter Good___ ___ ___ ___ *York Times Book Review*

"Stunning in its ___ ___ ___ ___ is more engrossing and e___ ___ ___ ___ City-based radio sh___ ___ ___ ___ ___ ___ arily provocative writing___
> —Roberto Sa___ ___ ___ ___ *Dealer*

". . . [a] bull's-eye men's-room ___ ___ ___ that became the fastest-selling book in Simon a___ Schuster's 72-year history."
> —Rick Marin, *Rolling Stone*

"Howard Stern's PRIVATE PARTS is raucous, riotous and undeniably funny. Stern finds his voice in print, in all its smart-alecky, profane, funny candor."
> —Marshall Fine, Gannett Suburban Newspapers

"PRIVATE PARTS is sure to offend. . . . There is something refreshing about reading the words of someone who so joyfully delights in exercising free-speech rights."

— Larry Platt, *Philadelphia Inquirer*

"Think of Howard as the pure embodiment of irreverent, adolescent id. Only a complete stuffed shirt will find nothing in this book to laugh at. On the other hand, almost everyone will find something to be offended by. . . ."

— Fritz Lanham, *Houston Chronicle*

"The poet laureate of urban American white trash, Stern has written a book that reads like a direct transcript of his radio show. . . ."

— Joe Queenan, *People*

"For every jibe of Howard Stern's that makes me want to push him down a manhole, there's another that makes me shriek with laughter. . . . The text hurtles along. . . . very entertaining."

— Margo Jefferson, *The New York Times*

For information regarding special discounts for bulk purchases,
please contact Simon & Schuster Special Sales at
1-800-456-6798 or business@simonandschuster.com

# HOWARD STERN
## PRIVATE PARTS

**POCKET BOOKS**

New York   London   Toronto   Sydney   Tokyo   Singapore

POCKET BOOKS, a division of Simon & Schuster Inc.
1230 Avenue of the Americas, New York, NY 10020

ISBN: 0-671-00944-3

First Pocket Books printing October 1994

15  14  13  12  11  10  9  8  7

POCKET and colophon are registered trademarks of
Simon & Schuster Inc.

Designed by Bonni Leon

Printed in the U.S.A.

TO DR. JOHN SARNO,
for ridding me of back pain and
obsessive-compulsive disorder.


TO RAY AND BEN STERN,
the two most giving people on the planet.
I thank them for their love, guidance,
and understanding.


AND MOST OF ALL,
TO MY WIFE, ALISON,
who stuck with me
through thick and thin,
who never gave a shit about material things
or put any pressure on me,
who let me finger her on the first date,
and who loved me
before I had a radio show.

# ACKNOWLEDGMENTS

Writing a book just might be the hardest thing I've ever done, besides trying to get laid in college. I had no idea I could write a book when I signed on for this project, because quite honestly, I've only read about three books in my life. Anything longer than *MAD* magazine has always been a problem.

Most people assume that the author of this kind of celebrity book just hires a guy to write the book for him. I always assumed that as well, so I went right out and hired Larry "Ratso" Sloman.  Ratso's first job was to inform me that I'd have to write the book myself. I should have fired him for insubordination. Ratso was a great collaborator. He understands me and has that same sick, stupid, juvenile sense of humor. In other words, like me, he's a disaster as a human being. Ratso worked day and night focusing me on my best material. He didn't get laid once during the writing of this book and received only one blow job while sitting at his computer. When he called to tell me this sodomy story, I threw up. Ratso helped me find my "voice" on paper—whatever that means. He's a real brother and a good friend.

This book would not have happened without the guidance, wisdom, and beautiful pouty lips of my editor, Judith Regan. An editor's job is to push you, teach you, and to wear miniskirts with black mesh stockings, all of which Judith did so well. She's a wonderful mother and professional and I don't know how she does it all. She is quite simply brilliant. Judith put in ridiculously long hours, gave up many weekends while helping me out, and put a lot of faith in me as a writer, despite the fact that there wasn't a shred of evidence indicating I could write. She went way beyond the call of duty and her bosses at Simon & Schuster should worship her.

I must acknowledge my radio comrades Robin Quivers, Fred Norris, and Jackie "the Joke Man" Mar-tling. Robin, next to my family, is the most impor-tant person in my life. There is no one else who has lovelier jugs or the ability to draw out the best in me. She is the catalyst for all of my material. Jackie and Fred spend their day making me funny. All of the song parodies and endless one-liners come from these two great minds. They help me to be funny and are willing to stay behind the scenes while I get most of the attention. We all spend way too much time together.

Laura Lackner, my tireless executive administrative assistant (can you believe I have one of those?), enabled me to be creative while she did all the nuts-and-bolts hard work and organization. She gave up many nights and weekends overseeing the entire project and no one cared more about the outcome of this book than Laura. Special thanks to her son Bobby, the coolest fourteen-year-old in the country, and the ever-present Mike Gange, for all the hours he sacrificed, which cost him his relationship with the only woman he ever loved.

Don Buchwald, my agent and good friend, is the one person responsible for not only putting this book deal together with Judith Regan, but elevating my entire career beyond that of an asshole disc jockey. If it wasn't for him, I'd still be getting the shaft from creeps like the guys at WNBC. His guidance has enabled me to go where no radio guy has gone before. If anyone deserves the title Super-agent, it's Don Buchwald.

Also, I'd like to acknowledge the contributions of Mel Karmazin, the bravest broadcaster in the world, who has always believed in me.

Let me list a bunch of other folks who busted their balls for this book. All of these people worked very hard and I want them to know how much I appreciated their assistance:

Gary Dell'Abate: His memory of everything that ever happened on the show made researching a breeze.

Gary is my main dude.

Ralph Cirella: For making sure I look good. He put my look together for the cover and did all the celebrity impersonation makeup in the book.

Bonni Leon: Who designed the book and made this more than just some text with pictures thrown in the middle. She was devoted to me, worked well beyond the call of duty, and gave up many afternoons with her son.

John Gall and Paolo Pepe: Great paperback cover design.

Cathy Tobin: Who toiled late into the night, researching and transcribing.

Drew Friedman: For inspiring the back cover and for all the great illustrations.

Jonathan Basile: Personal trainer to the stars, who got me in shape for the cover.

Fran Shea and Lee Masters at E! Entertainment Television.

To all the photographers and illustrators who allowed me to reprint their material: Jack Adler, Paul Aresu, Jim Cabett, David Crout, Peter Faris, Bill Farley, Frank Jacobs III, Jeff Kravitz, Manny Newhouse, Kerry Rae, Ted Shell, Natalie Silverstein, David Sobel, Beryl Sokoloff, Harvey Wang, Tim White.

Archie comics, Rex Babin, Chris De Fazio, Danny deBruin, David Jacobson, *MAD* magazine, Charles McLaren, David Miller, Jack Ohman, R. P. Overmyer.

Special thanks to Barry Morgenstein, who chronicled my TV career so well and really knows how to take a picture.

Thanks also go to Ellen and Peter Dunn: I love you guys; Ronnie Mund, who is always there for me; Leslie West, my musical inspiration; Neil Drake, for everything; Dominic Barbara; Gabriela Schwartz; Captain Janks; and Dr. Matthew Kaufman of Great Neck, dentist to the stars.

Transcribers: Eugene Corey of Brave New Words, Carol Decon from Soho Wordpro, Kevin Renzulli, Linda and Steven Schwab; without their help I'd have nothing.

Interns: Chris Ailes, Tara Bernie, Leslie Boghosian, Richard Christensen, Michael Falk, Steve Grillo, Sandi Kirkman, Randi Klein, Dennis Lopez, Ted Ranieri, Eliana Salzhauer, Richard Virgilio, Russell Weston.

Cover girls: Tempest and Amy Lynn Baxter.

Models: Michele Bale, Cindy Lynn Bodner, Christina Bonnici, Lynn Bratti, Michele Brindley, Terri Colavtoni, Cherlynn Dooley, Priscilla Dorinas, Jeannie Evans, Heidi Fiatz, Kathleen Gibbons, Deborah Grommet, Denise Grommet, Lisa Havel, Kirsten Kappenberg, Alexis Khoury, Jessica Lisi, Andrea Lorah, Gwen Lucas, Theresa Lynn, Stacey Marra, Karen Martinez, J. J. North, Sandra Pandelios, Lisa Pittuis, Gina Rose, Laura Shapanus, Trish Stratten, Pina Tondo, Joan Torino, Michelle Tyrrell, Tricia Zocchi.

Michael Catino and the New Jersey Swimsuit Calendar Girls.

Chauncé Hayden, *Steppin' Out* magazine.

And finally, thanks to Greg Aull, Nina Castro, Tom Chiusano, Charles DeFranco, Dan Forman, Mark Garten, Steve Herzfeld, Bill Knaub, Jr., Jim Lackner, Jr., John Melendez, Charles H. Menut, Al Rosenberg, Scott Salem, Dee Snider, Billy West.

# CONTENTS

PRIVATE PARTS

# My Philosophy

## *Lesbians, Lesbians, Lesbians*

CHAPTER

1

**WHAT YOU ARE ABOUT TO READ
IS A TRUE STORY**

I was driving to work on the Long Island Expressway.

It was mid-morning. Not much traffic. I turned the radio on. About half an hour later, it happened. I put my hand on my pants. I couldn't believe it. I had to pull over.

I pulled over into the shade. Someone one or two car lengths behind me certainly could have seen what I was doing, that's for damn sure! It was the first time I had ever done anything like this before. But the show was making me nuts that morning. I was beating off to a radio call-in show! Here I was in my business suit. I didn't want to spill my love gunk all over my pants. What the hell could I come on? The only thing I could find was an old leather glove. I grabbed it. The girl was young, and she was being seduced by an older woman.

When she started talking about her 34D breasts and the fact that she was wearing no bra, that really got me turned on.

LISA: I'm a blonde. People tell me I look like Catherine Oxenberg. I have a really good body.

HOWARD STERN: How big are your breasts?

LISA: Thirty-six D, I think.

HOWARD: What do you mean, "I think"?

LISA: I never wear a bra, so I don't know how big I am. I think a D.

HOWARD: What about your waist?

LISA: Twenty-four.

HOWARD: Hips?

LISA: Thirty-six.

HOWARD: And you really dig lesbian sex?

LISA: Yes.

HOWARD: How old were you when you first had lesbian sex?

LISA: Eighteen.

HOWARD: Who with, a friend?

LISA: No, my mother's friend.

HOWARD: An older woman seduced you?!

LISA: Yes. She was thirty-two. I was very frightened when it happened but it ended up feeling good.

HOWARD: And you were fully developed at eighteen, were you not?

LISA: Well, yeah, I guess so.

HOWARD: Your breasts were a full D cup, your body had developed, you had hair on your body.

LISA: I sprouted out early.

HOWARD: Do you shave?

LISA: Yes, I do.

HOWARD: You groom very nicely?

LISA: Yes.

HOWARD: Yeah—close-cropped?

LISA: Yes, very close-cropped.

HOWARD: Are you blond, uh, all over?

LISA: Light brown.

HOWARD: Really. Excellent!

ROBIN: Well, now, let me ask you something. This friend of your mother's, what did she look like?

LISA: Really dark hair. She looks like Demi Moore. With long legs and big breasts and stuff. She was thin and tall. She had a beautiful face.

HOWARD: So your mom was real young when she had you?

LISA: Yeah.

HOWARD: So, how did you end up with your mom's friend?

LISA: She would always come into my room and watch me change.

HOWARD: Had she ever seen you nude growing up?

LISA: Yeah, yeah.

HOWARD: Had she seen you nude at eleven, twelve?

LISA: I would say so.

HOWARD: Had she seen you nude at fifteen?

LISA: Yeah.

HOWARD: Oh, man, I'm so turned on. I'm aching, that's how horny I am for you because you look like Catherine Oxenberg from "Dynasty." The long blond hair, the perfect body—perfect. And you've runway modeled. I'm offering you to the lesbian community today. Am I not the greatest friend of the lesbian community? Do lesbians adore Howard Stern? If any o' you friggin' homos say a bad thing about me again, I am going to complain to somebody in the gay organizations. So what were you wearing the day she came over? You were probably in your sleepwear, weren't you?

LISA: No, I was wearing a sundress.

HOWARD: Oh, my God—I love that! A sundress! God, I'd have fun with you as my girlfriend. You know what I'd do? I'd just put you in different outfits every five minutes. Dress you like a Barbie doll. So there you are, eighteen, you're in high school, your mom's friend comes over, and you're wearing a sundress, with a kind of a low-cut top, short skirt . . .

LISA: Yeah.

HOWARD: . . . and you're showing off your beautiful long legs, right? And you're wearing heels?

LISA: Yes.

HOWARD: I can't stand up right now. Do you believe that? Why don't you stand up, Jackie ["the Joke Man," one of my writers]? You big-bellied bastard.

JACKIE: I don't have a hard-on.

HOWARD: Yeah, I don't know what you have. You got a one-inch penis, that's why. You're probably aroused—no one can see it. All right, anyway—where were we? So why did your mom's friend come over?

LISA: She was in the clothing business, so she brought a big bag of leather clothes and stuff, and she had this blue leather outfit for me to try on.

HOWARD: So she said, "Hey, this is a great outfit. Do you wanna try it on?"

LISA: Yeah, and I said, "Great." So we went upstairs and . . .

Listening to her first lesbian experience was more arousing than I imagined.

I wanted to come while she was telling the story. I loved Howard's lesbian stories. At least five different guys told me that they jerked off to the show. Especially the lesbian stories.

The story was getting better and better. I stroked and manipulated my shaft, careful not to hit the steering wheel. Careful not to pump too hard. I wanted this to last. I wanted to milk it for all it was worth.

HOWARD: So you go upstairs, you're in your sundress, you go in the room together, and you say, "Hey, I'll try this on. No big deal to try it on in front of her." Now, here you are, with one of the best bodies I've ever seen, and all of a sudden you take off your sundress. Now, under your sundress, are you wearing a bra?

LISA: No.

HOWARD: Panties?

LISA: Yes.

HOWARD: Are they thong panties?

LISA: No, just little white panties.

HOWARD: Little white panties.

LISA: So she said, "Well, why don't you take your clothes off so we can try the dress on?" So I did—I unzipped my dress in the back, took it off, and put it on the bed. And I took my high heels off.

HOWARD: Mmm-hmm. So you're completely naked except for panties. And then what happened?

LISA: So I tried on the leather dress.

HOWARD: Was it very tight?

LISA: Very tight.

HOWARD: And skimpy?

LISA: It was really nice. And she zipped it up for me, and she looked at me, and she told me, "You look wonderful! You look great!"

HOWARD: And she's holding you when she tells you this?

LISA: No, she was standing behind me. We were looking in the mirror, and she was standing behind me, and looking at me. So I just said, "Thank you very much." And then I started walking toward the bed, to take the dress off, and she followed me, and she kinda like turned me around and sat me down on the bed.

HOWARD (low voice): Talk slow.

LISA: And then she . . . she held me.

HOWARD: She hugged you?

LISA: She put her arms—yeah.

HOWARD: And you said . . .

LISA: She put her arms around me, you know.

HOWARD: From behind you?

LISA: No, in front of me.

HOWARD: In front of you.

LISA: She sat me down so I was facing her, and she put her arms around me and my face was . . .

HOWARD: . . . close to her . . .

LISA: Chest.

HOWARD: Your face was on her chest?

LISA: Yeah.

HOWARD: She held you and hugged you against her chest.

LISA: Yeah. I was very nervous. I didn't know what to do.

HOWARD: Did she kiss you?

LISA: She started caressing me and touching my arms and all.

HOWARD: And it felt good.

LISA: And I started to get aroused.

HOWARD: You got excited.

LISA: Yeah, I did.

HOWARD: You didn't resist.

LISA: Absolutely not.

HOWARD: You didn't say, "Hey, what's going on here? This is very unusual." Nothing.

LISA: No, no. No, I was—

HOWARD: And what did she say?

LISA: There were no words spoken after that.

HOWARD: No words spoken?

LISA: No, no.

HOWARD: She started caressing you, and then she did everything to you.

LISA: Yeah.

ROBIN: Did you do anything to her?

Oh man! I was about to come but I held back. I was late for work but I didn't give a shit. I cranked the volume up and closed my eyes.

LISA: She instructed me for about an hour.

HOWARD: Oh, I can picture that. Oh, man! My head's exploding!

LISA: Then she leaned over and kissed my mouth while she gently cupped my breasts.

> My penis exploded like a volcano and my hot molten liquid poured into my leather glove, just as Howard said, "Oh, man! My head's exploding!" I threw the glove out the window to destroy the evidence and sped off to work. FUCKIN' HOWARD, RADIO GOD!

Can you believe this?

My producer, Gary Dell'Abate (alias Baba Booey), actually knows this guy. And he knows five other guys who beat off to my show! It's a fucking epidemic.

Now, when I think of my radio audience, I envision guys driving to work on the expressway, guys who need an opportunity to hear about lesbians.

**The Lesbian Dating Game from my TV show.**

**LESBIANS**

Lesbians bring home the ratings. Lesbian Howie-wood Squares (left) and below, Kirk (me) and Spock (Gary) visit the Planet Lesbos . . .

. . . a planet of wild Lesbians.

Lesbianism, let's face it, is a godsend. Every man in the world is totally fascinated by those sisters of Sappho. I know I am. To have two girls doing wild things to each other with me in the sack would be unbelievable. And since I never got to experience any of that because I got happily married so fucking young, I have to do it vicariously.

## EVERYONE LOVES GOOD LESBIAN STORIES

I had a caller named Jean tell us about her initiation, courtesy of her counselor at Girl Scout camp. Jean was a ripe fourteen at the time and her counselor was seventeen. They started by hanging out on rocks and having long talks.

"You mean you'd start talking about, 'Gee, what if other girls liked other girls?' " I asked.

"No, this was in the days of Donna Reed. We didn't even talk about sexuality per se. I didn't even have the word *lesbian* in my vocabulary," Jean said.

"I'm getting nervous with this story," I said. "I'm not hearing enough sex stuff."

"You're not giving me a chance!" Jean protested.

"It's a Friday! My audience isn't looking for Oprah," I prodded her. "What did your counselor look like? Was she cute?"

"Stunning," Jean said. "I only went for the good-looking ones. Absolutely gorgeous. She was five-ten, athletic."

"So she just all of a sudden starts kissing you?" I asked.

"I think I started kissing her first. Then we'd find opportunities to get in bed together. We slept in a tent and I had my bunk carefully positioned at the back of the tent, with the flap that faced the woods. She'd sneak out at night, slip up through the back flap, and climb into my bunk," Jean said.

"Were the other campers there?" I wondered.

"Yeah! The other five Girl Scouts were sleeping," Jean said.

"Wow!" I marveled.

"Yeah, and we'd fondle and pet and . . ."

"I'm *never* sending my kids to camp," I said.

"Years later, my mom said if she'd known that that's what I was going to camp for, she never would have sent me," Jean laughed.

"HEY ALISON, IF YOU'RE LISTENING, CHAIN THE KIDS TO THE BED," I warned my wife.

"It was like Club Med," Jean went on. "I had two counselors at one time the following year. I did it in a church with a counselor. There was a chapel out in the woods and we did it in the church on an overnight."

"LESBIANS—OH, I LOVE LESBIANS! I LOVE LESBIANS!" I ranted.

## WE'VE GOT THE KINKIEST LESBO STORIES, TOO

One woman called in who said she looked just like Cindy Crawford. She was five-nine, weighed 130, with a 38–26–38 Double-D body. She told me that when I have lesbian calls, she lies in bed and "takes care" of herself. But her best story was the story of her lesbo induction.

"I have a really, really best friend in the whole world, even hotter than me. She looks like the red-head on 'China Beach.' There was always an element of sexual tension between us. She was also very promiscuous in the days when promiscuity was safe. From time to time, before we'd go out, she'd get dressed and I'd see her breasts and everything, and I'd just try to hold it in. I would be dying, you know. She knew about my lifestyle, that I was into girls, and she used to tease me without trying. I think she wanted it, but she didn't know how to go about it either.

"She was always kinda hot for my brother. We lived on an island and our parents went away for the summer. So one night, I went down to the nightclub at Ocean Beach and I met a friend. We were just going to have some drinks . . ."

"What were you wearing that night?" I interrupted her monologue.

"I had on a Danskin that was like a tank top. No bra, hard nipples. Minishorts. So me and my friend walked back to my parents' boat and the boat was moving. I said, 'Hmm, somebody must be down there.' It was my brother and my girlfriend. And they were very nude. They were doing it. And I almost died. I wanted her. I turned around to the person I was with and said, 'Oh, you gotta go—my parents are on the boat!' He gave me a hard time but he left. So I went down in and I saw them and she was facing away from him, looking right at me. I just took the straps down off my Danskin and I pulled it down around my waist, and I was just standing there, topless, and she stuck her hand out like to come here."

"Oohh! And your brother's there!" I screamed.

"My brother didn't know what was going on. And I walked over and I started to—"

"Kiss her? Touch her?" I gasped.

"Kiss things," she laughed.

"Oh, man, my sister never got it on with anyone in front of me!"

"Howard, you've got to stop, I'm getting so horny," she said.

"You are?! You're a minx! And you grabbed her?" I guessed.

"I was very gentle. We got it on, but I didn't do anything with my brother. While she was doing stuff, I was doing her."

"This is the sickest, sick . . ." I feigned disgust.

"Oh, it is not! I wanted to make sure that she reached, because in that position you really can't."

She talked a bit more and then she hung up.

"Horny girl. In front of her brother. That's the sickest thing—sick animal. Perverts." I was delirious. "This country's doomed. Where am I? I'm not doing anything! I haven't gotten it in three months."

One of the hottest lesbian stories I ever heard came from the lips of a twenty-six-year-old listener who had just had her first experience the night before she called in. She was a successful businesswoman who was in sales. She said she had always thought about trying lesbianism but had never really done it. She claimed to be a very good-looking woman so I asked her if a lot of women came on to her.

"No, I've never had another woman come on to me," she said.

"Do you dress provocatively at work?" I asked her.

"No. I wear very nice business suits."

"Underneath your business suit, do you sometimes wear—"

"A camisole," she said. "Very lacy, silky, satin."

"And do you wear panties with those garters?" I asked.

"No, but I wear the thigh-high pantyhose with just elastic and lace on the top. Very, very sexy."

She reported that she was five-eight and weighed 120 pounds and that her measurements were 34D-26-36. I started getting really horny. Then she said she looked like Phoebe Cates.

"No, c'mon—be serious," I moaned.

"No, it's true. I have long dark hair and full lips, like the kind that people are collagening."

"All right. So what happened to you yesterday that caused you to enter the world of lesbianism?" I couldn't wait to hear this.

"Well, I was going to meet a friend to grab a bite to eat and have a drink. I got to her neighborhood early, and I had a few hours to kill, so I thought I'd go into a club that I thought looked nice. I walked in, and there weren't that many people there. But it was early. So I sat down at the bar.

"The girl behind the bar was dressed outrageously,

and was very sexy, and she was just really pleasant. Then somebody sat down next to me, and she was really attractive. She had on a miniskirt and a shirt that tied. She didn't have a bra on. She kind of looked like Cindy Crawford. I mean, this is stretching it, but she was very, very pretty. And very buxom . . ."

"Hey, how many guys are aroused so far? Jackie—you got one?" I asked.

"Flying," reported Jackie "the Joke Man."

"Me, too—I'm flyin'," I said. "Fred?"

"Cindy Crawford did it for me," said Fred Norris, the man from Mars and one of my writers.

"I've been flyin' since she told me that she wears those camisoles. Robin, anything flyin' on you?" I asked.

"I don't even know what the story's about," Robin said.

"So you're at the bar, and she sits down next to you, and you go, 'Hey, she's a pretty girl,'" I said.

"Yeah, we just started talking, and we were very comfortable together. The conversation just kept flowing. And then my drink got low and she said, 'Can I buy you another drink?' At first I didn't even think anything of it."

"But were you thinking to yourself, 'Hey, this is a pretty sexy woman'?" I asked.

"Yeah, I actually was thinking that, as I started getting a little—you know—it took a couple o' drinks to start really . . ."

"And were you touching each other when you were talking? Did she put her hand on your back?" I asked.

"No, she didn't do anything yet. Then I kinda looked around and was wondering why there were no men in here. I said, 'Isn't this bizarre that there's like no guys in here?' And she said, 'Do you know where you are?' I said, 'No.' And she said, 'This is a gay bar.' And I said, 'It is?' And she said, 'Wow, I'm sorry. I was really coming on to you.' It was really bizarre but I just looked at her and I said, 'Oh, I don't know that I would have minded that.' I don't know why that came out, but I guess it's because I was feeling it."

"You were feeling sexy with her," I said. "Nothing wrong with that—don't feel bad about that."

"Well, it was really strange. And, as it turned out . . ."

"Wait, wait. Slow this down," I said. "So this happens—now where did you two go?"

"Well, what happened was I went into the bathroom and I looked around the place—there were things going on," she said.

"Like there were people makin' out and stuff—girls?" I asked.

"Right. And when I went into the bathroom I didn't realize, 'cause I've never been in one of these places, but there were regular stalls to go to the bathroom, and then there were longer stalls—and they have those loungers in them. And they're not the kind that fold down—they're just straight, like beds, and they're curved a little."

"You mean you can lay down with another girl?" I was beside myself.

"Isn't that incredible?" she laughed.

PRIVATE PARTS **17**

"And when you walked in, you saw two girls gettin' it on in the bathroom?"

"Well, they're behind the stalls, but there're big gaps, so you could definitely see in. They were going wild, and I could not believe how turned on I got," she said.

"It's like individual hump parlors," I marveled. "And you got really hot?"

"Well, I'm sure the alcohol had a little to do with it . . ."

"Right, and you were getting turned on. You said to yourself, 'I want this,' " I said.

"And all of a sudden she came in behind me, and cupped me from behind. Do you know what I mean? And I just turned around, and at that point she kissed me."

"She started to kiss you with her tongue?" I asked.

"Oh, mmm-hmm," she moaned.

"Fred, come over here and cup me. C'mon, man. C'mon, gimme a break, pal."

"You *know* this is a great story," Jackie said, "because Fred stopped eating."

"So she cupped you and you turned around and you started kissing. Then what happened? She started to disrobe you in the bathroom?" I prodded.

"Mmm-hmm."

"Did you go to one o' those little parlors?"

"Yeah."

"And she started to remove all your clothing?"

"Yeah."

"And then did you undress her?"

"Yeah."

"And then you had full lesbian passion?"

"We did everything. We did it all," she said. "It was really wonderful, I must say. I don't know that I ever thought that this would have ever happened to me, but—"

"And she had a hot body?" I asked.

"Yeah, she was really, really gorgeous."

"What happened to the meeting with her friend, though?" Robin asked.

"Screw the friend—she's in the bathroom. Imagine the stink in there, too! Oh, man, what's goin' on? Like, aren't girls goin' in there and takin' dumps and stuff?" I asked.

"Well, you know something? I don't know. I didn't pay attention to anything else that was going on."

"What did you do first?"

"Well, I didn't know what to do, so she had to teach me. She started tugging at my shirt but it wouldn't come down because my breasts are so big."

"How big?"

"My breasts are so full. They even look bigger because my stomach is so flat and hard."

"And your hips are really narrow, too, right?" I said.

"Yes. She started ripping at my shirt, kissing me on my cleavage. I was getting really excited."

"You were turned on?"

"Yeah, my nipples were so hard and I got this really achy feeling all over my body."

"Where? In your most private of places?"

"Yes, I could barely stand up. She pushed me back on the couch. I was on the couch and I pulled my shirt off, exposing my breasts."

"Did your breasts fall to the sides?"

"No, they're really firm and full. They stood straight up."

"So they're not sloppy. Hey guys, they're not sloppy!" Fred lay unconscious in the corner. Jackie's big toe, I know, was up his asshole. He was a gymnast in high school. "Then what happened?"

"She played with me and caressed me and I was getting more and more excited."

"What about your thigh-high pantyhose?"

"I have really long, thin legs and I was wearing long, spiky high heels. She took off my shoes and she stripped me of my pantyhose and before I knew it, she was sucking . . . on my feet."

"Did that turn you on?"

"I loved it. No guy had ever done that to me."

"So did you do anything to her?"

"At first, no."

"What was she wearing?"

"She had no bra on. She just untied her top and her breasts just fell out. They were incredible. She rubbed them against my legs as she sucked my toes. She kept her miniskirt on, but she wasn't wearing any underwear."

"Was she shaved?"

"Completely!"

Whore! Slut! Bitch! Lesbo! Radio sucks. . . . We had to cut off her story. It was getting too graphic.

> "He's completely anarchic, outside the establishment. He's bawdy, lewd, lustful . . . constantly attacking sacred cows. He's also genuinely funny."
>
> —Camille Paglia

I was going crazy. I tried to persuade her to come down to the studio and pose nude so we could paint her. I was going through my Van Gogh stage. But she was resistant. She claimed she was too busy at work.

"Oh, c'mon—you do sales. You can screw off a little bit. You've had time to be in bathrooms with women!" I protested. She still claimed she was too busy to come in. I used a harmonizer to make my voice sound deep, like Satan's.

*"Abandon everything! Now that you've had lesbianism, come to our studio and let us paint you! Let us paint you, my dear! You want to be naked in the room with me, Jackie, and Fred. Don't you wanna be painted and immortalized?"*

"I must say that this is like the most bizarre thing that's ever happened to me," she said.

I kept trying, in my normal voice. "Hey, why don't you ask your lesbian to come on down with you? You guys can be in bathing suits, and we'll paint you while you guys get to know each other better. 'Cause I need nude models," I suggested.

"I know you do, I know you do. I'm not sure that I'd be into that," she said.

"All right." I gave up. "But I got Clapton tickets for you. That was a good story. Now I'm even more sexed up than I was fifteen minutes ago. Hey, do me a favor—go meet another girl tonight and call us back to-morrow."

She hung up. I felt drained. Then Gary came into the studio.

"Can I tell you what a twisted world we live in?" he said. "We got a ton of phone calls from women, begging me for the name of the place, which we're not giving out. And I also got a call from a private investigator who wanted to know if we wanted to hire him to go in and videotape what's goin' on in there."

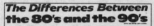

**The Differences Between the 80's and the 90's**

CONGRESSWOMAN FELNER, ARE YOU WILLING TO **ADMIT** YOUR ROLE IN THE S&L FIASCO?

**In the 80's** *radio personality Larry King made it big in television.*

CONGRESSWOMAN FELNER, ARE YOU WILLING TO **ADMIT** THAT, DESPITE BEING A **LESBIAN**, YOU FIND ME ATTRACTIVE?

**In the 90's** *radio personality Howard Stern is making it big in television.*

# Hate Mail

Dear Mr. Stern,

I am writing in response to the insulting remarks you made about The Blessed Virgin Mary, lately. I am having a mass said for you, and Robin, for God to have mercy on you for the remarks you made about his mother.

I will keep you in my prayers, and ask you to cease offending people and the Mother of God, who is by extension, mother of us all.

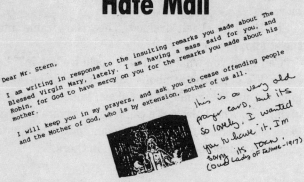

this is a very old prayer card, but its so lovely, I wanted you to have it. I'm sorry its TORN (OUR LADY OF FATIMA - 1917)

Dear Mr. Stern:

Recently, you stated on the air that Chris Burke, the young man who plays "Corky" on "Life Goes On" is not an actor. You explained that he is not really acting because he has Down Syndrome, as does his character. In other words, because he is a retarded man and as such is limited to playing the roles of retarded young men, therefore, he is not a true actor. To this argument, I can only say:  what an <u>ignorant</u>, <u>moronic</u>, <u>asinine</u>, <u>infantile</u> and, yes, <u>retarded</u> thing to say.

So lay off Chris Burke and his acting. And good luck with your acting career. I advise you, though, to change your character's name from Fartman to Fartbrain, although in either case you might be accused of not being a "real actor" because rude, flatulent behavior seems to follow you everywhere.

Dear Howard "the honky cracker kike" Stern,
You ought to be ashamed of yourself for critícizing a great black man like Spike Lee. You seem to have a problem with black people who are doing well in this country. People like Bill Cosby, Arsenio Hall and David Dinkins. You're just pissed off because the brothers used to kick your ass when you lived in Roosevelt. Couldn't your Kike father teach you how to fight you honky faggot. I'm sorry I forgot, Kikes can't fight. I hope Lenrick Nelson Jr. comes down to your studio and carves you up like a Thanksgiving Turkey.

Sincerely,
Angry Black
Woman

# It Was the Worst of Times, It Was the Worst of Times

## *The Stern Family*

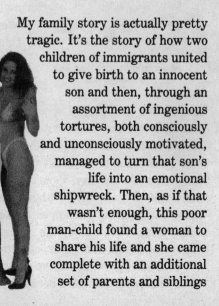

CHAPTER
2

My family story is actually pretty tragic. It's the story of how two children of immigrants united to give birth to an innocent son and then, through an assortment of ingenious tortures, both consciously and unconsciously motivated, managed to turn that son's life into an emotional shipwreck. Then, as if that wasn't enough, this poor man-child found a woman to share his life and she came complete with an additional set of parents and siblings to torment him. Yes, this is my story, A Tale of Two Dysfunctional Families. *It was the worst of times, it was the worst of times.*

## RAISED LIKE A VEAL

"Mrs. Stern, you have a really happy baby," the doctor said at my birth. "Howard's very smiley. He's as happy as a Mongoloid idiot." Who knew I'd grow up to be so miserable?

Basically, my mother, Ray, raised me like a veal. It

was like growing up in a box with no lights on. Sure I was tender—because my mother would never allow me to do anything. She was constantly attentive, totally overbearing, and would always put

**At six months, drooling like a Mongoloid.**

fear in me. If I played sports, I'd get hurt. If, God forbid, I left the house without a coat on, I'd catch cold. I always had to have rest periods to collect my energy. She had these kooky rules for everything. But it worked. To this day, I can't go out of the house for more than five minutes without worrying that something bad is going to happen to me. I live in fear of everything. I can't enjoy life so I sit in my house and vegetate. Under dim lights, of course.

I confess. I'm an obsessive-compulsive, anal-retentive, miserable neurotic because I was raised by a

woman who ran her household with the intensity of
Hitler. Now, let me clarify things. I love my mother.
She had the best intentions. She's a very moral, up-
right person. In fact, my mother broke the world
down into a battle between good and evil. And anything that didn't conform to her worldview was definitely evil. Man, did she put me on a permanent guilt
trip. One time I was walking down the street with my
wife, Alison, and I saw a wad of bills on the ground. I
picked it up, started to walk away, and all of a sudden
I heard my mother's annoying voice: "Don't pick it up!
Don't pick it up! That belongs to someone else!" Idiot
that I am, I felt bad for the poor slob who dropped it
and had this lunatic idea that he was going to come
back to look for it. So I ran back and put the money
down exactly where I found it.

And boy, did this woman have wacky ideas and bizarre practices. First of all, I couldn't have any pets
growing up. My mother was convinced that pets actually drain energy out of the humans who own them.
To this day, I swear, if I'm feeling a little rundown, I
walk around my house thinking that our cat is like
Cujo or something.

But some of the strangest of her practices centered
around my underpants. My mother was obsessed with
them. First of all, the minute she bought me underpants, she would have to sew big name tags into them.
She was always concerned about me losing things.
This I never understood. If I lost them, and someone
else found them, what were they going to do? Drop
them into the nearest mailbox? Who would even want
to touch these dirty things?

Plus, my mother kept this up all through college. Can you imagine my embarrassment when I was in bed with some lady and she's taking off my underpants and she slips her hand beneath the elastic waistband and says, "What's this tag on the back?" My mother never stopped. She went on archaeological digs in the dirty clothes hamper. She was like a research scientist and my underpants were her petri dish. She could even tell what I'd eaten for lunch.

And God forbid she should find a little stain on a pair. She'd run upstairs to our only bathroom, run hot water in the sink, and rub soap into my underwear. The whole family would parade in and out to use the sink only to be stopped by the soaking underpants. You might as well have had a neon sign flashing: STAY AWAY FROM THE SINK. HOWARD HAD ANOTHER ACCIDENT. Was this total emasculation or what?

My mother had me so crazy that, in kindergarten, when I pooped in my pants, I was always afraid to come home. I would come home with a full metal jacket in my underpants, run up to my room, take off my underpants, and sneak out in the backyard to bury them. Somewhere in Roosevelt, Long Island, there's a BVD tree with some pretty fertile soil around it.

One time I ran out of underpants. So my mother told me to wear her panties to school. I actually put them on. They were huge and very soft, and as soon as she left the room I took them off, fished out the least crusty pair from the hamper, and wore them to school. Can you imagine the humiliation I would have faced changing for gym class? I might as well have moved out of state.

The funny thing is, sloppy underpants weren't even my fault. My mother never toilet trained me right. She never taught me the proper method of wiping. When I was four, I developed a bad case of rectal worms. I had to take a dump in

"Uh-oh! I think I had an accident!"
Me at seven years old.

a cardboard box and my mother and father drove me and my turd to the doctor's office, where he made the diagnosis.

The worms cleared up but a much more chronic condition ensued: anal fissures. I itched like crazy. I would bury my finger so far up into my underpants that I would poke holes in them. I had no idea how bad it was until a doctor fresh out of medical school took one look at my sphincter and told me I had a hole the size of a garage door down there. It was like a blowhole. And all because I never learned how to wipe properly. Now don't laugh at me, because judging from the amount of hemorrhoid creams and ointments being sold, a lot of you don't know how to properly care for your sphincters, either.

### HOWARD'S RULES FOR A HEALTHIER RECTUM

So, as a public service to my readers, I will now impart to you the wiping wisdom I've learned from sources other than my mother. Pay attention because you will never have another hemorrhoid or problem back there again. I used to overwipe. I would scrape and strain. But you must only take three swipes and that's it. Oh, and stay away from dyed toilet paper. Use white and you'll be all right. If you feel dirty down there, jump in the shower and scrub down. But stick to the three-wipe maximum. Also never push. Wait until that bowel movement is sliding out of your ass before you go to the bowl. If you're pushing a lot, you probably need oat bran cereal for breakfast plus three tablets of Evening Primrose oil, one with each meal. That should grease it all up.

My mother also had this kooky compulsion to constantly monitor my temperature. And, of course, she used a rectal thermometer every day of my life until I was eighteen years old!

It's amazing I didn't become a mass murderer like John Wayne Gacy. When my mother dies I'm going to have her mummified. I'll prop her up in my attic and tie her to a chair. I'm going to save all her clothes and I'll wear a bad wig and parade around the house in her housecoat and panties.

Mom, I love you. And thank you for putting me in touch with my feminine side.

RAY: Howard, I can't believe these stories you're making up. You exaggerate everything.

HOWARD: Don't say you didn't make me put on your panties.

RAY: I never did.

HOWARD: Well, what about taking my rectal temperature until I was eighteen years old? You humiliated me by raping me with that piece of plastic!

RAY: Don't make a big deal out of everything. You grew up to be a very well-adjusted individual.

HOWARD: It's a miracle I'm not a homo.

RAY: That's what a homo comes from?

HOWARD: You better believe it. Before you know it, you're putting ashtrays up there. It's a miracle I'm normal. Although I did pay a woman $150 the other night to take my temperature with a drumstick. Thermometers just don't satisfy me anymore.

## "SHUT UP! SIT DOWN, YOU MORON!"

My father, Ben, is a no-nonsense guy who has guided me in my career and stood by me no matter what. He loves me, but he was tough on me. It was understandable, though, because his dad had been real hard on him, too.

My father was a radio engineer who eventually bought his own recording studio with five other guys. He never made big money, though. We were living in Roosevelt in a house that cost my old man $14,000. A good house would have cost about double that back then, but my father didn't mind driving an extra fifty miles to save money. Every day he'd drive to Queens, park, and take the subway to work. Then he'd come home and sit down at the dinner table and expect to

be served like a king. Even today, he just sits there
with a miserable expression on his face until his wife
serves him.

As a kid I was disturbed that my mom had to serve
my father like that, but then I started to analyze it
and I realized he was right. In fact, I try to do the
same thing with Alison. I just sit there while Alison
sits down with her plate all full and eventually she'll
look over at me and go, "Oh, Howard, you don't have
anything." Then I get up and get it myself.

King Ben would come home and sit on his throne
and everything had to be just right. One of the nightly
rituals was serving him a Rob Roy, his favorite drink.
I swear they tasted like paint thinner. But my mother
didn't mind making him toxic drinks because she figured they'd tranquilize him. She'd spend half the day
preparing the Rob Roy for his dinner. And he would
give her explicit directions on how to do this. First,
she had to chill the glass. Then she took a lemon rind
and ran it around the rim of the glass. Then she mixed
the alcohol—one part vermouth and one part whis-
key—and chilled it. Finally, my mom would put a
piece of Saran Wrap over the top of the glass in the
refrigerator so everything would be perfect when he
got home.

My old man could be a bastard sometimes. She
would kill herself for half the day preparing this stupid
drink and he'd sip it and go, "Hmmm. Not as good as
the one you made last night, honey." Meanwhile, we
were living in Roosevelt, an almost all-black community, a place worse than South Central L.A. There

wasn't a white neighbor in sight, and my father was in his little bungalow, making believe he was in some fancy country club, sipping away at his Rob Roy.

My mother let me make my dad his Rob Roy one night, which was a big mistake. I sure as hell wasn't going to go through that torture. I'd piss in that damn glass before I spent half my day making a stupid drink. If I got it just slightly off, my father would scream his head off at me.

Those drinks didn't tranquilize him at all. He would just get all lit and red-faced and then scream even louder. No matter what I did or said, he'd just yell at me.

"Hey, Dad, how was your day?"

"Are you putting me on? SHUT UP!"

"Dad, I'm just asking . . ."

"You don't care about my day! SHUT UP, YOU MORON!"

He'd be bitching to my mom about work and how his partners were screwing the business up and I would try to empathize with him and ask him questions.

"What?" he'd yell at me. "What did you say? I'm talking to your mother, you dummy. You don't know what it is to have a partner. You never even worked. GET OUT OF HERE! SHUT UP!"

I remember one time I told him that I wanted to be a millionaire and he chased me up the stairs. He was going to beat the fucking shit out of me.

"You dope, you don't even know what it's like to make money!" he screamed. "You say you want to make money? Let me see you work. YOU WON'T EVEN LIFT YOUR ASS TO MOW THE LAWN! SHUT UP!"

Meanwhile, if I even tried to mow the lawn, he would grab the lawnmower from me and complain about how he was the only one in the family that had the brains to know how to mow the lawn right.

My dad and I never did things that most dads and their sons do. I think he was a pretty good athlete but he never suggested we play sports together. Once I played catch with my father. I threw him the ball and he missed it and it hit him in the nuts and that was the end of that.

My father's favorite sport was yelling. And he was pretty scary. I'm surprised that he didn't just wake up one night and wipe us all out like a disgruntled postal worker. Maybe he got all his frustrations out by yelling at us. Actually, it was mostly yelling at me. My father would never yell at my sister, because she was his favorite, his little jewel. And my mother actually dug it when my father yelled at me because that would take the heat off her. I was the designated yellee.

He'd do it everywhere and under any conditions. We'd go out to a restaurant to eat and we all had to know what we wanted to order *before* we even got there. He'd get all embarrassed in front of the waiter for some stupid reason. My mother would fumble around with the menu, indecisive about what to eat.

"I know what I want to eat before we get here. You shouldn't need a menu!"

Then he'd get bent out of shape if we ordered out of order.

"Howard. You order your appetizer, *then* your salad dressing, *then* your entree, you moron!"

Here we are in some shithole Greek diner and my father's worrying about following the rules of Amy Vanderbilt and Emily Post.

I once asked for Russian dressing after my entree and all hell broke loose.

"What do you care what the waiter thinks?" I'd ask.

"THERE'S A PROPER WAY TO ORDER, YOU IDIOT!"

He's that way to this day. I should take Stuttering John out to dinner with him. He'd put him right through a wall. When we go out with my parents to dinner, I always order the same thing just to please my father. Meanwhile my wife's like a retard. She starts nudging me with her elbow. "I don't know what to order. Help me." My wife goes into a panic because if she doesn't order properly my father starts to get all agitated.

When I graduated college, my father came to the commencement ceremonies and then he yelled at me all the way home.

"WHAT ARE YOU GOING TO DO NOW, YOU IDIOT?"

"But Dad, I graduated magna cum laude."

"SHUT UP! I PAID TWENTY GRAND FOR THAT DEGREE. I NEVER WENT TO COLLEGE."

People always thought I was kidding or exaggerating when I talked about the way my father yelled. But then we found some evidence. I unearthed some old tapes that my father neglected to throw out and I brought them in to Scott the Engineer. The next day he came into my office.

"You don't know what's on these tapes," he marveled. Apparently they were tapes made of the Stern family at my father's recording studio when I was seven years old. Once a year, my parents would march me and my sister and my cousins to the studio and he would record us singing and fooling around. Except he didn't like it when we fooled around. In two seconds, my father would lose his patience and start screaming like a banshee. And now I had the tapes to prove it.

These sessions were supposed to be fun, but I dreaded them. Who wanted to be humiliated in front of his sister and cousins? My father would "interview" us and ask us questions about current events and stuff and I would sweat bullets because if I said one wrong word, that was it. My sister would just breeze through the questions, because he'd never yell at her. But just listen to this sample exchange:

BEN STERN: Do you feel the United States should remain as a member of the United Nations?
HOWARD: Yes, I really do.
BEN STERN: Are there any special reasons why you feel they should?
HOWARD: There should be peace in all the countries and we wouldn't have any war because we don't want the Japs anymore haa-haa-haa-haa. [I imitated the sound of a machine gun.]

# BEN STERN: I TOLD YOU NOT TO BE STUPID, YOU MORON!

See? See? Right away with the "moron" stuff. I was just doing some shtick, some humor, and my old man freaks. And being called a moron to me was real. I thought I *was* a moron. At seven years of age, you'd think he'd cut me some slack. But no, it was "SHUT UP! SIT DOWN!"

We played these tapes on the air and my father called in and said he felt like Nixon. We get along great now as adults, but believe me, at the time, he turned me into a basket case with all the yelling. The day after we played the tapes on the air, a neighbor of my father's came over to him and said, "Hey, Ben, how do I get my kids into that Ben Stern Day-Care Center? They're out of line." One of our classic bits was about to be born.

My father was definitely the disciplinarian, but during the day, when he was at work, my mother was in charge of giving me a smack if I got out of line. So one day she complained to him that her hand was hurting from smacking me. He told her to get a stick and hit me. So she got one of those half-wooden, half-wire coat hangers from the dry cleaners and she detached the wire part. My father came home from work and my mother told him that this wasn't good either because I held her arm so she couldn't hit me. So my father called me over for a little talk.

"Howard, your mother tells me you're not letting her discipline you," he said.

"Who in their right mind is gonna just stand there and let someone whack 'em with a stick?" I asked.

"Look, your mother has to express herself in some way," he told me. "Let her give you a couple of little bangs and we'll get it over with. Why are you making such a big thing out of it?"

But I always resisted being disciplined. "No, I don't want to go up to my room," I'd say, trying to brown-nose her. "I want to be by your side."

One time she forced me to go up to my room, so I started chewing up my furniture. I don't even think it was a protest or anything, it was just a fun thing to do. I was gnawing at my wooden dresser drawer, scraping my teeth against it, and by the time my mother came up to get me, there were big chunks ripped out of it.

Actually, that was probably a very rational thing to do given my circumstances. Can you imagine being trapped in that madhouse for eighteen years with no way out? I didn't have the balls to run away from home and live on the streets. All I had to do was go to Times Square and have sex with a few old men like Jon Voight did in *Midnight Cowboy* and I could have had my own pad.

Speaking of sex, I'm sure that's why my father used to scream so much. I know he wasn't getting any from my mother. I figured that out when he took me to see *Barbarella*, starring Jane Fonda. I was about fifteen and my mother was visiting her father in Florida. So my father said, "Let's go to the movies." This was great, because I really didn't get a lot of chances to pal around with him alone. Now, my dad's pretty knowledgeable, but I don't think he knew it was going to be a dirty movie.

Imagine you're fifteen and your hormones are going crazy and Jane Fonda comes on a big screen with those two plastic see-through things over her breasts. And right next to you is your dad. We were both pretty embarrassed. We left the theater and never spoke about it.

I just knew he wasn't getting it at home. So, over the years, whenever my mother called up on my show, I made it a point to ask her about their sexual practices. One time she was acting so crabby that I told her she needed to get laid. After we hung up, Gary stormed into the studio.

"I can't believe you told your mother she needed to get laid," Baba Booey marveled.

"She does," I affirmed. "But she wants to be celibate."

I called my mother back.

"You want to say you're sorry?" my mother asked.

"Admit you want to be celibate," I said.

"How can I be celibate? I'm a married woman," she said.

"So you're saying you're not celibate? You have a love life?" I asked.

"Yes," my mother said.

"Oh, I'm going to throw up," I said.

"I hate to tell you this, Howard; it's a shock-a-roo, right?" she laughed.

"You mean you like the pants monster of love? I just can't accept that. You and my dad doing it. If you *do* do it, it's gotta be once a month, tops. Just tell me how often you do it," I pleaded.

"It's none of your business," my mother maintained.

"Please, Ma, I got to know. You let that animal touch you? He bangs you? I can't believe it."

"That's your father you're talking about," she reminded me.

"Oh, man, I'm in shock. He touches your cans? Hey, did you know Robin likes anal sex? She's a three-input woman. Would you ever do that, Ma?"

"Do what? What's this three inputs?" she asked.

"Either you have two places to put it or three, Mom. Are you a three-input woman with Dad?" How many guys have the balls to ask their mom if she takes it up the ass?

"Please, Howard," she said.

"What about that stuff Chip did to Madonna? When

he guzzled water and relieved himself." I was referring to the exclusive story that Chip from Enuff Z'Nuff told us about urinating during a sex session with Madonna. "Does that excite you? Can you fathom that? Imagine if Dad did that to you. Dad, do me a favor, do that and videotape it. That'll be the greatest videotape that ever was. Does that excite you in some bizarre way, Ma?"

"I'm not talking," my mother said.

"I've seen Dad naked. Is the reason you don't like to have sex with him much because it hurts you?" I asked.

My father, unlike me, is hung like a moose. I'm sure my mother was frightened by his huge hose.

"Hurts what?" she said.

"Does it hurt?"

"It was wonderful talking to you." My mother was ready to bail.

"I love you, Mommy," I said dutifully.

"I love you, too," she said.

"You don't get up on all fours, do you?"

"Good-bye," my mom said and hung up.

## MY SISTER

My sister, Ellen, is the complete opposite of me. She's four years older but she's very quiet. We had a perfect relationship. I would beg for and suck in all the attention in the house and she could live her life

Ellen—Daddy's favorite.

unnoticed. She was the type who could just curl up with a book and be in heaven. I remember once, right after she got her license, she and I drove out to the beach. She lay down on the blanket, cracked open her book, and didn't move for hours. Me, I was going out of my friggin' mind. She wouldn't talk to me. She wouldn't move.

But we used to get along. Except when it came to watching TV. Another one of my mother's idiotic theories was that her two children should watch television together. As I said, my sister is four years older than me, and at ten years of age, she wanted to watch love movies. At six years of age, all I wanted to watch was Yogi Bear cartoons. To me that was the ultimate in entertainment. So my mother devised a plan that every other day the other person got to pick out what we'd watch.

But my sister was shrewd. One day when it was her turn to pick there was a Yogi Bear cartoon I was dying to watch. So she said that she'd let me watch it that day if I let her watch what she wanted for a year. So I said, "Okay." I'm a little kid, I have no idea what a year is. A couple of days went by and she was watching everything she wanted to watch and, finally, I said, "When's my turn to pick the show?" My sister then told me I couldn't pick for a year. So we went to my mother to arbitrate.

"What was the deal you made?" she asked me.

"Ellen can pick the shows for a year," I said.

"That's it," my mother said. "A deal's a deal."

I learned pretty early that life sucked.

The best time I ever had with Ellen, though, was when I saw her dancing naked in her room when she was nine. She was developing those trademark Stern woman breasts. But other than that, I didn't catch many glimpses of her. Our household wasn't exactly a nudist colony.

**Visiting my sister (center) in college while wearing my serial-killer glasses. I was thirteen.**

Although my father once said, "There's too much modesty in this house," and he walked out of the bathroom stark naked. My mother said, "BEN! BEN!" and my sister covered her eyes. And when I was about nine, I saw my mother naked. That was pretty frightening. Back then, women didn't know about the grooming thing. At first, I thought she was wearing panties. Mohair panties.

## LITTLE BIG MAN

All right, so I've got a small penis. It's so embarrassing. I would give anything for even another inch. I don't get it either, because my father is so well hung. He might be four inches, just hanging around. The trouble is, he never gets to do anything with it. My mother knew I had a small penis, but she ignored it whenever she'd take my rectal temperature. But one of the most humiliating memories of my childhood was when my father had to check me for a hernia and he actually touched me down there. I threw him out of the room, I was so embarrassed.

Having a small penis has haunted me throughout my life. Whenever I'm with a bunch of guys, like going to Atlantic City to gamble or stuff, and we have to make a stop on the way to urinate, I always make a beeline for the stalls. I can't do it at a urinal. God forbid someone should see my puny pecker. I barely clear the zipper. If all the stalls are filled and I *have* to use a urinal, I press up so close to it that it's like I'm humping the porcelain.

My biggest fear about the draft and going into the army was that my dad told me when you go to the bathroom in the army there are no walls or anything between urinals and toilets. So everybody sees everything. I was going to run off to Canada just for that reason.

## MY STRANGE CHILDHOOD

Is it any wonder that I had a strange childhood living in this nuclear family? Let me give you a few examples. My mother thought that playing with dolls was an excellent outlet for creativity. But even she didn't want me to be ostracized by all my friends, so she decided to get me marionettes. By the time I was seven years old, I had become an accomplished puppeteer. My father built me a little stage and I would reg-

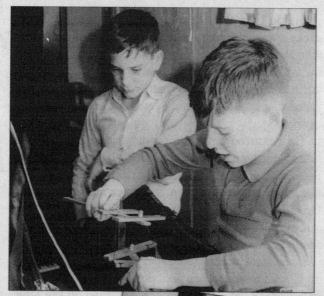

**Demonstrating my technique to my cousin Paul.**

**The X-rated ventriloquist preparing for his next pornographic puppet show.**

ularly put on shows for my friends and neighbors. In fact, I got so good at it that an old-age home asked me to do a production of *Fiddler on the Roof* using my marionettes.

The old people loved it and wouldn't stop complimenting me after the show. They just loved the sing-

ing. They were so out of it they didn't realize the
voices weren't mine—it was an actual recording from
the Broadway show.

At the end of the night, I was handed an envelope
with ten bucks inside! What a windfall! Getting paid
good money for something you enjoyed was definitely
a trip.

So I started entertaining my friends with puppet
shows in the basement. One thing led to another and
before I knew it, I was doing dirty marionette shows.
I had a nice girl puppet and a sailor marionette and I
would have the sailor fuck the shit out of the girl. Then
the pirate puppet would come in, knock the sailor out,
and grab his girl and bang her all over the place. My
friends went wild.

The shows got more and more perverse when I got
a horse puppet. I had the horse fucking all the other
puppets and it got pretty out of control. Plus, I kept a
running commentary the entire time. My friends loved
it. Once I started doing the dirty puppet shows, I
really lost interest in regular puppeteering, and
pretty soon, all the puppets were wrapped up and put
in storage. I had ruined a beautiful, innocent part of
my life.

Then my mother tried to get me interested in piano
lessons, but that also ended on a sour note. I took a
few lessons from a local piano teacher who begged my
mother to make me quit. "I'm just taking money from
you. I feel guilty," he said. A few weeks later, this
nice man went home and killed himself.

My mother didn't give up. She decided I should vol-
unteer at the local cerebral palsy center in my spare

time. This lasted four hours. It was an experience that separated the men from the boys. I was definitely a boy.

A boy *veal*. Thanks to my overprotective mother, I was the target of every bully in the neighborhood. A fat neighborhood kid named Johnny, who used to blow his nose into his Italian ices, then eat them with a wooden spoon, used to beat me up so regularly that my parents made me go to judo school to learn to defend myself. On the day of my first lesson I took a brush and scrubbed my feet down before I went. I knew in judo you had to take your socks and shoes off. I always hated to take baths or showers. I would go for days without washing until my mother would smell me and go "You stink!" and march me in for a bath. So I went to judo with my scrubbed feet, I took off my shoes and socks, and the Korean instructor looked down at my toenails and he freaked out.

"These are weapons!" he screamed. "You've got to cut these, you're going to kill somebody." Then, I looked around the room and saw all these young, athletic, Nordic Nazi types jumping over garbage pails and doing somersaults. There was no way I could do that. It was easier letting Johnny beat me up.

Is it any wonder that I wound up doing drugs? I smoked a lot of pot when I was in high school. But it wasn't fun because it made me so friggin' paranoid. All my friends would come over and we'd go out to my garage and smoke grass. I used to get Mexican. I'd go over to my friend's house and cop from his older brother. His older brother was in college and he was a big, fat, white Jewish guy who'd be lying naked on his bed liked a beached whale wearing a sombrero while reading *Penthouse* and playing with himself. This guy had the smallest penis I'd ever seen, even smaller than mine. We had to buy our marijuana from this fat naked guy. It was a disgusting experience.

I would smoke dope and cigarettes up in my bedroom, blowing smoke out the window, while my parents were downstairs thinking I was doing my homework.

One time, my mother staged a sneak attack. She crashed through the door as I was flinging a cigarette out the window.

"Howard. I smell smoke in here."

"What? I don't smell anything."

"No. I see smoke. I see clouds of smoke in this room," she insisted.

"I don't see any clouds of smoke," I lied through my teeth. "There's no smoke in here."

The room was filled with smoke. My mother stormed out. I was victorious. She never brought it up again and to this day she denies that I ever did drugs.

Being in the middle of this dysfunctional family I was able to come up with a great strategy for coping. Basically, I whined and whined and wore everybody down until I got what I wanted. My sister would always be amazed at my ability to do this. We'd be upstairs and we'd be talking about something that our parents wouldn't give us and I'd turn to her and say, "Watch me. I'm going downstairs and I'm getting it." I would march downstairs and ask for whatever it was they didn't want me to have and then I'd start whining and I'd wear and wear on them and then I'd start crying and I wouldn't give it up. I'd keep going and going and going and finally they'd cave in. My father always told my mother that I would have been one of the greatest trial lawyers who ever lived, the way I just wear people down. It was like Chinese water torture and great practice for the interviewing technique I use today.

## MY SECOND DYSFUNCTIONAL FAMILY

There is nothing bad that I can say about my wife, Alison, except for the stupid little arguments that we have.

She'll argue with me about really stupid stuff. I'm always on a diet, so I eat like a total of five things: tuna fish, baked potatoes, fruits (bananas and apples), Paul Newman salad dressing, and oat bran cereal.

We are always out of this shit, and I go crazy. How fucking hard is it to keep a few baking potatoes in the house? I know what you're saying: "Hey, Howard, why the fuck don't you go do your own food shopping?"

But that's just it. Alison doesn't have to food shop, either. We send out for food. They ship it out to the house. All she has to do is make a phone call and remember that her man likes baked potatoes.

"Hold it," Alison says, "I do remember. But you have to tell me when you're running out of something."

How fucking difficult is it to take a look in the fridge and see I need an apple? I tell her to order apples, anything—order a crate of oat bran cereal—but *NO*, at least once a week we need to have this fight.

And what a great husband I am. I pay the extra three dollars a box for cereal just so my wife doesn't have to go food shopping.

Also, twice a year I play in a card game with a bunch of guys. I have a few male friends and once in a rare while I need to get out and bond with the guys.

My wife says, "You're playing cards again? I have to spend Friday night alone? You don't want to be with me?"

I explain I need to do this once in a while the way Spock needed to mate on Vulcan once every seven years. We begin to yell and scream and the ridiculousness hits me. Here's a woman who spends every day with her clique of girlfriends gabbing it up, playing tennis, and going for lunches—and I can't have a card game twice a year without some shit being thrown my way?

I just threaten to go over to Jessica Hahn's house (if she has a house) and that quiets Alison down. But I know how lucky I am to have found a woman like Alison, who met me when I was a total loser in college with nothing but some big dreams. She's learned to suffer the bizarre personality that was a by-product of being raised like a veal in my parents' household. That's why I tolerate her PMS and her yenta friends and her snoring and her lunches at the country club. And that's why I haven't cheated on her for nineteen years.

But my in-laws! Don't get me wrong, I love my in-laws. First of all, they're cool enough to let me call

them Bob and Norma. I don't have to be a phony and
call them Mom and Dad. And they're really nice liberal
people. They even smoked pot once with Alison because they wanted to experience what their children
were going through. But two minutes with these people is enough to send you to Creedmore Psychiatric
Center for observation.

### TAKE MY FATHER-IN-LAW. PLEASE.

He's almost perfect, but I have just a few criticisms.
First of all, he talks in a monotone like HAL from
*2001*. Then he's got these annoying habits like lying on
my brand-new-God-knows-how-many-thousand-dollar
couch with his bare feet that he walked through the
grass on! Plus, he reads all these newspapers and
leaves them lying all over the white couch. Then, as if
that's not enough, he does the crossword puzzles in
ink and leaves the pen on the couch.

And he loves to watch movies on video. He's in the

**My future in-laws were great to me even though
I had NO radio show!**

house less than ten minutes and he's reprogrammed my VCR and my entire video collection is in disarray. He's got the videos out of the boxes, scattered all around the room. Between the tapes and the newspapers, it looks as if a windstorm hit my house. Then he starts going around trying to make home improvements. The next thing I know he's gluing tennis ball halves on the garage back wall so we know how far to back the cars into the garage.

But what totally irritates me is the way he leaves the doors in the house open. We have an indoor cat. We found it abandoned and we nursed it back to health. Because we declawed it, we can't let it go outside since there are a lot of raccoons in the neighborhood and they're all rabid. Even my seven-year-old understands that the cat has to stay inside, and we have to make sure all the doors are closed. We have a sliding door, you close it. Simple enough.

Every time Bob comes over, he leaves the doors open. He refuses to acknowledge that I have my own way of life. He always says, "Why don't you let the animal be an animal and go outside?" So I explain to him once again, it's an indoor cat. And, of course, he leaves the door open, the cat gets out, and he tries to blame the kids. Once when he did this I had to spend an entire day of my vacation looking for the cat. I went to the neighbors and asked them if they had seen it. They're from another country, they didn't know what was going on, so they called the cops. They thought I looked kind of seedy. Then the cops caught me on my neighbor's property and I had to go through a whole explanation with them. Finally, I called Jackie, one of the writers on my show, and his wife, Nancy, had a good idea. She told me to go outside with a can opener because that's the sound the cat always hears when it's about to be fed. So I took the can opener and plugged it into a thirty-foot extension cord and I was spending my vacation walking around outside with a can opener going. I felt like a moron, but it worked. The cat started meowing. We were a family again.

## MY MOTHER-IN-LAW? YOU CAN TAKE HER, TOO.

I love her a lot but there are one or two things about her that bother me. The minute she gets in the house all she wants to do is monopolize my children, which is fine with me. But she reverts to this baby talk not only with my newborn but with my two other kids, who are ten and seven. Then she starts talking to me in this baby talk with her thick Boston accent. My name instantly goes from Daddy to "Doddie."

"Hi, *Doddie*," she says when I come in the room.

"Hi, what?" I say.

"Hi, *Doddie*. Say hi to *Doddie*."

First of all, my name is Daddy, not Doddie. And she acts like I don't know my own kids.

Then she's got to examine everything I eat. Now I admit that this is a little more civilized than examining my underpants, but it's still irritating as hell. I don't like people watching me eat. One of the most annoying things in the world that anybody can do is to put his face in my food.

"Let's see what we're eating today," she'll say.

What do you mean "we"? She actually picks at my salad bowl with a fork, stirring everything around. I go out of my mind.

"You've got hot with cold, Howard. Hot rice with cold tuna?" Norma says. "I am fascinated by the combinations of food that you put in one bowl."

Great. What that really means is I'm disgusted by what you eat, you big, ugly, six-foot-five dork. And the fact that my daughter fucks you repulses me. Now I feel as if I'm a fucking zoo animal on exhibit. I felt like pushing her head into the damn food, she was so fascinated by it.

But the worst thing about my in-laws is the incessant questions they ask me. The second they walk into the room they start asking Howard Stern questions. This is my home. I want to relax. I don't want to think about being Howard Stern. But my in-laws don't let me forget it for a second. It's as if I've got two Stuttering Johns there, asking one stupid question after another. I made the mistake of showing them some of the tapes of my television show and that set them off.

"Howie." My father-in-law calls me Howie. God, how I hate that. "When did Kitty Carlisle Hart add the Hart to her name?"

"How would I know, Bob?" I said. I had her on the show as a guest and maybe I said two words to her off-camera. *Boom*, next question. Just like a press conference.

"How much is a person like Kitty Carlisle Hart or Arlene Francis or Dr. Ruth paid when they come on your show?"

I DIDN'T WANT TO TALK ABOUT MY TV AND

RADIO CAREER! I would have talked about their life or my kids or tennis or anything else. And quite frankly, WHO GIVES A RAT'S ASS WHEN KITTY CARLISLE CHANGED HER NAME TO KITTY CARLISLE HART!

My in-laws are just like my audience when they call up with these stupid questions. But at least I can hang up on my audience. Here, I was a captive. I couldn't leave. So I started making believe I didn't hear them and I made them repeat the questions two or three times, hoping they'd get annoyed. Like Muhammad Ali doing rope-a-dope, I hoped maybe they'd punch themselves out. But it didn't work.

When Bob rested, Norma piped in with more questions.

"How will they promote your radio show when you go into new markets?" she asked.

I actually started to answer her, but she was already asking the kids what they wanted for breakfast. It was as if she didn't even want to know the answer.

"How do you get guests for the TV show?" she started in again.

"Booker," I grunted. At this point, I was down to one-word answers.

"What do you mean 'booker'?" Bob asked.

"Booker, we have a booker. Frank Smiley," I said.

"And how does he know who to call? Does, say, a Kitty Carlisle Hart call you to be on the show?" Bob asked.

I was so woozy by this time that I was ready to pass out.

But I couldn't even find a couch, because every one

was taken. Bob was on one with his crosswords and pens and dirty newspapers all over the place. And one of Alison's brothers was on the other, watching sports on TV. Alison's brothers aren't as bad as her parents with the questions. But they can eat a person out of house and home in a shorter time than it takes Bob to leave the freaking door open so the cat can escape. I've never seen anything eat so much.

Uh-oh. "Entertainment Tonight" was coming on TV. My father-in-law was armed with more questions.

"Howie, Mary Hart, she's very perky. A very up personality. What kind of gal is she?"

"Don't know," I grunted, hoping to put an end to this nonsense. He had fifty more Mary Hart questions. "Do you think they show her legs on purpose on the show? What else does she do all day aside from 'Entertainment Tonight'? "

How the fuck was I supposed to know? I've never met the woman in my life. He kept asking nonsense questions that maybe only her mother would know the answers to. My father-in-law assumes I know everyone in show business, and when I don't, he's very disappointed.

But I have one surefire way of getting back at all of them—my parents, Alison, her parents, whoever. Whenever I'm with my family and I find myself getting irritated by something, which can usually be measured in nanoseconds, I run into the next room and I write down whatever they said on a little pad I keep there. And the next day, it becomes radio material. I write it in shorthand, too, so they can't understand what I've written if they find it. And after I talk about it on the radio I come home and Alison is all over my case.

"Can't we have a personal life? Does everything we do have to be grist for your stupid radio show? I don't want you to talk about our personal life on the air!" she yells at me.

Honey, if you'd let me out of the house once in a while maybe I'd have something to talk about. Maybe I'd experience other things besides your parents. Maybe at a card game I could have some funny things happen. But I'm locked up like a veal. Welcome to hell.

"Hey, I have an idea. Let me go over to Jessica Hahn's house! *Then* I'll have something else to talk about," I say. That shuts her up but good.

## STERN: THE NEXT GENERATION

I'm the only male in a household of five. And I love having three daughters. They're great kids and that's all because of Alison. I've told her that the kids are her responsibility. Believe me, it's better that Alison should raise them. If it was up to me, the kids wouldn't know that people have private parts. I'd teach them that the human body is filthy, and that all men are evil, you can be sure of that.

And just wait until they get old enough to date. Do you think there's a man on this planet good enough for my daughters? I look around at the creeps and mutants out there, the men who jerk off to my show in their cars, and the idea that these idiots are going to invade my life and marry my daughters at some point really frightens me.

Among the things I'm lacking as a parent are those really good hardship stories to tell my kids. Whenever I complained as a kid to my father, he would lay out his heavy Depression-era stories. He'd tell me how he didn't have a pot to piss in and couldn't afford a pair of shoes to go to school in. My grandfather would buy two left shoes from a pushcart vendor—the only pair of shoes that my father would have for years. My father would also tell me that he didn't have a desk to put his stuff in until he was thirty-five. And my mother! Her mother died when she was nine, so she had to go live on a farm with relatives for a year. She had only one pair of underpants, which she had to wash every night by hand.

Now these are good deprivation stories!

With my kids, I have no good tales of woe. What can I say about my childhood that was adverse?

*"When Daddy was young he had to buy pot from a big, fat, smelly Rush Limbaugh look-alike."*

*"Emily, when I was your age, Daddy had to break into Grandpa's liquor cabinet to steal his apricot brandy so he could get girls drunk enough to fuck them."*

*"Daddy couldn't score acid in college without writing home for money."*

*"Daddy had to roll his own joints before he went to see the math tutor."*

I have nothing to tell them.

*"When I was growing up, I had to share a bathroom with my sister. And I had to walk fifteen feet down the hall to get to it."*

Horrors!

The only thing I can tell them is that when I was their age we didn't have a housekeeper to clean my room, so they should clean their own rooms.

But I love my family. Alison's a great wife and I have three lovely daughters. A lot of people ask me whether I wish I had a son, but I tell them I don't really care. But they say, Aren't you concerned that the Stern name won't be continued? What, my family tree is so important? What are we, the Rockefellers, the Kennedys, the Munsters? I come from a long line of garbagemen, pants pressers, and butchers. What a loss. The Stern family crest will have to be taken down. So what?

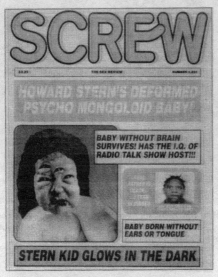

**Screw magazine honors the birth of my third child with a front-page headline. A new Stern is cause for celebration.**

# My Radio Crew

Back, left to right: Jackie "the Joke Man" Martling, Scott the Engineer, Howard, Billy West, Fred Norris, Robin Quivers, Gary Dell'Abate. Front: Stuttering John Melendez.

Boy Gary, pretending to work.

Gange, in my back office, keeping the log for my show.

Scott the Engineer, on the phone complaining about his hair.

Stuttering John, pretending to read.

Jackie "the Joke Man,"
killing time between weekends.

Gorilla, another intern, learning all
about radio as he demonstrates . . .

Howard (sex symbol) at the console.

Fred Norris, King of Mars, with stacks of cartridge tapes for playing sound effects and commercials.

Robin, following the top stories, in the world's largest litter box.

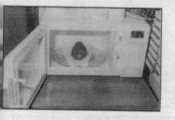

. . . microwaving Howard's infamous baked potatoes.

# A FAN'S-EYE VIEW

**This cartoonist's impression of the show was faxed to me on July 1, 1993.**

# Black and Blue Like Me

## *Howard in the 'Hood*

CHAPTER

3

Remember the book *Black Like Me*? It was about a reporter who dyed his skin black and traveled throughout the South to experience what it's like to be black. I could have written that book, only I would have called it "Black and *Blue* Like Me." I grew up the only white man in a black neighborhood in Roosevelt, Long Island, a pawn in my mother's little social experiment in integration. My mother is a wonderful, well-intentioned woman and I love her dearly, but one thing she was always rotten at was picking neighborhoods to live in. When my father started making a decent living with his recording studio, we could have lived almost anywhere on Long Island. But she had to pick Roosevelt, a little one-square-mile town that anybody with any sense would know was ripe for the realtors to start planting black people in. Overnight, there was an exodus of whites from Roosevelt. The Irish, the Poles, the Jews, the Italians—they all left. But my mother, the martyr, had to stay.

It was amazing. One day I'd go over to a friend's house to play, and the next day I'd go knock on the door and a big black guy would answer.

*"Hey man, who you looking for? We be in this house now."*

Every day another one of my friends would be gone. Can you imagine how traumatic that is to a kid? But did my mother care? Damn right she *didn't!* She had her nice middle-class black friends. Meanwhile, I was beginning to get the shit beat out of me every day by the welfare recipients who were moving into my neighborhood.

My mother didn't care; she wanted to build my character. Every part of life was about lesson builders—even the car pool. We used to have a car pool every day to get to school. My mother, always a conscientious neighbor, would drive my classmates a few days a week. Except for me. She thought I needed air. Air and ex-

**Hobble-along Howie, age seven.**

ercise. So I had to walk to school. And this was some walk; it wasn't just around the block. Every day I'd be walking to school with a heavy book bag and I would hear a car horn toot and there was my mother driving my friends, waving at me as she cruised by.

One day, I was walking to school and a bee stung me in the ankle and my foot began to swell. I was limping like a cripple. All of a sudden, my mother drove by. I saw her and I yelled, "MA!" *V-o-o-m*. She went right by. That afternoon, I hobbled home and complained to her and she told me I didn't need a ride. It was good for me to stagger home. This was what made the fiber of a person. Her and her fiber.

**Is this woman black?**

Anyway, one day there must have been a typhoon or a blizzard because she gave me a ride to school. I was sitting in the front seat of the car and my three remaining school friends were in the backseat and these guys started making fun of blacks. You know, stupid kid stuff. All of a sudden my mother turned to them and said, "Listen, boys, don't make fun of blacks. I'm part black, you know." There was a stone silence. I was sinking into my seat in the front of the car thinking, "I can't believe my mother just told my only friends she's part black."

"Ma, that's not true," I said.

"Oh, yes, it most certainly is, Howard, and you shouldn't be ashamed of it either," she insisted.

My mother had to pick this forum to make her social statement about racism? The car pool?

By the time I hit seventh grade there were only a

handful of white kids left in my school. That's when the beatings began to get regular. And lunchtime was the worst. I think I was providing lunch money for half the school. I'd hide my forty cents of lunch money in my sock, and black guys would come, choke me, rip my shoes off my feet, and take my money. One time I was able to sneak onto the line and actually buy lunch, but this guy Ronald came up to me and said, "I didn't get your lunch money. Think you tricked me?" Then he stuck his big black hand into my salad, scooped the whole thing up into his mouth, and swallowed it. It was like *Lord of the Flies*.

The lunch money thing got so bad that none of the white kids could bring money to school. One of my friends started bringing a bag lunch. The only problem was there was this black kid who would grab my friend's bag, and whatever chocolate snacks he had, like chocolate Ring Dings or Devil Dogs, the black kid would always steal. So my friend had a great idea. He took Ex-Lax, a large chunk, scraped off the word *Ex-Lax* on it, and wrapped it in tin foil. The next day the kid came along and swiped the chocolate. About two periods later we saw this kid running out of his next class. He was shitting his fucking brains out. "Yeah, revenge," my friend said.

There was no way to fight these guys. First of all, they traveled in six-packs. They all looked about twenty-five years old in the ninth grade. I don't even know if I had sprouted my first pubic hair, but these guys, who'd been left back at least fifteen times, were almost nineteen years old, with full mustaches and goatees. I would go home and say, "Ma, we love black

My trusted makeup man Ralph working on my transformation . . .

. . . me as Clarence Thomas with a wild Afro

. . . and today.

people but I don't think it's possible to live with them. They hate us. I'm not blaming them for hating us, but why do I have to be the one white person who lives with blacks?"

But my pleas fell on deaf ears. My parents were oblivious to my situation.

I wished Charles Manson were my mother. At least he protected his family. Half of the kids in my school were in a gang called the Five Percenters, kids from Brooklyn who had moved in. They had dietary laws like Muslims, never ate pork, and hated the white man with a vengeance. These guys would choke me and say, "You'll never live to see your fifteenth birthday"—nice stuff like that.

I was dealing with mutants who would take their penises out in class. Seriously. And what penises they were. These guys had rhinoceros penises. They would pull them out in shop and play with them. Remember when Clarence Thomas was being confirmed for the Supreme Court and he gave that speech about the hearings being a high-tech lynching because they were bringing up old stereotypes about the size of black men's penises? What is it with him? That's the one good stereotype blacks have. They get rapped on every stereotype—big lips, talk funny, nappy hair. The stereotype that God gave the black man a big penis is the greatest stereotype in the world. I'd like to walk down the street and have every person in the world think I have a big penis.

I tried to assimilate, but it was impossible. I was too tall to hide. I'd talk black talk but that didn't work. They even started up a black-studies program. The only kids who signed up for black studies were the few white kids left in Roosevelt. We all signed up thinking the blacks would like us better, but it didn't matter. We still got the shit beaten out of us. But I loved that black-studies class. Today, I could tell you nine thousand uses for the peanut, all invented by George Washington Carver.

Aside from my black-history education, there were some rewards for being in a school like that. I was one of the brightest kids in the school. I could have been valedictorian of my class. And I'm a dummy! They shipped all the bright black kids to a fancy school in East Meadow, so all the retards were left. In the ninth grade I was mistakenly thrown into a class for kids who came out of Brooklyn and Harlem who didn't know how to read. I got in this class and we were reading a book called *Itsy Bitsy*. *Itsy Bitsy* has got to be on a first-grade level. I was in ninth grade.

The teacher would say, "Howard, now you read." You had to read out loud.

**At my sixth-grade graduation with my sister (left) and mother.**

"Itsy Bitsy was a very little boy, and he . . ." I was reading, right? The other kids were like, "It-sy bit-sy." All of a sudden, I was like the genius in the class.

I had to put up with a lot of shit in this class, because every dredge was in it. Guys would shake you down. They'd go, "I like your pants," and they'd start to pull your pants off. They'd take your fucking pants! I'd be out of my mind. The teachers were oblivious, they didn't want to know about it. I aced this class, as you could imagine. But, of course, every good thing is ruined. I was about three months into it and I was the teacher's pet. I was a genius. I could do no wrong. I could read *Itsy Bitsy* backward, forward, whatever. I had the friggin' thing memorized.

My mother's good friend Estelle was a substitute

teacher at Roosevelt. She called my mother up and said, "Do you know that your son is in a class reading *Itsy Bitsy*?" So now my mother got hold of me.

"Are you reading *Itsy Bitsy*?"

"Yeah."

"Let me see this book, *Itsy Bitsy*." I gave her the book.

"WHAT THE HELL IS THIS!" she started screaming. "*ITSY BITSY*! YOU'RE READING THIS IN THE NINTH GRADE?!"

She called up the school; next thing I knew I was in the hardest English class, a new house of horrors.

It had the three white Polish kids who were the only other whites left by then in the school. They were sitting right in front of me. I was kind of feeling as if I was in a white school. The first day in this new class, I was sitting behind these three big Polacks, having a good time reading and everything, and one guy turned around to me, and he said, "Hey, Jew!"

*Pow! Smash!* Full fist right into my face. Hard as he could. I couldn't believe it. I finally got away from the blacks and the fucking Polacks were beating me up.

Today you're always reading about kids in the New York City public schools who get caught carrying guns to school. They should have *issued* me a gun to go to that school.

My parents finally realized it was time to move on when Alan, my one black friend, started getting hassled. Alan was a great kid; he would come over to my house and have milk and cookies and we'd play chess. One day, Alan and I were walking home and a bunch of black kids surrounded us. They beat the shit out of Alan for hanging out with a honkie. That was the final straw. My parents put the house up for sale. They decided to move to Rockville Centre. I'll never forget the day we moved. Everyone was crying. It was a real emotional experience. My mother was crying because our next-door neighbor, a really nice old black man, came over and was trying to convince us to stay, that Roosevelt needed white settlers like us. My father was crying because he was giving up a 3 percent VA mortgage on this house. And I was crying because I was afraid that my mother would listen to that old black fool and stay.

It turns out that it wasn't any better in Rockville Centre. I couldn't adjust at all. I was totally lost in a white community. I felt like Tarzan when they got him out of Africa and brought him back to England. I didn't know how to act around white people. I don't think I talked to anybody for three years. But I was thrilled to be out of Roosevelt. I promised myself that I would never, ever go back. Just thinking about it gives me the shakes. I remember before I married Alison, she would come to visit me in New York and she'd stay at my parents' home in Rockville Centre.

"I really want to go to Roosevelt and see where you lived," Alison decided.

"No, absolutely not." I was insistent. "I will not go to Roosevelt again."

"Why can't we go to Roosevelt?" she pleaded.

"Things could happen. Something could go wrong. Besides, I'm not even sure I know how to get to Roosevelt, I have such a bad sense of direction."

She wasn't buying it.

"Please," she started in with the whine, "I want to see how you grew up. I'm marrying you. I'm in love with you."

"I'll tell you the truth," I said. "I don't care where you grew up. Why do you care where I grew up?"

I finally relented. By now it was dark out.

"Okay, I'll take you to Roosevelt."

We got in the car. I drove a few blocks from my parents' house and made a few turns and then drove around that block about seventeen times. Finally, I pulled up to a house. We were maybe two seconds away from where we started.

"Roll down the window," I instructed Alison. "That's my old house." She had no idea we were still in Rockville Centre.

She peered out the window. She got all misty-eyed.

"That's my neighbor's house. That's my other neighbor's." I'm bullshitting like crazy.

"This is a beautiful community," Alison said. "How does it make you feel to be back here?"

"I don't know." I shrugged. "I just feel funny. But I'm glad you got a chance to see it. Roll the window back up."

Then I drove around the block about seventeen times again and *bingo!* We were back home in Rockville Centre. To this day, Alison thinks she's been to Roosevelt.

**My getup for my Black Men Who Look White sketch; hair inspired
by Kid 'n Play.**

## MALCOLM Z-Z-ZS

Spike Lee reminds me of every lame-o I ever met in Roosevelt. He's a trouble-maker who complains and bitches about the white man. He's totally unprofessional. You never see Steven Spielberg use race to raise money for pictures.

"The white man don't give me an Oscar nomination," he whines. Why should they? They gave him twenty-eight million to make that shitty Malcolm X movie and he flew all over Africa and went to the pyramids and went way over budget and then he resorted to a standard in the Lee arsenal—he bitched that the white man *be racists* for not giving him *mo'* money. I feel sorry for those poor jerks at Warner Brothers. He should have kissed their asses for giving him that money. Instead, he had the balls to go to his brothers and sisters in the black community with his little X cap out. He brought in Bill Cosby, Janet Jackson, Michael Jordan, Prince, Magic Johnson, Oprah Winfrey, and all they ponied in was $70,000 combined! What philanthropy! Warners chipped in twenty-eight mil but they were the white devil.

Spike Lee's movies are like amateur productions, worse than NYU student movies. His movies have ridiculous premises. The scenes are lousy because he's a bad director. The photography is bad. There's a loose, disjointed story line in most of his movies that makes no sense. Every Jew is a money lender. Every Italian is a dumb guinea on the corner who owns a pizza store and is out to get the black man. Lee doesn't do anything nice for the Koreans despite the fact that they're the only idiots who would open up a twenty-four-hour deli in a black neighborhood.

And the nerve of this schmuck to tell black kids to cut school and black adults to take off from work to go to the opening of that boring film *Malcolm X*. It's hard to keep black kids in school to begin with, and here he was inciting them to cut classes for his three-hour snoozefest. I know a lot of black men who called me up and said, "Howard, we've skipped work since 1978 to wait for the opening day of *Malcolm X*." That's been a big problem in the black community. "Why should we even take a job, when we'd only have to leave it to go see *Malcolm X*," they told me. I finally rented that film. I got news for you, it put me to sleep. They should have named it "Malcolm Z-Z-Zs." I guess that wouldn't fit on the hat.

Plus, that little dickhead is a coward, too. After I was talking on the show about how blacks don't go to see his films, he called Robin in the studio. In fact, let Robin tell the story.

ROBIN: What happened was Howard had been talking about Spike Lee on a Friday. He went through his usual litany of offenses—Spike's an amateur filmmaker, his films are worse than college-student films, they're not funny, black people don't go to them, the whole thing. I didn't say anything. I've said I like Spike Lee films, but I don't have to defend Spike every time—I just let it go. So, apparently, someone called Spike after that show and told him that Howard said no black people go to see his films. Well, Spike must have thought about this all weekend.

HOWARD: Good, I hope I ruined his weekend. Dumb little peanut head. Go ahead, Robin.

ROBIN: When he hit his office Monday morning, the first thing Spike did was call me. Now, I had no relationship with him, but I called him back out of respect. Spike immediately picked up and said, *"Robin!"*

"Yes," I said.

*"I heard that Howard Stern got on the air the other day and said no black people like to see my films,"* he said.

"Yes, that's his opinion," I said.

*"Well, that's bullshit, because lots o' black people go to see my films."*

"And that's your opinion," I said.

*"And you sit there and let him say anything he wants,"* he said.

Now I was pissed off. I said, "Excuse me, do you know what I do for a living?"

*"No, I've never heard the show,"* Spike said.

"THEN WHAT THE HELL ARE YOU DOIN' ON THE PHONE TELLING ME WHAT I DO!" I screamed. "I've been defending your stupid films for years. I say I like your films—everybody knows I'm black. I've been promoting your career for years. And yet the first time you call me to say anything is when Howard says he doesn't like your movies?! ARE YOU OUT OF YOUR MIND?!

Spike was speechless now. He didn't say, "You're a sister," or anything like that. What he said was, *"I sure hope they pay you a lotta money."*

"OH! AM I SUPPOSED TO QUIT MY JOB NOW?" I shouted.

*"No, I'm not tellin' you to quit,"* Spike said.

"JUST WHO THE FUCK DO YOU THINK YOU ARE? YOU FUCKING ASSHOLE!" I was really screaming, cursing him out.

And in the middle of this, I was thinking, "I'm yelling at one of the premier directors of film in America today." It was hysterical.
  *"Thank you for returning my call,"* Spike said. And that was the end of our conversation.

That was a great story except for the part about him being one of the premier directors. He's a knucklehead. How dare he talk to Robin about his problem with me. Her job on the show is not to sit and correct me every five seconds and defend the world. He's some black leader. HEY, BLACK PEOPLE, IF YOU'RE FOLLOWING SPIKE LEE, YOU'RE IN BIG TROUBLE!

## NIGGA' OF THE NINETIES

You know what the sweetest fruit of the civil rights movement was? The ultimate prize? We all know what the prize was. Porking WHITE BABES! And you know who enjoyed this benefit the most? Superstar black athletes.

One of the brothers who has attained the prize is the great basketball player Charles "I'm-the-Nigga'-of-the-Nineties" Barkley. Charles is so awesome, he once called us up and told me that he had just shared a hot tub with Donald Trump and some hot babes. I said that after that the water must have looked like egg drop soup! And this was when the Donald was still married to Ivana. I remember the time he called to tell us that he had just gotten married.

"So you're married now, what fun is that? Why'd you do that?" I opened.

"I got a two-and-a-half-year-old daughter," Charles said.

"Gary told me you married a hot white blonde. You got the prize, my man! She must go wild when you take your pants down. You're like an Adonis, big shoulders, strong muscles, tight ass," I said.

"That's from working hard, Howard. One day you'll get a job and have to work hard."

"Does your wife wear hot outfits when you go out? Miniskirts?"

"She has to dress her role," he said.

"How tall is she?"

"Five-foot-eleven."

"How much does she weigh?"

"One thirty."

"What cup size, C or D?" I was relentless.

"Probably a C. Jesus Christ, let me see."

She was right there in bed with him! This was great. "What's she wearing?" I asked.

"Nothing."

"She sleeps nude?"

"Totally nude."

"And you can easily palm her breast? Like a basketball?"

This was too much.

"Let me talk to her," I begged.

He put her on.

"Hey, honey, how you doing?" I purred.

"Fine, how are you?"

"I'm damn good," I said in my best Barry White.

"What are you calling her? Honey?" Robin butted in.

"She's naked. Be quiet, Robin!" I got back on the phone. "You got yourself a good man, don't you?" I buttered her up.

"Yeah, thank you."

"What are you doing naked in that room? You know Charles is a wild animal. He'll jump on top of you. Is Charles an animal in bed?"

"I guess he could be some kind of animal. Like an ant or a fly, something little."

"Is it true, once you go black you never go back?"

"I think so," she said.

"Is Charles the best lover you ever had?"

"He's the only one I ever had."

*This was too much.*

"You ever go to the gym and wear those aerobic tights with thong underpants?"

"Oh, yeah. All the time."

"Really!? *Whew!* Would you send me your sweaty shorts when you're done working out? I'd love to smell them. Let me tell you something, honey, I bet you if I got you alone, you'd mess around. I'd teach you a few things. I don't know how Charles is, but I do things that black guys won't do. I go the extra mile to please women."

"That's not true with Charles," she said. "He's white in that respect."

"Your parents give you any flak for being married to a black guy?"

"They don't care. He makes three million a year."

"You're set for life," I said.

"You're right about that," she agreed.

I got Charles back on the line.

"Your wife'll walk right out the door if you don't protect your money, you know these white women," I said.

"She ain't leaving with no money," Charles said.

"Damn right. You get her to sign a prenup?"

"No," he said.

"What? Are you kidding me? How will you stop her?"

"I'll have to call a couple of my boys to rough her up a little," he said. "That's the type of prenup you need."

"It's a preknuckle agreement," I said.

She got back on the line.

"If I do leave him, he says he's gonna dish out the bucks big time," she laughed.

"Smart woman. You sound like my wife," I said.

It was sad to read recently that Charles and his wife were separated. From that conversation they seemed like a great couple.

## RODNEY KING
### THE WORLD'S MOST DANGEROUS MILLIONAIRE

They didn't beat this idiot enough. He should be beaten every time he reaches for his car keys. Here you got a guy driving drunk going 100 mph leading the cops on a wild-goose chase. What if your kid was crossing the freeway then and got hit by him? I say beat him more. And beat your kid, too, because he's not supposed to cross a freeway! I would have run him over and then backed the squad car up and run him over again. Jerk! The fact that he lived after a high-speed chase like that means he didn't get beat enough. They should have tied his testicles to the bumper and then done 115 mph, see how much he would have liked that.

Those L.A. cops should have done what our New York cops have been doing for years: be real nice to Rodney, gently assist him into the squad car, give him a cup of coffee so he can sober up, take him into the basement of the station house, and beat the living shit out of him. No cameras. No riots. No nothing. Case closed. Justice is served. I love cops. Every time they're on a high-speed chase like that, they're taking their lives in their hands. Who knows what those cretins are packing when they get out of the cars? Cops, you deserve all the doughnuts you can eat. I just can't figure out why I still get traffic tickets.

Actually, Rodney should get down on his knees and kiss the feet of those officers that wailed on him. Have you seen the before and after pictures of this dude? It was the Rodney King makeover. He went in looking like Skid Row Joe, and after twenty whacks to the head he came out looking like Billy Dee Williams. Nice new 'do. Stylish pencil-thin mustache. He looks like a movie star. They beat all the ugly out of him. Now he's a superstar. He threw out the ball at the first Dodgers home game. Maybe Mike Ovitz will represent him for movie-of-the-week deals. He just turned down a $2 million settlement. This guy is going to be the world's most dangerous millionaire. Can you imagine what happens when he gets his Lamborghini? "UH, MR. KING! PLEASE PULL OVER. YOU'RE DO-

ING 375 MPH IN A 55 ZONE. PLEASE, MR. KING."

"Sheet, this be fun. What sucker gonna stop me, Rodney King? I gots my *own* video camera now. Sheet, I can drive a damn helicopter through the Lincoln Tunnel, nobody stop me."

## THE L.A. RIOTS SHOPPING SPREE

One thing's for certain. Those black folks in South Central L.A. sure know how to make good TV. I couldn't stop watching the live coverage of the riots after the first Rodney King decision. Didn't you love that on-the-spot coverage?

"We're here live as this supermarket is being looted."

In the background, guys were carrying garbage pails full of chickens. Women were running around filling up their carts as if they were on "Supermarket Sweep."

"Let me see if I can get a word in here with one of the participants."

Participants? Looters? Animals?

"Uh, miss, do you think this has anything to do with the Rodney King decision?"

This woman looked at him and said, "Whaaa? I'm busy shopping."

In the background, a woman was screaming, "IT'S FREE! IT'S FREE! PAYBACK!"

And they were all proud of what they were doing. I remember the good old days of the Watts riots when

Orchestrating a wild African jungle scene for the Miss Howard Stern Show contest. Cheetah is played by Stuttering John (far right).

the rioters covered their heads like Mafiosi going into the Federal Building. Now it was a friggin' photo opportunity.

"Hi, I'm looting."

There was no political agenda behind that rioting. This is what happens when we raise generations of kids who have never been told to do their homework, never been told to wipe their ass, never been told anything by their parents. In fact, it's more than likely that their parents aren't even around. They've got a senile grandparent raising them. Hey, they saw an opportunity and they went for it. And they blamed everybody else. "It's the cops! It's the Koreans! It's the government! It's white people! It's four hundred years of oppression!"

Hey, if things are going wrong for you, maybe it's

"Howard Stern is a cultural mirror of what is good and bad in American media. If Howard Stern didn't exist, white trash would not have a superstar."
— Reverend Al Sharpton

"If you want your radio to burn, stay tuned to Howard Stern."
—James Brown

**(Above) Here I am, shooting the shit with the Godfather of Soul, James Brown, and the Reverend Al Sharpton; and (left) using a metal detector on rap star Flavor Flav on the set of my E! Entertainment Television show.**

*you* who's causing the problem. That's a hard concept to come to grips with when you're used to blaming everybody else.

"Hey man, the summer's coming and there's no jobs."

Who's going to hire you? You've got thirty-seven earrings in your ear, you look as if you stepped off the set of a rap video, your hat is on backwards, and you've got your girlfriend's initials carved into your hair. Hey, if I walked in like that, no one would hire me, either.

And if you want to look like that, start your own business. This is America. Get off your ass. You don't have to answer to the white man. Start your own business right in the black community. Forget about four hundred years of oppression. If you wait for the white man to solve your problems, you're finished. You've got to be like those Koreans you're shooting. They bust their ass twenty-four hours in those delis. The whole family is working seven days a week.

"But the Koreans don't understand. They're rude to us. If I steal a fruit they yell at me, and they don't even yell in English."

Hey, they're rude to you? Don't go in the store. Open your own store. Everyone hated the Jews when they came over and lived in the ghettoes. You think the ruling class WASPs were so anxious to help the Jews develop businesses in this country? They couldn't care less if every Jew in America starved. They wouldn't let the Jews in their law firms so the Jews created their own law firms. They said, "Screw you, WASPs." You can do it, too.

## MY SECRET OF LIFE

Why doesn't everyone behave? Life is really so simple. Let me tell you the secret of life. You learn it young. The problem is after I give people the secret of life, they say, "Howard, that's not such a big secret." I know how they feel. It's like the end of an Ingmar Bergman movie. He takes you through hell and then at the end, all of a sudden, he says, "The secret of life is strawberries and cream." What the hell is he talking about? I just sat through three hours of boredom to find out that life is strawberries and cream? That rat bastard, I'd like to take his Swedish ass and throw it out the window. I went through a chess game with Death to find out that life is strawberries and cream?

You want the secret of life? Here it is: You wake up in the morning. You eat a little breakfast, maybe read the newspaper. You attempt to go to school if you're that age. If your teacher tells you to sit in the chair, you sit in the chair. If you don't feel like it, you force yourself, anyway. You get older, the routine doesn't change. You eat breakfast, you go to work, you come home. If you're lucky enough, you're married. If you're not, then maybe you have a boyfriend or girlfriend. You yell at your wife, you make up with your wife. If your testicles feel all right, you bang your wife. You watch a video you rented or maybe you go out to the movies.

Then you go home to your bedroom, you mellow out a little bit. If you're the late Sam Kinison you take a schnapps. Then maybe you get a snack, have some strawberries and cream, and wash it down with a Snapple. Then you snore away for eight hours, you wake up, and you do it all over again. You wait for the weekend, that's your party, the weekend. The secret of life is so simple. That's life. If you have kids, you live with the kids. You don't move out on your wife. You stay with her even if you've banged her nine thousand times and you're sick of it. *You stay with her anyway.* Nobody follows that. They don't realize that's the secret to life. When you've got kids, you raise them.

The secret of life, in one cliché, if I may sum it up for you, is: ENJOY, EVEN IF YOU'RE NOT ENJOYING. Stop looking for a big bang, stop looking for some kind of excitement. And if you can't go along with these rules, you're a misfit. Expect to be beaten by the police. It's like going on a diet. The secret to losing weight is to keep your big fat trap shut.

"But I got to have butter on my potato or I can't eat it." I'll put you in a concentration camp for one week, and you'll eat a potato without butter. It'll taste like ice cream to you.

"The secret to life is so simple," I declared on my show. "The reason I am announcing this secret is that perhaps one of the maniacs who is stealing a radio right now might accidentally tune to me and say, 'Uh-oh, I'm about to get the secret of life.' To him it would be profound."

Then Robin complained that my secret to life was

too honest. I didn't make it appetizing enough for the listeners.

Okay. Let me make it appetizing. If you follow the secret of life as Howard Stern expresses it, guess what will happen to you? You won't be beaten by the police. You won't be in jail. And you won't have to riot. You'll be perfectly happy.

That still wasn't good enough for Robin.

"You gotta say life will be sweet and all the rewards of the world will be yours," she said. "Lie, Howard."

I thought about it for a second.

"You're right, Robin, I should lie. I should tell all the rioters this secret of life. I hope they're tuned in. Here's the secret of life: Jump into a tub, get yourself wet. Put your finger in an electrical socket. That's the secret of life, you retards."


## HOLLYWOOD IN THE 'HOOD

MTV got me really pissed off during their coverage of the L.A. riots. What the hell was MTV doing covering the riots anyway? They flew in that baldy Montel Williams and imported a bunch of fifteen-year-old black kids who were sitting there looking angry and pissed off. MTV video jock John Norris got his combat boots on and they got a pretty young white girl host in a short skirt wearing a "No Justice" T-shirt. Who got no justice? The girl in the miniskirt? Montel Williams? I was furious at this knee-jerk superficial attempt by MTV to "solve" social problems.

Then they had Cosby on, making a "statement."

Cosby says, "Let's all pray that everyone, from the top of the government down to the people in the street, that we all have good sense." What the hell was he talking about? Why do the people in the government have to pray? What are they praying for, the idiots in the streets? Nobody wanted to say that those dickfaces in the streets had absolutely no agenda, no reason to do any of what they were doing, and they all should have been mowed down right there and then. Then they got that jerk Arsenio Hall. It's pretty sad when they have to go to a failed stand-up comedian to calm people down. Arsenio tried to deliver a message but nobody paid any attention to him. I did hear, though, that he was of invaluable assistance to the National Guard because they used the top of his head as a landing strip for their supply runs. Listen to this pretentious idiot:

"I'm a graduate of Kent State. I know that story about the National Guard, man. When they come tonight, it's gonna be insane. I don't want nobody getting killed. Imagine what they'll do to my young black brothers and sisters tonight if they're out in the streets. Please know where your children are because if you don't know where they are tonight, you might have to bury them tomorrow. I'm telling you, they killed white kids in Kent State, they will wear us out tonight."

Listen to that fuck face. What is he, a general? He's phonier than a Chinese redhead. What a stupid argument, too. At Kent State, kids were tragically killed when they were taking a moral stance in opposing a stupid war. He's comparing the lowlife scum looting

**Pissing everyone off, I played David Duke on my TV show. I pulled off my hood and shared the family photo album.**

and beating innocent truck drivers to nonviolent anti-war protesters? *Whooo! Whoooo! Whoooo! Whaaaat* a moron.

This politically correct Hollywood crowd should have gotten together to sing the peace song we wrote for L.A. It went to the tune of that old Billy Joel hit "Just the Way You Are":

### DON'T GO RIOTING

Don't go rioting, you African-Americans
Don't yank us whites out of our cars
Rodney is guilty, there is no question
The bastard should be behind bars

We need to know that you will all stay calm
And stay as gentle as Sinbad
Ahhhh—give us a break from all this violence
It's so inconvenient when you get mad

What will it take for us to wake you up?
We want to have the city calm . . .
Put down the guns and drugs and lose the hate
It isn't friggin' Vietnam

Don't go hitting TV reporters
Don't break the windows in the stores, mmmm—
Collect your welfare and watch Montel Williams
Instead of starting racial wars

Don't burn your houses, don't smack Koreans
That ain't no way to fix L.A.
Be calm and gentle, be kind to tourists
Or the cops'll blow you all away

---

### A SPECIAL MESSAGE

What we try to do with humor is
show the absurdity of the differences
between people, as Lenny Bruce did
when he used words like *nigger* and
*kike* and *wop* in an attempt to de-
mystify them and rob them of any
power they may have. Underneath
all the differences, we're all in
this together. So it's a drag to

get a letter like the one I got from a listener of my show who's in prison.

> I'm in prison, been here a few years. I was in a different prison a few years ago and I was working in the machine shop and we had a locked tool cage. Only one inmate was allowed in there and he was locked inside to pass out the tools. This cage is where the radio was, and the tool clerk and myself were the only white guys in the shop. He'd put on Howard in the morning and the black people would complain. A big argument broke out and some black guys threatened him. After work they jumped him with a steel pipe and he was beaten so bad that he died two days later. He got killed for the Howard Stern show. Prison murders are rarely publicized and his wasn't, nor was the circumstance. Just thought I'd share this with you.
>
> P.S. You guys help me laugh through hard jail time.

This is a distressing letter. If I can teach people anything, it's if you're surrounded by black guys who hate me, change the frigging station. Let them listen to whatever they want. This stupid show isn't worth dying for.

# My Sex Life

Short on sex, long on love. That's the story of my sex life.

I've been married to the same woman for over fifteen years. We've been faithful to each other for over twenty years. So, right off the bat, we're not talking about massive numbers here. Plus, I have to admit, I'm not exactly a sexual dynamo. I'm pretty typical. Dr. Kinsey reported that two minutes was the average duration for a man to achieve orgasm while lovemaking, and that's about how long it takes me. Of course, I'm including the time it takes for Alison and me to walk up the stairs and get to the bedroom.

I might be a better lover if I could only understand what is going on. Casanova Stern I'm not, but it's not my fault. I never had any sex education growing up. My parents wouldn't even say the word sex. I never even heard a peep coming out of their bedroom. When I was thirteen, my father called me into his bedroom and said, "Do you have any questions about sex?"

I got really embarrassed and turned red in the face. I looked at him and suddenly said, "I know more about sex than you do," and I ran out of the room. I think we were both pretty relieved that we didn't have to go any further in the discussion.

My sexual guru, Grandpa.

My entire sexual education came from my maternal grandfather, who was a fucking wild man. I never knew this growing up, because he was already old and he was presented as the loving grandpa, rather sedate and dignified. My mother, of course, would never say a bad word about her father, and as a result I was very close to him. We looked alike, and I loved this man very much. But my mother's mother died when she was nine and my grandfather raised her like a dog. She only had one pair of underpants. Plus, he had a really nasty temper. He would take my mother and her sister to the movies once a week and would yell and get into knife fights in the middle of the movie.

And from Grandpa, via my cousin Jack, I got this worldly sexual advice:

"I'm gonna give you some advice," my grandfather said. "When a woman locks up on you, punch her in the face as hard as you can and she'll unlock."

No wonder I was such a misfit. I obviously came from a long line of them. I was sort of a late bloomer, too. I was the last kid on the block to masturbate. One of my friends hinted about it to me, so I decided that I'd try it. I was about eleven when I first tried. My parents had left me alone in the house, so I went up to their bedroom and took off my clothes. I lay down on their bed spread-eagled and started playing with myself while watching "Gilligan's Island."

I really had the hots for Ginger and I was waiting for her to appear on the screen, but they kept showing Mrs. Howell III, that old bag. Finally, Ginger came on, and I really started pulling my pud. Mind you, I had no idea what happened during masturbation. After a few minutes, I started feeling warm all over and then I felt something building. "Oh, man, this is it!" I thought to myself. All of a sudden, warm liquid poured out of my penis, all over my legs and my parents' bed. I had urinated all over myself.

When Bob Denver came on the show, I played Ginger to his Gilligan.

I tried masturbating again over Anne Francis, who

played Honey West on TV. I thought she was the hot-test thing. They had adapted a book from the TV se-ries, and there was one scene where Honey West got captured and tied up against her will.

I got so excited reading it that I reenacted that scene in my bed with my legs spread and my arms out as if I was Honey. I started flailing away at my cock and, before I knew it, I had my first orgasm.

Then, I was over at my friend's house and his older brother came home fresh from fingering a girl, he told us. Some fat cow named Susan. We begged him to let us smell his fingers. We snorted that loving scent for a good half hour. Man, were we idiots! But my flaming heterosexuality could not be denied. I sought refuge in that Honey West book. I'd bring it with me into the bathroom and jerk off to the same passage over and over and over again.

Aside from seeing my mother naked once when she stepped out of the shower (ugh, what a nightmare), I had never seen a naked woman until I was twelve years old. I was walking home from my friend's house in Roosevelt and I passed a corner where I would al-ways find the weirdest things—like used rubbers and Kotex—just lying there in the hedges. One day I was walking past the bushes and I found an old, soiled, disgusting, ripped-up nudist magazine.

It was filled with pictures of naked women playing volleyball, naked women taking hikes, naked women cooking with their big fucking hairy crotches, with the fucking hairs running up to their belly buttons. No air-brushing as in *Playboy*. Real women. Real disgusting women. Playing volleyball with their big, fat, dimpled, cellulite-ridden asses hanging out. It was so disgusting. I loved it. I wanted to fuck everybody at the volleyball match. Even the ball.

I ran right home with that filthy magazine. But then I had a problem. Where was I going to keep it? I couldn't keep it in my room. Then I had a brilliant idea. I always stole my father's cigars. I used to smoke them down in the basement. Then I'd hide them in my sister's doll case, which was also in the basement. She had stopped playing with her dolls, so I thought it was safe. Thank God my sister never got the urge to play with her dolls again. They really reeked from cigars.

> "We were never privy to Howard's masturbation. Never saw him do it."
> —Ben Stern

I got totally into masturbation. But when you're living in a tiny, cramped house and your parents' bedroom is a foot and a half away, it becomes Mission Impossible to jerk off without your parents finding out. So when I wanted to jerk off I had to walk into the bathroom, grab a couple of tissues, and hide them in my underwear. Then I'd flush the toilet for effect and nonchalantly walk back to my room. I'd say goodnight but I couldn't close the door because then they'd get suspicious. I'd lie there totally quiet and jerk off like a jackrabbit. I trained myself to come so fast it's no wonder that I couldn't last more than a few seconds when I finally began to make it with real live girls.

A few strokes and *boom* I exploded into one of the tissues. "Honey! Honey West, I love you!" Then, my penis would drip, like a leaky faucet, so I would wrap it in another tissue. God forbid I should get semen stains on my underpants with my mother perusing each pair with a microscope. The whole process of jerking off was so complicated. It had to be so well thought out. I used to fantasize having my own apartment so I could jerk off in peace. My nightmare continued because the next trick was to get to the bathroom with that dangerous cargo. I had to flush that squishy load down the toilet without attracting my parents' attention.

One time I was on my way to the bathroom holding this scum-soaked tissue in my hand when, all of a sudden, my mother walked by me in the hall. I was cool under pressure. I immediately blew my nose into the soiled tissue. It was disgusting, the semen smearing all over my face, but it worked. My mother never caught me.

Then, at this tender age, I had my first homosexual experience.

Now, I'm all man; I don't want to mislead you. And I can't stand the thought of a man's ass as a sexual object. Have you ever smelled a man's ass with the hairs and pimples? I'm going to throw up.

But one day at my house one of my stupid friends suggested that we masturbate . . . each other. I wasn't interested in him seeing my little dick, so I reluctantly agreed to help him out. He pulled his pants down around his ankles. I started to rub his dick up and down when he told me I was doing it all wrong. He took his penis between his two hands and started rubbing his hands together like he was starting a fire.

This shit was all too weird for me, so I got the fuck

out of the room. And I never again thought about guys
. . . except for FABIO, my dream man. Ah, those lus-
cious lips. Just kidding, you pricks.

I first discovered real live girls when I went to
sleep-away camp. I was thirteen and I didn't look too
bad. I didn't have my big nose yet and I had short
hair. I always wore sunglasses to look cool, so my
friends called me Shades of Blue. That summer I met
my first girlfriend. Her name was Judith and she was
a piece of ass. She was much more mature than any of
the other thirteen-year-old girls. She looked like a real
woman—huge tits, curvy body, the works. I finally
got up enough nerve to ask her out and she actually
became my girlfriend. That meant we kissed on the
lips maybe once and she wore my I.D. bracelet. Hey,
we were going steady!

After we came home from camp, I wrote her from
time to time. She lived in a place that was alien to
me—Far Rockaway. Meanwhile, I was such a moron
because Far Rockaway was about a half hour's drive
from where I lived. But you have to remember, living
at my parents' house was like living in a prison. It
never even dawned on me to ask my father if I could
call her. Finally, that New Year's Eve, I got up the
courage and asked my father if I could make a long-
distance call to Far Rockaway. He said okay and I
called Judith and invited her to come visit me and she
said yes. I was jazzed.

Better yet, she was coming over on a day that my
parents were going away, which meant I had the
whole house to myself with her. The only problem was

I had no fucking idea what to do with her. There weren't any porno films back then for me to learn from.

Then I remembered a book my parents had sort of hidden with their other books in the living room. They probably thought it was safe to keep it there because they knew I never read any books.

It was a sex manual called *Your Wedding Night*. I opened the book. It had pictures of breasts and vaginas and penises and it showed intercourse. I concentrated on the part about french kissing and petting. So Judith came over and we spent the whole day talking. I was nervous as shit. Finally, I got her up to my bedroom and I leaned over and kissed her and that was it. I didn't even have the balls to put my hands on her tits.

But I had my first girlfriend . . . until we went back to camp the next summer. When I got there, my good friend Lewis Weinstein (who later became a doctor) came up to me and said, "What do you have a girlfriend for? Are you crazy? Play the field. Break up with Judith." I had no idea what "playing the field" was, but Lew seemed to know what he was talking about. I was a flaming asshole. I had the best-looking girl in the camp and I broke up with her. He told me all the girls would be lining up for me. Easy for him to say. He always had a remarkable ability to attract women. So, like an imbecile, I listened to Lew and I broke up with Judith.

Lew had a great summer. I, on the other hand, was miserable for the rest of the summer. No one would even look at me. Judith, naturally, found a new boyfriend in two seconds.

In fact, I didn't get another girlfriend until I was sixteen. Back home, no one would talk to me. I was a real misfit in high school. But that summer I went to Camp Wel-Met again. Right away, I met a really

**Eighteen years old and a fucking mess.**

cute girl named Nancy. We hit it right off. So one night, she and I sneaked off to the waterfront and started making out. We were buck naked and I was fingering her and I figured, this is it! I'm getting laid! There was no way that I was going to go home from camp and hit seventeen and still be a virgin. So we were going at it by the water, and suddenly she said, "Let's go in the water and skinny-dip."

Now I was really confused. I didn't know what I was doing, yet now I had to figure out how to do it in the water. We were standing in the water French kissing and I was trying to decide what to do. So I squatted while she stood. My balls and my ass were in this freezing cold water and she was looking at me as if I was crazy. Was I supposed to lay her down in the water and fuck her? Were we supposed to squat and fuck? Between my nerves and my dropping body temperature, I was shivering violently . . . like an epileptic. She was disgusted.

So back we went onto the beach, and by now I was freezing even more. I fingered her some more but she was really drying up on me. And my breath stunk because I had a nervous stomach. I was this skinny, shaking, smelly thing. It was amazing she didn't throw up on me. Here was my big opportunity to lose my virginity but I was also really paranoid that I would get her pregnant, because I certainly didn't have any rubbers. I was also nervous that we'd get caught and get thrown out of camp, so we got dressed really quickly. I threw my pants on and stuffed my underwear in my back pocket. I went to see my friends, who were hanging out in the main lodge, and they saw the underwear sticking out of my pocket and they went wild.

"Way to go!" they screamed. They figured I got laid. I didn't have the heart to tell them I didn't. But the next day I told Lew. We decided to drive into Monticello to get rubbers. Lew was, by far, the more sophisticated of the two of us. He had a full beard when he was thirteen, and he was really self-confident, so we decided that he'd do the talking to the pharmacist. We went into the drugstore and I was nervous as hell. Lew was like a pro.

"Could I have some lubricated Trojans, please? Do you have the ribbed ones?" He had this down cold. Meanwhile, I was standing next to him, screaming, "Me, too! Me, too!" like a demented little child. Lew was poking me in the ribs to shut me up. The druggist gave us each a three-pack and we were set.

The next night, Lew grabbed a girl, and *bang*, he used one of his rubbers right off the bat. Meanwhile, I was with Nancy, but after that fiasco, she wouldn't fuck me. She realized I was a virgin. That three-pack stayed unopened the whole summer.

After camp I called her and pleaded with her to come over to my house. She came over one weekend when my parents were gone and as soon as she was in the door, I was begging her to have sex.

"No!"

I gave her alcohol.

"No!"

I broke out my pitifully small stash of pot.

"No!"

"But I really love you, Nancy."

"No."

She was coming up with every excuse in the book, but I wasn't buying it.

"I've got my period."

"I don't give a shit, let's fuck!"

"NO!"

Finally, after three hours of begging, I wore her down. We went upstairs and she got naked and she looked great. We started to fuck and I lasted all of three seconds. But I wasn't a virgin anymore! I was elated.

"Let me get some wine. Let's make a toast." I was carrying on like a maniac. Meanwhile, she found some blood on the sheets and she was disgusted by the whole thing.

A couple of months later, I was at a party. I was no longer a virgin but I might as well have been for all I did with Nancy. I met a girl there named Janice. This girl was drop-dead gorgeous. A true blonde, with huge tits. She even had an older boyfriend who was away at college.

Normally, I'd have no chance with a girl like that who knew me from school because I was such a geek in high school. But Janice went to a different high school, so she was looking at me and all she saw was some guy with long hair. I offered to turn her on—again breaking into my pitiful nickel-bag stash—and she must have figured I was a major pot dealer. To her, I was a happening druggie. I had a license. I was driving my dad's Mercury Montego. I was cool. She fell head over heels for me. She was propositioning me all night. I didn't know what to do, so I got her number and said, "I'll call you."

Finally, I called her. I took her back to my house because at this point, my mother was working (Mom got a job as an inhalation therapist at Mercy Hospital, and her day consisted of extracting globs of disgusting-looking mucus out of diseased lungs). This was the perfect opportunity to score.

I called upon all my seduction skills.

First, I broke out the pot, but I made her go out to the garage to smoke it, so my parents wouldn't smell it later. That really must have made her feel as if she was with a grown man.

"Janice, do you mind going out to the garage to smoke this pot?"

How debonair.

How Long Island.

Then I broke into my father's liquor cabinet to make her an apricot sour. While she was drinking alone, I immediately had to run into the kitchen to wash out the blender so my mother wouldn't see a dirty blender and put two and two together. This had to be a dream date for her. Sitting alone on my parents' stupid couch while her hot man was in the kitchen tidying up.

**The toastmaster general at my sister's wedding, during my senior year in high school.**

How romantic.

How seductive.

How fucking lame can you get?

Finally, I took her upstairs to my room, where I was going to put the final touches on the seduction by playing some music on my little stereo.

So what does the ultimate Casanova choose for lovemaking music? Neil Young's "Down by the River, I Shot My Baby." This had to be the most depressing music on the planet. Even *I* was ready to slit my wrists.

While this music was on she started getting all weepy about her boyfriend in Albany, but I just kept plowing on. I didn't want to hear about her stupid fucking boyfriend.

I started to try to take her shirt off.

"No, don't take off my shirt," she said. "My boyfriend always keeps my shirt on when we have sex." I started thinking that maybe she was missing a breast. I asked her if I could feel her up under her shirt. "Oh, sure," she said. "Just don't take off my shirt." I started to pull her hiphuggers off and she was wearing tiny little panties. I slowly pulled her panties down and saw the most magnificent thatch of billygoat light blond hair. Oh, man! I started fingering her and she was hot and wet and turned on. She pulled down my pants and she grabbed my cock as if she was uprooting a carrot in the garden. She was saying, "Oh, yes! Oh, yes! That's it! C'mon already, do it to me!"

I had done this once before, for about three seconds, so I was fumbling with the rubber. When I got it on I said, "Guide me in."

"What?" she moaned.

"Guide me in."

"What do you mean?"

"Put me in you." I sure as shit wasn't having any luck getting in there by myself.

"You never did this before!?" she started screaming at me. So we started arguing back and forth.

"I did, I swear I did. I just prefer women to guide me in," I was screaming.

So she took my cock—she was totally disgusted with me by now—and she started to put me in her. The second I felt her wetness, *BOOM*, I shot my load. She had no idea that I was done. I wasn't even all the way in yet. Meanwhile, she was crying hysterically.

"What's wrong?" I asked.

"I can't take this," she sobbed. "I'm not doing this because you don't know what you're doing!"

"Perfect!" I said. " 'Cause I don't want to do this either." Meanwhile, if I hadn't finished, I wouldn't have given up so easily.

"I have to call my boyfriend in Albany," she suddenly decided.

"WHAT?!" I screamed like a maniac. "My father'll kill me. You can't call Albany from my house! You're a mental patient. Forget it."

She was still hysterical, so I drove her home.

"You're not going to call me again?"

"Absolutely not," I said. I was a real moron. I should have called her again and kept banging her. So what if she was a mental patient? I didn't get laid again until that summer when I went to camp to work in the kitchen. For some unfathomable reason, I was really in demand that summer. I began banging several different girls on a regular basis. But I didn't know how to handle it. I was so emotionally stunted. If I had been a smart guy, I would have made friends with the girls and been able to fuck them all simultaneously. As it was, I was like a black widow spider, I'd devour each girl after I fucked her. I wasn't in love with any of them and I didn't particularly want to hang out with them, so I wouldn't speak to them again after I nailed them. I was really mature.

But I was on a roll. I was sharing a tent with a guy named Danny, and one time he came into the tent while I was about to fuck a girl, and he wouldn't leave.

But that didn't stop me. While he was talking I slipped my penis inside of her. It was actually kind of exciting. And of course I came in like two seconds. It was too fucking exciting for an asshole like me.

One of the girls I fucked that summer was named Patty. She was a counselor and we were flirting with each other, so one night she came to my tent. I was lying there sleeping and she came in with her flashlight and she kissed me awake. She was unbelievably sensuous. We went back to her cabin and she was great. We ripped off our clothes, I got on top of her, and I blew my load in three seconds.

I was so sexually immature. Patty tried to widen my horizons but I was such a loser. I had no idea how to enjoy sex. One time we were about to fuck and just as I was about to enter her she tried to stick her finger up my ass. I pulled my cheeks together like rocks, I thought that was so wrong. I was so flipped out that I stopped talking to her.

But I had my eyes on a friend of hers, Leslie. Leslie was a latecomer to camp. She was filling in the last two weeks for a counselor who left early. She was a kooky actress type but she had an unbelievable body, great tits, brown hair, sensuous mouth. I fell head over heels in lust with her. I kept trying to get her to go out with me, but she refused. She told me that I was a jerk because I dumped her friend Patty. But I worked on her and worked on her and finally I overcame her loyalty for her friend and she caved in.

I was in heaven. It was great sex. Uninhibited, wild animal sex. She blew me like crazy; I'd eat her for hours at a time. We did sixty-nine all over the place. I wanted to propose to her right then and there, even though I was eighteen and she was an aspiring actress—very affected. So when camp was over, I kept in touch with her. She lived in Princeton in a kind of communal arrangement with a children's theater group. A few weeks after camp, we got together at a camp reunion and it was magic all over again. We were making out like dogs on the steps, out in front of the whole camp, we didn't care.

When the reunion was over, we took a bus together back to Princeton. When we got to her house, we were fucking five times a night. She'd jerk me off in the bathtub. I would take her back to her room and eat her out for an hour. I would do anything to please her. I was head over heels in love with her. It was unbelievable. One morning when she got up, she was nude and she grabbed my hand and said, "Come with me." I stumbled out of bed and I got my underwear on because I was totally self-conscious about anyone else in that house seeing my little mushroom. She led me down the hall and then she opened a door and we were in the bedroom of two gay guys who were in the acting troupe with her. Leslie hopped into bed with them and she started to get physical and then she turned to me and said, "Climb into bed with us!"

I was so provincial that if she had been in that bed with two other *girls* and she had made the same offer, I would still have panicked. But there was no way in the world that I was going to get into bed with two other guys. I ran out of the room, called her out into the hall, and started yelling at her.

But a few days later, I had a much better opportunity with Leslie and I really blew it. Patty came over to visit us and she brought her new boyfriend. Right off the bat, Patty's stock dropped in my eyes because here she was with this little douchy guy. We were all sitting in the living room and Leslie and I started making out. So Patty and her boyfriend started making out, too. Then Leslie started taking her clothes off and it dawned on me that we could have a group scene going down here. But I was so embarrassed to show my cock in public that I grabbed Leslie and took her upstairs. I blew what would be my one opportunity in life to do something kinky.

That fall I started college at Boston University. Anytime Leslie called me, I'd run right down to Princeton. But then one night I got a disturbing call from her.

"I'm breaking up with you," she said.

"What? Why?" I was stunned.

"I met this guy," she said. "He's a redhead and I like him a lot. He's got a really big penis."

I was freaking out. Now my penis was really an issue. She didn't say I had a small penis. But she was leaving me for a guy with a REALLY BIG PENIS. Why was she saying this to me? Was I really that small? I was devastated. Once again, I was a failure with women.

So there I was, a freshman at Boston University and horny as hell. B.U. was supposed to be a big party school, but I couldn't get arrested. Every girl on campus was ignoring me big time. One day I was sitting in the cafeteria with Lew (yes, the same Lew who was my friend at summer camp ended up being my roommate in college) and my other friend Elliot and some other guys and an incredible-looking girl walked in. She was like a goddess. She was built like a supermodel: long, long legs; perfectly flat stomach. She was about five-nine and she was wearing a miniskirt, cut-off shirt, no bra, and platform shoes. And she was with an incredibly ugly girlfriend of hers. Beauty and the Beast.

They sat down and this gorgeous woman started looking over at us. I had such a horrendous self-image by this time that I agreed when Lew said, "Look at her, she's checking me out."

"Fuck you, she's checking *me* out," Elliot said.

Of course, the furthest thing from my mind was that she was checking *me* out.

That night I went to a party at our huge dorm, called the Zoo. There were literally thousands of students there. Back then, I used to chain-smoke, so I took out a cigarette, got ready to light it, and this goddess walked by me and said "Hello" and kept walking. *Oh, man!* I figured she wanted it—why else would she say hello to a jerk like me? So I walked over to her and she was with Quasimodo again and I asked her for a light. Great opening line, huh?

"You girls looking for a party?" I asked, after a few drags. As if I, with no life, would ever have known where a party was.

"Sure, we love to party," the goddess said.

So we went upstairs. Finally, I had a social life. I had two girls with me, even if one looked like a troll. We were going from floor to floor, no parties. When we got to my floor I said, "I have some outrageous pot. You want to get high?" They said sure.

So we went into my room and I sat on my bed and the two girls sat opposite me on my roommate's bed. Once again, I broke into my pitiful stash—my father was sending me only a hundred bucks a month for spending money, so I was always low on funds to re-supply my stash. There was less than a nickel bag of pot in there and two Quaaludes. I took out a small hash pipe and we started smoking grass. That is, *they* started smoking grass. I was faking smoking it because grass made me totally paranoid and I wanted to be on top of things if I was going to put any moves on this babe.

After a few rounds of hits, I looked at the pretty one and said, "Come, sit next to me." Now she was sitting next to me on the bed, but Quasimodo was staring at us from her perch. I was doing a fake inhale on the hash pipe every time it came around to me, but these girls were getting whacked. Then I grabbed Beauty's hand and held it. Meanwhile, her blimp friend didn't get the hint; she was still sitting there staring into space. I started making out with the gorgeous one and still her friend wouldn't leave. By now, I figured she was getting paid to be a chaperone.

Finally, we dumped the friend and went back to Beauty's room. We lay down on the bed, but she wouldn't take her clothes off. She just wanted to make out. We were making out for a while and then she suggested that I sleep with her that night. But she meant it literally—just sleep with her. I was so intent on having sex with this beautiful woman that I

"Apparently we lived together for a few weeks. My diary said he was sweet, shy, sensitive, one of the nicest guys I've known."

—Beth, former girlfriend

would do anything by this point. Two seconds later, she was out like a light and I was lying there the whole night, nursing a hard-on and blue balls.

The next day I was talking to some of my friends and I found out more about her. Her name was Beth and I knew at least three guys she'd already slept with. Now I really felt great. So that night, I went back to see her.

"I don't understand," I said to her, right off the bat. "Don't you fuck other guys? Why don't you want to have sex with me?" Some diplomat, huh?

"Why don't you try me?" Beth said. "Tonight, I'm ready."

So we went to fuck and she pulled her knees up behind her ears and she was wide open. I went in there and, *BOOM*, I lasted one second. But at least I got laid and Beth seemed to be really into me. The problem was she was pretty mindless. We had nothing in common. I had nothing to say to her. But she was gorgeous. So I fucked her again.

The next day I was talking to my friends again and I told them I scored. One guy said, "Did you notice when you fucked her, wasn't there some white shit on your dick?" He got me totally paranoid for a few minutes, but then I realized he was just jealous because he wanted to fuck her again.

Beth and I had intense sex for about a week. I mean this girl was totally into me. One time she was giving me a blowjob and I was about to come so I pulled her head away from my cock and I shot all over her hair. She gave me this dirty look as if to say, What the fuck are you doing? I had no idea she was so into me that she wanted to swallow my come. I was such a moron. But after a week of this I was going crazy. She was so boring. I couldn't tolerate being around her anymore, so I dumped her.

I realized, then, that I was totally insane. I had nothing else going and nobody would even look at me. I got laid maybe twice more the whole year. Once was with a mutant who made Beth's troll friend look like Cindy Crawford and the other time was with an Armenian chick who wouldn't take her shirt off when we did it. And I soon found out why. While we were making out, I put my hand on her back and

Trying to fit in. With my new coif, I was ready for action.

her back started to move. She had such a bad acne condition that my hand was literally sinking into a zit swamp.

So I decided I was playing it wrong. I was a long-haired freak, which put me in the minority because Boston University was filled with JAPs and "beautiful people." The "beautiful people" all went to a nearby disco called Zelda's, where everyone but a leper could get laid. So Lew and I decided we'd do a makeover and go to Zelda's. I cut my hair, got a "beautiful people" coif, and went to the beach to get a tan. Then I bought a huckapoo shirt, the silky kind that you open at the collar to display your gold chains, and black velvet pants. I looked just like an Israeli pimp.

That night we went to Zelda's. You have to realize that I was a total social misfit. Not only was I totally inept with women, I didn't even have a sense of direction of how to get home from Zelda's, so I was following Lew around like a baby duck. We stayed there for a while but it wasn't happening. I couldn't even strike up a conversation with a girl. I was the one guy who couldn't get laid at Zelda's. Then Lew got a brilliant idea. Nearby was an all-girls' college. So Lew and I and our friend Rich decided to drive over there. Rich, it seemed, knew some girls there, so we were able to get past security and get on campus.

We walked into this huge dorm and there was this big open room and there were a million girls sitting around in pajamas, watching TV. So we sat down among all these girls. Rich knew some of them, so right away he disappeared into a room. So it was Lew and I now. We were sitting there and a tall blonde walked in. She had blue eyes and huge tits and she took one look at Lew and he disappeared with her. Now I was in my worst nightmare. I was sitting there alone with these girls watching TV. An hour passed, no one talked to me. Two hours. Three hours. Five fucking hours later, not one girl had talked to me. Lew came down all disheveled. He had had a wild time. Then Rich came down. He'd scored. Meanwhile, they were both looking at me as if I was Mr. Loser.

Sophomore year was no better. I think I fucked one girl. So now I was a junior and I was studying hard.

My father was paying good bucks for me to go here so I figured I had to apply myself. But I was still looking for a real girlfriend. I was a year and a half away from graduating college and I had never had a normal relationship with a girl. My sexual history was a nightmare. When a woman dug me she was either a psychopath or a misfit or her back moved by itself.

So you could imagine that meeting a beautiful, normal girl like Alison was the most incredible highlight of my miserable life. I met her through my friend Ilyse, who transferred to Boston University from Ohio Wesleyan University. I knew Ilyse from camp and from Rockville Centre. But I never even went to visit her because, frankly, I wasn't interested in women as friends. So my meeting with Alison was totally accidental. Lew and Elliot and I were on our way to a party and it started to rain. We were still masquerading as "beautiful people" then and we were dressed in those ridiculous clothes. We were getting soaked and I was worrying about my coif being messed up when Lew remembered that Ilyse lived right near where we were. I decided I needed a blowdryer to dry my hair, so we went to see Ilyse.

On my way to the bathroom, I walked by the kitchen and I saw Alison talking to another girl. I looked in and I thought Alison looked great. She was just my type—real cute, great thin body. Of course, I figured I'd never be able to get her, because it was only freaky fucked-up bitches who were into me, but I stuck my head in anyway and said hello. She totally blew me off and went back to talking to her friend. I really wanted her to like me.

I blew my hair dry and went back to the living room, where we were all hanging out. Lew and I started goofing on Alison's friend. We were asking her questions and then making fun of her answers. I was vicious and funny. I was doing a great radio perform-ance, only I was How-ard Stern without a show. I was doing this whole bit to show off my rapier wit for Ali-son's benefit but she was sitting there and

Alison, when I first met her.

she wouldn't open her mouth. Later I found out that she was afraid to say anything because we were doing such a number on her friend that she thought we'd do the same to her.

After a while, we left to go to the party and I told Lew that I really liked Alison but I didn't think she was into me. Lew, like a good friend, agreed with me. A couple of days later I ran into Alison at the Student Union and she was really friendly—she actually talked to me. I still figured she wasn't really into me but this chance encounter gave me courage. So I came up with an elaborate scam. I had to do a junior film project for one of my courses. I decided to do an eight-millimeter documentary on Transcendental Meditation. I had to cast the film, so naturally, I would call Alison and ask her to star in it. This had to work. Everyone wants to be in a movie, right?

I called Alison and I said, "You've got a perfect face. You're my dream girl. You have to star in this movie I'm doing." I was babbling like a maniac to a girl I hardly knew. She said she was too busy to do it. I couldn't believe I was being rejected again, so I started begging her. She went into a long rap about a youth group she was working with as part of her social work program. She had to take some kids to a funeral. "Fuck the funeral, this is a chance to star in a film that may get shown on a large screen in the student theater." I was cajoling her. I couldn't believe there was someone on the planet who didn't want to be in a film. Finally, to shut me up, she said that if I was really desperate and I couldn't get anybody else, she'd do it.

So I hung up, and two seconds later I called Alison back. "I can't find anybody to do it. You've got to do it," I begged her. "Your face is the right face for this movie!" So she said she'd do it.

We went out in the middle of the winter and I had her meditating on a rock and running around in a long, flowing dress, barefoot. Meanwhile, she was freezing to death but I was like a young Scavullo. I was telling her she was beautiful. The oldest trick in the world, but it was working!

I was so punch drunk from getting knocked around by women that I couldn't imagine someone this dynamite would be into me. But I was turning on all the charm, and she seemed to enjoy my company.

The professors voted my film the best film of the year. I saw myself as the next Ingmar Bergman. Alison was definitely the girl for me, I told her, and we decided to go on a real date.

Alison's roommate Ilyse decided to dress Alison for this date, and she put together a nightmare outfit. Alison showed up wearing baggy green corduroy pants, tan work boots, a brown sweater, a tan overcoat, and white gloves. But who cared? I wasn't going to let clothes ruin the night. She had her own car, so I figured she was rich. We went to dinner and then we went to see a movie—*Lenny*, the story of Lenny Bruce, starring Dustin Hoffman, which was a pretty good indication of our life to come. After the movie, I took her back to my place and I broke out the special wine stash—a five-dollar bottle of Blue Nun.

I was living in a room the size of a closet, and I had a queen-size bed that took up almost the whole room. (My room was set up for seduction.) We were

At home in my bachelor lair in Boston. The bed Alison and I partied on during our first date.

forced to sit on the bed. We watched TV and sipped the wine and I made my move. We started making out. This was great! I couldn't believe she was into me. We got all the way to third base. I got four fingers buried in her, so I figured this was it and I withdrew my fingers and went to get the rubbers.

"No, I never have sex on the first date," she said.

"That's absurd!" I said. "Tell you what. I'll drive you home and pick you up two minutes later so it'll be our second date."

I had to have sex with her and close the deal, but she wouldn't bite. So she went home and I thought she was a little disappointed because she didn't want to piss me off. We both knew this was going to be a deep relationship. Sure enough, second date, we did it. I had my first normal girlfriend. I couldn't believe I was in a real boyfriend-girlfriend relationship. I was so into this that even when a gorgeous girl named Andrea invited me to a party, I didn't go because I didn't want to blow it with Alison.

We had been going out a month or so when Alison decided to bring me home to her parents. We drove to Newton, Massachusetts, and we pulled up to a huge house. I HIT THE JACKPOT! I had a great girl, she dug me, and her father was rich to boot. Alison told me that her father owned the Pullman Vacuum Cleaner Company. Her father even had a meeting with President Lyndon Baines Johnson!! Incredible! So we went inside and I couldn't believe how nice these people were to me. I had such a shitty self-image that I would have thrown myself out and puked if I were a parent whose daughter brought me home. But they were really nice to me, and her mother cooked a huge roast beef dinner and we sat down to the table to eat.

At the table, Alison's younger brother Louie started getting into an argument with her father. In the course of the fight,

My father-in-law, Bob, with LBJ. I figured I'd hit the jackpot.

he called his father an asshole. Now I was prepared for the worst. I was the "Shut Up, Sit Down, You Moron" son. If I even called my father a schmo, he'd run after me and beat the shit out of me. But Alison's father, Bob, calmly turned to Louie and said, "Did you call me an asshole? Remember one thing. If I'm an asshole, then you're son-of-asshole." And they all cracked up. I couldn't believe the looseness of this household. What a difference from my prison camp upbringing.

After dinner Bob and I went into the den and I felt he was checking me out. Then he started talking to me about a book about cancer that he was reading and he seemed really depressed. I thought he had cancer, but I found out that he was depressed because he had sold his company to a big corporation and his ten-year contract was expiring and they weren't going to renew it. So all of a sudden, they were leaving the house and

**College graduates. I learned a lot, but not about facial hair.**

moving to Florida and Alison's car was being repoed because it was a company car. And, of course, I thought, "There go my rich in-laws."

But I didn't care. I was totally into Alison. Within a week after our relationship began, I knew I was going to marry her. We had long discussions sitting in front of the library, where we would see a lot of old couples. "We're gonna be like those old people, growing old together," we would tell each other. And it was true. Every time I reject another *Penthouse* pet, that vision gets sharper and truer.

It's funny, but all the time that I've been with Alison we've never done it more than once a night. When we first started seeing each other, we'd have sex every night. The next few years, we'd average three to four times a week. After we got married and started having kids, it went down to twice a week. Now, after fifteen years of marriage, I'm lucky if I get laid twice a year.

But it's not just Alison's fault, I have to admit. Part of the time she was pregnant and I am just not into having sex with a mom, okay? I find nothing attractive about the pregnant form. I'm like Elvis. If a girl got pregnant, he couldn't go near her. There's something weird about a woman's belly moving during sex.

Then, after she gives birth, you've got to give it plenty of time to get back to normal. Don't volcanoes take hundreds of years to cool down? I mean, it's not even a vagina at that point, it's more like a garage door. We tried to do it once right after Alison had given birth to one of our daughters, but it was a disaster. We started to make love and I tried to touch her engorged breasts, but she wigged out.

"Don't go near those, they hurt!" she screamed. "Why don't you touch my arm instead?" Yeah, right. But I was getting aroused anyway and she got on top of me and she said, "I'm going to take my nursing bra off." I wanted to see her breasts because they turned me on. So she took off the nursing bra and she started spraying milk.

"Oh, I'm spraying all over you," Alison said.

"I don't care, let it spray!" I yelled. Two seconds later, I was soaked.

"You know what?" I said. "I do care."

So she had to climb off me and get the big sling-shot bra, and by the time she got that on, I had lost interest. Then she was hurt that I'd lost interest. It was a nightmare.

Alison and I have done only a few kinky things. One time I said, "Let's take a shower together, I'd really like to shave you." And she was bitching, "No, I don't want to. It gets all itchy and I get razor bumps and I'm uncomfortable."

But then she said, "Only if I shave you." And I said, "Fine. Anything. As long as you touch me."

I started shaving her. She started shaving me. Within a few seconds we were totally bored. She hated it. I hated it. We ended up just shaving ourselves. It was a nightmare.

Alison's favorite position is the missionary position. She'll never get up on all fours because she claims she has chondromalacia of the knee—some kind of rare problem that makes her joints swell and ache. Meanwhile, she's out every day with her yenta friends playing tennis, bouncing around like a circus clown on her allegedly weak knees. It doesn't take a Sherlock Holmes to figure out that she's horseshitting me. And we're definitely into only one entrance, too. Occasionally, Alison will favor me with some oral sex, but in all the time we've been together, she's never swallowed my male issue. She was a trouper and tried to on our ten-year anniversary but she almost gagged. It was the most unattractive thing. She was retching for five minutes. Still, I don't blame her. I can't understand girls who swallow semen, anyway. I feel bad for them. I could never swallow it.

And forget about ever seeing her third input. It's funny because, when we first got married, I never even thought about anal sex. Who knew you could even do it there? But with the advent of porno tapes, I started thinking about a little assplay and I went back in my mind to Patty and how exciting it was back there in that tent when she tried a digital insertion, even if I was too uptight to realize it at the time.

So one night I approached Alison. We were in the middle of sex and I asked her if I could do the deed in her butt.

"I don't think I want that, not tonight," she said. "Some other time, I promise."

Every night I asked and I kept getting the same answer. Finally, after a couple of years, I asked her if she had ever done that there.

"I don't remember," she said.

"WHAT DO YOU MEAN, YOU DON'T REMEMBER?" I exploded. "I remember every time my mother stuck a goddamn thermometer up my ass."

"Really! I don't remember."

"How can you not remember getting fucked in the ass?"

"I don't know, I think someone tried once," she finally admitted. What I figure is someone did fuck her in the ass and it was a disaster. All I know is that there's no drug or liquor strong enough on the planet Earth to get her to do that. I even tried to ease her into it by sticking a finger or two up there but she freaked out and said she was uncomfortable. Finally, I asked her if she would do that to me. I even went on my TV show and during a takeoff on "The Newlywed Game" that we called the Sternlywed's Game, I said that the one thing I'd like to do sexually that my wife won't do is have fingers up the butt. Still nothing. So far, she's gotten as far as spreading my cheeks apart. It got so bad that I tried to do it myself one night when I was in the shower. I lathered up my butt and put my finger up there, but I didn't get turned on.

We even tried bondage to add a little spice to our sex life, but that was a disaster, too. One night I tied Alison's ankles and wrists with my neckties. She was afraid that the kids would come up and disturb us. Alison wasn't a good subject for bondage.

"This is uncomfortable," she started whining. "My circulation's getting cut off. And that voice you put on when you tied me up was weird." How could she not like it? That was my love voice. It sounds like a cross between Dracula and Barry White.

I tried to spank her, but that was even worse.

"Get out of here!" she screamed. I felt so stupid, I had to untie her. She was pissed off that I was doing stuff to her that she didn't want me to do. I had to explain to her that the whole point of tying someone up was so that you could do stuff that you don't normally do. The whole fun of it was being at someone's mercy. She didn't give a shit. We ended up doing the same old things we always did.

The greatest aid to salvaging what was left of our sexual life was the vibrator. The vibrator came into our lives a few years ago when Robin gave us one as a gift. And we needed it. When we first met, Alison would get wet instantly. After a few years of sex it took like an hour rubbing Alison's clitoris before she would get hot for me. I just like to fuck. At my age, I don't really have the time for foreplay. Why can't she be instantly wet and ready to go? When we got the power tool, it was like magic. I could just lie there and not do anything to her and she'd have an orgasm instantly.

And what a vibrator! You strap it onto your hand.

It's called the Swedish Massager. I put it on and I looked like RoboStern. I'd lie on my side, kiss Alison a few times, touch her with the vibrator, fuck her, and five minutes later I'd be asleep. Perfect. Life was good.

But as the years rolled by, I found that the amount of time that I had to use the vibrator to get Alison ready was longer and longer. She must have built up quite a callus down there, because it was taking twenty minutes for her to get wet even *with* the vibrator. She's so desensitized from using it that I'm going to have to go to the next step. I already told Robin. I want a jackhammer for Christmas next year.

But thankfully, I found something that really solves all these sexual problems. Actually, refound something. Masturbation came back into my life a few years after Alison and I were married, and right now it's the greatest single source of sexual satisfaction I have. I jerk off at least five times a week. I actually use masturbation as a medicinal tool because I have to get up at five every morning and I've found that the only way to get to sleep early is to whack off.

So I've become quite adept. I always use my right hand. I don't need Vaseline or lubrication. I don't use magazines or porno tapes. I just lie in bed and fantasize. I can get myself off in three seconds. I used to have to replay my sexual escapades with my old girlfriends, but now I've got it to the point where I can just fantasize about the latest girl I've had in the studio. I whack off to Jessica Hahn a lot because I know that she's someone who would open every hole. Jessica told me she's only interested in pleasuring a man when she has sex. She even said that she likes to blow a guy and then fall asleep for the entire night with his penis in her mouth, like a pacifier. God, did that story turn me on.

I've come full circle, I'm back to hiding my tissues . . . this time from Alison.

But the amazing thing about me is that even in my sex dreams I can't cheat on Alison. I sometimes dream about strippers I've had on the show, and when they're ready to have sex with me, I run out of the room. Somehow, Alison works her way into the dream and I feel guilty and I never get to fuck the girl. I CAN'T EVEN HAVE FUN IN MY DREAMS! That's how sick I am.

Speaking of Alison, you know, I really don't know what her take is on our sex life. And she won't tell me. I've been trying to get her to answer the anal sex question for years now.

So I asked Larry "Ratso" Sloman to interview Alison and find out about *her* sex life. Here's what she told him:

RATSO: We've all heard Howard's version of your sex life. What's your side of it?

ALISON: My sex life is great. Well, let me put it this way. When we do it, my sex life is great. There're times it's more frequent than others but basically we have a very good sex life.

RATSO: Howard says that he has a very unusual penis. Flaccid, it's like an acorn, but then it grows to incredible lengths. . . .

ALISON: His penis size is fine.

RATSO: Tell me about the time he tried to tie you up and have a little S and M session.

ALISON: Howard exaggerates. Not all of what he says fits reality. In real life, I don't deal with a sex maniac. People are always saying to me, "Oh, my God, you're married to Howard Stern!" It's not like he has me parading around the room discussing my cup size.

RATSO: What about anal sex? Did you or didn't you way back when?

ALISON: I don't know. I really don't remember. Let's forget it.

RATSO: How can you not know if you did it or not?

ALISON: It's the kind of thing where I think I was attempting it once and I wasn't interested. I've never really done it but then he asked me about it! It's not like I did it with everybody but him. Let's just say I think it was attempted and that was it.

RATSO: Would you have anal sex with Howard?

ALISON: I said to him, "Howard, if you're really interested, fine with me." Then he says he's not interested.

RATSO: What about his masturbation habit?

ALISON: Look, he tells me he doesn't masturbate and he tells the audience he does, so I don't know. People have sat with us at the dinner table and said, "I masturbate as much as you," and I'm sitting there dying and Howard's going, "Yeah, yeah," and I'm going, "Oh, my God!" I do walk in the room after I've kissed him goodnight and he's not masturbating. I don't know when he does it because I've never caught him.

RATSO: How can you catch him if he can do it so quick? He says three seconds and he's done.

ALISON: I've never caught him, but then again, who knows? I don't walk back into the bedroom *trying* to catch him. I assume he's sleeping. But there's nothing on the sheets either.

RATSO: What about the vibrator stories?

ALISON: No comment.

# Mein Kampf
## "My Struggle"

*How I Became the King of Radio*

CHAPTER

5

It's weird, but I always wanted to be in radio. That was all I could think about from the time I was five years old. I used to do these shows up in my room and record them on a beautiful Wollensack tape recorder that my father gave me. In fact, by the time I was nine, I had actually begun to create the format that years later would send me to the top of the world of radio. I'd get together with a few of my friends, much as I do now, start the tape rolling, and I'd dial. While dialing, I'd break into dirty little stories about my friends and I'd do monologues. The idea was to make the best phony phone call. One guy would call a Chinese restaurant and ask for Itchy Balls. The next guy would call the liquor store and ask for white horse in a bottle. Mine were always a little more inventive. Either I was a game show host (usually Gene Rayburn) and I would award old ladies thousands of dollars in prizes or I would call drugstores using a female voice and try to make dates.

"Hello, you got LSD?" I asked in my best nine-year-old female impersonator's voice.

"LSD, yeah, sure we do," the pharmacist said, knowing full well that he was on the phone with an asshole kid.

"And a box of Trojans," I added.

"Oh, sure we do, honey. What size?"

Size? Hmmm. He stumped me because I had no idea what he was talking about. I had never seen a condom. I didn't get it. What does he mean, size?

"Thirty-four," I ad-libbed. I was nine. Thirty-four sounded right.

"What else you want? You want Prince Albert in a can?"

"Yeah," I said.

"How big?" the pharmacist wondered.

"A twelve-foot dick," I said.

"What else do you want in your mouth?" he said.

"Will you give me a lay?" I asked. "I need you."

"I know you do," he said.

"I want to meet you in a dark alley," I added.

"I know you do," he said.

I hung up, triumphant.

I think the fact that my father exposed me to the world of radio must have had a big subconscious effect on me. Ironically, my father worked as an engineer at WHOM, which later became WKTU and then K-Rock, the same station I work at today. He always used to tell me stories about working with this legendary disc jockey Symphony Sid, whom my father described as a man who would become very agitated at times. Sid was this crazy guy who played a lot of jazz and rhythm-and-blues, and had been busted several times for drugs. His show was a madhouse—not on the air, but off the air! One time, my father told me, he thought Sid was coming off a high and he started to get violent. He went to smash the control room window when they were about to go back on the air.

So my father jumped up, banged on the glass in his control booth, and screamed, "SYMPHONY SID! BY THE POWERS VESTED IN ME BY THE FCC, I COMMAND YOU TO GET ON THE MICRO- PHONE IN A SERIOUS MANNER AND CON- TINUE THE BROADCAST!" It worked. He settled down and did the rest of the show. Sid did all kinds of wild things. He'd have a lobby full of street people and black gospel singers during his show and he'd be run- ning back and forth during his radio program trying to keep order in the studio and in the lobby. He just should have put those people on the air.

I always used to love to go to work with my father when I was young. By that time, he was part owner of a recording studio where they used to tape cartoons and commercials. I'd go visit my dad and get to meet

My dad at his recording studio in the fifties.

Wally Cox, Don Adams, Larry Storch, all the great
voices of my favorite cartoon characters. Plus they'd
have these great lunches—big cold-cut buffets. Man,
I was in heaven. Even then, I realized that I wanted
to entertain people on the radio. My father would
drive into Queens and we'd take the subway from
there into the city. The driving part of the commute
was horrible. We'd always listen to the radio on the
way in, and if anything good came on, my father would

get totally into it. It dawned on me that if you were half a mutant you could probably get on the radio to entertain people and to make them forget about the drudgery of that shitty commute.

I never wanted to be on the radio to be a disc jockey. I never wanted to play records. I just wanted to talk. It's funny because nobody was doing wild talk shows on the radio then. If you were on the radio, you were a disc jockey like Cousin Brucie. But I ignored those guys. They sounded so canned and phony.

**My high school yearbook photo.**

It was weird for me to think I was going to be on the radio someday, because I was so shy growing up. It drove my father nuts that I never took an acting course in high school. I never did summer stock. I was too inhibited. I knew I wouldn't wind up onstage somewhere; I always pictured myself in a dark room, talking into a microphone. But no one else could believe that. My father kept telling me, "Howard, you gotta talk. You're not gonna be on the radio if you're quiet. You gotta have diarrhea of the mouth." What a way with words. That Stern charm.

I hardly talked at all my whole senior year in high school. I was in a psychology course and the teacher told me she was going to flunk me because I never once opened my mouth the whole term. She warned me that I had better do well on my final or that was it. I had a cousin who'd been under psychiatric care forever. So I sat him down with a microphone and I interviewed him. I asked him one question: "So, you've been seeing a lot of psychiatrists?" He talked nonstop for two hours. I brought my father the tapes, he transferred them to two discs. The teacher listened to them, flipped out, and said it was a classic. She wanted the records and I got an A.

Drama class, same thing. I wouldn't open my mouth. The first day the teacher said, "Each of you will get up and sing 'Row, Row, Row Your Boat.' " He called on me first. I nearly shit in my pants. I couldn't do it. I whispered it. He was furious.

Yet whenever the people at the counseling center asked me, I would say I wanted to be a disc jockey. Even they said, "No way. He doesn't speak, he doesn't have a professional voice." So to make my parents happy, the counselors came up with an occupation I should train for in college. They decided I should be a speech therapist.

To be a speech therapist you have to be good at science. I have no fucking ability in science. Meanwhile, I'm flunking all my classes.

So they told my parents there was one school that might take me with my moron grades. Elmira was an all-girls school, but they were taking boys for the first time ever. I heard this, I said, "Unbelievable." Five boys and two thousand girls. "Or," they told my parents, "if he ever wants a shot at radio, he could go to Boston University." They had a retard program called Basic Studies, where you took moron classes for two years, and if you proved yourself, you could go into the School of Communications.

That sounded pretty good to me. I knew I could

apply myself. I wound up studying hard. I had nothing else to do because no woman would come near me. I graduated magna cum laude with a 3.8 average. And I got my start in radio.

I didn't get up the courage to go down to the college radio station until my sophomore year. The first time I went over there, they immediately gave me an air shift. I tried to cue up a Santana record and I was so nervous my hand was shaking. Finally, I got it playing, I was on the radio, and I was thinking, "This is going out to millions of people"—but probably three people in the dorms were listening. So the record was playing and I reached up for a pencil, knocked all of them over, bumped the rack that the station kept their carts in, and the cart rack came crashing down onto the turntable—in the middle of the fucking show. It was a disaster. I was a horrible disc jockey. I hated the fact that you had to be organized. I used to have nightmares about the record running out and not being able to change it in time.

I did everything at the station. I did news, I did interviews. But I really wanted to do comedy. I wanted to put on a crazy, off-the-wall show. I hooked up with three seniors and we put together a comedy show called the King Schmaltz Bagel Hour. We were totally outrageous, especially for 1973. We used to talk about girls' asses, hebes, and blacks. One of the guys did a game show hosted by Father McNern called Name That Sin. The object of the game was to confess a sin that was so bad it would make the bishop blush.

"If you can make the bishop blush, you win a free trip to the Vatican," the announcer said. "If you say the secret sin, you win one hundred dollars. And now for our first contestant."

"Father, I had sex with my girlfriend."

"Nope, he's not blushing."

"I had sex with my girlfriend's dog."

"The bishop does that all the time, that won't make him blush," the announcer said.

This was outrageous then. We broke all format, we had long bits. Most of the other guys were these way-too-cool soft-voiced "progressive"-sounding disc jockeys: "Now here's Pink Floyd on a trip to the dark side of the moon." We were crazy. On that first show, we also played a bit called Godzilla Goes to Harlem. That would be the last bit we'd play on college radio.

It started out like a typical AM broadcast, playing a Grand Funk Railroad song. Then the broadcast was interrupted.

"We bring you a special report from New York City. A strange being has been sighted in the East River." It was Godzilla. After the police put out an all-points bulletin, Godzilla was seen again at 125th Street in Harlem. We went on the spot to Harlem.

"Hey, brothers, look at that big green dude!" one of the King Schmaltz Brothers said in his best black impression. "Hey, what's your name, turkey?"

"Godzilla," the monster roared.

"Godzilla? What you Italians doing in this neighborhood? Hey, you're not Italian."

"I'm the monster Godzilla."

"Hey, brother, take out your wallet. Hear what I'm saying. Up against the wall."

Godzilla roared.

"You gonna give me trouble, I'll have to fight it out with you, dude."

There was screaming and roaring and confusion. Finally, Godzilla moaned.

"Man, all he had was a dime. What a waste of time."

Seconds later, the phone rang in the studio. One of the other guys picked it up.

"King Schmaltz, what can we do for you?"

"Three guesses, the first two don't count." I immediately recognized the voice. It was Hank Sennett, the guy who ran the station. He was home with his family but he had a special line that fed the station right into his house.

"Is it Mary?" one of the other guys said.

"No."

"Is it a sturgeon?" someone else guessed.

"Let me give you a hint," Hank said ominously.

"I bet it's Hank," I said.

"You're fired," Hank said.

Fired during our first show! Hey, even I was impressed. That was a record I was never able to surpass. But I had the tape of that first show and I had the direction I wanted to go in. I sent a copy of the show to my father and he sent me back a nine-page letter that basically called me a moron. "You stupid idiot, this is terrible," he wrote. He was always blunt and to the point with me. "What are these sketches? I hear you go, 'uhhh,' which is annoying. Who takes phone calls on the air? They don't talk like that on real radio stations. If you want to be different, don't go into radio. You don't sound like a real disc jockey. You

gotta take this seriously. You gotta announce the record and give the temperature and the time."

Here I thought I was doing great innovative stuff
and I sat there reading this and thought, "Jeez, maybe
my father's right. I'm a fucking asshole. What am I
doing?" I was really hurt. I think my whole motivation
in life has been to prove to my father that I'm not a
douche bag.

Meanwhile, my parents kept busting my chops for
me to get formal training. "You want to be a disc
jockey, you have to have training!" they'd both repeat
like a mantra. But I told them I had it under control.
I was totally focused on making it in radio. I used to
write letters to Nancy, the first girl I ever dated, and
I told her that someday I would be the greatest disc
jockey in the world.

And lo and behold, as soon as I graduated, I got a
job at WNTN, doing daytimes at this progressive AM
rock station in Newton. This was an unbelievable
coup. No one got this. So I was doing the job and three
days later I went in for my paycheck. No pay. I guess
the station was having financial difficulties.

In fact, the station was being run by some guy who
just got out of Boston University and was a really
strange guy. One morning he was making a public affairs tape and he accidentally said, "Aw, fuck." He
figured that he had erased it but when the show
played, the "Aw, fuck" went out over the air. Big fucking deal, probably three people listened to that show.
Nobody called, nobody complained, but this guy went
into a panic.

"Oh, my career's over," he moaned. "Help me compose a letter to the FCC begging their forgiveness."

"Why? Maybe nobody heard it," I said.

"It's better to turn yourself in," this moron said. So he wrote this letter:

Dear FCC,
I have made a terrible error. As you know, I'm a broadcaster, in charge of this station, and I was making a tape . . .

He went into this whole story and he sent the letter and he was shitting in his pants, waiting for the FCC to show up. I can't imagine that anyone in the history of radio had ever reported himself to the FCC except this dude.

I didn't last long at that station. I wanted to be in radio, but not for free. But at least I had a tape I could send around. Soon enough, I got called in for an interview at this station in Westchester County, New York.

This was great. I wanted to stay in New York, because Alison and I were quasi-living together at this time and she was getting her master's in social work at Columbia. So this program director wanted to hire me as the evening guy at ninety-six dollars a week.

I freaked out. I got real nervous that I wasn't good enough, and I turned him down. I rationalized it by saying the money was shit. I wanted to get married and all my friends were getting out of school and making twelve grand a year. I turned down my first legitimate job and went to work for Benton and Bowles, an advertising agency. I lied and told them I loved math to get this bullshit, pencil-pushing marketing job. It was terrible. I had to wear a suit every day, and my boss said, "Don't worry. I want you to come in on Sunday, but you don't have to wear your tie." I was miserable. And I've got to hand it to my mother. She really helped me here. She said, "This job is not for you. You're a wreck."

I quit without giving notice. I had already applied to their creative department, to run the AV equipment, some entry-level job. The day after I quit I got a call and they hired me in creative. I wasn't there for more than three hours when I got fired again, because their personnel department realized that I was the guy who just quit the other department.

Then I went to work for this place in Queens that I had read about in the paper. It was a barter house and I was going to sell radio time—you go to a company and you trade advertising time on stations for an equivalent value of what they produce. And they paid me for this. So I went into two Chinese restaurants, and I made two deals. They didn't even know what they were doing. "You mean I get radio ad?"

"Yeah, yeah."

As I was closing the deal, I realized that the guys I was working for were crooked. The IRS was after them, their funds were frozen by the bank, and the guy who owned the place would take off his shirt in the middle of the office and spray himself with fucking deodorant. It was crazy. So I went back to the restaurants and said, "I think I'm working for crooks, don't even get involved with them." They said, "No, no, how about if we pay cash money for the advertising time?" I was a great salesman. I couldn't get rid of them.

All of a sudden I realized I had turned down a job in radio, and I could've killed myself. What were the odds that I could get a job in radio again? And here, I really owe all this to Alison. She turned to me and said, "Why don't you pick up the phone, call that guy in Westchester, and say that you're really sorry that you turned the job down. Tell him to keep you in mind if anything comes up in the future." I have one of these minds that says you don't call someone back if you turned down a job. That I could do this was a mind-blowing revelation to me. So I picked up the phone and called the guy. It was right before New Year's and he was working at KTU, doing overnights, in addition to being the program director of this dumpy radio station WRNW.

Bingo, he had an opening, some fill-in work, mid-days, ten to two. The reason the guy offered it to me was that he couldn't get anybody for New Year's Day, and I would be his fill-in guy. I said okay, nothing permanent, but at least I'd get a shot. He wanted me to work because he had to do this overnight shift at KTU and he didn't want to be woken up the next day.

So I went up there and the radio station was in an old house in the middle of a residential area of Briarcliff Manor. One of the bedrooms was the radio station studio, the other was a production studio. I was doing this show and I was fucking nervous and my voice was hoarse and I was croaking "WRNW" and talking soft like an FM disc jockey. I was no more than ten minutes into the show, playing a Crosby, Stills & Nash song, when I hit the microphone and there were two little stop/start buttons. The buttons got jammed. That meant the microphone was permanently on. I couldn't turn it down. When you have the microphone switch depressed, you can't even hear to cue up a record. You're fucked.

Now this was a music station. You were just supposed to say, "WRNW," and go on to another song. So as I was saying, "WRNW," I was trying to think fast. I took the record, and I got the needle on the outside of the record, and I was playing the first track and panicking. I didn't know what to do. I didn't want to wake this guy up, he was going to fire me.

Finally, I called him up at his house. He had obviously just gotten to sleep after doing his shift, and he said, "What the fuck are you doing? Why are you calling me? Call the engineer!" I told him I didn't even know how to call the engineer, I didn't know his number, and he screamed, "OH, I'LL DO IT!" and hung up the phone.

Meanwhile, I couldn't change records, so I opened up the mike between cuts, saying, "We're tracking a whole album here at WRNW." I was doing anything to kill time until the next song. You weren't supposed to play a whole album side. So I was trying to make it sound natural; you weren't even supposed to talk between the cuts. This was a disaster, and I knew all the other jocks were listening to me. I was so fucking embarrassed. An hour into this, another jock showed up, and I didn't know what to do. I was almost in fucking tears, because I knew I blew it. The guy was going to hate me, and he was going to fire me. So the engineer eventually showed up, and he started blaming me because I didn't know what I was doing, and I was not supposed to hit both buttons at the same time, and I was a schmuck.

The next day I went out to the station to see the program director, and I groveled. "Please forgive me, I didn't know what happened." I really apologized and he didn't fire me. The guy has since told me that he wanted to fire me after that first show. In fact, the only reason he hired me was because I had a first-class radio license and I had short hair. That was ironic because I had just cut my hair for the interview. I had a broadcasting teacher who told me, "Always go in a nice outfit and cut your hair. Even though you're interviewing at these hippie stations, you should really dress nice." So I had gone up there real professional-looking, and the guy told me he hired me because he was so sick of these long-haired motherfuckers coming in giving him shit and never showing up for work on time. Hey, I showed up on time, I just couldn't work the friggin' microphone.

Anyway, he didn't fire me and I hung around and eventually became the regular midday guy. Meanwhile, the other jocks started talking about getting raises and forming a union. Again, my father gave me good advice. He said, "It's great you're making ninety-six dollars a week. That station's a training ground. Those announcers are nuts trying to get a union and benefits. The station is charging six dollars a minute for advertising; the place'll go out of business with a union."

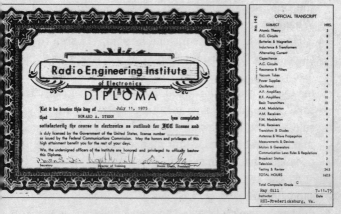

My radio school diploma. I had to take physics, which was a nightmare. Miraculously, I passed.

So I was doing middays and soon they made me production director, too, because I became really good at cutting tape and coming up with creative commercials. I did some spots for a local guy called the Cheese Wheel. Now this doesn't sound like much, but you have to understand that this was FM and everyone was too cool for the room and here I was doing commercials for the Cheese Wheel and I was calling the owner on the air and putting him in the spots. This was mind-blowing to everyone there. Plus I put sound effects and all kinds of wacky stuff into the spots. This was the only way I could be creative.

Meanwhile, the station was sold and new owners came in and they made this Israeli guy the general manager. This guy was a little bit cocky, a little overconfident, the kind of guy who would come up to me and say, "You know, my sign is Capricorn. Thees ees the best astrological sign!" And I would say, "Hey! Whaddya mean the best astrological sign?"

One day he came to me and he said, "I listen to your radio show. You are terrible. You will never be a great disc jockey. You're okay with the commercials, you do nice job. So why don't you become my program director?" This guy was so insulting, I swear, the day he said that to me, I told myself I was going to be the fucking greatest morning man this country ever had because I had to prove this prick wrong.

At the same time, he was offering me twelve thousand dollars a year, instead of my measly ninety-six dollars a week—twelve thousand dollars a year! This was unbelievable. So I went to my father and he told me to take the job as program director but stay on the air as a disc jockey because program directing is a shit job and on-air is where the action is. Good advice.

So now I was running the radio station. And the Israeli said, "Look, I can't make any money with this progressive format. Why don't you just get rid of all the records and play fifty of the same songs over and over again, like Top Forty does?" Hey, I just wanted the two-fifty a week, I couldn't give a shit about the music. I said to someone, "You're the music director, you pick the fifty fucking records." I couldn't believe I was getting a paycheck.

A couple of days went by and the Israeli said to me, "You're in charge of public affairs now, too, because you're the program director."

"What do I have to do?" I asked.

"See those records over there?" He pointed. "Religious broadcasters pay us to run those shows. And every week they come in and you open them up." I realized I had seen the old program director doing all this shit, and it was a whole involved library system, and I'm totally disorganized. Plus, I didn't give a rat's ass about the religious programming. So I figured I was going to get these religious programs and I was going to throw them in the garbage because nobody could possibly be listening to the Maryknoll Theatre with all the nuns on Sunday morning. I took one show and told the Sunday engineer, "Here's your tape. Just play the same fucking show over and over." I was right. We didn't get one complaint.

I soon started to realize that this was ridiculous. I was the program director, but I wasn't into it. Yet they loved me, they thought I was a great program director! I didn't give them any shit. If I lost a disc jockey, I'd take a college kid and throw him on the air. In fact, Bree Walker once asked me for a job there. She was on WYNY, a big station in New York, and she left the station. I met her at a party, I went to shake her hand, and she didn't have a fucking hand. Then she asked me for a job.

"Bree, we pay four dollars an hour. It's beneath you. You worked at WYNY!" I said. I wouldn't hire her, because I felt that she would intimidate all of us. She was a professional! We were not professionals, we were idiots, we were assholes! We were the worst assemblage of disc jockeys on the planet, and I put together the worst of them, because if I heard a tape and the guy didn't stutter I hauled him in and put him on the air.

So here I was, the new program director, and one

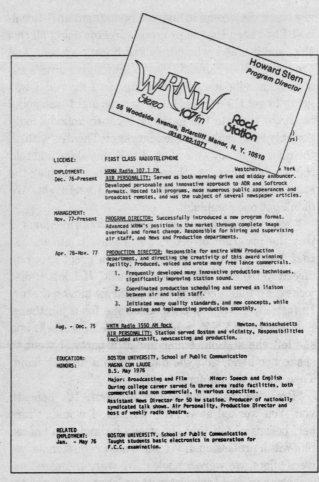

Howard Stern
Program Director

W<sub>stereo</sub>RNW<sub>107 fm</sub>
Rock Station

55 Woodside Avenue, Briarcliff Manor, N. Y. 10510
(914) 762-1071

LICENSE:           FIRST CLASS RADIOTELEPHONE

EMPLOYMENT:        WRNW Radio 107.1 FM                              Westchester, New York
Dec. 76-Present    AIR PERSONALITY: Served as both morning drive and midday announcer.
                   Developed personable and innovative approach to AOR and Softrock
                   formats. Hosted talk programs, made numerous public appearances and
                   broadcast remotes, and was the subject of several newspaper articles.

MANAGEMENT:
Nov. 77-Present    PROGRAM DIRECTOR: Successfully introduced a new program format.
                   Advanced WRNW's position in the market through complete image
                   overhaul and format change. Responsible for hiring and supervising
                   air staff, and News and Production departments.

Apr. 76-Nov. 77    PRODUCTION DIRECTOR: Responsible for entire WRNW Production
                   department, and directing the creativity of this award winning
                   facility. Produced, voiced and wrote many free lance commercials.

                   1.  Frequently developed many innovative production techniques,
                       significantly improving station sound.

                   2.  Coordinated production scheduling and served as liaison
                       between air and sales staff.

                   3.  Initiated many quality standards, and new concepts, while
                       planning and implementing production smoothly.

Aug. - Dec. 75     WNTN Radio 1550 AM Rock                          Newton, Massachusetts
                   AIR PERSONALITY: Station served Boston and vicinity. Responsibilities
                   included airshift, newscasting and production.

EDUCATION:         BOSTON UNIVERSITY, School of Public Communication
HONORS:            MAGNA CUM LAUDE
                   B.S. May 1976

                   Major: Broadcasting and Film        Minor: Speech and English
                   During college career served in three area radio facilities, both
                   commercial and non commercial, in various capacities.

                   Assistant News Director for 50 kw station. Producer of nationally
                   syndicated talk shows. Air Personality, Production Director and
                   host of weekly radio theatre.

RELATED
EMPLOYMENT:        BOSTON UNIVERSITY, School of Public Communication
Jan. - May 76      Taught students basic electronics in preparation for
                   F.C.C. examination.

**My résumé and business card. I was so proud of my meaningless job and my meaningless accomplishments.**

Now that I was making that big twelve grand a year, I married Alison.

"Hey baby, spend the rest of your life with a guy with a bad mustache."

My father and I share a slow dance.

of the jocks told me someone in the station was stealing from her pocketbook.

"What am I supposed to do?" I asked.

"Do something," she said.

"We'll set a trap for them," I said. "We'll put out

your pocketbook, and I'll stand in the other room, and we'll see who's stealing from your pocketbook." Sure enough, we found one of the jocks stealing from her pocketbook. He took twenty bucks. He was making ninety-six dollars a week, he had to pay rent and help out with his family's bills. He was taking twenty from her pocketbook because he was desperate.

So I went to the Israeli and told him what went down.

"If you want to truly be management, be a man, and fire him yourself!" he told me. "You go fire him! Be a man!"

I got it in my mind that, holy shit, if I was really going to be the manager, I really do have to fire this guy. And I was like pukin' over this, I was sick to my stomach. Even though he was stealing from the pocketbook, I felt really bad for the guy, but I had to go fire him. That's when I made the decision: I wasn't going to be in management. I probably could have done that whole trip and been a program director, but it was bullshit. I knew I had to get back to what I had wanted to do since I was five. I had to become a wacky morning man.

## HERE'S THE LEATHER WEATHERLADY

I picked up *Radio & Records*, which is a trade publication in radio, and I saw that WCCC, a station in Hartford, Connecticut, was looking for a "wild, fun morning guy." I had fantasized about working for this station many times because it was right between Boston and New York, and every time I drove back to college I had picked it up in the car. This was a fifty-thousand-watt FM station and it had a sister AM station that simulcast in the morning. So I put together a tape. I knew that deep inside I wanted to do wild stuff, but you can't do wild stuff sitting by yourself in a room.

The craziest thing I did on that audition tape was say, "Okay, let's listen to some Robert Klein!" and *boom*, I played something off a Robert Klein album. Then I played some Cheech and Chong. Those were the only two comedy albums we had at the station. And I mixed in a couple of one-liners that I'd written. Other than that, it was mostly Robert Klein being funny. When I finally met Robert Klein, I told him I owed my career to him.

So I sent this tape off to CCC and they called me for an audition. I went up there, I was shitting in my pants. The guy said, "Go in that room, put on the mike, here's five records. Go do a radio show."

I went into the other studio, and I was in shock. I didn't know what to do. I just felt weird. But I did it and I gave the guy the tape, and it really pissed me off that I fucked up, so I called him up and said, "I haven't heard from you. What'd you think of the tape?"

"Your tape is great," he said to me, "but that shit that you did for me in my studio was terrible! You didn't do anything."

I told him that I had felt very uncomfortable, I wasn't prepared. So I went back up and I did another tape for them, and this time I just let loose, I went wild. I nailed it and the guy hired me. They hired me for twelve grand a year, so I was maintaining my salary, but I needed money to move. I called the owner and I asked him to help me out.

"I've got to move me and my wife to Hartford. Where am I gonna live till she moves up?" I asked. "I have no money."

"Well, all right. I won't pay for your move but I'll give you a hotel allowance of sixty dollars," he said.

"All right, sixty dollars a night . . ." I said.

"No, sixty dollars for the week."

"Where am I gonna find a hotel for sixty dollars a week?" I complained.

Well, it seemed he knew a place right there in Hartford. So I moved up there. First night I was there, there was a shooting at this hotel. They were shooting right through the fucking walls and I was going out of my mind. I was scared shitless.

Plus, I was alone. Alison was convinced she should keep her job in New York. She had this good social work job. We were actually going to live in Bridgeport, Connecticut. I tested it out but it took an hour and a half of solid driving. By the time I got to the station, at five in the morning, I was exhausted. And this job was fucking torture. From six to ten I was on the air in the morning. From ten to two, I had to do commercials. Not just voice commercials—I had to produce finished commercials. And if the sales guy didn't like it, I had to go in and produce it all over again. It was like a torture chamber. It was just an unbelievably exhausting job. There was no way to explain how bad it was.

I was up there every day. I worked Saturdays from six to noon, trying to be funny. Then from noon to three, I had to be the production guy. Plus, I was the public affairs director. I had to do half-hour interviews on Sunday morning. But I would tape those during the week. It was funny because my public affairs show was the most interesting thing about the job, because at least I got to talk for a half hour straight with no music. I would interview local people, such as the head of the ASPCA.

But I would get into these bizarre lines of questioning. I'd ask them about their dating habits, whatever. I can't tell you how bizarre this was, because nobody was doing anything like this in radio at this point. People have told me that Imus was doing amazing stuff on the radio back then but he wasn't doing shit! He got on the radio, and he used to say: "Quack-quack, who loves you, baby?" I don't know how he got that irreverent reputation. But he had it because nobody was doing anything. Anybody who sounded a little different was irreverent.

But there was one good thing about Hartford. I met Fred "Earth Dog" Norris there. Fred was going to college and he was the overnight guy. He was a funny guy and a good writer and he had a knack for doing impressions. After his shift he hung out with me in the studio while he put away his records. He was half asleep and I'd say, "Fred, in thirty seconds, you gotta be Howard Cosell."

In Hartford, I began to conceptualize what I could really do with a morning show. I started off by demanding that the governor recognize my birthday as a state holiday. No response. I called aides to the mayor of Hartford. They told me I'd have to be dead. Finally, I got the majority leader of the state senate to send me an official-looking document that "for the rest of eternity" January 12 would be commemorated in Connecticut.

When Paul McCartney got busted in Japan and imprisoned for possession of grass, I called Tokyo to protest. When Yale and Harvard medical schools announced there was a shortage of dead bodies for research, I ran a cadaverathon on the air. But the one thing that got me the most publicity in Hartford was my "To Hell with Shell" boycott. It actually wasn't even my boycott, it was a listener's idea. During the summer of 1979 we experienced some gas shortages. I read a chain letter that was sent out to people in Hartford urging a two-day boycott of Shell products because Shell was foreign-owned and was the first company to ration its supply. We discussed the letter on the air and I suggested that people drive with their lights on to protest the rise in fuel prices. "Turn the lights on bright until they get the prices right" was the rallying cry.

Pretty tame stuff. But you have to remember that this was at a time when disc jockeys kept their mouths shut and never bad-rapped anyone. We were the stations' goodwill ambassadors, and controversies were to be avoided. Advertisers are gods in radio, and the rule is you never upset them. Two people from Shell even called our station, but we kept up with the campaign. Why not? Shell wasn't advertising with us.

I was doing well at the station, I had been there for

a year, and I asked for a raise. A lousy, stinking twenty-five-dollar-a-week raise. The owner, Sy Dresner, told me he had to think about it. That really pissed me off. I got on the next morning, I was doing my show, it was a Saturday, and I put on "Free Bird" and all of a sudden I was overwhelmed, I was on my knees, praying that somebody would hear me from Hartford and get me the fuck out of there. I just couldn't believe I was wasting my time at this annoying job.

Plus, I had the worst living conditions. I was living in this connected town house with neighbors who became obsessed with my show. At four in the morning they would play their stereo super-loud and if I banged on the wall they'd go even louder. And then they started a campaign against me. They started hanging all these signs on my front door. They said it was freedom of speech. "You can say what you want on the radio, we can say what we want on your front door." They were like mental cases. We were living in an apartment where you flushed your toilet and the next morning you woke up and there was shit all over the floors and water was everywhere. It was just unfucking-believable. I was living the nightmare of being a famous person who was poor. I couldn't afford to live in an unattached house. People always think that you're rich if you're famous.

So I was praying to get the hell out. The next day, I got a call from Dwight Douglas, one of the biggest radio consultants. He said, "I heard your show. I think you're fuckin' brilliant."

"You're kidding! That's fantastic," I said.

Then he told me he was going to put me at one of

his stations. Now, Dwight's company was so powerful at that point, it was like the touch of God coming to you.

"We've got a great opening in Columbus, Ohio," he said.

Now, to me, Columbus sounded like Hartford.

"You don't understand. This is the hottest station in Columbus. They have a real ratings book, four times a year, the whole thing. Hartford had a ratings book once a year," Dwight said.

So I put together a tape to give to their people in Columbus, and a week or so later he called me and told me the jock had decided to stay in Columbus.

"But don't worry, I've got you in mind," he said.

Meanwhile, I was ready to kill myself.

Again, I was looking through *Radio & Records* and I saw that a station in Detroit was looking for a morning man. Detroit sounded like a big market. But I'm bad in geography, I had no idea where Detroit was. I didn't know it was north of Canada! I called Douglas and he said the opening wasn't for me. I thought, "Fuck him." So I called the GM of the station, Wally Clark, and sent him a tape by overnight mail. That night I got a call.

"You're hired. We're flying into Hartford to do the deal."

"You're kidding!" I said.

So we arranged to meet at the Marriott, the biggest hotel in Hartford. I couldn't believe this was happening. I said to Alison, whom I'd kept in the dark about all this, "I'm going to meet with some guys from Detroit. They want to hire me."

"You applied for a job without telling me?" she said.
"You don't even know where Detroit is!" I gave her
my whole radio rap about how we had to travel around
the country building my career or we were doomed
to be stuck in Hartford. My philosophy was that you
needed a résumé with nine hundred call letters on it.
I was always shocked at the number of disc jockeys
who were willing to stay in places like Hartford with
owners who wouldn't even give them health benefits.

So I went to meet the guys and they told me the
station was an incredible rock station called W-4. They
were in the process of moving the station to the Renaissance Center, which was a brand-new series of
beautiful high rises with crystal and the works.

"I'll do it!" I said.

Clark handed me a piece of paper.

"This is the salary."

I opened it up nonchalantly. Twenty-eight thousand
dollars. Holy shit, twenty-eight thousand dollars! This
was it! Finally, I could tell my father I was making
twenty-eight grand.

So I went home and told Alison—she flipped out. I
told the radio station to go fuck themselves. I called
Douglas, the consultant. He told me he was hoping for
a better station for me, because W-4 was having some
problems. I didn't want to hear about any problems. I
didn't care, I was pulling in twenty-eight. Then I
called my father. And I was thinking maybe I should
go for thirty. He told me twenty-eight was great but
there was no harm in calling the guy and asking. So I
called Wally back and he said, "Okay," and now I was
pulling down an even thirty.

I was totally jazzed. I packed up all my stuff and drove up to Detroit alone, because Alison had to give a month's notice on her job. They put me up at the Renaissance Center. It was beautiful. I said, "Where's the radio station?" "Oh," they said, "we're not in the Renaissance Center yet. But you just drive down the block, into downtown Detroit, and the station is straight down this road." So I got up the next morning at four o'clock, I was ready to go to work. Meanwhile, I had talked to the program director and he had given me a whole list of rules. Don't take phone calls from women because you sound wimpy when you talk to women. Only talk to men. Program directors were always burdening me with their *lame* theories. I figured, if they knew anything they'd be doing the morning show. How the hell am I going to control who's calling?

So I left the Renaissance Center and drove to the station. As I was driving, the neighborhood was getting progressively worse. Finally I saw the station. It was a bombed-out old house. I swung into the parking lot and parked the car and got out and there were fucking rats nipping at my feet. I was flipping out. The station was a toilet bowl, but who cared? I was the morning man in Detroit! *A major market.*

What I didn't know was that Detroit was going through one of the worst economic crises in its history. The auto industry was in the toilet and everyone was getting laid off. The whole town was depressed! Including the staff of the station, who were all pissed off that I was making at least ten grand more than they were. So I figured to get noticed I'd riff on the hard times. I tried to think up some bits. I decided to call the Kremlin and apply for five billion dollars in foreign aid for Detroit. I called other countries and tried to sell off New Jersey to raise money. We had a big promotion and I led hundreds of people who donated $1.06 (our call numbers) to smash the shit out of a Toyota, then we turned around and donated the money raised to Chrysler. I started to get national coverage on some of these stunts.

I did all sorts of crazy things. I had contests where I gave away sixteen cents, which was my pocket change. I called dentists' offices on the air and begged them to change their reception room radios to our show. I called the governor and tried to get Ted Nugent's "Wang Dang Sweet Poontang" declared the official state song.

We had Go Back to Bed Day where we got bosses to let the lucky winners go back to bed, with pay. I did a lot of Dial-a-Dates, which I started in Hartford, but this time I got *Penthouse* pets as contestants. That presented a problem once when we found out one of the winners was a convicted sex offender who had served time for one offense and was awaiting trial on a similar charge.

I began to assemble what would later become our famous Wack Pack. This woman Irene called up one day and I found out she was a real-live leather-clad, whip-carrying dominatrix. So I dubbed her Irene the Leather Weatherlady and every day I'd call her for the weather and she'd say outrageous stuff, like "Bitch, this is the weather and if you don't like it I'm going to come over and beat the crap out of you." One time she even recommended that people buy their mothers a red leather enema bag for Mother's Day.

I did anything to get noticed. I entered a local Dolly Parton Look-a-Like Contest. I wrestled women (and lost!) on the front lawn of the station at 8:00 A.M. in front of two hundred screaming maniacs. When the Republicans came to town for their convention we organized a protest in support of the Equal Rights Amendment. It was "Burn your B-R-A for the E-R-A" and again, I humiliated myself in front of hundreds of people, parading around in a bra and then collecting a few dozen others and burning them.

But the worst had to be the public appearances outside the station that we had to do. Let me tell you, promotion people at radio stations are usually assholes. They're always talking as if they have their finger on the pulse of the public, when, in fact, it really makes little difference what you do out on the street. If you put on a good radio show, people are gonna listen. They couldn't give a shit where you're showing up. But the promo people had this idea that you had to do promotions—promotions, promotions—and they got you so crazy with it that you had to go do them or you're considered "an enemy of the station."

Now, to me, promotions reeked of these bad djs who go out and do bar mitzvahs. I always felt disc jockeys were lowlifes. When I worked in Westchester I used to see some of the old WMCA Good Guys, who were now working up in places like Westchester, and it was depressing. They'd do these appearances in blue blazers with their big dumb voices. They looked about a hundred and fifty years old and sad. And they had been the biggest radio personalities. They used to be the WMCA Good Guys! If they were once at the top of the radio profession, and this is what happened to them, what did the future have in store for me? I was really frightened of the whole business.

I was in Detroit and I was the morning man for this failing radio station, and I had no listeners to start with, so every weekend I had to go out on a wacky promotion. I was the moron my father always said I was, I agreed to this stuff. So Halloween night they dressed me up as Dracula and I was supposed to appear at three or four different showings of *The Rocky Horror Picture Show.* I had to get on stage and introduce the movie. Well, first of all, nobody knew who I was. Number two, if you've ever seen an audience for *The Rocky Horror Picture Show,* they don't want anything interfering with the movie. They're all in costume, they got their toast, they know the friggin' movie by heart, they live for this movie. Plus, Detroit's a very angry city to begin with. Everybody's unemployed.

So I went to do the introduction and all these lunatics were marching up and down the aisle. I felt as if I was at some kind of PTA meeting in hell. I started to speak and all of a sudden toast and garbage started flying, I was booed unmercifully; people were screaming, "GET THE FUCK OFF THE STAGE, YOU FAGGOT!" They were going nuts. This happened four straight times.

The next weekend, they sent me to Windsor, across the border in Canada, to a little punk club. I took Alison with me. Again, I was supposed to do the introductions for the bands. So I got up on stage and said, "HI EVERYBODY! MY NAME IS HOWARD STERN AND I'M FROM W-4 IN DETROIT . . ." Now, I'd been in Detroit maybe a month, nobody knew who the fuck I was, so again, everybody started booing. Then this one imbecile kid in a mohawk ran up on stage and *boom!* He smashed me in the face with an egg. Everybody cheered. *Boom!* Smashed me with another egg. I stood there stunned. *Boom, boom, boom!* Three more eggs. I was drenched in egg. Alison was sitting there, she couldn't believe it. I just said, "HEY! FUCK THIS!" I threw the mike down, and we split.

I vowed never to do these appearances again. But the following weekend they booked me to race another disc jockey at a racetrack. And the Leather Weatherlady showed up, too. By now, she really had the hots for me. She frightened me because she was a real dominatrix who really wanted to dominate me sexually. I mean, I had never seen leather people before this. She really came on strong, and quite frankly, it was pretty exciting. But she was really living the lifestyle. Even her little daughter had a whip. This was a sick crowd.

So they decided I was going to race another disc jockey. Now, I don't race cars, I can hardly drive a regular car, I didn't know what the fuck I'm doing. And they got me in this dragster and I was racing this other guy in front of thousands of people. This was such a dumb promotion that I got really pissed off and I grabbed the loudspeaker and I was yelling, "WHO

THE FUCK CARES ABOUT THESE FUCKING
CARS!" I was out of my mind.

I got a ride back to town from another dj and the
Leather Weatherlady was sitting in the backseat next
to me. Now she was always attacking me with lots of
sexual innuendo, always coming on to me, the whole
thing. I was sitting back there and she started going
"Oooh, I want you, I want you."

I had had enough of her bullshit, too.

"You fucking want me?" I said. "My cock is right in
these pants. If you fucking want me, go in and take
my cock out and do something."

Now, I never do this kind of shit. All of a sudden
she was unbuckling my pants and was starting to
move her hand down. The disc jockey who was driving
was watching all this from the rearview mirror and
couldn't believe what was happening. She was looking
at me and she couldn't believe I was letting her do it!
I finally called Irene's bluff, because it was just getting out of hand. I never thought someone could be
this fucking annoying; every minute she was coming
on, grabbing my ass, taking the whip, hitting me, and
I couldn't take it, I was so angry. So as soon as she

had an opportunity she goes, "Oh, I don't believe you're gonna let me do this," and she never laid a hand on me again.

After a few months my show in Detroit became really wild. I was taking no prisoners. I had whole biker gangs in the studio. One of the gangs came in one day and whipped out coke and started snorting it, and I said, "You can't do coke," and they said, "Oh, yeah? What're you gonna do about it?" I couldn't stop these guys. I was thinking, "Oh, my God, I'm going to lose the station's license." But I'd rather lose it than my life. And I got wilder with Dominatrix Dial-a-Dates with the Leather Weatherlady. One time, in the middle of another Dial-a-Date, I decided I was gonna drink and I got so loaded I passed out on the air during the show. I woke up an hour later, and these people were still talking.

So I was plugging away at this job, the station was going downhill fast, but I was getting some major attention. I won the *Billboard* Award for best AOR disc jockey, I won the Drake-Chenault Top Five Talent Search, and one of my bits went out on a record to everyone in the industry. So I was starting to get well known. I was getting some job offers when, overnight, the station went country. I looked at Alison, told her to start packing, and I ran out to get a copy of *Radio & Records*, an industry trade paper with lots of classifieds. It was time to hit the road again. Somehow, I couldn't see myself as Hopalong Howie.

## NEXT STOP: THE FUNNY FARM

One of the job offers I got was from an album-oriented station in Washington, D.C. — DC-101. Again, it was Dwight Douglas who wooed me to come to D.C. I was considering offers from Chicago's WXRT and a station in Toronto. I told Douglas I wasn't sure about the D.C. station because the general manager seemed slow on the phone and not really aware of what I did. He told me not to worry. I should have. Between the time W-4 went country and our move to Washington, I was holed up in my office in our second bedroom at home and I plotted out my show. After a few weeks of deep thought, I knew exactly what I wanted to do.

First of all, I decided that whoever worked with me on the air must be simpatico. Then I decided that I was going to kill my competition. I was going to say whatever the fuck I wanted to say. I vowed that I wasn't going to blow this chance in Washington because Washington was the Northeast and my eventual goal was to make it in New York. I know it sounds corny, but when I was still in college, I was so totally focused on winning that when I flew over New York, I'd look down at the city and say, "One day everyone will know my fucking name in New York City." I wanted to be famous partly because I wanted to get back at all the women who rejected me in high school. In my warped mind I thought they would feel bad that they rejected me. Bad girls! They needed to be punished.

So Washington was a step toward New York, and

there was no way I was going to lose. I decided that the Washington show was just gonna be off the wall. The first step was to put my team together. It was time to find my newsperson. I realized how important the news segment was to my show. Since so much of great satire is topical, I wanted to find a newscaster with a good sense of humor who could riff with me on the current stories. I wanted to tear down that artificial wall between the show and the newscast. I found my ideal partner in Robin Quivers.

Robin had been a nurse and had just broken into radio. She was doing consumer reports for a small station in Baltimore. She'd been in radio less than a year, but Denise Oliver, the program director of DC-101, played me a tape of Robin and she sounded great. So I said, "Go get her." But for some reason, Robin was playing hard to get. Right, Robin?

I wasn't playing hard to get, Howard. I was at my third job in less than a year and I didn't want to move again. Baltimore was my home. But Denise started wooing me, taking me out to lunches and dinners. Finally, she said, "Let me play you a tape of the morning guy I want you to work with." I was thinking, "Right, like this'll make a difference." She put this tape in the machine and here came this voice and I thought, "Oh, my God." Howard was interviewing a prostitute on this tape and I had never heard anything like it in my life. You know how people immediately take on a sort of adversarial position when they're talking to someone like a prostitute? Like, you horrible person, you must have been abused in your life. Howard wasn't like that at all. He was asking stuff like, "How much do you charge? How many people do you service a day?" He was like a giddy kid, just curious about this other person. It wasn't condemnation, it wasn't "We're up here and we look down on you,

you poor dear." He was just treating this prostitute like everybody else.

I immediately lost all reservations and I just said, "Where do I sign?" He blew me away. I said, "I gotta meet this guy." So I was taking a job just to meet him. Then he said, "Wait a minute, I don't know if this'll work." So she put me on the phone with Howard to see if we could talk to each other and he started talking to me as if he'd known me all my life. I can't describe what that's like, for a total stranger to be instantly familiar with you. I thought, "He's nuts. I just agreed to work with a crazy man. What have I done?"

I knew Robin was the partner I'd been looking for that first day we went on the air together in March of 1981. I was going to open my show with a bang, as usual. I remember I called the mayor's office and asked them for a police motorcade and a parade for me to honor my first day on the air and I got some mayoral aide on the phone and I started screaming like a lunatic about Washington's mayor, Mr. Marion Barry.

"WHAT KIND OF GUY CALLS HIMSELF MARION? THAT'S A GIRL'S NAME!" I ranted.

Then I pulled out my other standard opening ploy. I would tell my audience how to get women and I'd give them tips from some cheesy paperback book about picking up girls. I got guys on the phone, I'd interview them about women. When was the last time you nailed a girl? Robin came into the studio, it was right before her newscast was about to begin, and I turned to her and said, "So Robin, this guy who wrote this book must know what he's talking about. He's slept with a ton of women. And his tip to get women is you have to wear tight pants."

Robin gave me this look like that was crazy.

"No, it's true," I insisted, "it's tight pants."

Robin looked at me and said, "This guy has slept with a ton of women?"

"Yeah," I said.

"If he slept with a ton of women, when did he have time to put on pants?" Robin said.

I reeled back in my chair and thanked God. She could talk!

We went to commercial and Howard was saying, "That's wonderful! That's brilliant! You're great!" And I was saying, "What did I do? Leave me alone—you're making me crazy." But that was the way he was. If I farted it was "Oh, that's wonderful." I just thought thank goodness I was in another studio when I did my broadcasts because he would say, "Oh, please, do this, say that." He wasn't putting words in my mouth, he just wanted me to react. And then they finished construction on the studio and I was now behind glass in another studio behind Howard. So we couldn't even look at each other unless he swung all the way around.

So I'd be in the other studio and Howard was on the air doing his thing. I'd listen to him and laugh out loud, because he was so crazy and outrageous. First of all, he never rehearsed anything. He didn't tape anything, he didn't prepare, he just hit the button and talked to whoever was out there and made something hilarious out of it. It's hard to realize how revolutionary that was because everybody else in radio then was rehearsed and prescreened down to the last letter. And he didn't care at all about format. We were constantly breaking format.

And the content was hysterical. Howard wasn't telling jokes, it was life happening in front of your eyes. He was catching people with their pants down. People would get up in the morning and call and they would think that they weren't going to be the fools and, invariably, they would be the worst fools. The people who thought "I think just like Howard," or "I know exactly what to say," Howard would drive them nuts. He'd take a wild right turn and do exactly the opposite of what they expected. Then he'd scream at

> them or he'd hang up on them. Nobody ever did that before on
> the radio. You can't yell at your callers, you can't treat them bad,
> you can't hang up on them. You can't take too many women callers
> because this is a rock station. You can't mention the other stations'
> call letters. Howard would break all the rules and I'd just be in
> there cracking up saying, "Oh, God, here we go again!" Then
> Howard started saying, "Robin, you have the greatest laugh. I love
> it when you laugh on the air. So when you come in the studio, turn
> on your mike as soon as you get there. Just say whatever comes
> into your mind." I told him, "You're so sweet," but I wouldn't do it.
> I had control of my mike. But he kept at me and at me and at me
> and he finally wore me down. He got me to do it.

The only thing holding me back was, again, I had
to start from square one with management. I had to
educate the general manager, educate the program director, talk them into letting me do little things. I kept
pushing the envelope just a little further every day,
just a little bit, then a little bit more. And what a pair
of management types I had at that station.

First, there was Denise Oliver, the program director. Denise was a real nice-looking woman with huge
breasts. Now right off the bat, I have trouble with
women as authority figures, especially if they have
huge breasts and come in wearing jeans and a tight
work shirt. How the hell are you supposed to concen-
trate in a meeting when she's leaning over, showing
you a memo or something, and those melons are staring you in the face? And she was always in the meetings. Right away, she didn't like Robin and me talking
to each other. I couldn't believe it. She'd go over to
Robin and say, "Should I stop him from interrupting
you?"

Robin would say, "No way. This is great!"

"Robin, I want you to stop him when he does this. You have to take a strong stand." I have always thanked Denise for pairing me with Robin but it upset me that she wanted us to act traditionally. It got so bad that in the beginning, Robin would meet with Denise and me but soon she banned Robin from the meetings because Robin always took my side. I was frustrated because my program was being slowed down.

Denise also had to have a strict format. We were doing regular features like Dial-a-Date and What's Your Problem?, where people would call up and I'd solve their problems. But Denise would say, "Now you seem to do What's Your Problem? on Mondays, so why don't we make that official so when I wake up on Monday, I know it'll be What's Your Problem? day." I didn't want a format. I wasn't comfortable with these restrictions. Then she had these elaborate grids. The grids made me feel as if I was back in elementary school. She wanted me to fill in the grids every week in advance with what we were going to do each hour. This woman was a great music program director and really had a great sense of direction for the station. But we were breaking new ground. I think she wanted to take control, and that was her job, but the constant interference was killing me. How was I supposed to know what I'd do on the show next Friday? Didn't she realize I was a spontaneous performer?

Then she'd bring up research. I had to play a lot of music. "The listeners we surveyed don't want to hear phone calls between records. We asked them," she said. But how did you ask them? They didn't explain in the survey that the disc jockey doing the talking is a fucking mutant and he's going to take these phone calls and talk about women's tits. Of course, the research showed they didn't want talking.

She had other theories. She wanted me to memorize the names of the high schools in the area. I had to learn the goddamn street names of every neighborhood. I had to make local appearances. Again with the appearances. Rules, everybody had rules. One time I was on the air and I decided to eat breakfast. So I ordered breakfast on the air, and it went on for eighteen minutes. Denise went ballistic.

*"I can't believe you ate breakfast for eighteen minutes on the air! THIS IS INSUBORDINATION!"* she ranted. "And the most embarrassing thing about it is that I didn't know you were going to do this. You're supposed to clear things with me ahead of time. The program director from WPGC, Steve Kingston, called me as soon as I got in my office this morning and said, 'Do you know your morning man ate breakfast for eighteen minutes on the air?' *What's wrong with you?!*"

I turned to her and I said, "Denise, a competing program director called you and told you he sat and listened to me eat breakfast for eighteen minutes. And he timed it! Do you think there were other people in the audience who couldn't believe I was doing this, too? Do you think that it's a possibility that this was compelling radio, that you all thought I had lost my mind, and just had to stay tuned to see what would happen?" She just couldn't understand what I was saying to her. Every day it was like this, me trying to educate her, and her wanting me to make a grid. But

Denise didn't torture me for long. In a few months, I tripled the station's ratings, and because the station was on such a roll she was able to get a job in New York. It was a great opportunity for her and now I was free from our daily meeting routine.

The general manager was another story. This guy, Goff Lebhar, was the biggest pain in the ass I ever worked for. Well, at least until I got to NBC. Goff would pontificate every day as if he was damn Einstein. He had theories, cockamamie theories about rebuilding the station. He had a five-point plan. Number one was antenna strength. If you had good transmission, nothing else could fail. Number two, the sales force. Once you had a good sales effort, you'd have the money forever. Numbers three and four were equally inane and number five, last, was programming. In other words, it didn't matter who was talking into the microphone or what they said, as long as the damn signal was clear.

This was what I was up against. But I kept chipping away at management's archaic approach, and we began to assemble the program I had envisioned. We did parodies like Hill Street Jews. We did Beaver Breaks, bits where Wally made love to an inflatable doll or Ward got a sex change. I introduced God and had Him do the weather. Who could be better at forecasting? Then I had God reveal that he was gay and living with a guy named Bruce. I savored every letter of hate mail and read the best ones on the air. I even called the haters up and got them on.

I formed a new Wack Pack. Somehow I got it into my head that we had to have sports coverage on the show—but not just any sports coverage. I started auditioning people who called in. We got this guy who sounded like he was having a nervous breakdown while he was giving scores. I brought him into the studio for his reports and Robin would find him lying in a corner crying, in the fetal position.

"He's crazy," Robin worried.

"Yes, but he's great on the air," I said.

One day he got really scary and we had to reevaluate our sports team. Our guy had held it together for the first few sportscasts, but he was withdrawing more and more as he became popular. Finally, when he was balled up in the fetal position mumbling to himself and sounding suicidal, we could no longer get him to the mike.

But I had other nuts I could work with. Alison was working as a psychiatric social worker in Washington so, after work, she was always telling me about her patients. What a fertile source of material! She was working with severe schizophrenics who would burn themselves with cigarettes, bang their heads incessantly, and think that their radios were sending them personal messages. The next day I'd imitate these patients on the air. Boy, did she get pissed. She'd say, "They listen to your show and they think you're having the same hallucinations."

Once a year they had a family picnic for these kooks. I'd be cooking hamburgers and Alison would tell me to go play Frisbee with some of her patients. Have you ever played Frisbee with schizophrenics? You throw the Frisbee to them and they make no attempt to catch it. It just hits them in the face. They won't pick it up and throw it back. I kept fetching it and throwing it and they'd just stand there and let it hit them. Finally, I quit playing and I turned away and one guy picks the Frisbee up and flings it right into my neck. That was my last picnic.

I always resented the label of "shock jock" that the press came up with for me, because I never intentionally set out to shock anybody. What I intentionally set out to do was to talk just as I talk off the air, to talk the way guys talk sitting around a bar. To me, that was always the most fun, when I would get together with guys and we'd all start bullshitting about getting pussy or that girl's tits or even political events, but doing it in a goofy way, where nobody's taking anything seriously. If I could eliminate the notion of the microphone, so that people would get loose and be real, that was the ideal. You don't know how many times I have guests on who think we're still in a commercial, and they start talking, and then they say, "Oh! We're on the air?" That's why ultimately radio is better for me than television, because on TV they never forget they're on. When that camera's in the room, everybody's on guard.

In Washington I approximated this ideal by creating the Think Tank. The Think Tank was a bunch of guys I put together: Harry Kohl, a lawyer; Steve Chiconas, a salesman; and Steve Keiger, who managed a record store. They came up every Tuesday and we went wild. Anything could happen. We were just a bunch of guys goofing on everything. It really was my college radio show all over again. In fact, out of those sessions evolved the "rankouts," which were the first things to get me in trouble in Washington.

We used to have rankout contests on the air. Listeners would call in and try to beat me in ranking out each other's mothers. "I heard your mammy is so fat that her gynecologist has to put up scaffolding to do the job." "Your mammy is like a Seven-Eleven. Open all night, hot to go, and for thirty-five cents she'll give you a slurpy." Stupid stuff like that. But immediately we got attacked by all sorts of moronic uptight PTA groups.

But I was no stranger to controversy. Hey, I was going for ratings. A large percentage of my audience in Washington was black, and I used to watch this local militant self-help positive-thinking black guy named Petey Green who had a UHF television show on Sunday mornings. I loved this guy because he was a real showman. He was always talking about the "niggers" and the "crackers" and jiving and rhyming and sitting in this big wicker chair in his expensive fine clothes, sort of like Huey Newton meets Superfly. I always talked about this guy on my radio show, how all whites should listen to him because he was giving away the militant blacks' game plan. So Petey invites me to be a guest on his TV show.

This was my first TV appearance in D.C., and even then I always felt that whenever you have a chance to be on television, you should do something memorable. So I went out and rented an Afro wig and brought some props and went to the taping with Robin and Fred. In the dressing room I put on the Afro wig, smeared black shoe polish all over my face except for

a big circle around my mouth, and went out on the set
carrying a big boom box and huge Afro pick.

The audience was almost totally black and didn't
know how to react until Petey saw me and cracked up.
Our interview was great.

Petey then paid a poetic tribute to me at the close
of the show:

> His name is Howard,
> his last name is Stern,
> but there's a C somewhere
> and that C stands for Concern.

> I don't think he's hateful,
> deceitful or mean,
> and he even gets up in the morning
> and watches Petey Green.

> So grab your hand
> and make a fist,
> just listen to me
> and know this:

> I'll tell it to the high,
> I'll tell it to the cold,
> I'll tell it to the young,
> I'll tell it to the old.

> I move so fast
> that sometimes I burn,
> but tonight I'm glad
> to deal with Howard Stern.

I kept the pressure on Goff to constantly push the
parameters of the show more and more each day. One

day I said to him, "I want to do a Gay Dial-a-Date." Immediately, he said no. But I kept pushing. I told him that the gay audience was demanding it, they were jealous of the regular Dial-a-Dates. I told him that I would handle it with class and decorum. Sure I tried all sorts of tactics to make it seem legitimate just so I could go on the air and mess with gays. In fact, I even suggested that we do it first with lesbians to ease into the whole gay area. Right. I just wanted to hear those hot lesbo stories. Finally, he relented. *The Washington Blade*, D.C.'s leading gay paper, wrote about it:

---

## DC 101 AIRS GAY DIAL-A-DATE

Washington Gays may have been done a great service by a radio disc jockey. Howard Stern recently made a "Gay Dial-a-Date Game" the focal point of his popular broadcast . . . [Stern, who is twenty-seven years old and married, has been holding Dial-a-Date games on radio for three years.] When homosexual listeners wrote him suggesting that it would only be fair to have a Gay version of the game, he agreed. Stern often wields his voice on the air to mercilessly puncture the pretensions and underline the stupidity of the people who call his show. Therefore, there was concern that he would use the occasion of the Gay Dial-a-Date to ridicule homosexuals. Instead, on Friday a.m., the Gay community was treated to one of the best, most sensitive treatments of Gay themes ever to air on the mainstream media.

For the first Gay Dial-a-Date he decided it would be best to feature Lesbians because the audience would be more likely to accept them, but he promises in the future there will be a Gay male version. Stern gave "Miss X" and her three suitors—bachelorettes numbers one through three—the opportunity to refute the idea that all Lesbians are ugly women with hairy legs and hiking boots, and the misconception that most Gays molest children. Listeners who called up to scorn or mock Gay Dial-a-Date while it was on the air were made short shrift of by Stern.

---

I was pushing the boundaries all over. I didn't know how far I would go. Anything that happened to me became grist for the mill of my show. I was with Fred doing an appearance on the local Charlie Rose television show when we saw Arnold Schwarzenegger, who was there to tape an

> "The American people are smart. They hear Howard on the radio and they realize that's the program to tune in to."
>
> —Arnold Schwarzenegger

earlier show. I loved Arnold and I had just read that he was about to do the Conan film. Now, normally I'm not a star-struck kind of guy. I don't just go up and approach celebrities and say, "Hey, I'm a big fan." But I figured maybe I could get something for the radio show, so Fred and I started following him. He walks pretty funny because he's so muscle-bound his thighs are like hitting each other. So we were following him and he went into the men's room. Fred and I looked at each other and we followed him in. He was sitting in a stall, with his pants down around his ankles, and he was taking a monster dump. A loud, big, smelly shit. I knew this was the rudest thing to do but I also knew I could talk about this for years on the air, so I said, "Arnold!"

"Yes." His booming voice filled up the bathroom.

"Hey, I'm Howard Stern and this is Fred Norris. We do a radio show in Washington."

"Yes, boys," Arnold says politely.

This was great. You're always vulnerable when you're crapping out, no matter how big a star you are.

"Hey, I just want you to know I'm a big fan of Conan the Barbarian and I think it's a superior move for you to do it," I said.

"Thank you, boys," he said. "I really appreciate you saying that."

We had this whole conversation with him and then we walked out. Later we ran into him on the set and introduced ourselves to him again. I thought it was really nice of him to even answer us. I would have been embarrassed as hell. Years later I had him on my show and I told him I was sure his penis was as long as his last name.

It didn't take long for Robin to realize that I would talk about anything on the air. In fact, let her tell this story.

I'll never forget the day I realized that nothing was sacred. I had started to gain weight. We had been under attack from management all the time. Goff hated us, and the other djs hated us because we were getting so popular. It got really depressing even though the show was doing great. We were both drowning our sorrows every day at Roy Rogers with bacon cheeseburgers, fries, and shakes. We both ballooned up.

One day I got up in the morning to get ready to go to work and I couldn't get my pants buttoned. I walked into Howard's studio and I said, "I can't believe how fat I'm getting. I couldn't get the top button on my pants done today," and I showed him. I went back into my studio, because we were gonna do a break, and he got on the air, and he immediately said, "Guess what, everybody? Robin has gotten so fat she can't button the top button!" I was horrified! This is the worst thing you could do to a woman. He just got on the air and told all of Washington, D.C., that I was so fat I couldn't button my pants. I couldn't believe he had done that. He was so sweet and understanding just seconds before. I looked at him and he gave me one of those little-kid shrugs like, "I couldn't help it."

But that was nothing compared with what I did to Alison. We had been married almost four years and we decided to have a baby. It was February of 1982 and we went to Aruba on a vacation because that's a nice place to bang away and try to make a kid. In Aruba we met these other people from Washington who invited us over when we got back. They had a nice house and a fancy hot tub and Alison went in the hot tub. Meanwhile, I started calling Alison every morning on the air with the Pregnancy Patrol report. Fred played some ambulance sirens in the background and I'd ask if she got her period yet. She missed her period. So we were telling everyone she's pregnant. We flew up to Boston to visit her parents and grand-parents and immediately told them. Alison's grand-mother, this great woman who was in her nineties, said, "If I were you, I wouldn't broadcast it." I al-ready had.

So Alison was about six weeks pregnant and she started cramping and bleeding. I took her to the doc-tor and he put her down on the table and he said that she was expelling the fetus. It was about the size of an aspirin but we were totally bummed out. We didn't know if Alison could get pregnant again. We felt like total failures. So to keep our sanity, we started kid-ding about it. I said that we should take some Pola-roids of the blood blob and send it to our parents so they'd at least have a picture of their grandchild. After a couple of days, Alison was joking about it, too. So I decided it was okay.

The next day I got on the air and it was time for God to do the weather:

"Let's check in with God. Hello, God. Yo, God! Your holiness!" (Thunder and lightning sound effects.)

"This is God."

"What's the weather like, man?"

"Hey, Howard, I see your wife had a miscarriage."

"Hey, you're not supposed to talk about that!"

"You tried to have a baby and you failed."

"Don't bring that up on the air! I didn't tell anyone."

"You couldn't even succeed in getting that right. Boy, are you a loser."

"I don't think this is funny."

"You're not a real man. Ha, ha, ha. You must be half a man. A real man would have done it right the first time. You're an embarrassing creation."

I started crying.

"Howard, I will make it mostly sunny today. Maybe you should go out and breathe some fresh air and go do it and get it right this time."

When Robin came on, we continued the discussion.

"God let the cat out of the bag. I didn't want other people to know," I cried.

"I'm sorry," Robin said. "Pull yourself together."

"That was my kid," I bawled, "and now he's lying on some laboratory floor. My kid's gone. And with him all my dreams and fantasies. MY STUPID WIFE HAD TO HAVE A MISCARRIAGE! IT'S ALL HER FAULT!"

"It's not her fault, Howard," Robin said.

"You know what it was? All the LSD I took in the sixties. I'll tell you kids out there, don't be like your pal Howeird and take LSD. I did it a long time ago and now I'm paying for it. It's my fault my wife had a miscarriage. I've got pulverized sperm. Chromosomal damage. Just because I wanted to see rocks move and watch trees melt. I blew it. I'M A WUSSY. I'M SHOOTING BLANKS. MY WIFE SAID IT'S MY FAULT, I HAD DUD SPERM." I sobbed hysterically. "Don't tell my wife we talked about it on the air," I said.

"You should talk about it, get it off your chest," Robin counseled.

"They made us put the kid in a bottle so they could examine it and see what was wrong. DO YOU KNOW WHAT THAT WAS LIKE? My wife and I wanted to save the bottle. He's our kid. We even named him. Ethan. We got him in formaldehyde. We're going to carry him in the bottle and take him to the zoo next weekend, buy him some popcorn. Every slob on welfare has kids, why can't I? What did I do to deserve this? We're going to have a birthday party for him. We're gonna act like he's alive. Just because he's in a bottle doesn't mean he can't have a life of his own."

"So I'm gonna be Auntie Robin?" Robin asked. "Should I buy him toys?"

"Don't get him toys," I said. "Get him fresh formaldehyde every once in a while. DON'T LAUGH AT MY MISERY, ROBIN."

I opened up the phone lines and we were flooded with calls. The first call was a woman who had been pregnant nine times and lost seven.

"If you were my husband, I would divorce you. That

was the cruelest thing I ever heard. I care!" she yelled.

"You care about what?" I asked.

"Your wife."

"I care about my wife, too, lady," I snapped.

"You made a boo-boo. You're cruel. Talking about the miscarriage and then referring to it as a blob on the floor. My God, man, put yourself in her shoes for just a minute and think how she might feel," the woman said.

I let her have it. "HOW DO YOU THINK I FEEL? IT WAS MY KID! MY KID! I LOST MY KID!"

I hung up on her. "I'M NOT GONNA TAKE THAT FROM HER. I COME ON THE AIR AND BARE MY SOUL TO YOU AND THIS WOMAN HAS THE NERVE, THE NERVE, TO MAKE FUN OF ME. I'M REALLY UPSET. WHY DO YOU THINK I WASN'T HERE LAST TUESDAY! I WAS IN THE HOSPITAL WITH MY WIFE WHEN SHE LAY THERE." I started acting as if I were sobbing. "IT'S MY KID, TOO. HOWARD JUNIOR. WE HAD TO PUT THAT KID IN A BOTTLE AND THE DOCTOR STILL HAS OUR KID AND I WANT HIM BACK."

I composed myself. "I even bought my wife roses when she told me the good news. I spent thirty bucks on those roses and then I called up the florist and said, 'Look, the kid didn't make it. Give me at least fifteen back.' The guy said, 'I don't care, pal.' I'M NEVER USING THAT FLORIST AGAIN! THAT IS MAN'S INHUMANITY TO MAN!"

That night I went home and went to sleep early. I should get Alison in here to tell you the rest of the story.

Twelve years and three children later, this whole thing is pretty hysterical, but I didn't feel that way then. I got a call from a local reporter who asked me how I felt about Howard talking about the miscarriage on the air. Howard was already asleep. The more this reporter told me, the angrier I got. He got me completely crazy and I stayed up all night and yelled at Howard. I was pissed. I felt really violated by him for the first time ever. I was mortified. I was furious. I was up the whole night, I felt so betrayed by him.

This reporter Dennis was writing positive articles about me, but this time he acted like all of Alison's gossipy friends who listen to the show and then report back to her on what I said. This guy prodded her. "Didn't it make you feel bad? Don't you realize it was your baby he was talking about?" He got to her and she went ballistic on me. "You're an asshole! You're a moron!" she screamed. What was I supposed to do? Once she was joking about it I figured it was okay to talk about it on the air. My personal life has to be my material because I hate to go out anywhere. Hey, I have to fill up five hours a day. I thought this would be strong material for at least a week but I had to nip it in the bud. Bitis interruptus.

The next day I went on the air, all contrite.

"We'll do Dial-a-Date tomorrow. I also want to tell

you that due to the fact that I told you about my wife's miscarriage yesterday, my wife isn't talking to me now. Just because I wanted to be honest with you people. She said, 'That isn't the kind of thing you should tell your audience. You can't talk about that on the radio, you just should have said it was a false alarm.' I said, 'No, no, you don't understand. The whole premise of this radio show is that I'm honest with the people.'

"So we're not talking now. We're having a fight. She's not into talking because she's embarrassed. A lot of women have miscarriages. I know why we had it. Because I eat all that artificial sugar with the cyclamates. In my coffee this morning I'm having regular sugar with that fake milk. Come to think of it, there's a lot of chemicals in that nondairy creamer. Maybe that's what's destroying my children."

I started reading the ingredients. "Corn syrup solids, partly hydrogenated vegetable oil, coconut oil, cottonseed oil, palm oil, then something called sodium caseinate, you know that's going to kill my kid."

Then God came back on to do the weather. And He apologized to me for talking about my wife's miscarriage:

> "I'm sorry I made fun of you. Just because you're not a real man doesn't mean I have the right to make fun of you. [A baby cries in the background.] By the way, do you hear that baby in the background?"

"Yeah."

> "That's yours. He's up here with me now."

"Oh, man."

"Not to worry. We're having a good time. I'm going to introduce him to Jim Morrison of the Doors."

"You better not, that guy's a derelict."

"I will make it a nice day today. This is God on DC-101."

"God, I'm sick and tired of you. You're out! I'm gonna get me that guy from Channel Four, what's his name?"

I wanted to climb under a rock. I started getting all these letters from people whose children had died. I got a letter from a woman who had a stillbirth and mine was the size of an aspirin! I was so embarrassed. When we went out in public, I felt that people could see right through me. But I could never stay mad at Howard. I understood it wasn't so horrible. Within two seconds, he can talk to me and he has such a sweetness. I know this sounds corny, but he can turn to me and say, "I didn't really mean to hurt you, I really love you," and then it's all over with.

That was the turning point. I knew that nothing was off bounds. I thought, "Here we go." He always says that nobody knows if this is true or not because he embellishes stories, but I still get angry when he talks about our personal life, even to this day. It's weird, but if I have a problem with something I have to say to him, "I have to talk to you but I don't want it on the radio." Then he'll say, "I wasn't even thinking about it for the air, but now that you mentioned it, it would be great radio."

But the thing that got me the most notoriety in Washington was the famous Fourteenth Street Bridge incident. This event has been so distorted over the years by the press that I want to set the record straight, once and for all. It started when that Air Florida flight crashed into the bridge in February of

1982. The plane crashed because they didn't de-ice the wings. I was outraged that people lost their lives because of this stupid airline fuck-up. So I made believe I was calling Air Florida and I said, "What's the price of a one-way ticket from National to the Fourteenth Street Bridge? Is that going to be a regular stop?" I was seriously coming out against this negligence. I didn't make jokes. I didn't actually call and speak to someone from the airline. But that riff became legendary. In fact, six months later, when I was leaving Washington to go to WNBC in New York, a reporter from *The Washington Post* wrote that I had been fired from DC-101 for that call. That bullshit article still haunts me. Everybody says I got fired over this incident. It's not true. In fact, no one ever complained about it.

Anyway, after a year on the air, we had quadrupled our audience. It was insane. We were real celebrities in Washington. We'd go out to do public appearances and we'd be mobbed. People would come up and press coke or pot into our hands and we'd politely refuse. We did an appearance at the big department store Woodward & Lothrop and it was out of control. They set us up in a little booth in front of the store window and I was supposed to greet people. Well, it was a rainy day and the mall was packed with people. Thousands and thousands of people showed up and they were lined up outside and when they finally let them in, they almost tore the store down. We had to be escorted out of there because the people just rushed in and trampled over all the merchandise and knocked over the racks and started stealing everything in the fucking store. They had to evacuate the mall. It was unreal.

That was the last public appearance I ever did, except for one right before I left Washington, when my album *Fifty Ways to Rank Your Mother* came out. Fred and I went down to a record store to promote it and a young girl came up to get her album autographed. She said, "I want your autograph for my mother."

"Your mother? Where's your mother?" I asked.

"She's out in the car waiting for me," she said.

"You should bring her in. Is she nice-looking?" I asked.

"Don't you talk about my mother like that!" she yelled and *wham*, she kicked me right in the nuts and went running out of the store.

But with all that popularity do you think that our general manager Lebhar would be happy? No! He was pissed that I had made his station successful! This guy was reaping all the rewards of my success, he was making about half a million a year because of his deal, and I was still pulling in about forty thousand. And *he* was pissed. Meanwhile, Robin and I went to a party at his house one night and he was living in some huge, tacky house with one of those stupid naked kid sculptures that pee into a fountain in the middle of his foyer. It was so disgusting it looked as if it should be in a mausoleum. I was sitting there eating my heart out that this character was making a half a mil a year and living in a big house because of my success. Meanwhile, I was driving a 1970 Valiant.

Then he pulled me into his office and he said, "Why don't the newspapers mention me? They only write about you."

This guy was giving me shit because I was getting credit for my accomplishments.

"Why don't they mention *me?* I was the architect of this station's success."

He was one of those guys with dry mouth, and as he was talking, I was watching this little piece of white spit get caught on his lip and go up and down like a cobweb. And I realized that this guy was angry at me for being successful. I asked him for more money and he said, "Absolutely not."

So I knew it was time to move on. I had my sights set on New York. I had gotten a lot of other offers, even an offer from WPLJ in New York to do nights, but I didn't think that was the right move. Meanwhile, Goff got wind of my offers and he tried to nail me down to a contract. All that time he didn't want to give me a contract, now he said if I didn't sign one within a month, I'd be fired. But he didn't want me to be represented by a lawyer. I was whining that I wanted to be represented; he wouldn't let me be represented. While this was dragging on, he got sick. He was home, he was missing work. He was getting sicker. They didn't know what it was, but it looked as if he was going to die. I couldn't believe my good luck.

"He's going to drop dead. We're going to get our wish," I told Robin.

All of a sudden, his wife came in, all smiles.

"You aren't going to believe how lucky we are. They

found a tick in Goff's head. He has Rocky Mountain spotted fever." They took out the tick, he got completely better, he was coming back.

So Goff came back and we worked out a one-year contract with a nothing, shitty raise, which I signed. A few months later I signed a contract to go to WNBC in New York after my Washington contract expired. Well, this pissed Goff off and they started to make my life miserable. They took away my office. They harassed me in a million different ways.

In August of 1982, with two months to go on my contract, they hired this no-talent jerk called the Grease Man and they gave him all the money I had been asking for. Another disc jockey getting a boatload of money off my hard work. The day they hired him, they decided to fire me and get me off the air right away. They made up some excuse, saying I had violated station rules by talking about other disc jockeys. That made no sense, because I had always talked about other disc jockeys. They really just wanted not to pay me for the last two months of my contract, but I took them to the union and they were forced to pay anyway. I was thrilled. I was getting away from Lebhar and I was finally getting my shot at working in New York.

I was going to work for the world-famous, first-class National Broadcasting Company. This was my dream come true, I thought. Little did I realize it was more like "Welcome to My Worst Nightmare."

# Pig Virus

*It Sucks at NBC*

CHAPTER
6

I had done it. This was the culmination of all my dreams. This made all the shit I ate in Westchester and Detroit and Washington worth it. I was on my way to New York, the nation's number-one market, my hometown. I was the afternoon drive-time air personality for WNBC. I thought back to all those commutes I had made with my dad. Now I was going to be the guy who could come out of your car radio and make that drudgery magical. I was jazzed. I wouldn't be for long.

There were hints even in the first meeting

I had with the NBC people. NBC's management came to Washington to meet with Robin, Fred, and me, and at one point in the meeting they asked Robin and Fred what they would do if they weren't hired by NBC. At the time I ignored it and focused on the positive aspects of the meeting, but later I was to find out that the dickheads at NBC had a systematic plan to break up my morning team. Years later, Bob Sherman, the executive vice-president of the NBC radio stations, admitted to *New York* magazine that they had developed a strategy to tame me before I even came to New York.

"We wanted Howard without his aides-de-camp, so he'd be as naked and vulnerable as possible to good management," Sherman said. "Naked and vulnerable"—this sounds like he's talking about a bondage video. Little did I know that wasn't far from the truth.

For starters, they did succeed in busting us up. They refused to hire Robin after they told me they would. I assured her that I would keep trying to get them to bring her up, but she got really mad at me and she went back to an all-news station in Baltimore. So it was just Fred and I going to New York, but before we even got there another asshole intervened to make my life miserable. This scumbag also worked for NBC, but he was one of the network's television news talking heads. His name was Douglas Kiker, a name that, to this day, summons up my vomiting reflex.

This story started in Washington. Douglas Kiker contacted us and said he wanted to do a favorable report on the Howard Stern phenomenon. I thought, "That's cool." I had already done a few good interviews with Charlie Rose for his television show and Kiker's piece was going to appear on "NBC Magazine," which was a national show. Great publicity, I thought. At that time, we were doing a lot of live shows and they decided they'd bring their cameras down to Garvin's comedy club where I was scheduled to do the next one. Those shows were a whole story in themselves. I would come out in a bathrobe and we'd all be sitting behind tables and we'd do our normal morning show in front of an audience of rabid fans.

So Kiker and his crew came down and filmed us. They interviewed me later. While they were preparing the piece, I signed with NBC radio in New York. Fine. Now Kiker and I were working for the same corporation. A few weeks later, the piece aired. I sat down with Alison to watch it and I couldn't believe what I was seeing. The piece was called "X-Rated Radio" and it started with Kiker saying this:

> What you're about to hear is going to shock you because it's vulgar, even obscene. A warning: If there are any children in the room you might not want them to watch this report. It's X-rated radio, barnyard radio, and there's more and more of it on the air because kids love it.

That was just the friggin' introduction! I was going out of my mind. Then they went to a close-up of a radio and coming out of that radio was the voice of, you guessed it, me! "I hear your pappy is so disgusting that he takes a bubble bath by farting in a mud puddle." Okay, so it was a fart joke. Big fucking deal. But then we saw a hand reach into the frame and shut off the radio; the camera dramatically pulled back and we

saw the hand belonged to Douglas Kiker and he was
sitting in his living room with a six-month-old baby
that looked as if it came from Ivory Soap central cast-
ing! Give me a break! And now Kiker spoke again:

This is my home in Washington. It's secure enough. I've got
locks on the windows, locks on the doors, even an alarm
system . . .

What's the matter, Dougie? Afraid of the schvartzes
breaking in? Show us your Uzi, why don't you, you
big jerk.

. . . What I cannot prevent entering my home are the sounds
that come over this radio. The idea for this story originated a
few weeks ago when I heard my seven-year-old son, this one's
older brother, coming down for breakfast saying the same
things you just heard this DJ say.

Hey, his son was quoting me! He should be thrilled!
What's wrong with a seven-year-old kid into fart humor? Is that a crime? Asshole. Okay, then they cut to
me on the stage at Garvin's and I was singing "Fifty
Ways to Rank Your Mother," to the tune of Paul Simon's "Fifty Ways to Leave Your Lover."

*My friends always enjoyed your mom they said to me*
*She was so generous, she did so much for free*
*Until they found she gave them all a social disease*
*There must be Fifty Ways to Rank Your Mother*

Then this jerk Kiker came back:

His name is Howard Stern. His station is DC–101. He's on
the air from six to ten in the morning when grownups are on

their way to work and their children are off to school. And he is hot.

Back to me onstage, singing:

> *I heard she's frigid tho' she might just*
> *be hard to please*
> *But if that's so why does she douche with antifreeze?*
> *She says she likes it 'cause it also kills her fleas*
> *There must be Fifty Ways to Rank Your Mother*

I liked this song! But Kiker didn't. Then he said that when "word got out" that he was doing this piece, a group of "concerned parents" contacted him and requested to be part of the show. Yeah, right. "Word got out." Who's he kidding? Anyway, they assembled a group of these mutant parents and here's what they had to say about me:

"I don't consider it humor at all, adult or child. I think it should be completely off the airwaves."

Oh, this housewife was a comedy critic? And she wanted to ban me from the airwaves? Thank you, Mrs. Hitler.

"Kids are looking for rock 'n' roll music and they get a guy pandering smut to kids."
"Kids call in with their own rankouts on mothers and I'm a mother!"

But my favorite one was this guy:

"Vietnam at dinnertime was bad enough, but this stuff over my cocoa puffs is driving me crazy! It just doesn't need to be there."

Great, he was comparing me to Vietnam. Who were these people? And what's more important, why were they giving these people so much time to propound their theories when they hardly mentioned the fact that I was number one! People wanted this kind of radio. And you, Kiker, you big jerk, you didn't need bars on your windows. You weren't being invaded by your radio. He sounded like one of Alison's mental patients. IF YOU DON'T LIKE WHAT YOU'RE HEARING, TURN THE FRIGGIN' RADIO OFF!

The piece went on and they showed some other no-talent disc jockeys in other markets who were doing naughty humor. But the real kicker was the ending to the piece. After they ran the report, Kiker was in the studio:

> That is X-rated radio. And you could be hearing it next in your hometown. This is a story with a little twist to it. While we were in the process of producing this report, Howard Stern was lured away from his Washington radio station by a New York City station which offered him a big increase in salary. That station, you guessed it, is WNBC-AM, which is owned by NBC. Dom Fioravanti, the station general manager, told us that WNBC-AM, and I quote, "is mindful of its responsibility to present programs in accordance with acceptable public taste."

Great way to start a new job. I couldn't even get the NBC guys in New York to return my phone calls after that piece. That one piece poisoned my entire relationship with NBC for the next three years and all because Douglas Kiker didn't like his son going around telling fart jokes. Man, I was happy when I heard that Kiker kicked the bucket. Big jerk!

Finally, I got a letter from Dom Fioravanti. He said they were excited about me coming to the station and that my show should blend "satirical, farcical, and absurd comment" to expose "the inconsistencies and hypocrisies inherent in certain public standards, mores and norms of conduct." Sounded good. Then he told me what I couldn't do.

---

## NO

1. jokes or sketches relating to personal tragedies
2. slander, defamation, or personal attacks on private individuals or organizations unless they have consented or are a part of the act
3. jokes dealing with sickness or death
4. jokes dealing with sexual topics in a lascivious manner
5. scatological or other "barnyard" type material
6. ridiculing religion for the sake of ridicule or making fun of the religious faith people may have
7. use of the so-called seven dirty words

---

Great, I was the number one radio personality in Washington, D.C., and these guys had to remind me not to say "fuck" or "cocksucker" on the air. What was I, a baby? I tell you, they really knew how to make a new employee feel good. And it only got worse.

They had no idea what to do with me, and that was evident from their first advertising campaign. "Howard Stern Returns," they were trumpeting all over. Well, it was true that it was a return because I grew up in New York, but I had never been on the radio there before. Imus was the one who had been in New York then got fired and then came back.

I was scheduled to go on the air right after Labor

NBC press photo. I was fat with a bad mustache.

Day, 1982, but the station program director, Kevin Metheny, decided he wanted to "test" me out before that. He wanted me to do an overnight stint before my actual afternoon show. First of all, this was totally demeaning. They had hired me away with big bucks from a major market and now they were treating me as if I was a college kid doing an audition. But what was worse, Metheny and Fioravanti kept telling me that I should develop "characters" for my show, just the way "Mr. Imus" had. They sat me down every day and forced me to listen to tapes of Imus's show while they cooed how "brilliant" and "creative" Mr. Imus was.

It was amazing the way everyone at that station was kissing Imus's ass. And he was doing a lame, tame show with "characters" that were older than me! He had his Reverend Hargis bits, and this stupid Moby Worm routine, which was just his voice put through a synthesizer. The whole bit was that Moby Worm was coming to eat your high school. So he'd warn you a hundred times, "Coming up next hour, Moby Worm is gonna eat Rockville Centre High," and then they finally did the bit and they played a few sound effects and Moby Worm ate your school. No real conversation, nothing innovative, just the same stupid bits over and over. Lazy radio. If I had my preference, I would have come to New York, gone on in the morning, and just beaten the crap out of him.

I didn't get it. But "Mr. Imus," "the genius," did characters, so they wanted me to create characters for my show. I told them a hundred times that I don't do characters. I'm me on my show. But they wouldn't relent. They got me so crazy with this characters stuff that I decided I'd give them a character for that first overnight. As a matter of fact, I did the entire show in character. I was Lance Eluction, a hairdresser who was getting his big break in radio, and Lance was joined on the show that night by his life mate, Bob, who was played by Fred. We were two over-the-top gay guys, thrilled to be on the air.

Now you have to remember NBC at that time had a Top Forty format. So while I was Lance, the prancing gay guy, I was also doing a parody of the typical Top Forty guys who would do these inane intros to a record right up until the lyrics kicked in. There I was in my falsetto voice, commenting on Andy Gibb's voice: "How does she get up so high, what does she do? Is it the tight leather pants or what? I just got a note from the program director, it says, 'Always say double-u-ennn-b-c.' Double-u-ennn-b-c. Ohh."

That was another thing. The program director, Kevin, whom I started calling Pig Virus because he reminded me of a kid I knew in camp who looked like a stupid porker, would always make me practice saying the call letters. He would come into my office and lie on the floor and make me repeat again and again, "Double-u-ennnnn-b-c." This Pig Virus would just lie there and shake his head and say, "Nope, that's not it. Do it again. You're not doing it like Mr. Imus does it." I wanted to kill that creep, but I later realized that he was just a pawn in this whole game. The NBC brass were putting heavy pressure on him to get me in line and he was just doing his job. But I resented the way he did it with such viciousness. I could never forgive him. So that whole first night I kept moaning "Double-u-ennn-b-c" almost like I was coming.

Around one in the morning, Fred came up and I put him on the air:

"Lance Eluction here at double-u-ennn-b-c. I'm here with my friend Bob who just dropped in because when you work here at WNBC, excuse me, it's not WNBC, its double-u-ennn-b-c, when you work here late at night your friends can drop in and the program manager never knows the difference. I'm so glad it's getting late here at double-u-ennn-b-c because I just spoke to the program director of the station and he's going to bed now and we're really going to have some fun as soon as all the network brass and my program director go to sleep. I'm going to gargle to all the songs here at double-u-ennn-b-c. THE FUN BEGINS WHEN THE BRASS GOES TO SLEEP. I LOVE IT, DOUBLE-U-ENNN-B-C."

"It's kinda dry in the studio, don't you think?" Bob said.

"It is dry, Bob. That's why I'm going to do the gargling thing now. At double-u-ennn-b-c they give you a pitcher of water for the djs."

"That's so nice."

"Let's play the next song, and I'm going to gargle over it."

Fred cued up "Don't You Want Me" by the Human League and I gargled through the song.

"I gargled the whole song. Pretty funny bit. My tonsils are killing me from this stupid station—you have to keep talking the whole time. And it's so dry in here."

"Would you like a neck massage?" Bob asked.

"Give me a neck massage. Bob's going to give me a neck message. This is the first time I've ever been on the air anywhere. This is sort of an unbelievable story for me. From hairdressing school right to the studio. Double-u-ennn-b-c is the most liberal network in the whole world. Is it marvelous? Only in America. God bless America. God bless double-u-ennnnnn-b-c."

We went on like that all night. And the reaction was incredible. The switchboard operators at WNBC were so flooded with calls that at one point they actually called upstairs to find out if there was something wrong. They said they never got a response like that before. I was thrilled. We came in the next day and Pig Virus was beet red. He said, in that slimy Southern accent of his, "You ruined us. Do you know how many phone calls we got?"

"But you guys want characters," I protested. "I did it in character."

He brought me in front of five other empty suits sitting on a couch, the board of censors, and started telling me what I couldn't do. I was flipping out, because these guys didn't get it at all. They should have been thrilled with the reaction they got. All of a sudden, I was having a flashback to DC–101. I hadn't even started my show yet and these guys were trying to kill me.

That was the way it was for the next three years. Except for one guy, Randy Bongarten. He came in as general manager and understood what I was doing. These morons had no clue whatsoever and tried to kill my show from day one. Meanwhile, I was desperately trying to reunite my team. I kept nagging and nagging them to bring Robin in from Baltimore. They wouldn't do it. Divide and conquer, right? So I started doing my show, in this incredibly restrictive format, and I was on the air a little more than a month and, bingo, I was suspended.

Again, it was God that got me in trouble. I was dying to do bits on my show but these guys thought the comedy was distracting from the real value of the show: the Trini Lopez and Neil Diamond records I was spinning. But I was able to squeeze in a bit or two an hour between all the music and the double-u-ennn-b-c bullshit. I figured if they wanted characters, I'd give them characters. So I put God back on the air:

> "Okay, now it's time for me to unveil another God video game. You've heard of Donkey Kong, haven't you? Now, are you ready for this? Virgin Mary Kong."

"Oh, my God, are you crazy?" I said.

> "The object of the game is Virgin Mary is being chased by all these guys in a Jerusalem singles bar. You have to keep her away from those guys or she won't be the Virgin Mary anymore, if you get my meaning."

At the end of the bit the Virgin Mother was impregnated by some dude who pushed her up against the wall of a singles bar. Anyway, I thought it was a great skit. I had no idea they'd suspend me for something like that. I was shocked by their reaction. Maybe that's why they call me a shock jock, I am always genuinely shocked by people's reactions to what I do.

But the suspension was a blessing in disguise. I went to Pig Virus and Fioravanti and told them that I did that bit because Robin wasn't there. She was the one who made sure I didn't do stuff like that. Of course, it was all bullshit. Robin didn't rein me in. Robin's whole thing was after I did something outrageous on the air, she'd go, "Oh, Howard, that's terrible." But they thought bringing Robin in would keep me in line. What was really happening was we were about to go to war and I wanted more troops.

I'll never forget Robin's introduction to Pig Virus. Her first day at the station, she was just sitting in the studio, getting familiarized. I went on the air, and I was rapping and we were about to go into some music and then we heard this loud thud coming from the other engineer's booth. It was really dark in the engineer's booth, so we couldn't see what was happening, but Robin turned to me and said, "What's that?"

"Oh, I think Kevin just threw the phone at the wall," I said nonchalantly.

"What?" Robin was incredulous.

"Yeah, he does that. I must have broken format."

For the next three hours, she stayed in the studio, sitting there a little shell-shocked. She was afraid to even go to the bathroom because she might get hit by a flying object. Finally Robin turned to me and said, "What the hell have you gotten me into?"

"I told you it wouldn't be easy." I smiled and put my headphones on. Pig Virus made my life miserable every day for the next year. He sounded and acted like a real rube tourist with his Southern accent. "I pay twelve hundred dollars a month for rent for a studio apartment. Ain't that sumptin'? But I love it. I luuuve it. I ate at Mr. Chow's the other day with Mr. Imus. Whee doggie, Jethro." This guy was supervising my creative talent.

After Virgin Mary Kong, I had to get every bit approved by committee before it could go on the air. Pig Virus would yell at me because the scripts weren't typed. He'd yell if the bits went longer than two minutes. He'd say real encouraging things like "If the people don't like you, and if you only talk for two minutes before they can get so disgusted, you'll be back into music." Nice, huh?

But what was worse was that he would memo me all these idiotic rules and ideas he had. And it wasn't just to me; he would cc everybody at the whole damn station, including accountants and security guards! This man was trying to publicly humiliate me; to break me and make me quit. It took every ounce of strength I had to keep from doing that. I got so paranoid, I forgot I was funny. It was like water torture in Vietnam. You begin to think you're an animal and the VC are gods. I was walking around a station full of untalented people who thought they were more talented than I was. Robin and I decided that Imus must have

made a pact with the Devil so that he didn't have to
be funny but could still get ratings.

You have to read some of these memos Pig Virus
sent. He came up with this complicated terminology
to make it sound as if he knew something, but it was
all mystification. Any idiot could go into radio. But he
knew the vocabulary:

> You did say "NBC" which is *not* the call sign, and it is *not*
> the primary identity of the radio station. As we have discussed
> before, "WNBC" is the primary ID, and that which should be
> stated first. In a "double sell" set, that is, a break (in a sweep,
> or on either side of a stop set) in which you have the opportu-
> nity to ID the station more than once, you may use "WNBC"
> twice or "WNBC" and "NBC" once each. But in a break where
> you only ID the station once use "WNBC."

I would look at Fred and say, "What the hell is he
talking about?" This was just a lot of bullshit trying to
make a simple job look complicated. There's more:

> JINGLES: Please refrain from singing along with jingles,
> and play them per schedule. No more jingle-thons, no more
> playing of other jocks' jingles.

In other words, don't have fun. Don't let the listeners think you might be having fun. God forbid, they
might think the show is funny. Clearly I had a different point of view. I was breaking all the rules and it
was his job to control me. I was his nightmare.

> BIT PLACEMENT: One bit per break is the maximum. Con-
> sider the Moreau Blanc live spots a "bit," which will preclude
> another bit in the same break.

Great, now he was telling me (and the janitor who got cc'd) that doing a fun commercial was the same as doing a comedy routine. According to his calculations, I could do three two-minute bits an hour, and that was my show.

**THE STAFF:** I'd appreciate it if you'd discontinue making deprecating remarks regarding the other Talents' capabilities, styles, and performances.

Again, no kidding around here. This was a serious comedy program.

**MUSIC:** Discontinue making derogatory remarks about the music you play.

God forbid I should make fun of Olivia Newton-John.

**IN GENERAL:** There's not a lot positive in this particular memo, because I feel it's time to start moving forward again with the project of making The Howard Stern Show sound like an organic part of WNBC Radio. So, *yes,* on balance I am pleased. Yes, WNBC *does* continue to have a strong commitment to personality radio, to Howard Stern. Yes, I acknowledge and appreciate your efforts to date. And *now* there's still a lot of ground to cover.

Is it any wonder that I would want to slit my wrists? But it wasn't just memos. Pig Virus was actually monitoring my show. He installed a "dump" bell that worked from a hotline in his office. Whenever he didn't like what I was doing, whether it was what I was saying or a bit that was running over his cherished two-minute time limit, he'd pick up the phone. That would light up a light and ring a bell in the engineer's booth, and the engineer then had to immediately go to a commercial or a jingle with no explanation. Can you imagine if you're listening and all of a sudden a bit is interrupted by a jingle? You'd think these guys were total amateurs. Then to top it off, he sent a memo about this to the engineer and cc'd the whole world:

### Subject: Remote "Dump" Procedure

During Howard Stern's airshift, *at all times,* there should be loaded a basic jingle, *and* a record. If the dump bell/button goes off, instantly dump: close all mikes, fire the jingle and record *immediately.* Do not pick up the phone and check, do *not* advise Howard over the talk-back to get out of the bit— simply DUMP PROGRAMMING and roll the jingle and record.

Pig Virus was single-handedly ruining my show. He took away my ability to talk for any duration, he took away any control over my show with this dump button bullshit. Then, to add insult to injury, he sent around another memo:

### Subject: Non-AFTRA talent

A reminder that only currently active AFTRA members may speak on WNBC Radio, and only via prior arrangement with the Program Director. This precludes regular appearances of friends of the family, engineers, and any others not officially in WNBC's full-time or part-time employ for the express purpose of appearing on our air.

There went the rest of my show. I couldn't call Alison or my mother. I couldn't talk on the air with the engineers or the cleaning lady or the security guards. Pig Virus had issued his edict. I was fucked. My show was like nothing anyone was doing and they were trying to make me sound like everyone else.

Besides all this, Robin told me that Pig Virus tried to undermine our relationship. He called Robin into his office and, out of nowhere, he told her that he didn't have any money to give her because "Howard has taken it all." Luckily, Robin is an intelligent woman who didn't fall for that.

But it was so demeaning to have any contact with him. He got a few of the interns to cut out pictures of happy, smiling families from magazines and paste them into a collage which he hung in the studio to remind me of the target audience of the station. I can imagine how the other jocks were laughing their asses off at me every time they saw this work of art hanging there.

One of the people who was really supportive during those years was comedian David Brenner. Brenner would come in and do the show from time to time. He truly admired my style. "David, these assholes are attempting to squelch all my creativity and train me to be a boring fuck like Imus." We'd have these discussions during commercials and David could tell I was at my wit's end. "Who's in charge of the station?" he said. "Dom Fioravanti." With that, David marched into Fioravanti's office. He was in there for ten minutes yelling at him about how he had a genius at work and they should get off my fucking ass. This was a pretty spectacular gesture and I loved him for it.

As bad as it was to go to work every day, I somehow knew that, eventually, they would all be worn out dealing with me—just like my parents when I wanted

Early NBC. I was broadcasting from listeners' homes.

Here I even talked with a guy in his home who was bathing in a tub of red Jell-O.

my own way. A drop in the bucket every day—get away with a bit one day, and then maybe get suspended the next. But in due time, I would get things my way!

Pig Virus just had no clue where I was coming from. Neither did my general manager. One of the worst things they ever did was have me cohost the Easter Seals Telethon. I had been at the station a few months and they decided that I needed a good-guy image, so they arranged for me to do the telethon. I was trying to be a team player, so I went along. I got dressed up in a tux, but this isn't my scene. You can't be funny talking about crippled kids. I didn't know what the fuck to say. I was on for about seven hours and by the end of my slot I was crazed. I was saying stuff like: "I'm gonna be a father in two weeks and I've been going shopping for baby furniture and it's expensive. But what if I should have to go shopping for a wheelchair? Or an artificial limb? That's really expensive."

By the end of the night, I was sitting in a wheelchair, doing my pitch: "I'm about to fall asleep and this wheelchair is pretty comfortable. But at least I can get out of it. So many kids can't."

The whole thing was a total nightmare.

Even the engineers humiliated me at NBC. I'll never forget one engineer. This jerk was so busy filing union grievances that we could never get him to do anything for the show. It was hell. But this guy had plenty of time to walk around the halls of NBC when the ratings came out like he was a fifth-grade teacher giving out grades.

"Let's see how everyone did!" he'd shout. "Howard

Stern show, uh-oh." This was our art, the stuff we lived and died for, and some asshole engineer was walking around with a ratings book, evaluating us. It was amazing we survived. That's why Robin and I ballooned up in weight again. Every night on the way home on the subway . . . oh, I forgot about the subway! Those bastards made us take the subway. They wouldn't even give us a damn car to use. I was begging them to help us out because we were making personal appearances after each show. After a while, when we were getting well known, we had to deny we were those people on the radio. Meanwhile, vodka breath Imus had a twenty-four-hour company-paid limo. Robin said he was the only guy who looked as if he was being limoed to a park bench.

Getting back to the subway, every night on our way home, we'd devise ways to torture management, to keep our sanity. Robin's boss in the news department was this woman Meredith, and all I'd have to say is "How are you gonna do it tonight, Robin?" and she was off.

"I'm gonna hook Meredith up to a wall and take some five-inch spike-heel shoes and invert her nipples with them."

One day we were on the air and I could see that Meredith had fucked with Robin in some way. I started talking to Robin and soon I got her saying that she wanted to do a Bic pen test on Meredith. She wanted to take the Bic pen and put it in a rifle and shoot it through Meredith's head and then use her whole head to write "BIC." We went off the air and we heard these footsteps rushing down the hall and

Robin looked at me as if she was about to be fired. The door was thrown open and it was Pig Virus and he looked at Robin and said, "God, I wish I could say that!"

Meanwhile, life struggled on at NBC. I got suspended again for a skit Fred and I did called Das Love Boot. It was a high-concept bit. Doc Mengele was running the Love Boat and he was experimenting on the passengers.

"Sea sickness, Mrs. Cohen? Come down to the infirmary and I will remove your ovaries."

Eartha Kitt was the rotating guest star on that episode and Doc Mengele got to mate her with a black angus bull for his latest genetic experiment.

But basically we were working on one cylinder. Pig Virus would always be butting in, presiding over the content of our show. When Princess Grace died, her body was still warm and Piggy was running in, forbidding us to talk about her.

In fact, the only fun I was having at all professionally was on television. Judy Licht and Doug Johnson were hosting a local talk show called "Good Morning, New York," and they were about to be canceled when I made my first appearance on the show. It was actually supposed to be a joint appearance but Doug informed everybody that Imus couldn't make it because of the snow.

"What kind of snow are we talking about?" I wondered, a sly allusion to Imus's coke habit.

I then proceeded to do a magic trick in which I handcuffed Judy in a most revealing bondage pose and then threw a blanket over her and tried to remove the handcuffs by ESP. Of course, I couldn't, so I just left her on the floor, cuffed. But the best part was yet to come. They mentioned that the show had been canceled and they were going to be off the air soon.

"Hey, if this was my show and they canceled, I'd bust up the set," I said, and I started knocking all the furniture over. The audience went wild. They loved that bit so much that they asked me to come back in three weeks for their last show. That time, I showed up in a hard hat and I backed a huge pickup truck onto the set and with the help of four hard hats, we actually packed up all the furniture and carted it off. The whole time these guys were lugging the furniture away, I was chopping the set to smithereens with an ax.

But the funny thing was, even though the jerks at NBC had emasculated my show, we were still getting ratings. We were really beginning to show some numbers. Then Fioravanti left the station and NBC brought in Randy Bongarten as the new general manager. Randy was my savior.

Randy was young, hip, and a keen judge of talent. He had to be, he thought I was great. He basically let me do my show and that meant trashing the format, playing a lot fewer records, and re-creating the ambiance I had started in Washington. By now we had added Jackie "the Joke Man" Martling and Al Rosenberg as writers and we hired Gary Dell'Abate as our boy producer. We were ready to roll.

Jackie was a Long Island comic who had sent me a few of his home-made albums. I liked what I heard and I envisioned him as the perfect good-time party guy to hang out in our studio. When I brought him in,

The NBC radio softball team, playing before a Mets game at Shea. I hated softball but this was one of those mandatory radio promotions I had to do to prove I was a team player.

he proved to be an exceptional talent and collaborator. While we never hung out together outside the show, we had a magical meeting of the minds when we wrote the radio show. It was the same magic I felt with Robin and Fred. I knew we belonged together. Throughout my career there have been managers who've tried to get me to abandon these people I work with, but each of them is just as important to the show as I am, and no one will break us up.

A major indication of the change in atmosphere was the way we dealt with Randy. I had bitched on the air about Pig Virus from the start. But now Randy got management off my back and allowed me to go crazy. I began to call his wife, Fran, and she became a semi-regular in our cast of characters. Whenever Randy gave us any kind of trouble at all, I'd call Fran on the air and beg her to give Randy some sex so he'd be in a better mood.

In fact, sex loomed larger and larger as a topic of our show. We even instituted a feature called Sexual Innuendo Wednesday in which we asked women to call in with their stories about sexual harassment, child abuse, or rape. These women would call in and say, "Well, my coach took me down to the locker room . . ." and I'd say, "Whoa, slow it down, slow it down. What were you wearing?" All in the interest of public service, of course.

We began our great tradition of Christmas parties around then. Whoever wanted to come had to apply over the phone and had to promise to do something weird to be invited. For a guy, it would be something like belching out Christmas carols. For a girl, getting naked would do just fine. On the day of the party, girls were running around topless, couples were making out in the corner. It was wild.

Anything that came to mind, we tried. One time I had to take a piss during commercials but I was afraid to go because if there are other men in the bathroom, sometimes I get intimidated and it takes me longer to pee. I started talking about that on the air and my engineer told me about his bathroom habits and one thing led to another and he challenged me to a race to see who could take the fastest whiz. We got a wireless mike and our first Bathroom Olympics were born. By the time we were through milking that bit, we had listeners calling in vying for prizes if they could guess the closest time.

The Bathroom Olympics evolved into the Mystery Whiz, in which callers had to guess who was peeing from the sound of the urination alone. This was a bit much, even for Randy, but when he complained, I found out that his wife had ratted me out, so I called Fran on the air and let her have it.

Radio was suddenly fun again. When the infamous Vanessa Williams *Penthouse* lesbo spread came out, I got an advance copy and I rerouted the NBC Studio tour *into* the studio, then I sold peeks at the pictorial to the tourists for five bucks a shot. We did so well that we decided to hold our own tours. We charged listeners a flat forty bucks to come into the studio, then we socked them for additional money depending on what they wanted to do. If they wanted to read the news, that was another thirty. It was fifteen to intro a record. We even had Gary go down to the NBC commissary and buy some food and resell it for double the price to the tour. We made over six hundred dollars on one tour alone.

Randy also encouraged me to do more television appearances. They booked me on "Donahue," but it was as one of a panel of controversial disc jockeys and the topic was totally lame. Donahue was bitching and moaning about the controversial lyrics of rock and I told him that I had no idea why the hell he had radio

personalities there to answer these charges since we
didn't write the lyrics, we didn't pick the records to
play, and we didn't particularly like playing *any* records.

But my best exposure was when I did the Letterman show. Dave was working in the same building as
we were and he was a big fan of my show. He was the
first guy, except for that other television genius,
Petey Green, to
have me on as a
guest in my own
right, not as one
of an assem-
blage of "wacky
disc jockeys."
And I killed. I
broke all the
rules of those
late night talk

> HOWARD STERN                    REVISED
>
> OUR NEXT GUEST IS THE NUMBER-ONE MORNING RADIO PERSONALITY
> IN NEW YORK AND PHILADELPHIA. THIS SUMMER HE WILL BE SEEN
> IN FOUR ONE-HOUR TELEVISION SPECIALS. PLEASE WELCOME
> BACK TO THIS PROGRAM THE ALWAYS LOVELY, THE ALWAYS TALENTED
> HOWARD STERN.

shows. I touched Dave's hair. I talked about the prein-
terview. I bitched about both my radio management
and his show's producers. And they loved it. Suddenly
every show wanted me as a guest and not me with
nine other djs.

We were on a roll. Our ratings were going through
the roof. Even Imus started coming around and dropping in on my show. If he wasn't there physically, he
would make sure to call in. That was pretty weird
since when we first got to NBC, nobody from Imus's
show would even deign to talk to any of us. But when
some of my bits started showing up on Imus's morning
show, I realized why he was suddenly my new best

friend. He was stealing my act. Suddenly, he was opening the mike, allowing guests to come in, breaking format. But he was so bad at it, it was laughable. He was very threatened by what we were doing. He had to change. It got so bad that Imus started calling up my mother on the air. But she knew how to get rid of him. She told him that he didn't want her for a mother because that would make us brothers.

Things were almost too good to be true at NBC. In fact, things got so good that Randy got a nice promotion to president of the radio division. To fill his vacated post they brought in a young, clean-cut new general manager from San Francisco. His name was John Hayes. Soon I would know him as the Incubus.

From the minute Hayes got to NBC, it seemed as if he had one goal in mind: to get his highest-rated, biggest revenue-producing, most creative on-air radio personality fired. We knew we were back in battle mode Hayes's first day when Robin bumped into him after our show was over. She made an offhand comment about how funny the show had been that day and Hayes gave her a look as if he wanted to vomit.

But I had learned my lessons in my struggles with Pig Virus. The best defense is a good offense. I was all over the Incubus from day one. In fact, even before day one. When we heard that Hayes had been hired, I dialed his station in San Francisco.

"I'm not even having lunch with him. If this guy comes on the air, I'm gonna lay it on him. For all you people out there, this is the way to deal with management."

Someone answered.

"Is John there? This is Howard Stern and tell him to hurry. I don't have a lot of time. I got his secretary reeling, Robin. He's under the impression he's my boss. *Capo di tutti capi.* Who the hell does he think he is? Mr. Boss Man with his newfangled ideas. You should hear the deejay on the air now."

They had me on hold. Way too long, I thought.

"You should hang up on him when he comes to the phone for making you wait," Robin said.

Hayes got on.

"Hello, is this John Hayes? This is Howard Stern. You kept me waiting. I understand you were busy. WELL, YOU DON'T KEEP ME WAITING!"

I slammed the phone down. "That'll teach him," I crowed.

I called him back a few days later. He was out but I left explicit instructions with his secretary. I wouldn't have lunch with him. I wouldn't meet his wife. I didn't do remotes. I didn't go to shopping centers, circuses, or dopey animal hospitals. He couldn't bring any of his stupid friends into the studio when I was working. He had to meet with my agent before he could even meet with me. All my material was copyrighted and he was not allowed into my writing meetings. He had no say over anything I did. And if I wanted to, I would belch on the air. That should set him straight, I thought. I made his secretary read back my message and hung up.

Hayes finally got to the station on October 1, 1984. I met with him briefly that day and then went on the air and reported on the meeting. "I spent two minutes with him," I told Robin and the world. "I don't have time to sit in meetings with the GM. He started in, 'It's great to be here.' I'm going, 'Oh, man, what a douche bag.' Of course it's great, he wouldn't have come here otherwise. He seems to not have any ideas, which is great. He was respectful and kind of timid. It's great when they shake in their boots. I think he's a pushover. I think this show is gonna get dirty as hell."

Well, I was wrong. Not about the show getting dirty. Hayes did have ideas, even if they were all lame. His major idea was to bring Soupy Sales to the station as the personality between Imus and me. Now, as a kid I idolized Soupy. I thought it was brilliant when he told a kid who called his show to go through his parent's pockets and send him all the pieces of paper with the presidents' pictures on them. But I was now the personality. I deserved the perks. But no, they were still treating me like a child. Soupy came into the station as if he was a conquering God.

Right off the bat, Hayes gave Soupy a limo while Robin and Fred and I had to squeeze into a Fugazy fleet car every night and hear the driver bitch about how he wasn't getting paid.

Hayes had a real investment in Soupy doing well: Soupy was his idea. Soupy even had Hayes bring a grand piano into the studio and hired a pianist to accompany Soupy on his show. Whatever Soupy wanted, Soupy got. And I was jealous. So, of course, I got on him unmercifully.

Soupy and his crew were always leaving food debris around and stinking up the place for when I came in. One day they spilled some salad dressing on the floor. I decided to make a bit out of it so I called them on the

NBC's Dream Team (left to right): Soupy Sales, that idiot Don Imus, me, and Wolfman Jack.

air and told Soupy if his producer wasn't in the studio in two minutes cleaning up their mess, I was gonna cut his fucking piano wires. Fred went out and got some wire cutters and sure enough, the deadline passed and I started snapping away. I think I had about four notes out before they finally cleaned up the mess. After that, Soupy stopped talking to me.

After a few months, my relationship with Hayes deteriorated totally. He was fucking with my show just like Pig Virus and I was fucking with his head every day on the air. I would rant and rave about Hayes being some punk kid who was born with a silver spoon in his mouth, whose father gave him everything, whose wife was smarter than he was. He would sit in his office listening to this, seething. After nine months of this, things came to a head when we actually got into a fistfight on the air.

I don't even remember what specifically caused the fight. I had met earlier with Hayes and he was insistent that I not talk on the air about what we discussed. But you know me, when someone tells me not to say something, I've got to say it. So I called his office to get him to talk about our earlier meeting.

"Could you put that idiot on the phone with me?" I asked his secretary.

"No, I can't, Howard, he's in a meeting," she said.

"He's always in a meeting."

"What can I tell you, he's an executive."

"Who's he in a meeting with?"

"Very important people."

"Who?"

"I can't divulge that."

"Tell him to put down that magazine and zip up," Fred yelled in the background.

"I hear him talking," I said.

"I have the radio on. That's how I know what you're doing," his secretary said.

"That's how the Incubus knows all. Poke your head in and say I want to speak to him on the radio now. That supersedes anything he could be doing," I asserted.

She wouldn't comply with my wishes. I sent Gary back and he reported that Hayes's door was closed and his "Privacy" sign was up. I sent Big Al Rosenberg and Gary back to bang on the door, all the while forcing the secretary to stay on the phone so we would be broadcasting all this.

"The Incubus is back there talking to his father, the Devil," I mused as we waited for Gary and Al to get back there.

Rosenberg banged on the door and Hayes opened it, told them to go away, and slammed it shut.

"He's too busy planning a bumper sticker promotion. He's an idiot. He's a big moron," I ranted.

"I told you he was in a meeting," his secretary crowed.

"Scum," I cursed.

"He came out all authoritative," Gary reported. "He said, 'This isn't funny.' "

"What's funny? Soupy?" I smirked.

I decided to go back there myself, get on the telephone, and yell at John.

"Who can he be in a meeting with?" I mused. "Maybe he's giving the program director hot beef injections."

I made my way toward his office.

"This could be it," Robin prophesied. "Either he'll resort to physical violence or he'll freak out."

I got on the phone to Robin.

"I'm back here. First I'll yell. I won't bang on the door, he's got his 'Privacy, Please' thing up. JOHN! JOHN!"

Hayes came to the door.

"I got him!" I exulted.

"Another monument to radio," he said.

"Hey, nobody's in here with him," I noticed. "He's just working. Hey, John, come on the air with us."

"This is great radio, Howard. Boy, what a bit," Hayes sneered.

"What are you working on, man? How come you can't talk to us?" I was petulant.

"Because I'm working."

"On what?"

"I'm not telling."

He started closing the door on me.

"YOU IDIOT SCUM! DON'T TALK THAT WAY TO ME!" I shouted. "IDIOT, YOU WORK FOR ME! I told him off, huh, Robin? He's really mad. He looked like he was gonna cry. He's got papers on his desk. He was doing budget stuff. He was seething. You should have seen the look on his face. Now he's not even coming out. COME OUT AND TALK TO ME! He's a baby. He's an idiot. Oh, here he is."

He had come out again and he was pissed. But, hey, this was great radio. And it was going to get better pretty quick.

"Howard, go back and do your show."

"You can't take it, can't take it," I taunted him.

"Howard, this isn't fun," Hayes snapped.

"It's fun for us," Robin piped in. "I love it when you squirm."

"I'm not squirming. I'm not even having fun."

While Gary diverted his attention, I rushed into his office and looked at the papers on his desk. Hayes had a desk full of papers that detailed everyone's salaries. I started yelling that I could see Imus's and Soupy's ridiculously inflated salaries.

"Hey, Howard, get out of there!" Hayes yelled.

He freaked out and started pushing me out of his

office. Actually shoving me forcefully and with bad intent. I couldn't believe it. I was doing a bit but he was dead serious. I went back to the studio.

"What a goofy guy to get upset like that. He doesn't understand me or my sense of humor. My audience loved that. He was all red and he was pushing me. Could you tell how angry he was on the phone? He hates us. He doesn't understand why it's funny when the Marx Brothers screw around with Margaret Dumont because he is Margaret Dumont. He dropped the phone, he was wrestling with me. He's an idiot. I can't deal with him."

This was really war. Fred and I went into the studio and made a promo that we started running on my show:

---

*YOUR FRIEND HOWARD STERN IS IN TROUBLE AND HE NEEDS YOUR HELP . . . HERE ARE THE FACTS:*

ITEM 1: Howard Stern has the biggest ratings at WNBC.
ITEM 2: John Hayes, the general manager of NBC, was born with a silver spoon in his little mouth.
ITEM 3: How can a little rich boy possibly understand this radio show?
ITEM 4: John Hayes wants to radically change the "Howard Stern Show" . . . that's right, change the "Howard Stern Show."
ITEM 5: Would an intelligent, caring general manager tamper with success?

*WHAT CAN YOU DO TO HELP? BE A PART OF A GRASS-ROOTS MOVEMENT TO FIRE JOHN HAYES . . .*

Here's an officer from the 106th precinct . . .
Officer: Hey, John Hayes, know what I wanna do? Tie him down and poke him with a sharp stick . . .

*NO, NO, DON'T DO THAT. LET'S GET HIM FIRED.*

Here's a Manhattan art dealer . . .
Art Dealer: I want to take him up to Rockland County, fit him with

a leather mask, you know, the one with the zipper, and chase him
naked up and down the hillside throwing walnuts at his anus.

*GOOD IDEA, BUT THAT'S NOT WHAT WE'RE GOING FOR. THE
BEST THING TO DO IS TELL ALL YOUR FRIENDS ABOUT THE SHOW.
AND WITH THE BIGGEST AUDIENCE IN HAND, WE'LL VANQUISH
THE DEMON JOHN HAYES.*

Here now is Cosima von Bülow . . .
Cosima: Hey, if John doesn't knock this off, I'll tell my . . .

*JOIN MILLIONS OF NEW YORKERS IN AN EFFORT TO DRIVE JOHN
HAYES OUT OF THE RADIO STATION. AND REMEMBER, NEVER
APPROACH JOHN HAYES IN THE EVENING WHEN HIS POWERS
ARE THE STRONGEST.*

We were really going wild. We were attacking management, we were dealing with sex and bodily functions and every known radio taboo. I was pretty out
of control but I didn't care. I just wanted to do great
radio. I've always felt you can't back down after a certain point.

Randy Bongarten tried to give me a little message
one evening when he insisted I let him drive me home
to Long Island. As soon as the car got out of the parking garage he began to work on me.

"Your ratings are great, Howard. But I'm telling
you, back off a little. You're doing very strong material. And the powers that be don't like it," he said.

"Be direct, man," I said. "Who doesn't like what I'm
doing? We'll go sit down with them and explain the
jokes to them. I'm trying to revolutionize radio."

I was on a high horse, but I was serious. I wasn't
going to back down. I was too fucking popular. I didn't
even know how to hold back. I didn't know what

Randy was driving at and, frankly, I didn't care to know.

A couple of weeks later, I got on the air and announced my greatest Dial-a-Date ever. I was going to do Bestiality Dial-a-Date! I was fantasizing on the air about how I was going to set up a listener with an animal. That night, Randy came over to me when I finished the show. It was time for another ride home.

"What are you going to do on the Bestiality Dial-a-Date?" he asked.

"I don't even really know what I'm going to do. I was getting into a thing on the air. I've done lesbians. Triplets. I've done it all."

"Just don't do the Bestiality Dial-a-Date," he said.

"Are these guys thinking we're going to fuck a dog? What are you talking about?" I said. It was obvious he wasn't understanding.

We were still fucking with Hayes, too. He called us into his office for a meeting and he was talking his usual shit about how we had to clean up our act so he could get better, more prestigious advertisers on the show, and Robin and I looked at each other and just got up and walked out of his office in the middle of a sentence.

As we were walking down the hall, Robin looked at me and said, "Are you sure we haven't gotten a little crazy here? We just walked out of the general manager's office while he was in the middle of a sentence."

"What are they gonna do to us, Robin?" I shrugged. "Fire us?"

Meanwhile, I was out of control on the air. New

York was in the middle of that stupid Statue of Liberty two hundredth anniversary and Robin was reading a news story about how Lee Iacocca had raised $200

million for the statue's restoration but he needed to raise another $200 mil.

"What do they need all that money for?" I wondered. "What are they gonna buy her, a bronze tampon? They gonna get fifty thousand gallons of copper so she can douche?"

Here I was the number one radio entertainer in the world. I was invincible. Everyone wanted me . . . and no one could touch me.

I don't know, call me naive, but I thought I could just go on and entertain my millions and millions of listeners at NBC as long as they were happy and still tuning in and the network was making millions and millions each year selling my ad time. Well, I was wrong. The bastards were going to fire me.

Except God intervened in the form of a major hurricane. On September 27, 1985, New York awoke to howling winds and torrential rainfall. Most New Yorkers took the day off, but I called Robin and Fred, and we decided to go in and brave the storm. It never occurred to me to stay home that day. Dale Parsons, my program director, called to beg me to stay home. The truth was Dale was told by NBC management to make sure I didn't go to work because I was supposed to be fired that day. It was a Friday and this way the Saturday newspapers would carry the story and it would be forgotten by Monday. None of the execs were available to fire me that day because the storm kept them home. They just figured I wouldn't come in. I came in and did one of the most vicious shows ever. Ironically, I even predicted my own firing.

The show was going fine until I heard that Soupy had announced on his program a few days earlier that he had just signed to do a syndicated version of his show on the NBC network. I became livid. For years I had been trying to get my show syndicated on the network. I had been promised that they were working on it, but it was all hot air. And now Soupy got to do his show nationally. I totally freaked on the air. I refused to believe it until I got confirmation from my bosses. The problem was, they weren't at work; they were all hunkered down in their suburban homes waiting for the hurricane to blow over.

I frantically tried to call Randy at home but I couldn't get through. I reached Hayes and I put him on the air and he denied knowing anything about it. His denials sounded hollow. All the while I was ranting on the air that if this information was true, that was it, I was quitting NBC.

Now here I was embarrassing all the execs by throwing them on the air, and they were freaking out because I shouldn't even have been on the air! They had promised Grant Tinker, the president of NBC, that I would be fired.

I threw open the phone lines. All my listeners called in and said they'd hate to see me go but they'd understand. Putting Soupy on national was too much of a humiliation for anyone to take. It was nearing time for my shift to end. Jack Spector had already come into the studio to prepare for his show. I took one last phone call. It was the guy we set up for the Bestiality Dial-a-Date.

"Howard, this is your dog lover dial-a-date. No one called me yet," he complained.

"It might take a month or two," I said.

"By the way, I heard Soupy talking about the show, too. You really not coming in Monday?"

"I'm not sure how the scenario will play out. We have three offers from other stations. There's a lot to consider," I said.

"By the way, I hope your bathroom has towels in it. It didn't when I was there. I had to wipe my hands on my pants," he complained.

"Here's a guy who made love to a dog worrying about wiping his hands on his pants. I don't see how that would disturb you."

"It was a clean dog," he said.

That was the last call I ever took at NBC.

I went home that night bummed out. Over the weekend, I went jogging and tripped over some of the tree debris from the hurricane. So on Monday morning I reported for work on crutches. Robin and I were supposed to have had a big meeting on Friday but since the top brass couldn't make it in, they had rescheduled it for Monday before we went on the air. We were to meet at 12:30, but I didn't arrive at NBC till 12:45. Fuck them and their meetings. John Hayes met me in the hall and escorted me to an elevator. "Randy wants to see you alone." He smiled and put his arm around me like the priest who visits death row. Little did I know that Hayes had been given orders to make sure I got on that elevator. Hayes couldn't wait to get me on that elevator because it was his job to fire Robin while I was upstairs being fired.

I hobbled into Randy's office.

"Sit down," Randy said.

I sat.

"I'm going to have to put an end to the show," Randy said soberly.

I figured he meant the syndicated show. So they were right, Soupy was going to get his show syndicated.

"Okay," I said, getting up, "I gotta go to work."

"No, I mean the afternoon show."

"Okay," I said again, and started for the door. I was in shock.

"Do you want to sit down?" Randy said.

I said, "No. If I'm fired, I'm leaving. I have no reason to be here."

I hobbled downstairs to my office and called my agent, Don Buchwald. Within minutes, Buchwald strolled into the office with a cold bottle of champagne in hand, singing "Happy Days Are Here Again." Robin, who had just been fired by the Incubus himself, looked warily at Don. But Don was thrilled. He was certain we'd be back on the air shortly, making a lot more money.

I sequestered myself in my inner office. Hayes came

```
        STATEMENT FOR CALLS RE: HOWARD STERN

The Howard Stern Program has been taken off the air at WNBC.

The reason for this move, as explained in the statement broadcast,
is that conceptual differences exist between Howard Stern and
WNBC regarding the program.

If you wish to state an opinion we ask you to write to:

        John Hayes, Vice President & General Manager
        WNBC
        30 Rockefeller Plaza
        New York, N.Y. 10020

Thank you for your call.
=============================================================

GUIDELINES:

A.   Be as polite as possible to all callers -- this is very
     important.
B.   John Hayes is not accepting phone calls on this matter. --
     Please write if you want.
C.   We will forward mail to Howard Stern and Robin Quivers.
D.   If caller becomes abusive, politely end the [call] by
     thanking them  for their interest, then hang up.
```

around and tried to see me but I wouldn't let him in. He sat in the outer office and talked to Robin.

"You know, my greatest fear is that you guys are going to go across the street and kick our butt," Hayes told Robin. He said that, but he didn't mean it. I know he really thought we were not employable. He also figured it would be a snap to replace us.

Meanwhile, in place of us, they were playing music and periodically interrupting it with this prerecorded message:

*NOW, WNBC VICE PRESIDENT AND GENERAL MANAGER JOHN HAYES:*

WNBC ISSUED THE FOLLOWING PRESS RELEASE THIS AFTERNOON. AS OF TODAY, MONDAY, SEPTEMBER 30TH, WNBC HAS CANCELED THE HOWARD STERN PROGRAM BECAUSE OF

CONCEPTUAL DIFFERENCES THAT EXIST BETWEEN HOWARD
STERN AND WNBC MANAGEMENT AS TO THE PROGRAM. I
ENCOURAGE ANYONE WILLING TO EXPRESS AN OPINION
ABOUT THE CANCELLATION OF THE HOWARD STERN PRO-
GRAM TO WRITE TO ME,

> JOHN HAYES
> GENERAL MANAGER
> WNBC
> 30 ROCKEFELLER PLAZA
> NEW YORK, NEW YORK 10020
>
> YOUR COMMENTS ARE WELCOME.

While this announcement was being made, Robin
and I were standing outside of 30 Rockefeller Plaza,
surrounded by a few boxes containing all of my valuable tapes and bits, waiting for an NBC car that would
never come. We finally took a cab. Later that night,
Fred and Gary penetrated NBC security, using a
forged pass, and emptied the entire contents of my
office into a U.S. Postal Service van that Baba Booey
had borrowed from a friend. They started at midnight
and took load after load out past an uninterested-look-
ing security guard. Finally it was 3:00 A.M. and they
had packed up the last load and were almost out the
door when the guard spoke up.

"Hey, you two!" the guard yelled.

Fred and Baba Booey froze in their tracks.

"You know what time it is?"

We were home free.

The next day, every paper blared the firing in its
headlines. The *New York Post* ran a full front-page picture of me and Alison and our first daughter. One cam-

Front page of the *New York Post*. The unemployed at home.

era crew accused me of staging a disc jockey hoax. That afternoon, I hit each local news show and told my side of the story, which was that I had no idea why I was fired. Not one NBC executive would take credit either, but I had my theories.

One theory, which later surfaced, was that Thornton Bradshaw, who was chairman of the board, was riding in his limousine and said to a friend, "I think we own an AM station here in New York." For the first time ever they tuned in, and heard me setting up the dude with a dog for Bestiality Dial-a-Date. Bradshaw screamed, "Fire that guy immediately!" and told Grant Tinker he'd better not hear me on the air again.

I confronted Grant Tinker several years later on the air. I was at the Emmy awards show and Tinker had just been given the prestigious Lifetime Achievement Award. Here he was beaming, glowing, stepping into the press room to answer very respectable questions. I stood up screaming, "GRANT TINKER, WHY DID YOU FIRE HOWARD STERN? WHY?" He wouldn't answer.

"Bless my wife, bless this house and bring back Howard Stern."

The first few days at K-Rock, knocking Imus off his perch.

Meanwhile, my agent, Don Buchwald, starting sorting out the various offers we had immediately received. There were a few good ones coming from Los Angeles. But there was no pressure to take anything. NBC had just renegotiated my contract and they still had to pay me for the next three years. NBC acknowledged this in their conversations with Buchwald and they also told him that if we went to a station in L.A., they would pay us fifty thousand dollars.

"You call them and tell them to shove their fifty thousand," I told Don. "I will never go to L.A. Tell them that I'm going to stay right here and destroy that radio station. I'll make it so bad for them that they'll have to sell that piece-of-shit station. I'm going to rob them of all their fucking ratings."

I was crazed. But I was right. A few weeks later, I signed with K-Rock to do afternoons. A few weeks after that, K-Rock asked me to switch to mornings so I could go head-to-head against Imus and destroy him. I said I would do it and I did. My ratings soared and I dragged Shit Stain down to a one share. NBC wound up selling the station for millions less than it was worth. Pig Virus wound up in some station in the Midwest. The Incubus is back in San Francisco, humbled. Thornton Bradshaw, the former chairman of the board of NBC, is dead of a painful cerebral hemorrhage. Grant Tinker, the other moron who now publicly takes credit for firing me, hasn't had a hit TV show for years and will probably die a very painful death.

> "If Howard Stern beats me, I'll eat a dead dog's penis."
> —Don Imus

# DON'T FUCK WITH STERN!

# Spill It

*Celebrity True Confessions*

How do I get celebrities to talk? I keep the studio dimly lit and I try to keep them in there for hours. After a while, I just wear them down, and then they forget they're on the radio.

That's the secret.

Plus, I can't stand bullshit. I never like doing typical interviews. When you're on the radio, you have nine hundred competitors, and there's no loyalty. Your audience will abandon you in two seconds. That's why I hate my audience. They're so damn fickle. You'd think they'd have some allegiance. Just because I'm having a bad day doesn't mean they should ruin my career. And just because a celebrity is going to come on doesn't mean he is just going to come on and plug. I want people working hard for me.

And besides, I don't need guests on my show because I've proven that I can get ratings without them.

You come on my show, you'd better perform. I'm busy telling everyone that I jerk off every night and stick fingers up my own ass; you'd better open up, too.

Here's a bunch of celebrities I like because they're honest and can laugh at themselves:

## SANDI KORN
Penthouse *Pet*
*Runner-up* Penthouse *Pet of the Year*

Sandi is one of my favorite guests—great to look at and incredibly naive about simple world events. Her claim to fame on my show has been her remarkable inability to answer questions that any sixth-grader would know. Sandi told me *Penthouse* pets were smart and that she was practically valedictorian of her school.

"Sandi, what country did *Saddam Hussein* invade during the Gulf War?" I asked. Fred played some "Jeopardy" music as Sandi contemplated.

"Uh . . . what is . . . Jerusalem?" Sandi smiled.

Who gave a shit if the answer was Kuwait, Sandi was wearing a skimpy bikini. The lump in my pants grew heavier and thicker as I thought about tying her up and eating her for an hour . . . while I talked about world events.

"What political party is *President Bush* a member of?" I asked.

"I know he's either Republican or the other one . . . but I don't know. I would say Democrat."

"Close enough," I exulted. "What is the capital of New York State?"

"Albany."

"What does the FBI stand for?"

"I don't know, I have no idea."

"Where is it located?"

"It's everywhere!"

It was fascinating watching this mind at work. I decided to give her a hard one.

"What's in iced tea?"

"Water," she said brightly.

"And?"

"Tea!"

We got such a great reaction to her quiz appearances that we decided to milk this thing for an entire segment on my TV show—the I Couldn't Get into College Bowl. So we brought Sandi back

Sandi Korn being interrogated on the set of my TV show.

and had her match her intellect against a girl in the seventh grade named Jessica and a man with the maturity of a seventh-grader, Kenneth Keith Kallenbach, a charter member of our Wack Pack.

Suffice it to say that the seventh-grader wiped everybody out. Here's a breakdown of how Sandi did:

## QUESTIONS SANDI WAS ABLE TO ANSWER CORRECTLY

1. How many days in a year?
2. Name an even number.
3. What is a clarinet?
4. What is Bush's wife's name?
5. What does E.T. stand for?
6. Who was the first president?

## QUESTIONS SANDI WAS UNABLE TO ANSWER CORRECTLY

1. What does ESP stand for?
2. What country did the United States declare independence from?
3. What substance do diamonds come from?
4. Who built the pyramids?
5. Who was the host of "The Twilight Zone"?

Sandi with Chuck Norris and Shadoe Stevens on the set of $20 Pyramid.

Of course, Sandi didn't do that badly compared to Kenneth Keith. He thought diamonds were a "substance unto themselves" and that Pete Rose was the host of "The Twilight Zone." To this day, Sandi maintains she is intelligent. In fact, she wants to reaffirm that right here.

No matter where I go, everybody remembers that show. And it's weird because I am smart. I really am. But Howard asked me about the war and I was traveling around modeling so much I didn't keep track of things like that. I really could have sworn that we bombed Jerusalem because I have a friend who lives in Jerusalem and I'm sure he told me Jerusalem was bombed. But Jerusalem, Iraq—it's all the same, anyway.

**Sandi's most recent photo; she's totally changed her look.**

I like Sandi a lot because of her honesty. She once revealed that Donald Trump came up to her apartment and got on top of her and kissed her and dry-humped her. Trump denies it, but it's a good story, anyway.

> "Howard Stern broke the mold."
> — Ed Asner

## BOB HOPE

There're two great things about having Bob Hope on my show. First, I never know if he understands half the questions I'm asking him. It seems as if he hears every other word. I've asked Bob Hope questions nobody else would ever dare to ask him and there's no way of telling if he's just avoiding answering them or he's too zoned out to understand.

"What about Martha Raye? Did she ever come on to you?" I asked.

"Martha Raye? Oh, sure! We started together."

"But the two of you were never lovers?"

"We started together at Paramount . . ."

"Hey, are you glad Carson's packing it in?"

"Yeach," Bob growled.

"To heck with Carson already. It's enough," I said.

"Yeah, I'm doing Carson Friday night."

"What about Ann-Margret?"

"Oh, Ann-Margret . . ."

"I heard you said I was the brightest talent you'd seen since Ann-Margret," I said.

"Isn't that something?"

He had absolutely no idea what I was saying. I don't know if he's on the same planet with the rest of us.

# THE BEST IN TOWN
## It's time to stop picking on Howard Stern

**KINGS OF COMEDY:** *It's a meeting of comic minds when Howard Stern interviews Bob Hope tomorrow night on "The Howard Stern Show."*

By ADAM BUCKMAN
*Post TV Editor*

IT'S time to stop bellyaching about Howard Stern and to begin considering him for what he is: the most original TV and radio talent in New York.

With his morning radio show, which runs anywhere from four to five hours every weekday, plus his weekly TV show on WWOR Ch. 9, Stern has become the hardest-working man in New York show business.

And no matter how hard he works at it, he still draws complaints from those who don't share his sense of humor, or are offended when he jokes sophomorically about genitalia and women's breasts.

In fact, those who are offended by Stern should probably not tune in to his TV show tomorrow night.

And that's too bad.

Why? Because they'll be missing the funniest home-grown comedy show on New York TV.

"The Howard Stern Show" has been a hit-or-miss proposition since its debut last September.

Tomorrow night, however, Stern has come up with his best TV show yet — an hour that's both savagely funny and nakedly honest.

It's funny because of the spectacle of the long-haired Stern interviewing Bob Hope in a Garden City, L.I., hotel room.

Or because of how he manipulates Dr. Ruth Westheimer into saying the word "penis" so that he and his off-camera crew of writers and sidekicks can hoot like grown-up adolescents.

Or because of longtime panel show stalwarts Arlene Francis and Kitty Carlisle Hart, who agreed to participate ¬along with Stern sidekick ¬

ers) in a game show spoof called "What's My Secret?" in which the three poker-faced panelists try to guess

**"Howard Stern Show"**
Tomorrow night at 11
WWOR/Ch. 9
★ ★ ★ ★

a secret held by a bikini-clad contestant.

It's honest because on "The Howard Stern Show," the camera never blinks.

Instead, it stares — revealing the truth about Stern and his guests.

On tomorrow's show, Bob Hope sits on a hotel room couch with little or no stage makeup and without a hairpiece. He looks older than he usually does on TV and, after nearly 70 years as a performing comedian, he still compulsively spews one-liners and glances around the room for appreciation.

Ruth is revealed not as a kindly diminutive grandmother, but as a head-strong celebrity who's fiercely protective of her right to publicize her latest book or pet project on someone else's TV show.

With Hope, Stern reveals himself as an awestruck fan who's anything but tongue-tied in the presence of his idol. With Dr. Ruth, Stern does his best to fend off her efforts to dominate his show, and then brings out his wife Allison to listen to some sex advice.

And, as for "What's My Secret?," the absurdity of Arlene Francis and Kitty Carlisle Hart asking serious questions of Heather the contestant has to be seen to be believed.

So forget about tomorrow night's "Saturday Night Live" ... ¬rn,

But one thing he knows is how to promote whatever stupid NBC special he's got coming up. He called in to plug his new program and it was right after the L.A.

riots. I tried to get him to comment on the riots but he wouldn't bite.

"I hate that looting," I said. "I hope with all those TVs they stole they watch your special."

"Yeah, right."

"You know what I'm saying."

"Saturday night!"

But the one thing that Bob loved to talk about was the fact that he used to play golf with George Bush's father, Prescott Bush. Like clockwork, every time I interviewed him he'd say exactly the same thing. "Do you know that George Bush's father's name is Prescott? Prescott Bush. I played golf with him and Eisenhower. He was a senator from Connecticut."

I don't even know if he remembered that he had told me that story nineteen times before. So the last time I interviewed him I told Robin I would find a really creative way to make him tell me the story. "Robin, I'll get Bob Hope to tell the Prescott Bush story without asking him about George Bush, watch me."

I then called Hope and about fifteen minutes into the conversation I asked Bob if he was going to remember me in his will.

"Are you gonna leave me anything in your will?"

"I think so, Howard."

"You're considering it?"

"Yes, sir."

"Seriously, how about remembering me, Howard Stern, in your will? You have so much money a few million would be like nothing."

"I'll think about that today."

"There would be no greater honor to me than if Bob Hope, in his will, left me five million dollars. That's nothing to you."

"Something like that."

"Think about it, I'm a good guy."

"We may cut down on the zeros."

"By the way, Bob, my middle name is Prescott. Howard Prescott Stern. Make sure you put it in your will just like that."

Bob suddenly came alive. "PRESCOTT!? COME ON!!"

"Yeah, Prescott."

"Do you know that George Bush's father's name was Prescott? Prescott Bush. I played golf with him and Eisenhower. He was a senator from Connecticut."

There you are.

## PATTI DAVIS REAGAN

Not only did Patti tell me that old Nancy "Just Say No" was zonked out half the time on Valium and that Patti had actually gotten banged in the White House, but she then spilled the beans about a threesome she had once participated in. She said she found it distracting. "Logistically, you had to sort of figure out who was gonna do what to whom—you know?"

I pressed her for details. She did it with her boyfriend and his best friend. They'd been doing reefer or drinking and they all wound up sleeping together. She slept in between. She thought that was cute, but she wasn't a three-input woman.

All this talk was getting me crazy. I started to fantasize on the air about having my way with her. I asked her if she'd ever been spanked or tied up. She said no, but that being tied up might be an interesting idea.

"You have to trust someone a lot to let them tie you up. I don't even trust people to be nice to me, so trusting someone to tie me up would really be a stretch," she said.

"I'll teach you trust," I promised. "I'd tie you to the bed, spread-eagled, with my neckties. I'd tie your wrists to the headboard and I would take a tie and tie up your ankles. Now you're completely spread-eagled in your clothes and I walk out of the room. I'd leave for ten minutes."

"See, this is why I wouldn't let someone tie me up," Patti protested. "What a schmucky thing to do!"

"No, that would be just to make you think about what was gonna happen."

"But that's really mean," she said.

"But that's *taming* you! In my mind, that's getting you ready for the session."

"This is why I'm never gonna do this."

"Oh, you're gonna do it," I asserted.

"That's abusive to abandon someone there," she complained.

"Of course! That would piss you off! When you tie someone up you don't do stuff they necessarily agree with. So you're tied up, you're lying there pissed, but meanwhile you notice, five minutes into the session, that

> "I listen to Howard every day."
> —Patti Davis Reagan

you're getting sexually aroused. Even though you're mad and upset about it, you're getting sexually aroused—that's the sick thing about it. And you're going, 'This is the stupidest, schmuckiest thing. I hate this guy. When Howard comes back into the room, I'm gonna make him untie me.' But meanwhile, this is like Foreplay From Hell, because when I come back in the room, you're completely excited."

Patti started laughing now, this really weird piercing laugh from Mars. She was really getting into this scenario. I told her that she wouldn't be laughing like that if I was dominating her.

"And you're not laughing either," I continued.

"I wouldn't be laughing," she agreed. "I would be really upset."

"Actually, I could hold out a long time with you, because if you laughed like that, I would definitely not be too quick."

I went on with the scenario. I'd come back in, she'd yell at me, I'd tell her to shut up. I'd put some spiked heels on her feet. I'd cut four holes out of her leotard. Two on top, and then the other two. Then I'd leave her again, and then come back in and shave her completely.

"Now you're really pissed. You're furious. But you're completely sexually excited," I said.

"Has any woman ever let you do this to her?" Patti asked.

"No, of course not."

I pressed on.

"I'd do stuff to you for over an hour. I'd lick you. You'd have fifty orgasms and then you'd pass out. But

I still wouldn't untie you! I'd leave for two hours. You'd hate me but you couldn't wait for me to come back.

"I'd come back, feed you lunch, and then we'd do it all over again. Then I'd untie you. That would be some session. Then I'd take the video out of the camcorder and sell it to 'Hard Copy': 'PRESIDENT'S DAUGHTER HAS SEX WITH DISGUSTING ANIMAL!' "

I could have sworn Patti would go for it but she had to go to another show to plug her new book. But my seed was planted, and my deep eroticism took hold. She's now writing a book on the subject of, you guessed it, bondage.

## TORI SPELLING

If I wasn't married to Alison I'd go after that Tori Spelling. She's really cute, she's on a hit show, and any guy who bags her can back the Brink's truck up to the house. I had her on the show with Melissa Rivers once when we were broadcasting out of L.A. and I brought up the fact that people accused Tori of being an airhead.

"That's my character, not me," she said.

We decided to test her. I gave her a battery of questions. She knew that Daryl Gates was L.A.'s ex-police chief, that Woody Allen was being investigated for child molestation, and that Rodney King was the guy who was beaten up by the L.A. cops. But then I gave her a hard question.

"What's the capital of New York State?"

She hemmed and hawed. "C'mon, say anything," I implored her.

"New Jersey?" she guessed.

"I'm sorry," I said. "But as a consolation prize you get to kiss me goodbye while I grab your buttocks."

"What would I have gotten if I won?" Tori asked.

"The same thing," Robin said.

## DONALD TRUMP

> "I tune in to Howard to hear what you rarely get these days— straight talk and very close to the mark."
>
> —Donald Trump

**The Donald and the Howard rating women.**

Donald is probably the only person on the planet who's more afraid of germs than I am. We were talking about his germ phobia once when the conversation shifted to his womanizing.

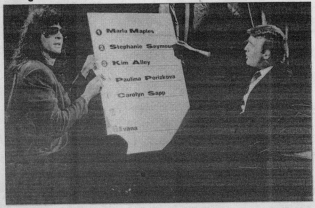

"With all those girls you're screwing around with, aren't you afraid of AIDS?" I asked.

"Germ phobia is a problem," the Donald admitted. "You have to be selective. It's pretty dangerous out there. It's like Vietnam! Dating is my personal Vietnam!"

I love that quote. He's always one of our best guests.

## AXL ROSE

The first time I ever had Axl Rose from Guns N' Roses on was when a listener gave me his New York hotel phone number and we called him cold.

"Axl, it's Howard Stern! You're on the radio, man!" I greeted him.

"Oh, yeah. What's happening?"

"Uh-oh, you're sleeping," I said.

"Waking up," he said.

"I bet you're there with a babe," I said.

"No."

"Come down, man. I'll put you on Dial-a-Date," I offered.

"Maybe I need a breather," Axl said.

"Did you ever get Jessica Hahn?"

"I didn't go after Jessica Hahn. She needs a diet."

"Did Slash get her?" I said, figuring someone from the band had done the honors.

"Slash used her for a spittoon. He really enjoyed that," Axl said.

"Hey, you must be getting, I'd say, ten women a week," I guessed.

"Let's say psycho-bitches," Axl corrected.

"You get tattooed women?"

"We just get crazy people. If they last twenty-four hours, it's amazing. We give them like a twenty-four-hour test. If they act normal for more than twenty-four hours, they get to stay."

"I bet you've had three women at the same time. What's that like?" I needed to know.

"Usually someone gets pissed off," Axl said.

"Can't you get the other girls to get it on with each other? That's what I would have done."

"Yeah, that happens," he said nonchalantly.

"Oh, man!" I was dying with envy.

"The problem is they all get upset. They don't want me looking at another girl. So I say, 'You didn't pass the twenty-four-hour test.' Then I call a friend and they politely escort the person out."

That's what I need. A twenty-four-hour test—to weed out every kook and asshole in my life. I learned a lot from Axl Rose that day.


## JOAN RIVERS

Although I like Joan a lot, there are two odd things about her.

How is it that a rich woman can go on TV and sell that fake jewelry with a straight face . . . *and* say that she thinks it's beautiful?

And how much longer can she go on milking the

"C'mon, baby, you know you need a hot sausage . . ." Coming on to Edgar's widow.

death of her husband, Edgar, for ratings? At first she did a few magazine articles, then a book. Okay. That was cool. She got it out of her system. Then she had her daughter, Melissa, on the show and they both cried, embarrassingly, on national TV. I envisioned Joan's ultimate sweeps week line-up as she ran out of ways to milk Edgar's death for ratings:

"On Monday's show I'm going to have my doorman. You know, when Edgar died the doorman came up to me and opened the door. You want to talk about class. He's a very special doorman."

Joan starts sobbing here.

"Tuesday, we'll have Edgar's embalmer. He's the man who last touched Edgar. A real class gentleman. He put the formaldehyde in Edgar, who looked so handsome. He was a handsome man."

Now Joan's hysterical.

"All next week, the man who built Edgar's casket. And during sweeps week we're going to get the guy who dug the hole in the ground. He was the last man to see Edgar."

Joan's inconsolable.

"For my Christmas show, I'm climbing into the hole with Edgar to decorate him and I'll cry the whole show. I'm going to decorate his skull like a *hamantashen*. We're going to put Edgar's skull on top of the tree. We'll be right back, I can't go on . . ."

Joan sobs all the way to the commercials.

Now, as soon as Joan comes back from commercials, it's time to sell gold jewelry.

"This jewelry is replicas of all the jewelry Edgar has given me over the years. Of course, I have the real thing. You're going to wear this fake shit that I wouldn't be caught dead in.

"Now this is a replica of a bee Edgar gave me right before he died. The Greek word for bee is 'Melissa.' That's why he gave it to me.

"I'm all about class and now you'll be full of class, too. Now I have this next item on sale, available only through QVC.

"This is a solid-silver miniature booze bottle, the same booze bottle that Edgar drank from right before he committed suicide," Joan weeps bitterly.

> "He's honest, he's forthright, he says what we all think. He has no fear, he's a great showman and a loyal friend. My hand would go into fire for him, but I'd make sure there's a fire extinguisher nearby."
> —Joan Rivers

"This is a solid-gold replica of Edgar's thumb. Different Edgar body parts are available to wear around your neck. I'm wearing right now a tiny diamond-studded coffin, the same coffin that Edgar put himself in. A class box. And these are my eggs. Edgar put his sperm on these eggs and we made Melissa. I had my eggs removed like caviar right before I stopped menstruating and they've been petrified and I've made copies of them, so you can wear them around your neck."

Can anybody else turn personal tragedy into ratings like Joan?

How Joan remained friendly with me after all those Edgar routines I did amazes me to this day. She even invited me on her show. One time I went to her show carrying a hidden video camera. I put it in my dressing room and called Joan in before I went on. I gave her this long sad rap about how I was not getting along with my wife, Alison, and how much I'd like to take her out that night. I made a move to grab her, but she ran away. I don't know why, but she was repulsed by me.

## DAVID LEE ROTH

I once got pissed off at him because he was making the rounds of the rock stations to promote his album but he neglected to come on my show after he promised me he would. I really like David and think Van Halen sucks without him. So, naturally, I was angry that he didn't show up. I was so mad at him that I grabbed his record and scratched it up pretty good and then I smashed it into a million pieces.

> "At any given time, Howard says what is really on his mind. Most of the time, Howard says what is really on your mind. This makes Howard unique on American radio."
> —David Lee Roth

"I've always been good to him," I whined. "I've even avoided talking about his new hair weave. I've been kind to him. Hey, screw him. I'm going to talk about this. He's David *Weave* Roth. He looks like my Jewish accountant without that hair. I've had it with him." A listener called up with his New York hotel room number but he didn't answer.

"He's probably putting on his hair!" I fumed. "Hey, whenever you see him just call him 'David Weave Roth,'" I instructed my listeners. That night I got a call at home. It was David Weave. "You're killing me," he said. "Everybody on the street was fucking with me."

The next day I went on the air.

"So who calls me at home but David Lee Roth," I gloated.

"You mean David *Weave* Roth," Robin said.

"You better keep your mouth shut, Robin," I said. "He's going to be here in about twenty minutes. He's making the peace." Well, David did show up, and he proved to me he wasn't wearing a weave.

## SANDRA BERNHARD

Sandra used to come on my show a lot before she got a job with that fatso Roseanne and Tom Ono, who, because they hate me, have prevented her from coming on my show. But Sandra was really open about her relationship with Madonna. I had her on my TV show the night we did a roast. While she was roasting me, I leaned over and pulled something out from between her teeth.

"I always wanted to see Madonna's pubic hair," I said.

Whenever Sandra would come on the radio, I'd ask her if she ever got it on with Madonna.

"I've gone to some dumps before, but I've never gone to that place. I have a little bit of dignity," she said.

"Did Madonna steal your girlfriend?" I went on. "A real friend wouldn't steal your girlfriend."

"I know and I couldn't be happier. It worked out beautifully."

"I can't stand Madonna," I said. "I think she's the biggest bitch phony."

"Beyond," Sandra said.

"When you girls don't get any penis, you all fall apart," I observed.

Sandra plugged her show and hung up. "I would do Sandra," I said. "She's got a good body. And those lips. Lips o' plenty, lips to do things with, lips to make up for everything else, lips that, maybe after you finish with her, might make you a little nauseous. But I don't care. I'm proud to admit I'd fuck Sandra."

## JESSICA HAHN

How we first got to know each other is a great story. Jessica was an obscure young girl from Long Island who was propelled into the headlines when she was caught up in the Jim Bakker sex scandals. I really felt sorry for her. It was clear that she had been manipulated and used by these phony preachers. Meanwhile, she was holed up in her little trailer on Long Island, hiding from the press.

Jessica carries a pocketbook full of lingerie when she visits my show in case I ask for a striptease.

Baba Booey had gotten hold of her home phone number from a friend of a friend who worked for a television station. Apparently the entire New York media had her number, but Jessica would never pick up the phone when someone from the press called. We decided to give it a try. I dialed the number on the air and got the answering machine.

"Hello, Miss Hahn, my name is Howard Stern. I don't know if you've heard me before but I'm a reporter. Not a reporter. A friend. I'm a deejay."

Suddenly, we heard a click. "Is this really Howard Stern?" a female voice said.

"Yes," I said.

"Do you listen to the show?" Robin said.

"Yes, I do," Jessica said and we all cheered.

"This is really cool, you're like a newsmaker," I said.

"I appreciate it," Jessica said. "At least you guys make me laugh. It's a great way to wake up."

I immediately began a role that would continue throughout our relationship. I counseled Jessica on dealing with her newfound celebrity.

The next day we called back with a gift for Jessica: an all-expenses-paid trip to Montego Bay for seven days. Of course, I made her promise she wouldn't talk to any other New York radio stations, especially WNBC. And, in this second phone conversation, I began a sexual flirtation with Jessica that over the years has put tremendous strain on my marital vows of fidelity.

The strain was intensified when Jessica came into the studio for her first live appearance, almost four months after that phone call. Jessica had just gotten back from Chicago, where she had done the Donahue show. In fact, I was furious when she told me that the Donahue audience had the nerve to laugh when Jessica revealed that I had been giving her advice. Morons!

"I have fun with you, Howard," Jessica said. "People don't want me to relax. They want me to start preaching or sit in a corner and cry."

"I stuck by your story the whole time," I told her.

"I know. I love you for that," Jessica gushed. "I just love you so much."

 You could cut the sexual tension in the studio with a knife. In fact, it got so heavy that Alison called in. Gary came in and conveyed her message: "She loves you, but watch it." We got Alison on the phone. She exchanged pleasantries with Jessica. Dominic Barbara, Jessica's lawyer, offered Alison his services for the divorce.

"Alison knows she's on the gravy train, she ain't jumping off for anybody," I said.

"Listen, I trust you and I know when you're carrying on for the show," Alison said. "But Dominic, if anything happens, I'm taking him to the cleaners."

We had a lot of fun with Jessica over the years on the show. One time I made a phony phone call to her posing as Bob Trellis, a fictitious editor with Doubleday. She once told me that she wanted to write a book, but nothing dirty or pornographic. I wanted to see if she would stick to that premise if I offered her a lot of money. I told her that after hearing her talk on the "Howard Stern Show" about how she exercises her vaginal muscles, I realized it would make a perfect book.

"A step-by-step instruction guide would be fabulous," I said.

"But I'm not a pro on anything," Jessica said, not recognizing my voice.

"We're interested in your talents as a reproducer," I said. "Perhaps we'll have drawings. Dating habits, safe sex, lubricants, whatever."

I offered her a fifteen-thousand-dollar advance.

"It's a fledgling idea," I pitched her. "The idea of the inside mechanism of a woman's parts being exercised and used is an incredible concept. Obviously, a strong book would include the story that you used a milking machine for sexual use."

"I have to see this whole thing in my mind to be able to accept it and see if it'll work," Jessica said.

"It *will* work," I pushed. "You could do a whole chapter on using a candle. Or a loom rack. Or a plumber's helper's handle. A whole chapter on that would be fabulous."

"I really don't know," Jessica said.

"Look, I don't want you to get perverted for the book. If Jessica Hahn had used a propane hose, then we do a chapter on propane hoses," I said.

"Look, *Playboy* paid me a million dollars and they asked me to do one percent of what you're asking. I am not going to put myself on the line like this, this is too far out!" she said.

I barreled on:

"Let's say we find someone who uses road flares, for example. Then we'd put it in the book. Not necessarily you using a road flare. I don't think you'd use a road flare, you're a very beautiful woman, but some people are desperate."

"Look, I can only go so far," Jessica said. "I've done

a lot of things that I don't regret at all, but this is going a little beyond that."

"So you're saying you're opposed to posing with weird gadgets and strange people?" I said.

"Yes," she said firmly. She began to act a bit suspicious. She asked me for my phone number.

"Would it be out of the question to name the book 'A Red Snapper Ain't Just for Fishing'?"

Jessica's best breast press photo.

"Can I ask you a question? Is this a joke? Did Howard put you up to this? I cannot believe in my wildest dreams that anybody from a book company would call me up like this."

I ignored her. "You have to be willing to put out when it comes to books. Books are bucks."

"Who is this? This makes *Playboy* look like church," she said.

"Your breasts were made for print," I whispered. "You know, a picture of you watching a guy spank his Franklin while looking at your *Playboy* spread would be unbelievable for a book."

"It's short-term bucks. There isn't enough money

on the face of the earth for the idea you have," Jessica decided. "No! I'd do this and I couldn't get a job cleaning toilets."

"You know, squeezing a man's Jolly Rod with your Hay Nanny Nanny means dollars," I urged. "If we could just shave you down like a four-year-old . . ." I started cracking up and I couldn't go on and I let her in on the joke. Another five minutes and I swear I could have signed her.

Jessica became a regular on the show. We found a pattern to her phone calls. She'd leave New York to go to Los Angeles for the weekend and she'd call in to say good-bye.

"I love you," she said.

"No, I love *you*," I'd reply.

"I miss you guys," she'd come back.

"No, we miss you," I'd say.

After a while we started taking bets on the air to see how long it would be before she told us she missed us.

It got to the point where she was calling in so much that we had to brush her off a few times. Then she started leaving messages on Gary's answering machine at home. Gary would call in for messages and there'd be eighty messages and seventy-eight of them were from Jessica. Gary would bring the tape in the next morning and we'd play it on the air. Jessica was shrewd enough to know that this was another way of getting on the air. One day before Thanksgiving we were bickering with Jessica and I told her not to call anymore if I was causing her too much pain. So it was the day before Thanksgiving and Gary got stuck in the office until four. He left and went to rent a car to go to his Thanksgiving dinner the next day and he drove back home and he had to circle the block about ninety times before he could find a spot. So it was six now and he was really bumming. He walked in the door and the phone rang. It was Jessica, ranting and raving. "You fucking people are supposed to be my friends!" Blah, blah, blah.

Gary lost it. "You're a fucking nut! Fuck you!" he screamed.

"No, fuck you!" Jessica yelled.

They told each other to fuck off for ten minutes. Finally, she hung up. Seconds later, Gary called me at home, hyperventilating.

"Boss, I can't take this anymore," he said.

**While Jessica teases, she pleases the crowd at the outdoor funeral that I staged for my competitors.**

**The King of L.A. celebrates at the ratings death of his morning competition.**

The Friday after Thanksgiving, Gary got the phone company out and they installed a second line and he's never had to pick up his phone for Jessica again. She drove him to a second line.

But I'm proud to report that I never did have a physical relationship with Jessica, although, to be brutally honest, I could have nailed her any time I wanted. It was especially hard resisting her temptations since Jessica began to make it a habit of undressing in front of us. It began when we were all out in Los Angeles during Grammy coverage. Jessica was so homesick that the minute we came to town she rushed over to our hotel. We were hanging out in Baba Booey's room and Jessica flipped out over Gary's K-Rock T-shirt. Gary had brought a bunch of them with him, so he told her to take one. She grabbed the T-shirt off the top; it turned out that Gary had cut the sleeves off it. Jessica was so excited, she rushed into the bathroom to put on her new gift. She came out wearing the T-shirt. "What do you think, guys?" she said and put her arms out, like Jesus on the cross. *Boom!* Both her tits flopped out on both sides. We went crazy.

With each succeeding Jessica appearance for us she's worn less and less clothing. It culminated finally when we were shooting our last video, *Butt Bongo Fiesta*. I came into her dressing room and she had like nine hundred outfits laid out.

"What do you want me to wear?" Jessica asked me.

"Why don't you get something really sexy?" I said.

"Well, I have this," she said and held up a piece of silk that was smaller than a G-string. My heart dropped. This was gonna be the world's greatest videotape!

"Put it on. Let me see if it's sexy," I said, trying not to froth.

Jessica asked me to turn my back while she put it on even though I'd already seen her naked about nine hundred times. So I turned, and

With each ratings victory, Jessica's outfits got skimpier and skimpier.

when I turned around again I saw she was like completely nude through this thing. I couldn't believe she wanted to go on the video totally nude like this.

"That's pretty good," I said.

"Do you think it's too revealing?" she worried.

"No," I lied.

I left her dressing room and ran downstairs.

"Don't make a big deal when Jessica comes down," I lectured everyone. "If we make a big deal, she'll get nervous, and if she gets nervous, she won't do it."

So she came down and nobody reacted because she was wearing a robe. We started to roll and she took off her robe and she was standing there almost totally naked and everybody went nuts!

But a few months later, we would get an even better view of her physical attributes. We were out in L.A. again, this time for the funeral of those two idiot djs, Mark and Brian, whom I had just usurped as the number one show in town. Jackie, Gary, Fred and I were hanging out at the bar of our hotel. It was a Saturday night at about ten and I told Gary to give Jessica a call and get her over to our hotel to give us a fashion show. He left a message on her machine and ten minutes later he got paged by the bartender. It was Jessica. She was throwing some things into her bag and she was coming right over.

We went up to my room. By now, besides us, we had Stuttering John, some guys from Fox, my L.A. program director, Andy Bloom, and half the L.A. Police Department in the room. Jessica and I went into the bathroom to prepare for the show. I dragged Gary in there, too, in case she tried to rape me. Instantly, she was completely nude and doing the whole grooming ritual. She was shaven down and she was putting baby powder all over. I swear, she even pulled a piece of lint out of her love canal. Gary and I were cracking up whenever she turned her back to us.

We started out showing the natural progression of

her nakedness. I went out and introduced Jessica to the crowd in the room. "This is the outfit that Jessica made famous at the Philadelphia Zoo funeral." Then I told her she had to show more, and she came out with the miniskirt and heels, but she'd lost the top. The guys were whooping it up and they started chanting, "Take off your dress! Take off your dress!" So she took off her dress and she wasn't wearing underpants. She acted as if she was embarrassed and she went back to the bathroom. We followed her in.

"Why don't you just come out naked in high heels?" I suggested.

"I don't know." She acted coy.

"It's just Jackie and Fred and the guys!" we begged.

She agreed and she came out totally naked! She was naked but demure; she was holding her breasts.

"Turn around!" the guys started yelling.

"I don't know if my ass looks good," Jessica worried as she turned around. Two minutes later, she was running around the room, totally nude and totally unself-conscious.

But it was Jessica's total obsessiveness about her personal hygiene and grooming habits that made for one of her most memorable appearances on the show. I knew that if I pointed out the slightest imperfection on her body, she'd go into a total snit. So one day Jessica was in the studio and, out of the blue, I stuck my finger in her belly button.

"Let me smell your belly button," I demanded. "Whoa." I started coughing. "Hey, Fred, come over here and smell this. My finger stinks."

"You probably stuck it in somebody else's!" Jessica screamed.

Fred picked up on this. "It smells like she was picking her toenails."

"It does not!" Jessica protested. "I put baby powder on it. I use Nivea. It's not true." She actually began to cry.

Robin wondered if it was Jessica's time of the month. That got her going even more.

"Just because I detect a little belly button odor, you're freaking out," I said. I tried it again. "Hey, there's something living in there!" Jessica was beside herself. She said she used half a bottle of Nivea skin creme a day.

Four months later, Jessica was in the studio again, so naturally, I brought up her belly button odor. She went into this whole rap about how she'd consulted a doctor and now she goes through elaborate belly button rituals.

"I haven't been the same since. I've done so much to my poor belly button that I probably can't have kids now," Jessica said. "You ruined my life, Howard."

## RICHARD SIMMONS

Dietmeister Richard is one of the greatest all-time nuts I've ever encountered. He's a warm and generous person and I love him. And that lovable TV guy has a lot of pent-up anger and hostility that surfaces every once in a while. Actually, we're a lot alike.

The first time I had him out to my house, he was

totally manic. It was summertime and we were sitting outside by the pool and we brought him a tray of cucumber dip and he said, "This is wonderful," and started throwing the food into the pool.

"Asshole, what are you doing?" I yelled at him.

He started giggling like a maniac. I told him to calm down and relax. We went into the house and there were two big grapefruits sitting on the counter, so Richard picked them up and started juggling. Then he started running through the house singing Streisand songs. All of a sudden, he grabbed our housekeeper and gave her a bear hug and picked her up. Then he ran up to Alison and did the same to her. I swear to God, Alison thought her ribs were cracked. She was moaning in pain. Then he went after my kids, grabbing them. He was like a terrorist. It wasn't really funny. It was frightening. My daughters' ribs hurt for two days.

Besides his general nuttiness, I was always fascinated with Richard's sexuality. I never got a straight answer out of him on the subject, but he's one of the most effeminate men on the planet.

In fact, one time Richard showed up in my studio with a beautiful woman and he told us they had just gotten married. He even showed us the ring. He said he had hit forty and it was time to have kids.

"How long has she been a woman?" I asked. "Is today April first?" We broke for a commercial.

"Hold it, I just got some calls. The flags are flying at half mast on Key West and Fire Island," I said when we came back on the air. "In San Francisco, the whole town is in mourning."

That wasn't the only joke Richard tried to play on us. A few months later, Robin was in the middle of her newscast when a nurse walked into her room. "Uh, excuse me, ma'am, you can't come in here," Robin said. Then she realized it was Richard. He was in full nurse regalia, with fake nails, earrings, a beehive hairdo, the works. Then he spent the rest

Richard dressed up as a real man for my TV show and later went so far as to make out with Sandra Bernhard.

of the show denying he was dressed like that. He did the same thing a few months later when he showed up on Ash Wednesday dressed as a nun!

Even though he was showing up in full drag, we still didn't really poke fun at his sexual orientation on the air until Richard himself gave us the go-ahead in an indirect way. One time he came to town to promote one of his charity events and he was going to make appearances on a number of different radio stations. The night before he did our show, Scott Shannon's producer at Z–100 called Richard and told him that if he did our show, he shouldn't bother coming to their show. Richard explained it was a charity event and he was trying to promote it in as many places as he could. They still wouldn't budge so Richard told them to screw off and he came on our show. About a year later, the Zoo morons realized they had fucked up, so they called him the night before he was supposed to do our show.

We were in a commercial break and Richard was recounting the conversation.

"C'mon, come back on," Scott Shannon's female producer said. "Don't hold a grudge."

"You tell Scott Shannon I would rather eat pussy than do that show. And I think you know how much I like doing that."

We were all silent, we didn't know how to react. Then Richard went into his little cackle of a laugh. Little did he know it, but Richard had just unleashed the floodgates.

The next time he came up, Richard entered the studio singing. He was dressed normally for him, which meant he was wearing shorts that were cut up to his navel.

"Could those shorts be any shorter? Do you design each pair of shorts so your sack'll hang out?" I asked. "I can see your meat. You know what this outfit is? He's trolling for Cub Scouts this morning."

Another time Richard called in and I invited him out to my house for dinner.

"So Richard, what do you like to eat?" I asked. "You like hot dogs? Sausage? Carrots? Zucchinis? Bratwurst? How about a giant cucumber for dinner?"

"You get so ugly and it isn't even seven o'clock yet," Richard hissed.

"Hey, for dessert, how would you like three Cub Scouts?" I said. Richard hung up.

"I guess I'll be dining alone," I said. I didn't want Richard to leave with a sour taste in his mouth, so I called him back.

"Hey, my newsboy asked me if he could meet you," I told him. *Click*. He hung up again.

"Why doesn't he calm down and take a Valium enema?" I wondered. "And I was planning on serving cream-of-anything soup, too. Good thing I didn't tell him I was going to cook the lamb in KY mint jelly." We got him on the phone again.

"Hey, do you think the Zodiac killer is attractive?" I asked him. Again he hung up.

But he did make it out to my house for dinner. My parents were there and Alison had made a really great spread. Chicken, fish, the works. There was even a tray stocked with the most incredible desserts, all sorts of cakes and chocolates. But Richard wasn't doing too well with the eating. He was just picking at the food. Then I got a phone call and I left the table. Richard was sitting there and Alison came running in.

"Richard, Howard had to take a private phone call!" she screamed. With that, Richard grabbed the dessert tray from the center of the table and he started shoveling the food into his mouth. My mother told me it was the most incredible thing she'd ever seen.

We always used to give Richard a hard time about his diet program and those fatsos he was constantly dragging around with him. In fact, I booked Richard and his human balloons for my third TV show. Richard came out with two assistants who put baskets of fruits, flowers, and balloons all over the set. The highlight was a poodle made out of mums. I told you this guy was nuts. After we calmed him down, I told him that we were going to play some clips from his exercise and diet tapes.

"Howard, what have you done to my tapes!" he yelled. He guessed right. We started out showing Richard leading a bevy of fatsos in sweating to the oldies. However, off to the side of Richard we had superimposed Fred in a full leather S and M outfit, including a hooded mask.

"Stop teasing me," Fred was saying on the tape. "Let's go upstairs and play house. Why are you ignoring me, Richard?"

I stopped the tape. "All right, all right, we're just kidding. Let's show the real sweating to the oldies now," I said. We ran the tape. There was a line of blimps on either side of the screen. Then one fatso who had lost a few pounds would run up toward the camera, the way football players do when they're introduced. We let a few legitimate ones go, and then a fat woman we had superimposed on the tape ran right up to the camera. She looked straight at the camera and then barfed her guts out and fell down. Richard was flipping out.

"All right, you know I love you," I told him. "Let's bring out the two fatties he's got with him. Hey, Richard, your wallet weighs more than your porky friends."

The two blimps came out and sat next to Richard. Richard was bragging about how well they were doing on his Deal-a-Meal program so I decided to put them to the test. While we were interviewing them, I grabbed a fishing pole that had a huge bag of Lay's potato chips hooked onto its end and I dangled it in front of the fatties' faces.

"Can they resist?" I said.

"Howard, how could you?" Richard yelled.

I put the pole away, but a few seconds later an entire roast chicken was lowered down from the ceiling almost into their laps. I guess his program worked. They didn't eat it.

Richard kept making appearances on the radio show and we kept ragging him endlessly about his suspected sexual proclivities. The last time he appeared in person we were relentless. I was talking about the time Richard had gone to Baba Booey's house for dinner.

> "Damien has a brother and his name is Howard Stern. No one has ever made me cry and broken my heart like Howard has. He's the bully in every school yard and for some reason I love him very much."
> —Richard Simmons

"You just wanted to put a black leather hood over his head and stuff a rubber ball in his mouth, put clamps on his nipples, and squeeze them," I said. "Hey, you ever been tied up?"

"Tied up? Mercy!" Richard said. He was laughing strangely under his breath. He was eating a bagel and extending his pinky as he ate.

"Hey, I just noticed something about you, you're very effeminate," I said.

"This is something new?" Richard joked.

One of Richard's fatso friends called and was upset about the way I made fun of fat people. We had to shut off Richard's microphone because he was blabbering too much.

"Pipe down," I told him. "Your belly is hanging out like your nuts."

Richard almost started crying and he bolted for the door. Jackie blocked his way.

"You have picked on me from the moment I got here. All you've said is horrible things," Richard complained. "I can't take it anymore. Let me out the door."

"Hey, I'm just trying to make you interesting, you're boring otherwise," I said, to make him feel better. He calmed down.

"Be a man, Richard," I said. "Let's beat off and smoke cigars."

"I just want to know, after all this time in our friendship, why you have to feel that you have to put me down and be so mean every time I come on the show," Richard asked.

I told him I wasn't being mean, just honest. "You're outrageous today. Did you ever kiss a man on the lips?"

"What is wrong with you today?" Richard laughed.

"Where are you off to now? Where will you flit around, a shopping mall?"

Richard barged out of the studio but Gary dragged him back in. He started talking about his recent appearance on "Evening Shade." Then he said he thought Loni Anderson was beautiful.

"If you saw Loni Anderson nude, would it be exciting or would it be like looking at a building?" I asked him.

Richard laughed but he also said he thought it would be best if he didn't come on the show anymore. He didn't realize how prophetic he was.

The next time he called in was right after the *Globe* had printed a story that Richard had regularly paid young men to spank him while he dressed up as a young girl. Of course Richard denied it all.

"The only person in the whole world that I would actually let spank me is Howard Stern," Richard said proudly.

We read the article on the air. It alleged that Richard had had up to eight men in his house at a cost of four hundred dollars each.

"Do you know what my fantasy is, Howard? My fantasy is a buffet that costs nine ninety-five," he joked.

"Bad girl!" I yelled at him. "Have you been naughty? Did you wet your diappie? Hey, for four hundred bucks I'll give you such a session you won't be able to sit down for a month. No wonder he can't sit still in the studio, his ass is probably beet red."

I haven't seen Richard for almost a year and I really miss him, but he's pissed because he thinks I've gone too far discussing his sexuality. We had a lot of fun together off and on the air. He calls a lot and leaves messages that he wants to come out and see our new baby—after all, he did name her Ashley—but I refuse to see him until he returns to my radio show, the show that revived his career.

## AL HENDRIX
*Father of Jimi Hendrix*

"You shoulda had a lotta kids," I told Al, " 'cause you got talented sperm. Seriously, did you ever look at your own sperm and go, 'My God, I wonder if there's another Jimi inside me?' Did anyone ever approach you about your sperm?"

"No." He seemed befuddled.

"Jimi's male member was legendary. Mr. Hendrix, is he a chip off the old block?" I wondered.

> "I think he's great."
> —Sting

"Who's this?" he asked.

"Did Jimi inherit your huge size in the male-member category?"

"I'm ordinary," he said, modestly.

"Really?" I was surprised. "You're ordinary? Because Jimi was legendary for the size of his penis. When he was a little boy, did you know? Was that how you picked him up?"

"He was average," Al said.

It sounded as if the whole family was hung like horses.

"He was average? When did he get to be so large? I guess in his teenage years," I said. "Mr. Hendrix, seriously, didn't he get it from you? Because Robin'll be over there in a minute if you say yes. He did get it from you, didn't he?" Silence . . . Hendrix was befuddled. "All right, I understand. You're a little shy about that. What's the most embarrassing thing you ever caught Jimi doing?"

"Playing the broom's about the only thing," Al said.

We all laughed.

"He was making believe the broom was a guitar."

"Oh, I thought you meant something else. I call that playing the broom, too," I said.

## MARK HARRIS
### Husband of Martha Raye

One of my favorite guests in the sex revelation arena is Mark Harris, the young man who married the very ancient comedienne Martha Raye. The first time he came on, Mark was very reticent to talk about both

**MARK HARRI**

**Joining us for Homeless Howiewood Squares, where the downtrodden win prizes.**

his sexual relationship with Martha and his sexual relationship with the rest of the world, possibly because he was in line to inherit her five-million-plus estate when she finally kicked. But we did find out that the first time he met Martha he washed her hair, hair which hadn't been washed for over a year and a half. He also revealed that he was smitten with Martha because she, like his mother, was a stroke survivor.

He told us that he masturbated to relieve his sexual drive, but not with Martha in the room, doesn't use a picture of Martha to get off, and (SURPRISE!) he had sex with a man. Yes, he said, and a very *famous one* who he wouldn't reveal. BINGO!

It's always weird when a guy says to me, "Yeah, I've had homosexual sex, but not with that many guys." One sounds like plenty to me.

"Any farm animals? Did you pitch or catch?"

"Catch," Mark said. "Oh, you're talking about sex! I'm talking about baseball. No, I've never bent over, not even for a banana peel."

Everybody's a comedian.

Then he talked about the weirdest sex he probably ever had: making it with Martha! Martha proposed to him through her nurse, he told us. He wasn't sexually attracted to her at first; it was more of a business-type marriage, to protect her estate from relatives.

"Now what got you hot when you saw her? Was the wheelchair especially shiny?" I probed.

He avoided the question. I asked him about their wedding night, the night they consummated this strange union.

"You didn't plan to have sex with her?"

"No."

"Are you sure it wasn't the nurse you banged when the lights went out?"

He described the scene. Martha was in a trousseau and he was nude except for a silk robe.

"Are the teeth in or out?" I asked.

"In."

"Did the nurse do anything to prepare her sexually for you? Any jellies?"

"I really would have to ask the nurse," he said.

"You unwrapped your robe and you were completely nude in front of her?"

"No, I lay beside her, and we were talking and I was drinking champagne and she unwrapped me— let's say," he said.

"She unwrapped you like a birthday present!" I exulted.

"Like a cigar! This is getting crazy!"

"And then you leaned over and you began to kiss?"

"Absolutely. Lovingly."

"Were her hands scaly or smooth?"

"Very beautiful."

"And you went all the way with her that night?"

"Would you like to know that before the evening was over, in the wee hours of the morning, we all wound up in the hospital," he reported.

"Why? Martha had another stroke?"

"Abdominal pains," he bragged.

"So from your lovemaking she experienced some pain?"

"Take it as you wish," he said.

### ANDREW "DICE" CLAY
*Replies*

Not everyone loved hearing Mark. One time, when I had him on, Andrew "Dice" Clay called in. Dice is always brutal, always great. His call in to Mark Harris was a classic:

"I'm getting sick and tired of parasite faggots like you," the Diceman started. "You want to tell me you're in love with her? You want to tell me you fucked somebody that shoulda been dead thirty years ago and nobody told her yet?" Everyone went wild. Mark started yelling at Dice, but Dice kept at him.

"What about young girls with big boobs and great asses? You don't like that? What does he do when he sees a real chick, like one from this century, walking around? Harris, you're a parasite."

## DICK CAVETT

I always love having Cavett on because I know he's good for some juicy stories. They usually center on his various mental ailments and the drugs he was taking to combat them. I was convinced that he wasn't on antidepressants but antiratings drugs. Dick said that his mental problems were in no way connected to the abysmal ratings his shows always seemed to produce.

**Hugging Dick.**

"What's worse, Dick, when they cancel one of your shows or when they cancel one of your prescriptions?"

He didn't answer. He did come through with an amazing abuse story. He said that he was molested when he was a kid growing up in Nebraska. I claimed that this was merely a career move to get on the Arsenio show, but Dick gave us some details. He was five years old and at a Hopalong Cassidy movie and there was a guy sitting next to him with his raincoat over his lap. The guy said, "Put your hand under here and squeeze."

"Did you?" I probed.

"Sure, because I wanted to see the rest of the movie," he said.

"*Homo!*" I coughed.

"*Likes boys!*" Fred coughed.

"*Loves testicles!*" Jackie cleared his throat.


## SYLVESTER STALLONE

Sylvester called in to my show and didn't plug anything. That's a big plus. At the time he had just done two comedies and I yelled at him for a good five minutes. I gave him some good advice: "Keep doing action pictures." God bless Rambo. I love Rambo.

All you action guys always want to branch out. I would make action films all day and night. The more blood, the more gore, the more banging girls, the better.

After imparting my career wisdom, I told him that

if his girlfriend, supermodel Jennifer Flavin, was MY girlfriend, I'd make love to her three times a day.

"When you left the room there'd be nothing left but a black smoky hole," Sylvester said. Then he revealed that he especially liked the segment on my TV show featuring the Kielbasa Queen, a lady whose prodigious talent consisted of being able to deep-throat an entire massive sausage.

"You know what? We watched that show last week and I tried to ram a thermos down Jennifer's throat," Stallone wisecracked.

Then in a gesture of complete trust, he did something very un-Hollywood. He put his hot girlfriend on the phone.

In my own devious and subtle way I got her talking about sex.

"So, when you met Sly, what were you wearing?"

"A miniskirt," she said in her innocent-little-girl voice.

"Was it the miniest of micro miniskirts? Were you wearing panties under that miniskirt? Were they thong underpants? Were you wearing a bra under your shirt? Was the shirt the kind of shirt that exposes your rock-hard belly? Did Sly nail you on the first date?"

"No," she shyly answered.

"On the second date?"

"NO, NO!" she protested. I imagined she was fingering herself with her dainty nineteen-year-old feminine hand the entire time we spoke.

"Were you a virgin when you met Sly?" I whispered.

"Practically. I only had one guy before Sly. My high-school sweetheart."

Her pussy must have smelled like daisies, I imagined, as I clutched my hot beef. I shuddered.

"After a month, Sly asked me to go to Hawaii with him. But my mom wouldn't let me go unless she had a serious talk with him. Then when we got there, she called me every day."

"So, did you make love in Hawaii?"

"Yes." She giggled like the near-virgin she was. I imagined her clitoris was heating up with passion. All this sex talk had to be making her hot.

"Sly's a painter. Did he paint you in the nude in Hawaii? Did you wear a thong on the beach?"

"No." She giggled.

"A bikini?"

"Yes."

"Then Sly and you check into this room and like you guys had never made love before?"

"Right," she sweetly answered.

"Weren't you nervous?" I sensitively asked, as I gently fingered my asshole.

"Yes." She giggled orgasmically.

> "I love him, I really
> love him."
> —Sylvester Stallone

"Was Sly gentle?" I asked. "I would have been so rough." I would have tied her up spread-eagled, poured cement up her ass, and sucked it out with a straw. The bitch would have crumbled with desire. I would have filled her love pouch with my cock cheese while she did the schmega-hiney dance.

"Did you guys go to a nude beach? Did you fuck in the woods? Did you suck him off? Did you beat his meat? Were you jerkin' his gherkin?"—I forgot to ask.

Sly stopped the conversation and grabbed the phone: "She learned everything she knows from her first boyfriend."

Great guests. I'm still waiting for them to call back.

## THE WACKY STALLONE FAMILY

I could write a whole chapter about my exploits with the wacky Stallone family. You never know what's going to happen. Especially when Jackie, Stallone's mother, shows up. If she isn't making some cuckoo astrological predictions or claiming that Jesse Jackson offered her the vice presidential spot in 1988, she's having huge fights with her ex-husband. They were reunited for the first time in six years when Frank Sr. called in when Jackie was in the studio. They seemed to be having a pleasant enough conversation, but then Jackie got real and revealed that Frank was the one who got tired of sleeping with her.

"Let me tell you, when she was pregnant with Sylvester, she put on sixty-five pounds," Frank Sr. said.

"I did not!" Jackie maintained.

Soon after, he hung up and Jackie started whispering, not realizing she was still on the air.

"Thank God I said the right things about him, or he woulda shot me. He was the worst lay in the world."

We all cracked up. But we weren't laughing the next time these two tangled horns.

"He couldn't get it up when he was twenty-five," Jackie complained about her seventy-two-year-old ex-husband, who was now dating a twenty-five-year-old he'd met when she was seventeen. "What's he doing with her?" she railed. It didn't take long for Gary to come in and tell us that Frank Sr. was on the phone.

"I'm ready to jump through this phone. I just can't believe this wrinkly, messy, vulgar woman saying things about her own family that just won't quit!" he bellowed. "She is probably the lowest vermin that I've ever known in my life and it was a sorry day when I met her."

"Listen, you pig," Jackie countered, "let me tell you, you old son of a bitch. You beat me up and put me in the hospital so many times, and choked me to death so many times, and you like to go on the air and say you're basically a nice guy. You prick—you never supported your kids. You never gave a goddamn for—"

"You are the biggest goddamn liar!" he screamed.

"Fuck you!" Jackie said and we screamed. Thank God for seven-second delay.

"Get this slob off the phone!" Jackie ordered.

"You were nothing when I met you," Frank said.

"What the hell are you doing with an eighteen-year-old girl?" Jackie wondered.

"She's giving me more than you ever could, that's what."

"What the hell did you ever give me, you old bastard? I supported you for years. You goddamn half-ass hairdresser. I opened the business, I put you to work, and then you stole all the money. And I bought the house and goddamnit, you put a gun to my head and made me sign it over to you for another old broad married to a cabdriver with five kids who dumped you six months later," Jackie railed.

"You are absolutely insane!" Frank said.

"You can go to hell! And don't you ever talk to me again, you fucking creep! You gave me no pleasure. Goddamnit, you couldn't even fuck!"

"Whoaaa, wait a second," I jumped in. "You're gonna lose our license. I can't bleep you that fast." Jackie was still yelling off-mike while I waited for the delay to build up. I begged her not to use the f-word.

"I won't use the f-word, but as far as sex—twice a year, he'd say, 'Okay, if you're ready, lay down.' And then if I pretended I was excited, he said, 'Look, if you're gonna act like you're excited, forget it!' You're from hunger!" she screamed. "He'd bring home bushels of tomatoes and peppers and tell me to can them. I'm not an Italian housewife. What do I know about canning? He punched me in the jaw."

"Why don't you keep quiet and listen to the truth?" he said.

"That is the truth!"

"You're insane!"

"Well, I had to be to have you," she said.

"You are insane, woman."

"*But you two produced a movie star,*" I offered helpfully.

"No help from him. Any guy coulda done the job in three seconds. He didn't even want Sylvester—he tried to get me to have an abortion! Yes, you did! And I pretended I got one. You were very surprised to find out I had a kid."

"Is that true, Mr. Stallone?" I asked.

"It certainly is!" Jackie butted in.

"She's really off her rocker," he said.

"You didn't want this kid and you know it!" Jackie screamed.

"You remind me of an old crinkled-up Genoa salami. That's all you will be all your life. Good-bye!" he yelled and hung up.

"You know, you have to say to yourself, Why? Why? Why?" I questioned. "Why does this have to happen at ten-thirty? Why can't it happen during drive time at seven o'clock? I'll have to replay this tomorrow at seven."

## FRANK STALLONE, JR.

I even got Frank Jr. in on the act. I skillfully interrogated Frank on his relationship to his superfamous sibling, utilizing my best Perry Mason.

"You and Sylvester never tickled each other?"

"No."

"You never saw Sylvester naked?"

"Of course, he's my brother."

"Did you admire his large penis?"

"No."

"You didn't even look at it? Did you look at his genitals? Have you seen your brother's genitals?"

"Of course!"

"And you looked at them, is that correct?"

"Of course."

"So you do admit to looking at your brother's genitals?"

"Looking at—no. It was like a glance."

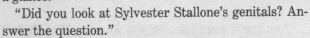

"Did you look at Sylvester Stallone's genitals? Answer the question."

"It wasn't like sitting there beaming in."

"No, but did you see them? Yes?"

"Of course I've seen them because we're brothers."

"Did you compare who was bigger?"

"Uh, yes."

"You did. So you admit now, not only looking at your brother's genitals, but doing . . ."

"No, I was doing this in my own mind."

"Oh, in your mind you were thinking about Sylvester's penis. Admit it!"

"No, no, no, no."

"All right, so there you go. You're as homo as I am," I said triumphantly. "I shoulda been a lawyer."

"His show is great! He possesses brilliance."
— Billy Dee Williams

## CHIP Z'NUFF
*ROCK STAR FROM THE BAND ENUFF Z'NUFF*

It started out innocently enough when I was asking Chip and Donnie, the two rock stars from the band Enuff Z'Nuff, if they got any famous women. Enuff Z'Nuff is one of my favorites, and I cannot believe that, after three albums, they are not superstars.

"Chip got Madonna," Donnie squealed. "He got her back when she was a drummer in L.A."

"Is that true, Chip?" I was out of my mind. "You nailed Madonna? Let me smell your hand!"

"I ain't telling," Chip said.

"Did you smack her around? I can't believe you got Madonna and you never told me in private!"

The next time they came on, Chip was foolish enough to tell me the details of what happened before we went on the air. He said he had sex with Madonna and peed inside her. We argued, because I said that it was impossible to pee inside of a woman. It was impossible to carry on with this graphic discussion on the radio, so I cleaned up the story a little. But I couldn't wait to talk about it.

"*These guys told me what went on with Madonna!*" I teased. "Robin, if I told you, you couldn't do the news. It would *be* the news!"

At a break we told Robin. Then she started in. "Was it out of disgust? Was it an accident or did you really want to?" she wondered.

It was time to go for it. "Chip, no kidding, Madonna goes for that? Did she get mad? These guys use women as a toilet and *I'm* sexist?" I blurted out.

"Hey, maybe Chip just had to go. He gets wild with women and he can't make the trek to the bathroom. When you see one of her videos, Chip, do you say, 'I've got to go to the bathroom'?" I asked.

> "Stern's conversation is . . . the national id run wild. . . . His over-the-top humor draws a road map of American society's taboos of public and private behavior and brings them audaciously, often hilariously, into the open."
>
> —Richard Zoglin, *Time* magazine

After they left, we told a less graphic version of the story. "How cool is that that Chip peed on Madonna?" I said, even though he insisted that he had peed *in* her. "That story should carry him for twenty years! And he's so casual about it. I would do bits on that endlessly for the rest of my life. Talking about it, analyzing it. And he's going, 'Why are you guys making such a big deal about the fact that I peed on Madonna?' Chip, don't you get it? *You peed on* MADONNA!"

Naturally, the next time they came on, I brought it up again. "Where's Madonna? I have to urinate," I said. "Poor Chip. Hey, you should be proud of that. That's a rock 'n' roll legend. It says something about you. It means you got street years on you. All these other guys are waiting to get Madonna and you just abuse her that way, just to teach her a lesson. *'Okay, shut up! I have to go to the bathroom now.'* That's so cool. *'Hey, there's no bathroom available and I'm a man. This is what I'm doing.'* That's so cool. But I don't understand it. Couldn't you go to the bathroom? You did this as a thing to turn her on, right?"

"It was a long time ago," Chip protested. "It wasn't like that at all."

"You see that guy Fred over there?" I pointed. "He farted in front of Gloria Estefan. It was really cool, she was all fouled out. But you take the cake. You're our hero!"

I began to fantasize them winning a Grammy: "We'd like to thank the Academy. We'd like to thank God. And we'd like to thank Madonna. When we didn't have a toilet, we used her."

Chip was uncomfortable. I tried to press him, but he would only say it was a one-night fling. Off the air, he couldn't stop bragging.

"Let me ask you something," I said. "If you had stayed with Madonna for a couple of weeks, do you think you would have built up to something? Like doing number *two* or something?"

Chip wouldn't answer.

---

"[The Howard Stern radio show] has made its own fairly major contribution to the rancid nature of public talk on the East Coast."
—Alexander Cockburn,
*The Nation*

"Howard is an improv actor. I don't think he believes half the things he says. He's picked his role well and he's given people the vortex to let the asshole in themselves come out."
—Sally Kirkland

Sally Kirkland (right) on set with Tawny Kitaen and me (as Larry King).

Another celebrity you have to love, Joe Franklin. I attempted male-to-male sodomy on the set, but he wouldn't hear of it.

> "Howard Stern without a radio microphone would be a goofy, lost child from the Aerosmith generation. Radio without Howard Stern would be a bore."
> —Geraldo Rivera

> "Howard knows I love him."
> —Steven Tyler, Aerosmith

**Yakking it up with actor/motorcycle-accident victim Gary Busey during the Head Injury Club for Men sketch on my TV show.**

# More Hate Mail

Howard:

Your show sucks. That person that says it's the Howard Stern show now here's Howard Stern. He sounds like a jewish guy eating corned beef in a deli.

Your jealous of Mark and Brian because they have national tv show. The reason there ratings on tv is not higher because there competing with the most popular tv show Sixty Minutes, why can't you get national tv show. Why don't you do plastic surgery on your ugly face.

Dear Mr. Stern:
So you're no. 1 in the ratings. That only proves that America is a land of perverts.

I received your reply to my letter and decided to try what you suggested about listening to Howard's morning radio show with an open mind. Attached is a typed copy of a daily diary of sorts with my notes on what I heard each morning for one week that offended me, insulted my intelligence and made me want to change channels.

7/25/91
In discussing Linda Lavin's divorce, Howard says it is OK for a man to commit adultery if his wife is ugly.

7/26/91
Howard says "all women should be skinny" with enormous breasts."

7/30/91
Pee Wee Herman is a pretty easy target this week but Michael Landon??? Howard bashes Landon as not being a real family man because he was married three times. Howard believes himself to be a real family man — he has only one wife and family. However, if his wife gets fat, he will be forced to bang the millions of women who hit on him because he is so famous.

# If You're Not Like Me, I Hate You

## CHAPTER 8

Every once in a while I have this fantasy that I should be lying in the sun somewhere on vacation. But where? To tell the truth, I hate every fucking place in the world. I hate Europe. I hate the Bahamas and all those islands filled with hostile natives. I'm uncomfortable asking black guys

to serve me. What about Mexico? They have a corrupt government, endless begging in the streets, and you get diarrhea from eating a piece of fruit. I also hate the hassle of going on a

A rare out-of-country experience, my honeymoon in Mexico. The Mexicans do everything to humiliate you. No Mexican would wear that stupid hat.

plane and feel no excitement for seeing strange and unusual places. I have no desire to expose my children to other cultures and give them incredible learning experiences. Hell, I hate leaving the house. I like the food here, and I got a pool for swimming.

---

HERE'S A LIST OF MY LEAST FAVORITE PEOPLES, IN ASCENDING ORDER:

3. The French
2. The Filipinos
1. Everybody else

---

## ZE FRENCH

Let me tell you why I hate the French. First of all, those bastards wouldn't let us fly our planes over their precious country when we were on our way to bomb that raghead Qaddafi. A lot of people forgot this; *I didn't*. That's some gratitude after we saved their snail-eating asses during WWII when they lay down like sheep for Hitler.

People talk about the French resistance. That was a myth. There was no French resistance. Those rat bastards were manufacturing more stuff for the Nazi war effort than any other occupied territory. Did you know that the French actually became the number-one producer of goods for the Nazis?! They couldn't wait to please those pricks. If I should ever go to France I'll pack a tape recorder so I can play a tape of Hitler's speeches every time a Frenchman gives me a dirty look for being an American. "Remember that voice," I will say. "That's who we saved you from. You should kiss my feet daily, worship my cellulite-ridden ass, and say God bless America for kicking some ass when you were lying down like sheep." *No one remembers. I remember.* I'd play that fucking tape every day. My tape recorder would blare Germans screaming *"Sieg Heil! Sieg Heil!"* through the streets of France. And if some asshole tried to fuck with me I'd scream from the top of my lungs, "LAFAYETTE WAS A PUSSY! THE BASTILLE FELL LIKE IT WAS CARDBOARD!"

Most people say, "Don't live in the past." But look at the French today. We offer them money, technology, and business opportunities, and they dump shit on us. And we take it. We bring them Euro Disney, a multibillion-dollar industry, and at the opening they have the balls to throw tomatoes at Disney chairman Michael Eisner because the Disney uniforms are not part of their precious culture. Would putting Mickey Mouse in a beret solve their problem? Those dirty scumbags with those stupid berets. They're not even hats. A piece of cloth should cover your head if it's going to be called a hat. That's not a hat, it's an oversized yarmulke. That ridiculous cowboy hat Garth Brooks wears is more sensible.

Think about it. Why would any sane American businessman want to invest good money with those dogs after they piss all over a new enterprise? *Screw them and their Eiffel Tower!* I don't know anyone who's been over there and hasn't been disappointed by the Eiffel Tower. They should knock it over on its side, point it toward Euro Disney, and use it as a road directional sign. This Eiffel Tower is a major tourist attraction? It looks like it was made with an Erector set. We should take all the French to New York and show them the Empire State Building. That's what the Eiffel Tower would look like if they ever completed construction.

But Howard, you might say, what about ze French women? The hell with French women and their hairy legs. Unless they're chambermaids and they're using their legs to pick up dust in the rooms, they're useless. We got the best women right here. Catherine Deneuve is fat and has small tits. Brigitte Bardot was okay in her prime but now she looks just like those fucking dogs she takes care of. And what's with those bidets French women use? I once asked a Frenchie on my show what the hell those bidets were for anyway. Something about cleaning the vagina and asshole. What about toilet paper? You mean this great French inventor felt a need to develop something beyond toilet paper? A porcelain water fountain for my asshole. This is overkill. You want to work on something? Work on a cure for cancer.

Unfortunately, the only time I get to rag directly on French people is when their broadcasters come to "observe" me in the studio. They really come to steal whatever they can understand of my radio show. One time I got a visit from this guy named Louique, who was the musical director of some station in Paris.

He was one of those smooth, good-looking French guys that women get a fondue going in their panties over. Radio in France must really blow 'cause his idea of good radio was to play a lot of so-called world music,

**At the mike berating the French . . . "Jerry Lewis is an asshole."**

which is mostly weird Japanese noises and a lot of African stuff, with people sitting around bongoing on rocks and every once in a while banging the plates in their lips to break up the monotony. So I really unloaded on Louique.

"Charles de Gaulle was a pussy. Maurice Chevalier sucks. Laurence Olivier sucks and Charo was a pussy."

"But Laurence Olivier *ees* English, and Charo, she is from Spain," he said.

"Big deal, it's all Europe," I said. "Your whole country is filled with snail eaters. Your only hero besides a hunchback is that little bastard Napoleon! And what's with Jerry Lewis being a genius? He's considered an asshole here. Know what else I don't like? You're hiding that child rapist Roman Polanski. Send him back."

I was on a roll but the lad was here for fatherly radio

advice. "Look, the only purpose for radio is to make money. You can buy a stereo and play weird world-music records in your house. This is a business, get the most you can, cut the balls out from under your competition. Screw 'em and make the most money. You French guys don't like the Jews, either. You're anti-Semites."

"No, we have no such—" he protested.

"You're anti-Israel! What's the beef with them, a bunch of Jews just trying to live in the desert? Hey, what's a dreidel? Do you know?"

"I don't know."

"What's a yarmulke?"

"I don't know."

"What's a Hanukkah?"

"I don't know, my English isn't so good."

"I rest my case. He's totally ignorant. Yves Montand sucks. Louis Malle's a creep. Toulouse-Lautrec was a troll. And we know most French designers are homos."

"Yes, that's true," he was forced to admit.

Since he'd come for my advice as a respected radio personality in America, here's what I offered: "The more money you make at a radio station, the better it is. Because when you have money you have power, and when you have power, you have freedom, freedom to bomb Libya. Just remember these words: Radio is business. Don't put up a fight. Repeat after me. Radio . . ."

"Radio . . ." He was doing it.

"is . . ."

"is . . ."

". . . a business. . . . Say it."

He repeated it like a frog parrot.

"Now you've learned and now my job is done and you can leave. Good luck."

"Yeah, good luck, too," he said.

"You're not insulted, are you?" I said solicitously.

"No, not at all."

"You should be. I don't understand. What, am I slipping? Did I forget anything? Jerry Lewis . . . Libya . . . the Eiffel Tower is ugly." I couldn't get to him. So I had Fred put on a Hitler speech with sound effects of sheep baaing over it. "Remember that voice," I said. "That's who we saved you from. You should play that on your station every day and say, 'God bless America for kicking ass when we were lying down like sheep.' Play this every day instead of all that Japanese music. Japan was bombing you. *No one remembers. I remember.*"

## THE KRAUTS

But it's not just the French. I get Kraut broadcasters, too. The Casey Kasems of Buchenwald all come to learn at the half-Jewish feet of the greatest radio personality in the world. I guess they can smell a gold tooth a mile away. And they all have such stupid names. Fritz, Hans, Claus; those names are no good for the radio. I give them good wacky radio names like Adolf the K, Cousin Nazi, or Wolfman Jackboots. One time I was invaded by six of them, at once. Six of Germany's future broadcasters were booked to come to my studio and observe American radio. These six sons of storm troopers were here to soak up all of my great radio wisdom so I put them through the usual drill.

When they first came into the studio, I told them, "I do crazy stuff on the air. Crazy stuff like 'Let's throw *ze Jews in ze oven*, we *haff* a contest today. All you Jews line up. Ninety-second caller goes in the oven. Shouldn't you give us your ovaries now? Okay everybody, it's Human Lampshade Thursday.' "

They looked at me with tight grins and steely blue eyes. They didn't think I was funny. Meanwhile, they were one generation away from the *shitheads* who *fucked* with us during World War II.

"Let me tell you." I suddenly got serious. "As Germany has known for years, gold is the way to invest. You guys have been into gold for years. In fact, my grandmother had a lot of gold teeth I want back. Nineteen people in her family were wiped out. Hey listen, let bygones be bygones. Seriously, some of my best friends are Germans. My grandfather thought he'd outsmart everyone, he swallowed his teeth before they took him to the chambers, but they found them in the ashes."

They weren't laughing. But I wanted the Germans to understand that this ugly American still held a grudge about that stupid Holocaust thing.

"Nobody would have gotten so upset if you didn't exterminate people. You moved too quick. Japan's got the right idea. Now they're our friends, and they're conquering us. Let's band together, let's be brothers." Now they really looked confused.

"Seriously, you guys are the master race, right?

**On the air teaching the Krauts about Human Lampshade Thursday.**

You're good-looking guys. Blond hair, blue eyes. Wish my parents would have been bred better. I'm wearing dark glasses to hide my big nose. Hey, I forgive you. Look how quickly we forgave the Jews for killing Jesus.

"Remember we're all brothers. Next time some drunk goes into a beer hall, ignore him. If he starts talking about world domination, say, 'Look, we're happy, our standard of living is way up. We have jobs in radio.'"

Just then my producer, Baba Booey, came into the studio. There was an angry listener calling in. We put her on the air.

"Is this Howard Stern? I think you're the rudest person in the world. Everything you said about Germans I found very rude and offensive and I don't know how those Germans can just sit there and let you talk about them like that."

"How old are you?" Robin asked.

"I am sixteen years old. I was born in Germany and I find everything you said very rude. Making fun of Germans, talking about Hitler, all that garbage." She was whining like a girl from the Five Towns.

"You don't think we should talk about Hitler?" I asked.

"It happened about forty years ago. Why don't you just leave it. You're acting like the Germans today still act that way. We're a new generation of Germans, we had nothing to do with what happened back then and most of those people didn't want it to happen."

Even though she was sixteen, I lost it. I started yelling. "Most of the people didn't want it to happen, honey, is that it? Your father ought to take you and spank you, you big dummy . . ."

"You're a real asshole," she retorted.

"Well, you are, too. Go to hell. The hell with you." I hung up on her. What a world-class philosopher this moron was.

Gilbert Gottfried, who was in the studio with me that day, started imitating her in a whining voice: "Stop talking to the Germans about Hitler and play more New Kids on the Block. Stop talking about the Holocaust, we want more Debbie Gibson!"

The Germans had had enough history for one day. It was time to wind this down. "You're gonna have to hide up in the attic with Anne Frank," Robin said cheerfully.

"God forbid, with my flatulence problem." I cut a big one. "Hah, a Jew."

---

## MY IMMIGRATION POLICY

Wherever I'm born, I stay, that's my rule of thumb. I don't try to go anywhere else. I'm happy where I am. The problem is, nobody else feels the same. Take the Mexicans. They're nice people. I got nothing against Mexicans, but if they're Mexicans, they should be in Mexico. And the ones that come here are so angry. Of course, I'd be confused and angry, too, if I had dark skin and white people's hair. Speaking of hair, how do you like those Hispanic chicks who dye their hair blond? That's an attractive look. No wonder some Spanish guys are ready to rape any white woman who comes along.

Look, if it was up to me I would open the world's borders to everyone so they could go anywhere. The only problem is that the United States is the only good country in the world. I don't see the Japanese opening their borders. The Germans try to rout anyone else out. Even Australia, a nation of criminals, keeps immigrants out. We take everybody's trash. We used to have an immigration policy in this country. During WWII a boat of nine hundred Jews tried to get into this country and we turned them away. Now no one's turned away. We used to get lawyers and professors coming here, fleeing intolerance. We got German rocket scientists, the crème de la crème. Now we get guys who aren't fit to be janitors.

HEY HOWARD HOW YA DOIN
HOW YA DOIN MAN
SO HOW YA DOIN
HEY MAN HOW YA DOIN
HOW YA DOIN
HOW THE HELL YA DOIN
HOWARD MAN HOW YA DOIN
HEY JUST WANTED TO KNOW HOW YA WERE DOIN

PRACTICING TO CALL THE HOWARD STERN SHOW

We're bank-rupt because it costs a fortune to assimilate all these immigrants. We're spending a fortune on social programs for people who come here with no skills, no jobs, and nothing to do. They have to be put on welfare. And we have to hire special bilingual teachers. Then they want signs in Spanish. *Excuse me, this is America. We speak English here.*

It's not just the Mexicans. A lot of people who come to this country don't want to assimilate. That's the difference between now and when my grandparents immigrated from Russia and Italy. They were so embarrassed that they couldn't read that they spent all their time trying to learn how to read and speak English.

When my grandparents came here, this was a huge, underpopulated country. Now it's filled up. But people still come and it's the fault of the damn French. They gave us that stupid Statue of Liberty to trick us. Some gift. Look what it's been attracting.

I remember one Haitian woman who called in to my show the day that I was discussing the Dominicans burning down Washington Heights, their own neighborhood, to protest a white cop who shot a drug dealer named Garcia. Hey, where I'm from, we give medals to cops who shoot drug dealers. Apparently, this Haitian woman was still steamed up about some comments I had made about Haitian immigrants.

"Hello, 'oward," she said.

"You got an accent. My grandparents worked their asses off to get rid of their annoying accents. You should do the same. Vere *you* from, honey?" I replied.

"Haiti. And I believe in voodoo. And if you don't stop saying bad things about Haiti, we gonna send a voodoo spell after you, 'oward."

"You know what, honey? You can do all the voodoo you want on me, it's okay. I'm not a backwards idiot who believes in voodoo. Don't embarrass the Haitian people."

She started screaming, *"I will! I will!"*

"A bitch like you comes over here and starts screaming about voodoo and Haitians everywhere are embarrassed by you. You know what, lady? Because you are such a moron I'm gonna put a voodoo spell on you. What do you think of that?"

All of a sudden she started screaming about Washington Heights. "And Garcia was shot in the back! Police are shooting people in the back!"

I couldn't take her irrational behavior. "Okay, lady. Here it is. I'm now going to reverse the situation. Because I'm the greatest radio man alive I will now put a voodoo hex on you. Here you go. *Ooh ga booga, ooh ga booga looga.*" It was an ancient voodoo curse I had picked up.

" 'oward, you're a jerk, 'oward."

"Shut up, lady. I'm not done. *Ooh ga booga looga.*"

"You think we're playing. We're not playing, 'oward."

"*Ooh ga booga! Ooh ga booga looga!*"

"We're gonna make a doll after you, 'oward."

"*Ooh ga booga looga.*"

"And Robin is sitting there, a black woman, and she's taking all dat shit from you!" she yelled.

"What? A filthy word came out of your mouth? Is that what you learned in America? *Ooh ga booga looga.*"

"Voodoo is a religion and it's my religion."

"Good. Voodoo is my religion, too, so, *Ooh ga booga looga.* I'm going to kill a chicken today. What's your name?"

"I'm not telling you."

"Tell me your first name so I can put the chicken's head on a stick and run around my house nude with it," I said.

"I'm going to make a doll and put some needles in the heart and you're gonna have a heart attack," she replied.

"Do me a favor. Answer me honestly. Do you own a television set?" I asked her.

"Yeah."

"You own a car?"

"Yeah."

"You got a car here, you got a TV here. It's pretty good here, isn't it?"

"NO!" she screamed. "I want to go back home!"

"*Ooh ga booga.*" I couldn't resist.

"I want to go back to my country. George Bush is a moron."

"Let me say something. In Haiti you don't have the balls to say anything about your leader, do you? You keep your mouth shut, Miss Voodoo. But all of a sudden you come to America and you got a big mouth about our president. How come if voodoo works you didn't stay in Haiti and put a voodoo curse on your president?"

She's screaming over all this. "No, I'm gonna put it on you and George Bush. George Bush is a KKK."

"KKK. KKK. I'm going to send you a friggin' inner tube and float your ass back to Haiti."

"Dat's what you think! Dat's what you think!"

I continued the assault. "Let me tell you something. Tonight with your voodoo, you cut up a pigeon and you put the pieces in your underwear, you smelly wench."

"YOU PUT YOUR FINGER IN YOUR BUTT AND YOU SMELL, SO I COULD DO THAT, TOO!" she screamed at the top of her lungs.

"This is America, the phone system works fine here," I explained. "This isn't Haiti, you don't have to yell out the window when you're on the phone."

I heard a male voice in the background.

"Who's in the background, Papa Doc?"

"Maybe."

I could sense that this poor woman was tense, so I signaled to Fred, and he pulled out a relaxation tape done by an Indian guru.

"You are completely tense, I want you to listen to this. Do what this tape says."

Suddenly mellow music filled the air, along with the heavy, wooden tones of an Indian.

"*Let's come to de neck area. Slightly roll de head to de right and then slowly to de left. Do this a few times and as you roll the head imagine that you are relaxing.*"

"Are you doing this, lady?"

"NO," she screamed.

"Do it," I encouraged her. "Roll your head. Roll your head right out the window."

"Do you have a job?" Robin asked.

"None of your business, Robin."

"You have no job and a TV and a car. God bless America, you should kiss George Bush's feet every night," I said.

"Oh, really! I spit in his face!"

"What has he done that's so horrible to you?"

"They kicked the president of Haiti out of the country and George Bush is part of this conspiracy."

"Why are you here?" I wondered.

"I don't want to be here."

"So why are you here?"

"Because of George Bush."

"George Bush brought you here?"

"I came here and I wanted to go back home."

"Do you want to go back home?"

"Yes."

"Okay, I'm going to do you the biggest favor of your life. I'm going to buy you a plane ticket to go back to Haiti, one way." But that wasn't good enough for her.

"Before you do that, there is a new government in there, get them out."

"Oh, now I have to topple a government. You know so much voodoo, why don't you go back there and get rid of them?"

"They have guns."

"So. You don't need guns, you have voodoo. *Ooh ga booga boo.* Tell you what. I'm gonna put you on hold, Gary will get your phone number and I will buy you a ticket. Leave your color television and car here and go home to your godforsaken Haiti."

I hung up on her. Just another day at the office.

## THE FILIPINOS

You can't even open your mouth on the air without having some interest group write a letter. Here's a letter we got that I read on the air. It was addressed to K-Rock's general manager, Tom Chiusano, from some California assemblyman who wanted to complain about my remarks about the Filipino people. I don't even remember what the hell I said about the Filipinos, but thankfully this group had "monitored" my show and they provided this guy with my remarks.

This guy is from the Office of Asian

**My leader:
Tom Chiusano.**

and Pacific Affairs. They got a whole office for these people. And he was writing to demand an on-air apology from me. Like I'll ever give him an apology. Anyway, he wrote:

> Dear Mr. Chiusano,
> I would like to bring to your attention the recent racial remarks made by Howard Stern. . . . "Filipinos are terrible people . . . Filipinos are the most depraved people in the world and probably worse than people from France . . ."

First of all, I never said that. I was talking about a segment of the Filipino population that caters to horny Americans by selling off their women. It disgusted me that so many Filipinos were so poverty stricken that they condoned the selling of their daughters into prostitution and, worse, slavery. And besides, I never said the Filipinos were worse than the French. They're not worse than the French. The French are the worst. If in a moment of frenzy I happened to say that there was somebody on the planet worse than the French, I stand corrected. Besides, what's so distasteful about my comments? The reason we have Asian Pacific Americans is because the Philippines is so despicable they left. Why are these people complaining about what I say? They should be back there and they wouldn't have heard it. I have to say nice things about Filipinos because a couple of guys came over here and suddenly they had balls? If they had such balls, why didn't they kick Marcos out? Where were they all those years with the shoes? It took them ten million years to get rid of Marcos. Everybody's so brave here in America. In their own countries they never speak up.

The letter went on:

> [Howard Stern said] "Parents are selling children for prostitution . . . . You can go in there and screw just about anybody . . ."

Well, prove me wrong.

> There was also said to be a comment by a caller. "He was in Manila and stayed at the Manila Hilton. He hired four midgets for sexual purposes and paid $1,000 for them." Mr. Stern responded, "You paid $1,000? For half the price you can own one of them."

It's true! Truth is my defense! It's unbelievable what goes on in the Philippines. There are men who will sell their daughters to you and it is documented. Why am I a bad guy for pointing that out? I'm not saying all Filipinos, I'm talking about a segment of Philippine society. By the way, this doesn't hurt the Philippines. Me saying that you can own a woman there for half the price of renting them certainly will help Filipino tourism. Most of the deviants in this country will run right over there.

Am I the first one to point out that you can get a Filipino bride for ten cents? I think not.

# Yes, I Am Fartman

Why is it that guys
who come from other
countries like India,
a country that's totally
destitute, a country with
no medical facilities, decide to
stay here after they get their
M.D.s? Why don't they go back and
help their own people? No, they
wind up here, buying expensive real
estate. Then they dress normal, in
business suits, and make their wives
wear those saris with their bellies
flopping out all over the place. It's
demeaning to the Indian women. I
don't see Indian men wearing those
diapers that Gandhi wore.

And what is it with the dots on their heads? Someone told me that the dot is actually a garage-door
opener. If the husband presses the dot, it opens the

double doors on the garage. Look, the Indians are very nice people but they worship cows and make bad movies and have dots on their heads. Then they move into white neighborhoods and ignore everyone in the town. They should loosen up.

This is America. They should assimilate. Here's my philosophy and it's very simple: IT'S VERY IMPORTANT THAT WE ALL ACT AS ONE!

I'm all for different races being here, but make an effort. Don't wear your culture like a badge of courage. Those wacky dots. Italian women don't walk around with pizzas on their heads. Jewish women don't go around with matzo on their backs. There are a couple of wackos like the Hasidim, but nobody takes them seriously. I'm trying to solve the world's problems. When they ask me to lecture before the United Negro College Fund (I know they will one day), I will tell them to try to act like white people. I tell the Jews to try to act like Christians. Everyone should try to act like white Christians.

But, you know, maybe it would be better if everybody just went back to where they came from. The Hispanics who come here and get into college by passing those ethnically weighted entrance exams (Question Two: Recite the words to "La Bamba"), go back to your people. Use your education to help them. Nobody wants to go back, nobody answers to a higher calling in life anymore. Except for me. I'm busy saving my country every day. I serve my country by marshaling my extraordinary superpowers in the pursuit of truth, justice, and the American way. *Yes, I am Fartman!*

## THE ORIGINS OF FARTMAN

Fartboy, age three.

Like all great superheroes, I had a traumatic childhood. My planet didn't blow up and my parents weren't killed, but I had hardships to overcome. I had a nervous stomach. And who wouldn't with a father who terrorized me so much.

My father would yell at me all week and then Sunday was family day. Sunday, my parents would take me and my sister into the city to get some culture. We'd go to a play or a movie at Radio City Music Hall, whatever. I hated going into Manhattan. I had a fear of the city. I don't handle things that well to begin with. I don't like walking around. I get confused. For me, it's better to stay at home where I know my environment.

But the main reason I hated going into Manhattan was gas. First, we'd eat a big meal at someplace like Joe's Pier 52. I was kind of a pudgy kid and I'd go wild. I'd have lobster bisque to start, and they kept bringing out this fresh hot bread so I'd eat a couple of loaves of that, then a whole bunch of salad and then a nice piece of fish and fries. Plus I ate real fast because at home when I got up from the table for a moment during a meal, my parents would assume I was done and would just grab my food. So I ate like a maniac and as soon as we left the restaurant the gas pains would start. During the show, I'd get horrible gas pains. I'd be moaning, fidgeting in my seat, and my parents would be really annoyed. I was ruining the show for everyone. "What's wrong with you?" my father would say.

"I gotta get home quick. I gotta go to the bathroom. I have bad gas."

"What's wrong with you? Why don't you pass some wind here? Do what I do. At the intermission, after the Rockettes are finished, go out in the lobby, walk over to the side, and let a few out." Fatherly advice.

"You're kidding. I should do that here in Radio City?"

"Who's gonna know it was you?" he said.

I couldn't believe my father was telling me to pass wind in Radio City Music Hall. At intermission my father took me out to the fancy lobby with the big chandeliers and everything. We walked over to the side and he said, "Make like you're talking to me. Just force it out while you're talking to me." I couldn't do it. I couldn't just force it out in the middle of the lobby of Radio City Music Hall. He was saying, "Go ahead, do it. Do it already. What's the problem with you, you're ruining the day." I'm sorry, I couldn't pass wind in the middle of a theater with my dad yelling at me to hurry up and fart. So we went back to our seats and I suffered through the movie. I was really in pain. I sat there for two hours wishing I was home. Misery.

Finally, fucking family day was over. We got in the car to drive back home to Long Island and I was in the backseat with my sister. My parents were in the front and I was holding my stomach and moaning.

My father was yelling at me to fart but I still couldn't, I was too embarrassed. I was moaning and my mother couldn't take it, so she said, "Ben, pull over and take him into a men's room and let him pass gas." We were in the middle of Manhattan, and my father was not too thrilled with all this. He was annoyed, he was yelling and screaming. My father saw a seedy hotel and pulled over. He grabbed me by the neck saying, "Come on, I don't see why we have to stop, we're going to be home in twenty-five minutes anyway." All this time, he was pulling me into the bathroom and pushing me in a stall. Now I'm sitting in this filthy stall in this seedy hotel with my old man pacing outside the stall, waiting to hear me pass gas. He's pacing, and my mother and sister are outside, alone in the car. How the hell am I supposed to be able to perform? You can't just let out gas on command, it takes a long time to let out gas. My belly is distended like a Biafran baby's at this point. I can't even move. *Oh, my God.* After pacing for five minutes, he said, "What's going on in there?"

"Dad," I said, "I can't fart."

The old man was steamed and he was screaming, *"Get out of there!"*

He pulled me out. Back in the car, I was moaning the whole way home. And then, at home, when I was comfortable, like a dog, I went into the bathroom and passed my wind.

I always had that problem with gas. Alison learned that early in our relationship. We were on a date. We had been going out a couple of months. Every time I'd be out with her, and we'd go to dinner, I'd have the same stupid problem. So we would get back to my apartment, and every couple of minutes I'd be talking to her and I would disappear for a few minutes, come back in, disappear another few minutes, come back in, disappear another few minutes, come back in. So finally she said, "When you disappear, where do you go?" Maybe she thought I was a drug addict or something.

"To tell you the truth, I'm a little uncomfortable, I'm a little gassy."

She said, "Why do you keep doing that? Why are you uncomfortable around me? You can pass gas in front of me. Feel free." Well, with that, the flood gates opened. I was farting day and night in front of the woman and she was nauseous. I smelled like death. Like a rat crawled up my ass and got buried way too deep in my sphincter and died. I was sure she was expecting to be gassed maybe once or twice a month. Never did she realize that she would be exposed to constant heavy doses. About a week after that, she was disgusted. "Listen," she said, "I want to go back to our original arrangement." But it was too late. I think that's why I married her. I couldn't go through that with another girl.

## FARTMAN TO THE RESCUE

How many people do you know who can turn their faults and disadvantages into something that works for a positive higher cause, a greater good? That, my friend, is what separates a common man from a superhero. I could have glided through life, making a nice living as a radio personality, secretly excusing myself from meetings and writing sessions to repair to the bathroom to rip off a rat. That would be the easy thing to do. But when your country cries out for you, when the greatest land in the world is threatened by the organized, synchronized, and simonized forces of evil, yes, when the going gets tough, the tough get blowing. There was no way for me to escape my destiny.

I had to be Fartman. I created this character out of frustration. Whenever there was a problem in the world I would call foreign embassies and yell at dignitaries in a very deep voice. When they ignored my demands I would fart into the phone. Real dignitaries, real people, getting farted on over the radio all over the world.

Fartman first hit the air when I was in Washington. I remember it well. A few miserable Poles had just declared martial law and poor Lech Walesa looked like he was going to have to organize a union of solitary confinement prisoners. This was a job for Fartman. I got on the air, called the Polish embassy, and actually got through to the Polish ambassador, farted into the phone, and the rest is history.

Years later, Fartman was called back to active duty. We were at K-Rock, it was July 6, 1988, and the United States had just made a dreadful but honest error. We had shot down an Iranian airbus, killing 290 people. The Iranians were outraged and milking the incident.

These were the very same people who had funded and orchestrated the terrorist groups that had taken innocent American civilians as hostages. As far as I was concerned, this was war. I decided to take some positive action. We would call the Iranian consulate on the air that day.

"I can say the things the president can't say, Robin," I said as I dialed the number.

"Is this the Iranian embassy? This is Fartman. We're on the radio."

"Yes."

"Are you Iranian?"

"Yes."

"Listen, douche bag," I told him. "I'm gonna try to talk sense to you and if you don't listen I'm going to fart into this phone." There was silence; I had his attention.

"Look, let me explain America's position. Sometimes in the heat of battle you look up in the sky and see a plane and feel you are being attacked. It was an honest mistake."

My logic must have stunned the madman because he remained silent. And silence pisses Fartman off.

"Now get ready." *PHHHHHT!* I unleashed a masterful gas missile. "That is all I have to say about this issue."

"If that makes you feel better . . ." was his reply.

He was nonchalant but the reaction was instantaneous. Our switchboards were flooded by calls from listeners who called to pay homage to their new superhero. It is not a coincidence at all that the Ayatollah soon shuffled off this mortal coil.

## THE RETURN OF FARTMAN

Unfortunately, we had to call on Fartman many times over the next few years. When a hostage was killed, Fartman called the Tehran Hyatt and chastised a reservations clerk. When the dreadful massacre took place in Tiananmen Square, he called the Chinese consulate and then called the world-famous F.A.O. Schwarz toy store and demanded that all their Chinese checkers be removed from the shelves. When Iraq invaded Kuwait, it incurred the full wrath of Fartman. Saddam has not recovered to this day.

Wherever injustice reared its ugly head, Fartman was there. When General Noriega ruled Panama with his pockmarked despotic face and hand, Fartman reached out to the Panamanian Marriott to offer his services:

"My tushy rules and drools, my digestive system pumps foul air for truth and justice. I squat and fart and whoosh my way into the hearts of my people, as my hemorrhoids sway in the breeze, my stenching toots burn nostrils and bowl over bad guys because *I am Fartman!* I can blow Burt Reynolds's toupee from here to Panama. I am calling the Panamanian people to offer my services. . . . Hello?"

"Panama Marriott."

"My name is Fartman. I'm calling from the United States. May I speak to the reservations desk?"

"Reservations. Can I help you?"

"This is a radio station, this is Fartman. Are you familiar with Fartman?"

My first appearance as Fartman, with Adam West on my TV show. I threw the costume together in five minutes, complete with a toilet-seat necklace.

Friends of Fartman: Fred Norris, the King of Mars Man, and Belly Button Man (Jackie Martling, right)

"Are we familiar with Fartman? No, sir."

"In the United States I am considered a superhero. Because of my unique colon, I am able to help the people of America. I would like to offer you help in your trials with General Noriega. If you need me in time of war I am *el farto stinko hombre*. Do you hear what I'm doing? Listen." *PHHHTT!* "Are you in fear of General Noriega or can you speak?"

"No, I cannot."

Poor woman. She was afraid to speak. "I will help you. I will come over with my farting power. I will blow up General Noriega and his armies. My flying dingleberries will put his eyes out."

"Okay, so whenever we need you, we can call you?"

"That is correct," I replied. She was completely out of it. What kind of a lunatic would take Fartman seriously?

"We'll be waiting for you then," she politely responded.

"And I'm sorry about Ricky Ricardo and Zorro."

## FARTMAN DEFENDS SALMAN RUSHDIE

Fartman's greatest test came at the hands of a Libyan peasant. It all started when we decided to support the great author Salman Rushdie, who was under a death decree from the Ayatollah for his book *The Satanic Verses*. I decided that Fartman should read from the book. When the Iranian embassy didn't answer, an alternate plan was hatched. I asked my producer Boy Gary to call any hotel in Iran in order to establish diplomatic ties. "I've got the Tripoli Hilton on the line," he proudly announced.

"Hello. Is this the Tripoli Hilton? This is Fartman calling from American radio."

Robin was the first to realize Boy Gary's error.

"Tripoli?" Robin said, confused. Boy Gary was in a state of confusion once again. We had called Libya in error.

"Oh, this is Libya?" I asked.

"Yes."

"Wait a second. This is Libya? I was supposed to be calling Iran but this will have to do." It wasn't the first mistake Gary had made and it wouldn't be the last. "Let's call Australia next, Boy Moron."

"Hello, this is Fartman, is anybody there? Hello? This is Fartman, you dothead. Somebody must be there."

Finally, "Hello?"

"Yes, this is Fartman. Can you speak English?"

"Yes."

"I am going to read from *The Satanic Verses*." I began my narrative. " '*You couldn't find your way to heaven or what? Insensitive words to speak to a woman.*' " Maybe Rushdie did deserve a death decree.

"Yes?"

"Can you say anything but yes?" I wondered.

"Yes."

We laughed.

"What's funny?"

"I am not afraid to read *The Satanic Verses*. Are you afraid to read them?"

"I think you are crazy," said the infidel on the phone.

**The sequels to *Fartman, the Movie*.**

"I am not, I am Fartman. I can blast you with just one fart. I will toot until all is well. Because my farts are wet."

"I think you're crazy, you know."

"I don't like Qaddafi. He sniffs camel farts!" I unleashed a mighty blast. *PHHHHT!* "I'm not afraid of him. One sniff of my gas powers and he'll be knocked unconscious. You know all those holes in Qaddafi's face? They're from the time that I met him and blasted him with one of my farts." This was war! "If I see you, I will fart in your face. Where do you fart? In your house, in the market, in bed with your hairy wife?" *PHHTTT!* "I am not afraid of Qaddaf—"

"Everybody is afraid of my leader!" he suddenly bellowed. Was it something I said? I'd found his weak spot.

"He's a coward! He's afraid of *us*! That's why he resorts to terrorism and cross-dressing."

"You donkey."

"I'm not a donkey, douche lips, I'm Fartman. America's the greatest country in the world, where everyone is allowed to practice freedom of religion. Unfortunately, even the Muslim religion."

"You are sick, I think," he said.

Robin suddenly interrupted. "I don't know why we're railing against the Libyans when it's the Iranians . . ."

"This is the only number Gary has. Gary, you're an idiot. Why am I talking to Libya?"

Gary stepped into the room. "He's Islamic. The whole nation of Islam is against the book."

"Let me tell you, your country stinks on ice. I wish

you were here so I could fart in your face. Are you wearing sandals?"

"No."

"Aha. You are wearing sandals. My rectum knows all."

*PHHHT!*

He grunted, obviously weakened by the cumulative effect of my blasts, then cursed, and hung up. At least we found an Islamic. We would have spoken to a Puerto Rican if it was up to Gary.

## FARTMAN GOES TO HOLLYWOOD

Hey, what's more American than doing something heroic and then wanting to cash in on it? Altruism goes only so far. I decided it was time to take Fartman to Hollywood . . . to the MTV awards.

The first problem was finding a copresenter for me. MTV couldn't get anybody to appear with me. For about a month they made phone calls to everyone in Hollywood, endless phone calls, and no one would appear with me. I wanted Cindy Crawford but she wouldn't appear with me. Then I wanted to get that girl from "Beverly Hills 90210," Shannen Doherty, but she's a friggin' Young Republican. She wouldn't do it. No one would do it. Then Luke Perry heard me bitching about it on the air and he volunteered to copresent with me. He was really nice about it.

A designer put together my costume to feature my ass cheeks. And I made the belt tight so my belly would hang out. I wanted this to be the most disgusting thing people had ever seen. I wanted people to retch over my outfit. I ate my ass off the weekend before so the costume would be extra gross. I also decided that I was going to fly in as Fartman. I figured I'd fly in about five feet above the stage.

When I got there before the show, the same guys who flew Peter Pan were going to fly me. Oh, great, this'll be a piece of cake, I thought. When I showed up for the rehearsal, they said, "You gotta go up there. Thirty feet in the air." Suddenly I'm a Flying Wallenda. Wait a minute. They want me thirty feet up in the air suspended by two little wires when I ate like a pig all weekend?

They had to raise me up in stages. And I'm shaking. I'm trembling with fear, because you have no idea how scary it is. They got me up there and said, "Stick out your hands. Let go of the wires." I couldn't even move. When I got down, the one thing they kept saying to me was, "When you're on the stage, don't spin around, because you'll tangle the wires. And if you tangle the wires, it's *not good*."

Backstage before the show, I suddenly felt like I was back in high school. Everybody there was trying so hard to be cool. The blacks were on one side, the whites on the other; everybody was going out of their

I put on twenty-five pounds so my belly and butt would look extra gross, hanging out of my costume. The backside needed full openings to gain maximum comedy impact. These are shots of the fitting session. Believe it or not, it took three fittings to develop this mess.

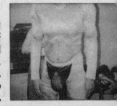

**Designer Ted Shell's working sketch of Fartman for the MTV awards show.**

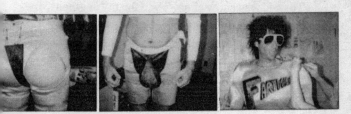

way trying to look like this whole gig was a burden, trying to outcool each other. That "My Prerogative" guy, Whitney Houston's husband, Bobby Brown, was back there with about nine hundred black guys hanging around, bodyguards or something. If you're a white guy, they all stare at you, and they don't smile. Nobody can smile at each other. When I saw Bobby Brown, I said, "What's going on in there?" He barely smiled. Hey, Bobby Brown's a multimillionaire married to Whitney Fucking Houston. How tough could that be? It's gotta be fun to get up and dance. On his worst day his feet are sore.

My ass was so fucking embarrassing, I kept covering myself. Everybody was staring at me. You have to remember, my buttocks were full of fucking pockmarks, cellulite, hairs, all kinds of shit. But the reaction from every celebrity I passed was unbelievable. I walked by Mick Jagger, and he was disgusted. I'm standing in this dressing room, and all of a sudden, there was a Michael Jackson look-alike in there and he was looking at me like *I'm* some kind of jerk. He was a fucking Michael Jackson look-alike, and he was staring at me? I passed by Shannen Doherty, and she gave me a look like, "You fucking piece of shit." It was a very strange vibe going up to do this.

Then it was show time. Time for my segment. I was thirty feet in the air and I looked down and saw Luke Perry being introduced. He went to the podium and said, "I would like to introduce my copresenter 'cause no one else has the balls to show up and do it." Pretty cool, I thought. "From a land far away and long, long

ago, it's a bird, it's a plane"—
hey he was really getting into
it—"it's a really bad smell.
Ladies and gentlemen, F-F-
F-F-Fartman!" Whap! I was
on my way down. The farting
noises were coming right on
cue, I was booming out, "Yes,
I'm Fartman. I'm the superhero Fartman." I landed on
the stage in one piece. So far,
so good. "Superman is nothing. Yes, behold the most
beautiful of sights. It is this." I turned my back to the
audience and stuck out my buttocks. The audience
was going wild.

We were stealing the show. Luke was going wild
applauding. "Yes, I am Fartman." I turned around
with my back to the audience again. "Is the camera

getting a good
shot of my beau-
tiful ass? Look at
it. It has pow-
ers." The place
was going wild.
"Allow me to
demonstrate the
greatest farting

powers of all." I bent over, tensed up, and *BOOM!*
the fucking podium exploded in a cloud of smoke. I
blew the podium apart with my fart! I couldn't believe

I was fucking doing this. I mean, I was almost forty years old. How sick was this?

"Luke, look at my ass." Luke was my disciple now. "Touch it for power. Rub it!" Luke held his hands up and grabbed my cheeks as if he were worshiping at the altar of my anus. Then he held his hands up, like he was cured. I felt like Jimmy Swaggart. "Yes, you may be laughing at my ass now, but when my movie *Fartman* becomes number one, all of Hollywood will kiss my ass." I farted to punctuate the sentence. "Do not adjust your televisions at home. This is really my ass." Another fart. There was no stopping me now. "Who of you would like to touch my ass?" The whole first ten rows started squealing in delight. A cute young girl jumped onto the stage. "C'mon up here, honey, touch it for power." I had this total stranger kneading my buttocks. This was too weird. "Yes, thank you, darling." It was time to present the awards, but I was on a roll.

"How did that ass feel, Luke?"

"Great ass, man." He pinched my belly fat. I was beginning to really like this kid.

"Now that you have saved us from the dangers of clean breathable air . . ." He was starting in on the business at hand but I wasn't through yet. I leaned over, grabbed his face, and planted a wet kiss on his cheek.

"He's the next James Dean," I crowed. "Let's get to the category filled with flashbacks and smoke machines, the best metal/hardrock video." They showed the clips of the nominees. When they came back from the clips, I had my back to the audience and I was shaking my Jell-O-ed ass. I opened the envelope. "The winner is Metallica," I boomed.

I love the band Metallica, and their last CD is some of the best music I ever heard, but these guys were taking the event way too seriously.

These two creeps from Metallica came down to accept the award. One of them, Lars Ulrich, was this total idiot who thought he was God's gift to the world of compact-disc technology. The other guy, a Carlos Santana look-alike, was wearing a beret. Enough said. This Lars jerk immediately went into a little self-pitying speech about how long it had been before these creeps won something from MTV. Meanwhile, the audience was going apeshit over me and Luke fooling around on the side. This jerk Lars started screaming at the audience to shut up. I couldn't believe he was telling his so-called fans to shut up. Then he started yelling at me, in the middle of his acceptance speech. "Hey, man, don't steal all the attention here, okay." What a dick.

Afterward, I was in the press room, having forgotten I was in my outfit. I was walking around and people were like nauseated. I went and posed for all these pictures, and they made every newspaper, with my disgusting ass and belly sticking out. Then there was all this debate in the press as to whether or not I should have done this, how it was such a terrible, terrible thing, how it brought a complete lack of decorum to the MTV awards. I'm going, "Excuse me. Decorum? This is MT Fucking V!"

## WHAT DO YOU THINK OF HOWARD STERN'S ASS?

*(Asked of celebs at the press conference after the MTV event)*

**ANTHONY KIEDIS,** *Red Hot Chili Peppers:* I was more impressed by other things this evening.

**DENNIS LEARY,** *Comic:* Watching Howard Stern's ass was the most fun I ever had, man.

**DANA CARVEY,** *Comic and Host of Show:* I'm still haunted by it. I tried the Fartman outfit on later and we took snapshots and compared our asses. I thought he was really funny. It was great . . . we love each other very much.

**CINDY CRAWFORD,** *Model:* I thought it was disgusting and if my ass looked like that I wouldn't show it on national television.

Hey, Cindy, you better hope your ass doesn't look like mine because your looks are the only talent you have. To tell you the truth, I'm thinking about stuffing a balloon up my ass to make it look better. Or better yet, maybe I'll buy Cindy's incredibly dangerous exercise video. Give me a break, idiot. You empty-headed bim. "It was disgusting." No kidding, honey, that's why I showed it. All she has is the ability to look good. Let me tell you, Cindy, I guarantee as soon as you start looking a little old, I bet Richard Gere starts seeing other women. What do you think, he's there for your brains? Believe me, in ten years we'll see if you're still together. I'm sure your religious husband, the cerebral Richard Gere, will stay with you when you look bad. Your personality is great when you look like Cindy Crawford, but Cindy Crawford at forty is not going to be Cindy Crawford. I want to be there the day Cindy Crawford gets into a disfiguring car accident and Richard Gere has to live out his years staring at a legless, toothless, titless Cindy Crawford. Oh, please, dear Lord, let me be there for that big event.

> "I wouldn't mind sitting across the table from Howard. He's cute."
> —Carol Alt

> "Jeers to shock jock and fledgling E! Entertainment Television talk-show host Howard Stern for his asinine appearance on the MTV Video Music Awards. Where was the infamous blue dot when we needed it?"
> —*TV Guide*, December 26, 1991

Lord, I offer you this prayer so that I might be a witness to Cindy Crawford's disfiguring car crash.

> *Dear Lord: I am a sinner. I need Jesus Christ to come into my life and become my Lord and Savior. I give my life to you in Jesus' name. For whosoever shall call upon the name of the Lord shall be saved. My prayer is that you will allow me to be a part of this tremendous event when Cindy loses all her looks and is forced to rely on that dynamic personality. Thank you.*

## WHAT DO YOU THINK OF HOWARD STERN'S ASS?

**SAMMY HAGAR,** *Lead Singer of Van Halen: Howard Stern is a jerk. He ruined the whole show. I don't know why you let him up there.*

Here's a guy who's desperately searching for an image. He has no image so his new image is he's street tough, a scrappy fighter, Hagar the Horrible. His big beef with me is that I don't enjoy him in Van Halen. That's pretty pathetic, isn't it? So now he's walking around strutting his stuff, "I'm gonna kick his ass." He's not kicking anybody's ass. A multimillionaire who's smart enough not to kick anyone's ass, who's he fooling? But

"If I were selling zero records, he wouldn't be on my case. He's a loser. I'll kick his ass if I ever see him."
—Sammy Hagar

he's going to come off like some scrappy young rock star. He's full of shit. He's a phony. I was sitting right there, three feet from him. Hard to miss me. He's a calculated businessman, that's all. I'm so sick of these millionaires trying to be street-tough gangsters. Wait until Van Halen starts going out in concerts and they start screaming out "Howard Stern" wherever he goes. Whenever you see Sammy Hagar just scream out *"Howard Stern!"* Make him nuts.

# More and More Hate Mail

Dear Robin and Howard,

This morning I happened to tune in to your talk show and I have a question. What is the aim of your program? It didn't entertain or inform or instruct. I also have some comments to make. Mother Teresa, Cardinal O'Conner, and the Knights of Columbus are all good people and should not be the butt of your "jokes." Concerning Mother Teresa's garb - she lives in India and is wearing the native woman's dress. Why did you have to emphasize anything about her derriere?

This USA founded By Christians has nothing Now to Brag About. The Howard STern Show out of N.Y is FilTering the People's Airways with dirty, FilThy Talk, Slut Too dirty To mention & SomeThing Needs To Be done, men's minds Are evil continually The Bible SAYs. Howard STern will eventually rot in hell!

Sirs: —

STERN, you CONSTANTLY USE THE Name of OUR Lord in VAIN. You ARE A FULL BLOODED Jew! You LOOK + SMELL LIKE A Jew, You ARE evil + SLANDER OTHERS LIKE A Jew. USE THE NAME OF your CHIEF RABBI — or MoSES WHEN you MUST CURSE. LEAVE THE NAME OF OUR LORD + SAVIOR JESUS CHRIST OFF OF YOUR DIRTY TONGUE. YOU ARE A DISGRACE TO THE HUMAN RACE - DIE JEW BASTARD DIE !!

DEAR MR. STERN:

I WAS VERY TROUBLED BY YOUR DISCUSSION WITH LINDA BLAIR IN WHICH YOU AGAIN ALLUDED TO YOUR WIFE'S "BREAST CANCER" FROM WHICH SHE IS EXPECTED TO DIE SUGGESTING MS. BLAIR WOULD BE A SUITABLE REPLACEMENT.

To Howard Stern "Sleeze",

I'm so incensed, and ashamed after listening to your program today where you "bashed" poor Mrs. Bush. I'll say this, if it were me, I'd get to that studio, and blacken your miserable crossed eyes, as you would deserve it throughly.

Here is a women who has done no harm to you or the American Public. You have demeaned and defamed her in your worst thoughtless manner. You have also offended all women regardless of what age they are. How about your mother Howard? Maybe she has cheese in her folds too.

# The Wack Pack

CHAPTER
10

I've always been fascinated by people on the fringe.
So it was natural that as soon as I got a radio show,
I started cultivating these very special people as regu-
lars. To me, they're much more interesting and compelling than any stupid celebrity who's touring to promote his latest mass-media drivel. And with repeated
exposure on my shows, these unusual people actually
become stars. Before we had him on the show, Fred
the Elephant Boy was an adult virgin working in some
crummy job in Manhattan and living in Queens. Now,
after we've made him a star in his own right, he trav-
els around the country introducing professional wres-
tlers when he's not working in his crummy job in Man-

hattan and living in Queens. But at least we got him laid!

On the following few pages, we present a pictorial gallery of my famous Wack Pack. These are the true stars of my program who, by virtue of their unusual talents, have attained a special status on my show. Long may their tongues aflutter, long may their neurons misfire, long may their penises burn.

### KING OF ALL MESSENGERS
#### *(CHRIS GIGLIO)*

*Defining characteristic:* Has a regular job, wife, and kids.

*Origins:* Made a phony phone call to Donahue and played it on Howard's radio show.

*Greatest accomplishment:* Was on CNN live during the coverage of the World Trade Center bombing aftermath. Told CNN he was trapped on the eightieth floor. Claimed that a gas leak from Fartman caused an explosion in the building. When asked why he wasn't evacuating the building with the rest of the people he said he was waiting to talk to Stuttering John or Baba Booey.

*Future ambition:* To produce a cassette of his greatest prank phone calls like his hero, Captain Janks.

### CAPTAIN JANKS
*(THOMAS CIPRIANO)*

*Defining characteristic:* Adopted the twisted persona of his commanding officer in the army.

*Origins:* Made the first phony Howard Stern call to the Larry King show.

*Greatest accomplishment:* The time he sneaked past the screeners of Jerry Lewis's MD telethon impersonating Larry King and asked, "What do you think of Howard Stern?"

*Future ambition:* To move out of his parents' house.

### KENNETH KEITH KALLENBACH

*Defining characteristic:* The ultimate airhead.

*Origins:* Wrote a letter to my TV show and claimed he could blow smoke through his eyes. When he attempted to do it, all he could do was vomit. A television first.

*Greatest accomplishment:* Blowing up his genitals at a bowling alley in Union, New Jersey, during the taping of my TV show and getting thrown off the set by producer Dan Forman.

*Future ambition:* To move out of his parents' house.

## SIOBHAN (pronounced Shivonne)

*Defining characteristic:* He cross-dresses. Also has a third nipple.

*Origins:* Wrote a letter to the show and went on Transsexual Dial-a-Date. Frequently propositioned me when he was trying to be a woman.

*Greatest accomplishment:* Asexual for over three years.

*Future ambition:* To retain his penis.

### FRED THE ELEPHANT BOY
*(FRED SCHREIBER)*

*Defining characteristic:* His speech impediment.

*Origins:* Was recommended to Baba Booey by a fellow employee who thought he'd be great on the show because of his speech impediment and because he was a twenty-eight-year-old virgin.

*Greatest accomplishment:* Finally got laid after a second Dial-a-Date.

*Worst moment:* Was walking across the room at Captain Janks's house and tripped over the phone cord. He fell face first into the phone and his nose disconnected the call while Janks was next on line with Larry King to speak to Governor Mario Cuomo.

*Future ambition:* To get laid for the second time in his life and to move out of his parents' house.

### VINNIE D'AMICO

*Defining characteristic:* Eats live worms.

*Origins:* Came up to the radio show and told Baba Booey he would eat a mouse if he was allowed on the show.

*Greatest accomplishment:* Eating a live mouse in a club in Manhattan after choking it and dipping it in olive oil.

*Worst moment:* Was prevented by armed agents of the ASPCA from doing the same thing at the taping of my live U.S. Open Sores show at the Nassau Coliseum.

*Future ambition:* To stick his head in a ceiling fan while it's on. Don't try this at home!

### VINNIE MAZZEO

*Defining characteristic:* So desperate for a laugh as a stand-up comedian that he sets his penis on fire when bombing at local comedy clubs.

*Origins:* Gave me a picture of himself lighting himself on fire.

*Greatest accomplishment:* Setting his genitals on fire and frying an egg over them at the Underwear and Negligee Party.

*Worst moment:* Immediately after setting his genitals on fire and frying an egg over them at the Underwear and Negligee Party.

*Future ambition:* To get a laugh without burning himself.

### DR. MARSHALL KING

*Defining characteristic:* Not wacky himself but he gets people to do wacky things. Can get beautiful semi-naked babes to think they're having an orgasm every time they rub their noses by giving them a posthypnotic suggestion.

*Origins:* Found at listener's K-Rock house party in Westchester.

*Greatest accomplishment:* Getting two beautiful semi-naked babes to sit on my lap and orgasm simultaneously.

*Future ambition:* To work your parties and Bar Mitzvahs.

### RACHEL THE SPANKER

*Defining characteristic:* Can smoke cigarettes using her vagina.

*Origins:* Sent me a dirty postcard in which she fantasized spanking me in the studio. Her fantasies were fulfilled.

*Greatest accomplishment:* Sucked my toes, attempted vaginal insertion of my big toe while under the console . . . nude.

*Future ambition:* None that we know of.

### DANIEL CARVER
(KKK GUY)

*Defining characteristic:* Was fired from his job because of his Ku Klux Klan membership and the lunatic race messages on his telephone hot line.

*Origins:* His KKK hot line was often played by me on my radio show.

*Greatest accomplishment:* Was center square on Homeless Howiewood Squares game show on my TV show.

*Worst moment:* On our Butt Bongo video segment, Guess Who's the Jew, he scored zero.

*Future ambition:* To cleanse his race of "niggers, kikes, faggots, and Mexicans."

### THE KIELBASA QUEEN

*Defining characteristic:* Is able to deep-throat thick, twelve-inch kielbasas.

*Origins:* Came to open call for Super Bowl girls. Recommended by her friend, the Snake Queen.

*Greatest accomplishment:* Got a Naples (Florida) affiliate to drop my TV show after she deep-throated a thick, twelve-inch kielbasa.

*Future ambition:* To become the Watermelon Queen.

### CELESTE

*Defining characteristic:* Drags her foot.

*Origins:* Called radio show.

*Greatest accomplishment:* Had sex with a blind man for our TV show.

*Worst moment:* Getting dropped by nurses and breaking her hip after undergoing radiation treatment for cancer in a hospital.

*Future ambition:* To live a long and healthy life.

### MELROSE LARRY GREEN

*Defining characteristics:* Holds up signs at the intersection of Melrose and Highland in Los Angeles at least once a day.

*Origins:* Hounded Gary and Stuttering John in a coffee shop until they noticed him.

*Greatest accomplishment:* At a

gas station, he ran into rap star Ice-T, who admitted to being a big fan. Larry said, "Of Howard or me?" Ice-T answered, "I never heard of you, but I like Howard."

*Worst moment:* Not getting on the show for months, therefore his celebrity dried up.

*Future ambition:* To be an unpaid Los Angeles correspondent for the "Howard Stern Show" or mayor of Los Angeles.

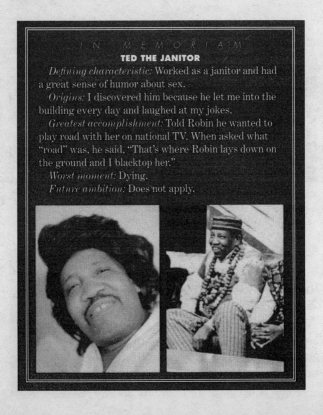

IN MEMORIAM
**TED THE JANITOR**

*Defining characteristic:* Worked as a janitor and had a great sense of humor about sex.

*Origins:* I discovered him because he let me into the building every day and laughed at my jokes.

*Greatest accomplishment:* Told Robin he wanted to play road with her on national TV. When asked what "road" was, he said, "That's where Robin lays down on the ground and I blacktop her."

*Worst moment:* Dying.

*Future ambition:* Does not apply.

# The Power of Negative Thinking

## *Celebrities Who Irritate Me*

CHAPTER

11

Oh, man, my blood is boiling just thinking about all the self-indulgent, narcissistic, self-important celebrities who walk around and act as if they're God's gift to the planet. I hate these arrogant jerks! They have a carefully cultivated show-biz good-guy veneer that

> "You ain't made it until you get hit by Howard Stern."
> —Tony Orlando

masks their insincerity and greed. With me, what you hear is what you get. That's why my listeners love me so much. I'm not afraid of the truth! I'm perfect. And that's the truth.

## OPRAH WINFREY

I have no idea why people like Oprah Winfrey. She just stole Phil Donahue's format and she gets all these poor slobs to go on TV, spill their guts, and she doesn't give them a dime, she just speeds off in her Rolls-Royce after the show. She's a big dolt with an empty, oversized head and $250 million.

She's always testifying before some committee in Washington on child abuse and telling about how she was molested by everybody in her family—uncles, cousins, guys coming in the door, you name it. No wonder she had to go to Capitol Hill, she had to get out of that house. And there's Teddy Kennedy going, "Er, ah, er, ah, bend over, tubby." I wondered if her family sent around one of those Xeroxed Christmas newsletters. Imagine the possibilities. Here's a parody we made up on the air:

Hi everybody!
Just wanted to let you all know what's gone on for the past year. Guess what? Oprah got raped by her uncle and then her

cousin came over and molested her. Then a few family friends stopped by and they molested her, too. The rest of the year went okay because in March, Uncle Al nailed Oprah in the seat. But, other than that, everything's fine. Dad is now working on a new project, and Mom is making quilts. The good news was that in November, Grandpa couldn't get it up, so Oprah was spared that humiliation. We'll check in with you next year. Happy holiday!

I don't know about all these stories. Oprah's got a sister who claims that Oprah was just promiscuous, so we don't know what the hell was going on. But if she was abused, it's great how she was able to take that tragedy and turn it into a positive by getting rich on other people's abuse stories. I'd love to follow the life of a person who's gone on "Oprah." This person admits to performing bestiality on a cat and, after the first euphoric fifteen minutes of being on national television fades, realizes that Oprah pays her guests nothing to ruin their lives in front of millions of people.

And I love the topics she comes up with. I remember one time she had a woman on whose husband was a doctor. They were in the middle of a messy divorce and this woman had to go into the hospital for surgery and while she was having her uterus removed, her husband came in and sewed up her vagina. And Oprah said, "He sewed up your vagina?"

"Yes, he sewed up my vagina."

"*He sewed up your VAGINA?*"

"He sewed up my vagina."

It seemed as if she said "vagina" twenty times. I had never heard the word said that many times in my whole life. Then this woman went into a detailed description of how her plumbing still dripped all day because she had no more bladder control and it hurt to have sex. *Every minute detail.*

Where does Oprah come up with this stuff?

Women who cook their fetuses for Thanksgiving dinner, on the next "Oprah." Dial 1-900-HI-OPRAH if you're a woman who has cooked her own fetus for a Thanksgiving dinner because I want to speak to you on my show. I want to get you up on stage, I want you to tell me your story for free, and then I'll just walk right away after we're done taping. Men who wrap their penises Christmas morning for their kids. If you're a father who's ever done this or you're presently serving time for doing this, I would appreciate your calling and letting me know. Trapeze artists who have left a testicle up on the high wire—on the next "Oprah Winfrey Show." If you're a trapeze artist who had this happen to you, dial me up at 1-900-HI-OPRAH . . .

## ARSENIO HALL

But if you think Oprah's bad, check out Arsenio Hall. So many of my black friends tell me they wish they were yellow, they're so embarrassed by this triangle-headed moron. He is everything that is wrong with show business, with that phony backslapping, kiss-ass sucking up to anybody who comes on the show. And fuck me if I'm wrong, but since when does someone use the word *posse* and not get kicked out of Hollywood? I wanted to vomit the one time I saw Assholio on the Oprah show. Those two show-business phony baloneys. Why can't there be just one honest TV talk-show host?

"You know, Arsenio, all you do on your show is suck ass," I imagined Oprah would say.

"Well, you a blood-suckin' ripoff, honey. Phil Donahue invented everything you ever done."

The Honest Oprah Show. Boy, would that audience go wild.

Instead we have this world-class no-talent sycophant Arsenio, who packs his show with that kiss-ass audience that woofs at anything he says. *Spy* magazine did a great piece on that awhile back. *Spy* actually clocked the woofs. Listen to these jerks. When Arsenio said that Haiti's new president resembled MC Hammer, they woofed for 12.74 straight seconds. When he impersonated his uncle eating grits, they woofed 15.89 seconds. Try that at home. Woof for 15.89 seconds right now, without stopping.

There. Don't you feel like a total moron?

I was a guest on Arsenio's old Fox show. That's probably where our feuding began. I had done a few TV pilots for Fox and the total idiots who run Fox had no idea what to do with me. Meanwhile, the producer of my show was producing their late-night show and Arsenio was the lame-duck fill-in after Fox fired Joan Rivers. For some reason, the producer thought that if I appeared on the show, he would show the execs that I was bankable and they'd go to series with my pilots. I flew out to do the show for one reason and one reason only: *to trash the shit out of Fox!!*

I went out to L.A. with Baba Booey and everybody was thrilled to see us. We got the full Hollywood hug treatment. Then we went backstage and they had lavish gift baskets in the dressing rooms with monogrammed JR robes and soap left over from Joan Rivers. Nice big spread of food, the works. Okay, I was the first guest.

"*Time* magazine called my first guest an equal-opportunity offender. The FCC called him on the carpet for his blue-tinged broadcast on WXRK. Let's welcome the meanest, nastiest, dirtiest deejay in the whole wide world. My man, Howard Stern," Arsenio said.

We shook hands and I sat down and surveyed the set.

"So, how does it feel to be part of a failing show? How long before you get the pink slip?"

I was going right for the jugular.

"You know, Eddie, you're great," I said to Arsenio, hoping to antagonize him about Eddie Murphy, the man who made Arsenio's career. "Eddie, I love your concert shows," I said, continuing the goof. "Seriously, I don't watch this show because I usually go to bed early. . . . I would never do a show for this stinking network. I think this network

**Robin and me on the set of my never-aired Fox pilot.**

blows. It'll last another six months and be off the air."

"Calm down." Arsenio was getting worried.

"Hey, I'll leave, man, I don't need this gig," I threatened.

Arsenio asked me what I had against Fox and I told the history of our pilots. "Fox blows. They did the Emmys and they came in third place in the ratings. How can you blow the Emmys? I wouldn't be surprised if Fox drove Joan Rivers's husband, Edgar Rosenberg, to his death. The poor man was going out of his mind, was he not?"

The audience was going wild. Arsenio tried to get me off track by going to his prepared questions. I grabbed his stack of lame questions and gave him some index cards of questions I had prepared on my own.

*"Is it right that a person comes over to this country and becomes a citizen just so he can own a TV network?"* Arsenio read from my list of questions.

"That Australian Rupert Murdoch, all of a sudden he comes over and he's gonna own a network. Arsenio, you don't own a network because you're black. But you've been in this country longer than Rupert Murdoch!" I exclaimed.

Arsenio read the next question. *"Do you think Arsenio Hall is talented, or does he have a picture of one of the Fox executives with a donkey?* Howard, we can't do these questions."

Arsenio pretended to faint. I looked at the camera and ignored Arsenio. "If Letterman is watching, I love you. I think your show is the best. I'm not even going to watch myself, I'm gonna watch the Letterman show tonight."

The segment ended. Arsenio told me to leave the set for now and then he would have me back on after completing a segment with a South African band. Then a page came up to me at the break and said, "Follow me." So this page took me and Baba Booey back to the dressing room. Empty hallway, empty dressing room. No producer, no Arsenio, it was like a ghost town. Gary and I were standing there thinking, "What happened?"

Before I knew it, two security guards escorted me and Gary out. Nobody said a word. No "You were great," no "You sucked," nothing. They show us to the limo and we got in to go out to the airport and the limo driver was cracking up. "You were great, man!" he said. "You fucking showed him. He's a fucking asshole!"

I was pissed. Just because I trashed Murdoch, the Fox network, and Arsenio was no reason for me to be thrown out of a building. So I went on "Letterman" and said that doing the "Arsenio Hall Show" was like being on the set of *Blacula*. The next thing I knew, Arsenio was trashing me a few nights later in what had to be the lamest monologue ever.

"What's his name . . ." He feigned forgetfulness, snapping his fingers. "Howard Stern, the deejay from New York. Oh, my man is a slimeburger to the max."

SLIMEBURGER TO THE MAX? You call this comedy? What a monologue!

"He's the reason why a lotta women are gay," Arsenio went on. "And Howard was on 'Letterman.' I'm surprised they were able to get all the Chap Stick off Letterman's pants during the commercial, because he kissed my man's butt for ten minutes."

That was it. The gauntlet had been hurled. I began a systematic attack on him. I played tapes of his various appearances on awards shows and analyzed them as if they were the Zapruder Kennedy assassination film. Arsenio laid off me but then he made the foolish mistake of getting in the middle of a controversy between me and another genius, Chevy Chase. Arsenio had Chevy on his show and while he was smart enough not to put me down, he gave Chevy a forum for a diatribe against me. The next day I went ballistic on Arsenio:

"Notice how Arsenio was afraid to even mention my name when he brought this up. He knows better. He knows I've bitch-slapped him a few times on the radio. He's well trained. He's my boy. He knows to shut his big gums about me. He knows I would go on a tirade and ruin his life. You dope. You remember that, Arsenio, the last time I started talking about you . . . you fool. You learned to keep your mouth shut. 'Cause now I'm on in California and you'd have to be a stupid fool to open that big Gumby mouth of yours. You're my boy! You do what I tell you. You heard him there with Chevy Chase. My boy did okay. 'Cause I got you trained like a pack mule.

"But that little comment you made to Chevy that he shouldn't waste his time, that could be interpreted as *sarcastic*. That implies to *me* that I'm not important enough to have Chevy Chase's time wasted on. Don't *ever* let me hear you say, 'I don't know why you waste your time.' You hear me? I got you trained like a dog with your big blackened gums. So be careful when my name crosses your stupid German shepherd mouth. You just keep banging those broads who are stupid enough to get in the sack with you. Imagine bangin' Arsenio, thinking he might marry you. First of all, if you're a stupid white broad, he's never gonna marry you, it's bad for his image. So go ahead, keep spreading your legs. And you, put your hat on straight, you phony twerp! He puts his hat on backwards at the YMCA every day. He's supposed to be a street guy. You're not street. You're a loser. I bet you he gets the AIDS virus, with all those broads he's doing."

"That's the plague. I don't wish it on anyone," Robin interrupted.

I was uncontrollable. "I didn't say I wished it on him. All right. I wish it on him. I wish the AIDS virus on him."

"Now you've gone too far," Robin said. "I know you don't mean it."

"Why not? I don't like him."

"Nobody needs AIDS," Robin said.

"Okay." I was amenable. "Then I wish painful testicles on him. I know what that's like. That would hurt worse than AIDS."

The next day, the media went crazy. Reporters were outraged, entertainment anchors cluck-clucked through their broadcasts. In L.A., a dumb talking head said, "Enough is enough. When is local radio sta-

tion KLSX going to give us all a break and show Howard Stern the door?"

But I was unrepentant. "What kind of gossip is
that, that I wish Arsenio Hall would get the AIDS
virus? I'd bet you ninety-nine percent of the people
you polled would wish Arsenio would contract some
disease." We went to the phones for our own poll. "If
you had a choice, would you rather see Arsenio Hall
healthy or with the AIDS virus?" Needless to say,
Arsenio got no calls that supported him.

He was definitely my bitch. I had trained that dog
well. When he went on the Larry King show and my
name came up, Arsenio had this to say:

> Howard Stern is an interesting guy. He's a gentleman I had
> on my show and we had words on the show and he said some
> things but Howard's one of the nicest guys in the world. He's
> a happily married man, a good husband, a talented guy. How-
> ard and I don't dislike each other. Howard and I, on the air,
> for some reason, act like wrestlers. You know how wrestlers
> are. You don't believe they're like that out of the ring. He does
> a lot of things to create controversy and he does it very well. I
> don't hate the man and I don't think the man hates me. As a
> matter of fact, we talk very kindly to each other during com-
> mercials.

Good dog, Arsenio, good dog. Woof, woof, woof.

## LARRY KING

How this guy has a television show *and* a radio show
*and* a newspaper column is beyond me. But when you
analyze it a bit, it isn't that formidable a feat. First of

"As a guy, I like him a lot. He's a family man, he goes home . . . every night. His show is not my kind of show. He's the best tasteless broadcaster in America."

—Larry King

all, his television show on CNN is actually a game show. Everyone watches to see how long it'll take one of my fans to penetrate Larry's idiot screeners and mention my name in the context of a question.

LARRY: Dubuque, you're on the line.

CALLER: Hey, Larry, Howard Stern's penis.

LARRY: Next caller. Montreal.

CALLER: Howard Stern. Baba Booey.

**Here I am in full Larry King makeup barking out marriage proposals every fifteen seconds.**

"People ask me how I write columns. Whatever thought comes into my mind, I just type it. Picking my nose in traffic is the most fun I have. . . . Call me a no-talent, but wasn't it a bitch coming to the blackboard with a boner? . . . Why can't I remove the mattress tag? . . . What is it about a junior high school girl in a Catholic school outfit that makes me want to wear a hood and get a net? . . . Did Mrs. Brown really have a lovely daughter? . . . I wet my *TV Guide* many times watching Miss Kitty in 'Gunsmoke.' . . . What the hell is my daughter's name? I've been married so many times I'm confused. . . . There's nothing quite as beautiful as the buttocks of a college quarterback."

But for me, Larry's special talent shines through in his regular *USA Today* newspaper column. I have never seen a greater collection of lame non sequiturs and idiot savant pearls of wisdom week in and week out. I always had a great time on my television show whenever I'd slick back my hair, put on my suspenders, don my bigger, craggier nose and be Larry King for a night.

One time on my radio show, I even gave Robin a quiz to see if she could tell which words of wisdom were Larry's and which were mine. Let's see how good you discerning readers are at this:

---

### A SHORT LARRY KING STUPID-QUOTES TEST

1. How about a hooray for whomever invented Q-Tips?
2. I miss those little Hershey's Kisses.
3. Isn't it about time we all started recycling toilet paper?
4. Sly Stallone must have terrific-smelling hands.
5. The tougher the Food and Drug Administration gets, the better I like it.
6. They should outlaw shorts on fat women.
7. Teri Garr is the finest little actress in this country.
8. Tony Danza plays light comedy as well as anyone on television.
9. Circumcision must hurt like hell.
10. I've never had an overnight delivery service disappoint me.
11. Maybe it's just me, but toe fungus isn't funny.

Time's up. If you thought Larry King wrote quotes 3, 4, 6, 7, 9, and 11, you're really far gone and you can no longer listen to my radio show.

---

# KATHIE LEE GIFFORD AND REGIS PHILBIN

Is this a great country or what if two mediocrities like these can make it? Let's skewer Kathie Lee first. Hey, that's the one thing I wouldn't mind doing with her. She's got a hot little bod, and I must confess, I've masturbated to her.

But I'm sick of living through her pregnancies, miscarriages, and births. I really pissed her off when, while she was pregnant with Cody, I suggested on the air that it would be a great movie plot if she were carrying the Demon Seed. She was going to give birth to Satan's baby. She must have been listening because a mutual friend once said to her and Giff, "Hey, do you guys listen to Howard Stern?"

Kathie Lee turned white. "How could you bring up that horrible man!" she screamed and went running, crying, into the bathroom. I consider that a compliment because I don't consider myself a man.

Then Giff said to my friend, "How could you do that?"

"What did I do?" my friend asked.

"He called my baby the Demon!" Giff wailed.

Then she had the kid and that's all we heard about for the next year on her show. She was on every morning showing pictures of the baby. What was coming next, pictures of the afterbirth? Would she be wearing the goddamn umbilical cord as a necklace?

Then she decided to write a book. She had a pretty good life up to that point, but she shrewdly figured that misery sells, so she had to come up with some hardship in her life. Okay, she wrote about her first husband, a real born-again great guy. She said this guy wasn't making love to her much. Now he had to be thrilled to be reading this in her book. What did that mean, he couldn't make love to her much? What is she implying? What was everyone going to think? If she was such a great born-again Christian, why was she saying anything about this guy? *If you don't have anything nice to say, don't say anything at all. Turn the other cheek*, isn't that what Jesus says?

So I was reading her boring book and I found out her real name was Kathie Lee Epstein. Hah! A Jew! Who knew she was a Jew with that whole Christmas rap! That's why I encouraged my audience to call her Kathie Jew Gifford. *In the morning, in the evening, ain't we got fun!*

But the worst part of that stupid book of hers was that ridiculous miscarriage story. The book was basically a bore and I guess she needed pain to sell, right? And apparently she had a miscarriage a few weeks into a second pregnancy with Giff. Anyway, she dropped this clot into the toilet bowl and she freaked out so much that she made a nosedive into the bowl to retrieve her little baby. What was this woman talking about? That wasn't a baby. That was a guppy. And then she wanted us to believe that she dived in. I guess Kathie needed some controversy and adversity to sell a book. But if *I* were writing about *my* miscarriage, it would go something like this:

> I cry when my husband plays with himself and everything dries up. I realize that could have been our baby. So I dive

into the garbage can and get that soiled Kleenex. I'm so glad
I dived into the toilet and saved our little clot. What a cute clot
it is today. It can even do the backstroke now. We have the
smartest, most intelligent blood clot in the world. We called
him Aquaman, because he lives in our toilet.

Meanwhile, Kathie Lee never had a minute of adversity in her life with a puss like that. She even told
a story in the book about dropping a ring into a toilet
after she peed. And what did she do? She went into
her little lost girl routine and had an assistant reach
into the piss and retrieve the jewelry. What a tragedy!
Then she had to go right out and get pregnant
again. Hey, poor Giff looks to me as if he's 177 years
old. Did he need this aggravation? Plus, he had to be
afraid he couldn't pork her for like four months while
she was pregnant. Hey, to a guy his age, four months
can be a death sentence. So she was about to give
birth and, frankly, I was surprised she wasn't filming
the birth as a special. Now, it was time to name the
kid. Again, I suggested Beelzebub on my show, but
she wanted a cute name starting with a "C" to go with
Cody. We offered Cucumberhead and Cokehead and
Coolie but Kathie Lee picked Cassidy.
But as vile as Kathie Lee is, Regis is ten times more
despicable. And he was the subject of one of our finest
hours on the radio: the Danny Philbin Radiothon. It
all started when we found an article in the *Enquirer*.
There was a picture of a sad-looking guy in a wheelchair. I began to read the copy: "This legless student
is the son of TV's Regis Philbin, ignored by his rich
dad and living in a slum."

Regis is pulling in at least two mil a year, and he's basically ignoring his crippled son. I read on: "Millionaire talk-show host Regis Philbin has a legless wheelchair-bound son who's desperately trying to scrape by on a $300–a-month disability check, but Regis isn't lifting a finger to help him."

It seemed that Danny was one of the children from Regis's first marriage to a woman named Katherine. Regis had gotten out of that marriage with a lump-sum payment of $30,000. While he was sending his daughters from his present marriage all over the world, he was barely giving this poor kid anything. Occasionally, Danny would get a package of old shirts that Regis had gotten from his show's sponsors. Danny was trying to get through college, but he suffered from internal infections, kidney problems, bladder troubles, and liver disorders.

A light bulb went off in my head! We would have a radiothon for Regis's son and present the money to Regis on the air. We dispatched Gary out onto the street with a wireless microphone, a big tin can, and a sad picture of Danny. Meanwhile I read on:

> Philbin personally declined to comment on how he treats his first family, but his attorney stated that Philbin denies he has failed to support his son and said the talk-show host has complied with and far exceeded previous contractual undertakings regarding his son. Danny told an insider, "I want to love my father, but I don't even know him. He's just some man I see on television."

By now, Gary was outside. He had fastened the blown-up pictures onto a sandwich sign and he had a

**Baba Booey collecting cash for Regis's son.**

big bell. He rang it and screamed, "Why does Regis
ignore his kid? Please help." In a short fifteen minutes, he had collected $230.76 and one subway token
for poor Danny Philbin. Meanwhile, the phones were

ringing off the hook with donations. Sam Kinison, with whom I was feuding at the time, called in with a $500 pledge. It broke the ice between us. Fred the Elephant Boy rang up with a $10 donation.

I tried to call the Green Room at Regis and Kathie Lee's show to ask their guests to contribute but I couldn't get through. A bus literally stopped traffic in the middle of Madison Avenue when the driver left to make a contribution. We read the tote board: $2,561.

"We've filled in three toes on our tote board for Regis's son, only seven more to go," I announced. I called an artificial-limb company. The receptionist told me that a new pair of legs cost between $6,000 and $20,000. But a consultation was only $75. When it was time to get off the air, we had collected $4,387.76.

The next day Gary spoke with Danny Philbin. While he was very appreciative of our efforts, his lawyers had advised him not to take the money we had raised. He told us to thank our listeners for thinking of him but there were other people in the world who needed the money more. He said it was Regis's responsibility and "that's a hell he has to live with every day." We sent the checks back and donated the cash to charity. But we got a great song out of the whole story. It was a parody of Creedence Clearwater Revival's "Proud Mary":

**ROLL HIM INTO TRAFFIC**

Left a TV job in Los Angeles
Headed to New York to work for ABC
Left my crippled son like a worn-out doorstop
I thought that pathetic anchor was through with me

That wheelchair leech is a liar
Embarrassed me in the *Enquirer*
I'd like to roll him . . . roll him . . .
Roll him into traffic

Flipper foot lives in a pesthole
While my two "normal" daughters live in luxury
Is it my fault that this goldbrick defective
Didn't get his check from me until last week?
That wheelchair leech is a liar
Embarrassed me in the *Enquirer*
I'd like to roll him . . . roll him . . .
Roll him into traffic

## RUSH LIMBAUGH

I gave this fat pig his whole career. He was so lousy at radio that, at one point, he had to give it up and take some lame job. Then he heard me and suddenly he was back on the radio trying to do me. But he blows. Look, anytime you see a guy who weighs like three hundred pounds, you know we're not talking about emotional health. As soon as one of these fatties gets thin, all his problems come spilling out. Typically, they'll say: "I used the fat to build a wall around me. I was abused as a young child," though I suspect that Rush's excuse is that he just likes to eat. There's always a reason for someone being that fat, and it ain't glands, man.

> "It apparently is lost on Stern that he's fuller of himself than Rush Limbaugh squared."
> —Ed Bark, *Dallas Morning News*, December 7, 1992

There's a whole wave of conservative disc jockeys in our country who don't have a true agenda unless it's to be dull and boring. And Rush is one of them. One of his big subjects is women. Women are Feminazis, women are wrong to have abortions. . . . Blah, blah, blah. I love these fat pigs who sit back and pass judgment on women. They all say things like "These women who say they're raped are just lying to get abortions." Let me tell you what I hope happens to any guy who's got a big enough mouth to tell women that they can't have abortions. I hope they, collectively, while walking down the street, get pulled into an alley, sprawled over a garbage dumpster, and boned right up their fat fucking asses. Then they'll be crying, "We got raped in the ass!" Good for you, you pigs. Then they'll be the ones screaming that they want to have abortions.

## YOKO OH NO LENNON

One of the "celebrities" I've ragged on for the longest time is Yoko Ono Lennon. I just thought she was some wacked-out so-called artist at first. She would do crazy things like go on "The Mike Douglas Show" with John and call up random people on the phone and tell them that she loved them! Some artist! Some spender, too! I read in the *Enquirer* that she even went out and invested a fortune in cows.

After John was killed, it seemed as if she was putting out anything she could get her hands on: "Wait, I think John once recorded something while he was on the pot here in the Dakota. Where's that tape? Sean, don't touch any tapes. I take tape, I buy cow. Two tape worth two cow. Sean, stay away from tape!"

And she sponsored a little fucking garden in Central Park, across from where they lived, and she called it Strawberry Fields! On the anniversary of John's death, Yoko is compelled to run down there to make an appearance with the same seven retards who show up every year. Yoko takes three of her biggest body-guards, comes out of her building, runs across the street to Strawberry Fields, says "hello," and scurries right back inside her multimillion-dollar apartment. A few years ago, I sent Baba Booey out to interview her for my television show and he wound up getting fan-tastic tape that we aired of Yoko almost getting run over by a car trying to avoid him.

But the height of Yoko's arrogance came when she went to the United Nations for a live celebration of John's fiftieth birthday. She figured out a way to get the broadcasters of the world to simultaneously broad-cast her hollow tribute on more than a thousand radio stations to more than 130 countries. Luckily for Lis-teners-Who-Seek-the-Truth, all this happened during my airtime.

I was pissed off at Yoko even before this phony cere-mony got under way because she was interrupting a hot Lesbian Dial-a-Date segment. I had a semi-boner when, all of a sudden, we had to cut live to the United Nations to hear this bogus tribute:

"People of earth," Yoko the Martian began, "how are you? How's life been for you? Today would have been the fiftieth birthday of my husband, John Lennon."

I couldn't control myself. "The good news is he doesn't have to sleep with you anymore," I said. I talked over the whole ceremony.

"I would like us to remember and celebrate his birthday as a day of love, as he was a man of love . . ." she droned on.

I imitated her droning voice: "*I didn't know he was John Lennon when I met him.* Yeah, right. She followed him around for months! HOMEWRECKER!" I yelled. "You STOLE John away from his real peace-loving wife Cynthia. You're a homewrecker, not a head of state! You're a rich foreign groupie, not the Pope!"

"Let's use the power of dreaming," Yoko continued.

"The power of dreaming? Okay, I dream that you would just shut your mouth," I hissed.

Yoko went on, making me vomit: "Let's dream of peace, birds flying in clear air, fish swimming in clear water, and—"

"*A stitch in time saves nine,*" I said in my best Yoko voice.

Yoko pretentiously went on . . . and on: "For a dream we dream alone is only a dream, but a dream we dream together . . ."

"Wasn't Cynthia Lennon dreaming that she could be together with John? HER husband?" I yelled over her stupid droning voice.

Predictably, they started playing John singing "Imagine." This was too much for me.

"I don't have to listen to that! I've got a lesbian in the studio. Hey, lesbian, can I spank you during 'Imagine'?" I asked.

"We're supposed to be listening to John Lennon now," Robin, the cop, reprimanded me.

"I'm not listening 'cause Yoko's merchandising everything of John's. Coffee mugs, everything. Hey, Yoko, *imagine there's no royalties! It's easy if you try.* We'll just take 'em away from you. We'll see how much peace you're into.

"You think John Lennon, if he were alive, would put his name on mugs?" I was telling her off. I was the only one speaking *The Truth*. Then a moron listener called to complain that I ruined her John Lennon moment.

"How did I ruin your moment? You could have turned to another one of a thousand stations. I create four hours a day for you, you thankless bitch!"

She called me a "motherless fucker" and hung up the phone.

"I'm wise to the whole scam. I'm not getting suckered into this," I said. "Everybody else wants to kiss Yoko's ass? Go ahead, not me! Not this boy. NO WAY! Hey, Yoko, if you didn't rip off Cynthia's husband, you might be scrubbing men with a sponge for twenty bucks a pop, doing the Chinese basket trick!"

## LINDA McCARTNEY

Yoko isn't the only ex-Beatles wife we've exposed. A while back there was a bootleg tape circulating of Linda McCartney singing backup at one of Paul's concerts. There's another witch for you. Here's one of the world's greatest musicians, he married this photographer, now he can't pick up a guitar without this bim singing along and pounding on the piano. Apparently, this even pisses off their own crew, because, rumor has it, it was a technician who circulated this tape of Linda isolated from the rest of the group. She was so off-key it wasn't funny. We started playing it on the air and the next thing we knew, we got a cease-and-desist order from Linda's attorney. But the damage was done. I had unmasked another hypocrite.

## MICHAEL LANDON

Another show-biz hypocrite who pissed me off was Michael Landon. Did you see the homages paid to him when he died? All the news programs showed him walking down the road as an angel from his TV show "Highway to Heaven." When was this guy an angel? I'm sure at least two of his ex-wives thought he was going to hell. And he has this great image as a family man. *Family man?* This guy had nine children from three different wives. He was a guy in his fifties having children with his third wife. He wrote family shows, meanwhile his family was in total disarray. Three different wives. He was a *families* man. He made a bunch of sappy shows about the family he would have *liked* to have. He couldn't be an angel, so he acted as one.

## PHIL DONAHUE AND MARLO THOMAS

It's funny, but most of the celebrities I really hate are talk-show hosts. Take Donahue, for example. I read that book by Phil and Marlo's butler, Desmond Atholl. Phil had a wife and kids and did what every other Hollywood guy does. He got himself *the* Hollywood wife. The trophy wife. But according to Atholl's book, she turned out to be a fucking shrew.

> "I'm actually a Howard Stern fan. I listen to him all the time. It's a voyeuristic show where you wouldn't listen to it in the car with someone else but 'Oh, great, I'm alone, I'll listen to Howard to see who he's trashing.' It was usually me."
>
> —John Tesh

This is some woman, this Marlo. All wrapped up in her little feminist causes. But when you think about it, what has she done for women? This yenta's always busy with the specials and the books about children's this and children's that. First of all, it's easy to write a children's book. I have to make up stories every night for my kids. Last night I made up one right on the spot for my daughters: *Once upon a time there was a daddy who ripped out a cat's uterus. Then he ripped off its claws. Then he chopped off its head. And it lived happily ever after.* The moral of the story is: Life sucks, shitty things happen to you along the way, but still you go on. Boom! You got a book. Big deal!

But what I love about this Marlo character is she's an expert in children's things. Hey, it was a good career move. She bombed as a movie actress so she does these dopey children's projects. But she's never had any kids of her own. She was on Donahue's show once and some nice woman in the audience asked her why she hadn't had any children and Marlo got this disgusted look on her face as if she'd just been asked when her next menses was due to flow. She said something like "Is there a polite way of saying it's none of your business?" The whole audience gasped. All she had to say was "Gee, it's a very personal thing," or "I really don't want to talk about this," or "I got dust bunnies on my uterus"—whatever. But "Is there a polite way of saying it's none of your business?" IS THAT HOW YOU TALK? WITH THAT *RUDE MOUTH*? WITH EVERYTHING HANDED TO YOU ON A *SILVER PLATTER* FROM YOUR FATHER? DON'T GO ON THE SHOW IF YOU DON'T WANT TO ANSWER THAT, YOU BIG JERK! AND IF YOU DON'T WANT TO ANSWER IT, AT LEAST BE POLITE TO PEOPLE!

Imagine how Phil's first wife would have felt if she had tuned in to this show. This hot bag of wind Marlo was up there talking about how Phil loves women; meanwhile, she was the actress trophy he'd picked up on his own show! Every once in a while the camera would flash to the old fat slobs in the audience. Why isn't Phil married to one of them since he can see right through to the inner beauty in people? Would Marlo have looked at him twice before he was famous and successful? And she was up there pissing all over his audience and he was loving every minute of it. Yet when our friend Jessica Hahn was on his show and Phil was interrogating her about being raped by Jim Bakker and she said, "I prefer not to answer that," he pressed Jessica for answers. HYPOCRITES! These are the very same people in show business who thumb their nose at me. Hey, I sleep easy at night compared to you two.

### JOHNNY CARSON AND HIS TWO ASSKISSERS

I'm amazed how reverential people get when they talk about Carson. "Oh, Johnny's a genius . . ." Hey, let's be honest here. Johnny's no genius. The guy who invented penicillin, Fleming, he's a genius. Johnny deserves his place in history as a guy who was a goofball on TV. Period. I look at Johnny Carson and I see just another Hollywood phony. I loved that crying routine on the air when his son died off the side of that cliff. Let's face it, this was no Father of the Year. You love your kids? Well, how about that little mulatto love grandchild you've got whom you refuse to acknowledge? That's why you're crying—you're guilt-ridden, in my estimation. And lay a few shekels on that first wife of yours, while you're at it.

I love slamming Johnny. He hates my guts. On my TV show we presented our own version of The Last

Tonight Show, starring Johnny *Carstern*. I was made up to look like Johnny, and one of my TV writers, Big Al Rosenberg, played Ed *McFat*. Dan Forman, my producer, played a bizarro Doc Severinsen named Dan *Formanson*, who led the All-Lesbian Orchestra, which was composed of the largest-breasted spokesmodels we could find. What a fitting tribute to a show-biz giant's career!

After I was introduced, I went into the monologue:

Hey, I haven't heard that much screaming since my first wife, Jody, didn't listen to me. Ed, you look particularly bloated tonight. I couldn't help but notice you broke wind tonight in your first HiHo! Thirty years, Ed, and your only contribution to the show has been four freaking letters, HiHo, you big leeching worthless no-talent fucking piece of shit. Hey, let's welcome Dan Formanson, our band leader. What happened to you? That suit is the color of Ed's vomit.

Our first segment was the last appearance of the great Sternac the Improbable. Ed went into the intro: "From the East, a man whose ass is bright, wet, red, and chapped from being constantly kissed, Sternac the Improbable!

"*Seem Salabim*," I said. Ed handed me the first envelope.

"*Punch and Jody*," I said, holding the envelope up to my forehead. "*How I spent most of my time with my first wife, Jody.*"

"HO HO HO HO HO, HO HO HO HO HO, HO HO HO HO HO!" Ed chuckled incessantly.

"*May you be feeling up Jenny Jones when her breast implants explode*," I said.

**Heeere's Howie . . . as Johnny.**

*"The next answer is black-eyed peas,"* I guessed, closing my eyes. *"What would peas look like if they were married to me?"*

Ed went wild with laughter.

*"Ed, you smell like crap,"* I said. *"May your brother share Pee-Wee Herman's buttered popcorn, you fat fuck."*

Ed handed me the last envelope. *"The answer is cauliflower,"* I said and opened the envelope. *"What did my first wife, Jody's, ear look like after she lost the car keys?"*

Then, to hammer home the point, we brought out my first guest, my first wife, *Jody Carstern*. A middle-aged nonbeauty of an actress came out.

**Howard Carstern with Zsa Zsa.**

*"Christ, you're still a pig. I know exactly why I divorced you. How long were we married?"* I asked her.

"Too long," she said.

I leaned over my desk and gave her a right cross to the jaw, sending her sprawling.

The segment ended with Ed and me both beating the crap out of her.

Then we brought out our next guest, Zsa Zsa Gabor. Mind you, our policy when we were doing the TV show was that the guests were completely kept in the dark as to what they were doing. So when Zsa Zsa walked onto the set, she had no idea she was part of a Johnny Carson sketch. She was floored.

"Take off that damn mask!" she hissed at me. Every time Zsa Zsa opened her mouth, Fat Ed started chuckling away like a banshee. I thought Zsa Zsa was going to belt him one. After I tried to get Zsa Zsa to model some S and M garb, it was time to end The Last Tonight Show.

*"I can see by the liver spots on the back of my hand, it's time to go,"* I said. *"You are such a big fat jerk, Ed, I can't say I love you. Over the years you've been loyal and faithful, though, and done what I've told you. I have one last request. I want you to kiss my bony ass one last time. But I mean really kiss it."*

I came out from behind the desk and walked over to Ed and pulled down my pants. Zsa Zsa was so horrified she couldn't even look. Ed thrust his face between my butt cheeks.

*"C'mon, you big marine! I want you to kiss it with your tongue."* Zsa Zsa was hysterical. We went to a close-up of Ed and his entire nose was dotted with fecal matter. We faded to brown.

But what really got me pissed off about Johnny and his two no-talent asskissers was the way they dumped all over poor Jay Leno when he took over the show. Jay Leno is one of the nicest people in the world. But he made a grave mistake. He didn't mention Johnny on his first show. Who knows with Johnny? Are you supposed to mention him or not supposed to mention him? What a crime. So this disturbed little man, Johnny Carson, who should be having the time of his life in retirement banging away at that beautiful young babe he's got out there in Malibu, sat idly by while his two henchmen, Ed and Doc, went to the Arsenio show, where they kissed Arsenio and conferred the mantle of "The Tonight Show" on him.

These two ungrateful no-talent scumbags, Ed and Doc! Why did they do this to Jay Leno? "The Tonight Show" was so bad to them? Do you think Ed McMahon would be hanging around those nubile "Star Search" candidates if he hadn't sat on that couch like a fat lummox and brayed for thirty years? And that Doc Severinsen stood there like a brick, night after night, conducting that cockamamie orchestra. A gorilla could have conducted that stupid orchestra. THIS UNDER-HANDED ATTACK ON NICE JAY REALLY BOILED MY BLOOD!

I got on my radio show and went after Johnny first. "I hope Johnny gets some sort of cancer. You know how his scalp is always pink, with the brown spots? I hope that it turns out that he goes to the hospital and they find out he's got brain cancer and it eats out through his skin. And I hope Alexis leaves him and marries me. Me and my wife. NBC made this guy a multimillionaire and Jay kissed his ass, and right away he's pissed at NBC and pissed at Jay Leno. How can you be pissed at Jay Leno? He's like a puppy. There couldn't be a better asskisser in the U.S. than Jay Leno but now Jay's his enemy."

I decided to get some help in my campaign against Johnny. I decided to pray to Jesus, on the air:

Jesus, my friend, who died on the cross for me. Jesus, dear sweet Jesus, please take away everything Johnny has except his liver spots. Amen, sweet Jesus. And make Alexis horny for Jay Leno. Jesus, if you please, Jesus my favorite nailed-up person, I pray to you to let that fat Ed McMahon burst open and let that Kuato from that movie with Arnold Schwarzenegger burst out of his belly. I pray that Johnny loses all his money and his big Malibu house and that his wife gets pregnant with Branford Marsalis's love baby. Jesus, please grant me this, you've come through for me before. Dear God, I am a sinner. I give my life to you in Jesus' name. Jesus, my pal, stuff Doc's trumpet up Johnny's butt. Amen.

But it wasn't enough to go after Johnny on my radio show. I had to do more to address this injustice that was being heaped on poor Jay Leno. So I decided to do "The Tonight Show." It became, with all due modesty, one of their most memorable episodes ever.

I had insisted, as per usual, on the number-one slot. After a lot of negotiating with Jay's then producer, Helen Kushnick, they agreed. But for a few days before the appearance, they were trying to get in touch with me for a pre-interview. I don't do pre-interviews. Pre-interviews mean one thing: Somebody is sitting there, editing your material. So I avoid them. In fact, I avoided it until fifteen minutes before the taping. They were frantically calling me at the hotel, but I had all my calls held.

My appearance had become the hottest ticket in the show's history, next to Carson's last show. I had been on the air in L.A. almost a year but I had never actually visited there. Everybody wanted to see the human oddity in the flesh. So it was literally fifteen minutes before taping, just enough time for me to go in and get some makeup on, when we pulled up to the studio. I got out of the car and there was a long red carpet waiting for me. Helen had the entire "Tonight Show" staff lined up outside cheer-

```
!ENTERTAINMENT!
-------------------------------------
BIG DEMAND FOR TICKETS TO HOWARD
STERN'S "TONIGHT SHOW" APPEARANCE.
-------------------------------------
(BURBANK, CALIFORNIA)-NBC IS HAVING NO
TROUBLE  FILLING  THE  SEATS  FOR THIS
EVENING'S TAPING OF "THE TONIGHT SHOW WITH
JAY LENO." ONE OF THE GUESTS IS MORNING RA-
DIO RAUNCH-MEISTER HOWARD STERN.
HIS FANS HAVE SWAMPED THE NETWORK WITH
TICKET REQUESTS. ABOUT 100 PEOPLE CAMPED
OUT OVERNIGHT AT THE STUDIO IN BURBANK,
CALIFORNIA, TO GET TICKETS, AND AN NBC
SPOKESWOMAN SAYS THERE HAVE BEEN MORE RE-
QUESTS FROM NETWORK EMPLOYEES FOR TICKETS
TO THIS SHOW THAN THERE WERE DURING JOHNNY
CARSON'S FINAL WEEK.

AP-NP-07-24-92 0410PDT<-
```

ing for me. They had cameras following me as I walked in. She had pulled out all the stops.

I got in my dressing room. Fifteen seconds later the door opened and Jay popped in and sat his ass down. "Howard, I gotta talk to you, I gotta talk to you. But we gotta do it quick, I have to go warm up the audience."

I couldn't believe my ears.

"Jay, you do the fucking warmup? What about being a big star? What about building anticipation? How about a little show biz?" It reminded me of the night I went to see Joe Walsh at the Westbury Music Fair and Joe just walked out on stage as his own opening act. So now, Jay finally had me cornered.

"Howard, I don't want you talking about Johnny Carson. You can't ta—"

"Jay, I'm very uncomfortable with this conversation," I interrupted. "I'm gonna tell you the way I operate. I don't know what the fuck I'm gonna talk about. Now that you told me *not* to talk about it . . . quite frankly, all I had planned to talk about was

Johnny Carson." Now I had a dilemma. I was planning to do a whole rap on how Johnny now looked like the crypt keeper from "Tales from the Crypt." I was going to paint liver spots all over my hands to do this rap but, out of deference to Jay, this one time, I backed off. I decided to blast Carson by going after his two no-talent henchmen.

It was time to do the show. Jay introduced me.

"He's radio's number-one shock jock." The audience started going wild. "We're here to prove once and for all that we here on 'The Tonight Show' are not members of the cultural elite. Howard Stern, ladies and gentlemen."

I walked out. The audience was primed. They were going crazy. "Jay, there's plenty to discuss, is there not? I'm excited to appear on the new 'Tonight Show.' This is truly marking a new beginning by having me on. I think . . ."

"I think hell in a handbasket would be a good description," Jay said.

"It shows a loosening up of 'The Tonight Show,' if I may say so. Let me address a few things. I'm going to tell you a secret. Jay talked to me backstage and asked me not to talk about Johnny Carson. Is that true, Jay?"

Jay started squirming. The audience went wild.

"Jay told me not to talk about Johnny and I certainly understand why. Jay is involved in a controversy. I'm not going to talk about Johnny so keep it in your pants. But I am going to say something. I tuned in Arsenio the other night and this moron . . . Arsenio, who couldn't even do stand-up comedy . . . Jay, true or false? Is Arsenio a good stand-up comic, Jay? NO! Say it, Jay! Say the truth."

"I will tell you, he's pretty good," Jay said, lamely.

I pounced all over him. "That's a lie. Ask Branford. This is the problem with this show. You have no killer instinct. He's a crummy stand-up. Anyway, I tuned in the other night and he calls Jay a punkass. What do you think about somebody calling you a punkass?"

"Well, I think it, uh, just hurts the person saying it more," Jay said meekly. I couldn't believe him. This guy was too nice to be true.

"YOU'RE A LAMB, JAY, YOU'RE A LAMB!" I jumped up. "Hey, Branford, what about you? You're a team player. What do you think about Arsenio?"

"That's between y'all," Branford said.

"Nobody on this show has a killer instinct. Is it he's a black guy and you're a black guy, Branford? So what? He's out to ruin you."

The audience was howling.

"Let me continue." I quieted them down. "I got a lot on my mind. The amazing thing to me, Jay, is here you're a nice guy, I never heard you say a bad word

> "Howard has his own agenda and you sort of follow along."
> —Jay Leno

about anybody. And I tuned in to Arsenio and I see Ed and Doc, who should really have come on this show. 'The Tonight Show' has been pretty good to those guys . . . Ed and Doc are two of the biggest loads on two feet. . . ."

The place exploded. Jay hid under his desk. Here I

was on the set of "The Tonight Show" destroying those two phony icons and cleverly complying with Jay's bullshit edict that I not talk about Johnny. But Jay looked worried.

"Hold it a second, Jay. I'm not talking about Johnny, I'm talking about Ed and Doc. Here you got two guys; this Ed, for thirty years he sat on this couch like the big fat blubber that he is, and he's making a great living. What's his problem with Jay? Why would they go on the Arsenio show—?"

"They did not talk about me," Jay got defensive.

"And then, Ed comes out and starts kissing Arsenio?" I jumped to my feet. I stared the camera in the face. "Ed?! If you're watching me at home, let me tell you something. You can be nice to this guy, Jay Leno. There's a certain relationship with 'The Tonight Show' that you should have. And Doc? You stood there in pink outfits leading that lousy band and did nothing. Doc? You're a crummy musician! Ed and Doc. Two idiots. The hell with them. You don't need them, Jay. You don't need them."

By now, Jay was fingering me under the desk. *Just kidding.*

The camera was on Branford. He was cracking up. The crowd exploded.

"This show is terrific, Jay! I don't care what Ed does. These are two no-talents that have absolutely nothing on the ball. They were lucky to have jobs here with Johnny. The hell with them. LET THEM GO KISS ARSENIO'S ASS. WE DON'T NEED THEM. SCREW 'EM! SCREW 'EM!"

The roar was deafening. We were making show-biz history. We went to a break and I leaned over to Jay. He looked pale. "How's it going?" I asked, always paranoid about my appearances. I couldn't judge this one, even though the crowd had never gone crazier. I never think I'm doing well, so I just keep pushing it and pushing it. That's why all this shit comes out of me, because I just think people want more. I think I'm not going far enough for them, meanwhile I'm completely over the line. But Jay was sitting there, ashen-faced. "I don't know. I don't know if you should have brought up that stuff about Ed." Can you believe Jay was ambivalent about this stellar appearance? He *should* have been fingering me under the desk. Meanwhile, Helen was brewing a fondue in her pants, she was so ecstatic about this appearance.

We came back from the break and Jay steered me away from Ed and Doc. But I had really knocked him for a loop. For the rest of the show, his timing was off because he kept looking over at me on the couch, figuring he had to deal with me if I exploded. Meanwhile, he was interviewing some actress from a sitcom and I was sitting on the couch with Lyle Lovett, pretending I was making out with him. Then I pretended to snore during this girl's rap. The whole show was off the wall. By the end of the show Jay looked as if he'd been through a war.

"I want to thank my guests, I think," he said. Think? He should have blown and reamed me. He should have fucked and sucked me. After all, I said everything he wanted to say but couldn't.

## CHEVY CHASE

This one is a really sad case. Here was a guy who was part of one of the coolest things around, the early "Saturday Night Live" crew. Groundbreaking, irreverent, creative. They would make fun of all the Hollywood establishment people like Cary Grant. And what happened? A little success and they became the very people they made fun of. Chevy Chase is pathetic. He's palling around on golf courses now with Gerald Ford, the doofus president he used to make fun of. Maybe all those painkillers Chevy took from those pratfalls affected his mind. He sure wasn't thinking straight when he decided to start a feud with me.

It started on Larry King's show. Chevy was a guest and one of my fans called in and said, "Howard Stern." Out of the blue, Chevy attacked me:

CHEVY: Is that that guy Howard Stern? Boy, he's an ass. Can't stand him.

LARRY: Have you seen his show?

CHEVY: I've never seen it, but I've heard him on the radio.

LARRY: And?

CHEVY: He's a very funny guy—got the brain of an egg timer.

They went to a break and this Chevy moron continued to obsess about me. It was clear that he was one of those guys who probably listens to me every morning, lying there in bed, beating off to my every word.

Probably all of his friends were talking about me and how I had the kind of buzz that Chevy remembers from way back when he started on "Saturday Night Live." But now he was bald and bloated and bitter and jealous. Listen to this guy talking about me when he thought he was off the air:

CHEVY: Boy, that Howard Stern is such an ass. I mean, really a nothing. Just nothing there, nothing. If he was just funny. Makes that Morton Downey look like Joyce Brothers.

Well! My fans called me up and played me the satellite feed of the "Larry King Live" show. And better yet, they called in and gave me Chevy's home phone number. Richard Belzer happened to be my guest at the time and Richard had been an old friend of Chevy's. We decided to call Chevy on the air. A woman with an accent answered the phone. We identified ourselves and asked her to tell Chevy we were on the phone and we wanted to speak to him. I even said "Thank you" at the end of our request, which will be relevant later in the story.

We waited a long time. Belzer and I filled the time working out possible scenarios for the call. Finally the woman came back on. She said that it wasn't Chevy Chase's house. An obvious, bald-faced lie.

"No, it is," I insisted. "What, you had to go figure it out? I don't understand why you're saying that. I know it is and Richard Belzer's here, his good friend. Can you just please get him?"

Note, I said "please." Again, she was gone. We started riffing on Chevy and his toupees.

"Hey, now everyone in California, when you see Chevy Chase on the street, go up to him and say, 'What's with your toupee, man? Why don't you take that thing off?' " I suggested.

After another interminable wait, I decided this was a job for Baba Booey. I wasn't going to wait all day for the woman to check to see if Chevy lived there. Gary dialed again and politely explained to the woman that he had spoken to Chevy at this same number the day before.

> "Howard Stern is an ass. He's really a nothing. I can't stand him."
>
> —Chevy Chase

Gary established that the woman worked there. He asked to speak to Jayni, Chevy's wife, another friend of Belzer's. Within seconds, Chevy was on the line.

HOWARD: Chevy, hey, Chevy.

CHEVY: Who is this?

HOWARD: It's Howard and Belzer and we're live on the air.

BELZER: Hey, Chev.

CHEVY: Howard and who?

HOWARD: Belzer, Richard.

CHEVY: Howard Belzer?

BELZER: And Richard Stern.

HOWARD: Howard Stern and Belzer. We're doing a radio show. Trying to talk to you. Why are you bad-mouthing me?

CHEVY: Howard who?

HOWARD: Howard Stern and Richard Belzer. We're on the radio.

CHEVY: What? Whose radio is on?

BELZER: Yours.

HOWARD: Larry King told me to call. Why are you bad-mouthing me?

JAYNI: Hello?

CHEVY: I've got it, Jayni, Jayni, hang up the phone!

JAYNI: Listen, he's not bad-mouthing you. It's early in the morning.

CHEVY: Hey, hey, Jayni, Jayni, get off the phone, please. Get off the phone. I want to deal with this.

HOWARD: All right.

CHEVY: Jayni, please hang up the phone! Will you please hang up the phone, we're on the radio.

JAYNI: I understand that.

CHEVY: Jayni, please.

JAYNI: Why is Howard saying things about you when you're a very nice person?

HOWARD: No, he's a nice guy but he's being real mean to me.

JAYNI: He's not being mean to you.

HOWARD: Do you want to hear what he said about me on Larry King?

At this point, Chevy was flipping out and did not want his wife involved in this nonsense.

CHEVY: JAYNI, GET OFF THE PHONE!

HOWARD: Chevy, I've always been nice to you.

CHEVY: Hey, Howard is this you?

HOWARD: Hey, we're on the air.

CHEVY: I've got news for you.

HOWARD: What?

CHEVY: I didn't bad-mouth you. But I do have some news for you.

HOWARD: What?

CHEVY: This is my home and I don't like you. Okay? Is that clear?

HOWARD: All right.

CHEVY: So don't call my house again.

HOWARD: Okay, fine.

CHEVY: See you later.

HOWARD: Bye. Who cares.

We hung up. "Did you hear him turn on his own wife because of his deferred anger toward you?" Belzer was amazed. I couldn't believe how much Chevy lacked a sense of humor.

"For someone who's done some of the greatest jokes in public, bad-mouthed executives at important dinners. Then you call him up and here's a chance to have like a great moment and he's the most humorless . . ." Belzer was astonished.

We started speculating on why he was so grim. Perhaps it had something to do with the reviews for his *Invisible Man* movie. It probably was because he realized that I was a thousand times more relevant to today's humor scene than he was.

I would have let it rest at that, but then a few days later Chevy went on Arsenio's show and *LIED!*

"He called my home early in the morning and berated my housekeeper. A lovely El Salvadoran woman—beat up on her basically, over the phone, to get me on live, at a quarter to eight in the morning. I thought that had a lot of class. I guess the guy's basically an egg timer. I'm not fighting with him, I just don't like him. When a guy calls your home and talks to your people that way, you'd be upset."

Oh, so now he's upset because of the way we treated "his people." What's the story here? GET A LIFE! GET A SENSE OF HUMOR!

The only good thing about this whole sorry incident is that Chevy is going on the air any day now with his own talk show and if it's still on the air by the time you're reading this chapter, I'm sure his glaring lack of a sense of humor will provide me with lots of material. Oh, and Chevy, say hello to Gerald Ford for me, babe. You old rebel you.

## MADONNA

I tried to be nice to Madonna. I really did. In fact, before she became "Madonna" I kind of dug her. I remember back in 1988 I even called her up at home when somebody gave me her home phone number and I left a twenty-minute message on her answering machine. I said all kinds of nice things to her:

> Hey Madonna, it's Howard Stern. How ya doin'? Don't get mad, somebody gave me your phone number. I heard you were a fan so I figured I'd call. Hey, I love your videos. I even rented *Who's That Girl* and *Shanghai Surprise*. And I'm gonna tell you something, your body looks great from all that running. Hey, we'd love for you to do the show. Tuesday would be a good day because Wednesday's Jessica Hahn and Thursday's

Gilligan so tomorrow would be best. Let's face it—it would help the ratings and since you like the show, you want to see us get good ratings. I figure you got a good sense of humor. That's why you'll understand this call because if some idiot disc jockey was calling my house I'd be pretty annoyed. But I have to do it because it's my job. I have to be a jerk or people won't listen. Just like you have to wear bras with the metal tips on them like an opera singer. We have so much in common. You have to do stuff for your career and I have to do stuff for mine. I mean, I'm on the radio so I can't have hairy armpits and stuff. I have to do outrageous things that people can hear, know what I'm saying? Oh, and that *Penthouse* thing. Forget about it, man. Your body is so much better now. I didn't think that was a big deal. I thought you handled it real well. You didn't get upset, you didn't threaten to sue. You admitted you did the pictures. Hey, who the hell needs you to show up here? We're talking to you anyway!

Madonna couldn't make it in the next day but it wasn't until she got really big that I really got annoyed with her. So by the time her documentary *Truth or Dare* came out, I had had it with this jerk. If there's a mountain called Egomania, she finally climbed to the top of it with that piece of garbage. Could you believe all the crap in that flick? How about those stupid prayer circles? Imagine if we did a live show again and I said, "Okay, everyone, come into my dressing room and let's form a prayer circle." Robin would have me arrested. And Madonna had *four* prayer sessions in that friggin' movie! Just once I wanted to hear God answer her back: "Hey, sweetheart! This is God! You know, there's like an AIDS epidemic. Don't you think you can stop wasting my time praying about a stupid concert?" I'd rather clean monkey shit in a circus than be in that prayer circle.

And how many ways could she humiliate the people she worked with? That one woman came to her and said that she was in a hotel room drunk and she passed out and she woke up and her ass was bleeding and this cunt face started laughing at her! You'd think Madonna would have the decency to turn off the camera and say, "I can't use this in my film. This is *this* woman's revelation, not mine." What kind of woman allows that to be aired? Meanwhile, Madonna didn't reveal any aspect of her own life that wasn't cunningly calculated. Hey, let me see *her* ass bleed a bit. If she picked her nose and put it in the woman's mouth, I'd say, "At least there's something of Madonna." She had a sore throat—that's real intimate. You see her go to the doctor's office to get her throat sprayed. Hey, if you're pretending to be intimate, let me see you on a bidet, cleaning yourself out.

Then she made fools out of her old girlhood friend and all the confused homos in her troupe and she even showed her brother in a bad light. How demeaning. You should be ashamed of yourself. How about the way she put down Kevin Costner because he came backstage to *compliment* her on her show? But she didn't like the word he used to praise her. Miss Hip here sticks her finger down her throat behind his back just because he said her concert was "neat." She is so hip. She's the hippest, man. God, does she make my skin crawl. Thank God I don't work for someone like that whose ass I'd have to kiss. I'd rather just be tied up and let ants eat me.

**Who's that girl? It's me striking one of my many Madonna poses.**

In fact, I was so incensed over her stupid movie that we decided to do the ultimate Madonna documentary on our TV show. I donned a Madonna wig and one of those stupid bustiers with the spiked bra cups and black garters and the spike heels and voilà! I was Madonna, sprawled across a big bed.

"Hi, I'm Madonna and I am so outrageous. Robin, do you know why America loves me? Because I'm constantly changing my attitudes and styles. Because I'm so outrageous. Let me show you why. Boys, come to Madonna."

Two leather boys in leather bikini briefs and chains and studded collars walked over to me like robots.

"Yes, Madonna."

**Boys, I want you to sit on my bullet bra! I'm Madonna, I'm outrageous!**

"Boys, I want you to hold hands."

"Yes, Madonna." They obeyed.

"Robin, I'm playing with homosexuality right now. Boys, I want you to sit on my bullet bra."

They each sat on top of one of my spiked bra cups.

I was suffocating. "Boys, get up! Watch this, Robin. Boys, I want you to put your genitals on that frying pan there and turn it on and burn them. Do it for Madonna."

"Yes, Madonna," they repeated and walked over to two hotplates.

"They'll do anything you say?" Robin was incredulous.

"Yes, we must break all sexual boundaries."

Smoke started rising as they burned their genitals on the frying pans.

"I'm so outrageous, aren't I, America? Robin, have you ever done this?"

I pulled a humongous booger out of my nose.

"But that's not outrageous enough, Robin."

"How far are you going to go, Madonna?" Robin asked.

"Monty, come to Madonna."

I ordered our bald cameraman to come up to me.

"I think all bald men should have boogers attached to their bald heads." I pressed my booger onto his head.

"Thank you, Madonna," Monty said.

"Why are you so emasculating, Madonna?" Robin wondered.

"Because all heterosexual men should be taught a

lesson. Do you believe how wicked I am? Can you do this, Robin?"

I lay back on the bed and grabbed some matches and lit a fart.

"This will outrage all America."

The flames shot up into the air.

"I am so wild. I am woman. I am child. I am virgin. I am whore. I am good cook. I am bad cook. I am so wild, sometimes I wear my underwear on my head." I pulled a pair of panties onto my head. "Try it, Robin."

I kept doing outrageous things. I rubbed myself all over with a porno tape. I wore my left shoe on my right foot and my right shoe on my left foot. I breast-fed my father. I even had our producer Dan Forman come out on a dog leash and I made him bark and roll over. I was totally outrageous.

"Robin, there's only one thing left that I can do. I WANT TO CUT MYSELF OPEN AND EAT MY OWN GUTS!"

"You're going to eviscerate yourself?" Robin was shocked.

*"Yes, I've always wanted to rip at my own belly . . ."*

I clawed at my belly and pulled my guts out.

*". . . and to eat my own guts!"*

I stuffed my mouth with my entrails.

"This is it!" Robin shouted. "Madonna has finally crossed the line!"

*"Oh! Oh! Oh!"* I moaned orgiastically.

"Are you dying, Madonna?" Robin asked.

*"I've done it all! I've done it all!"* I screamed as I swooned.

That was some bit. That fart lighting scene cost us our first NBC affiliate when WGIT in Hartford canceled our show. But it was worth it. After all, Madonna and I are artists and we'd do anything for our art.

## SHARON STONE

This loser is the newest one on my case. I can't figure these dumb bims out. It took this bitch thirty-three years to find the right role for herself, that of a crazed lesbian ice-pick killer who forgets to wear her panties at police interrogations, and now she wants to jeopardize everything by getting into a vendetta with yours truly. C'MON, BITCH! I'M WAITING FOR YOU! The nerve of her.

This jerk opened her fat yap to *Us* magazine and claimed that I got her so upset at a Letterman show that we were both on that she had to leave the building and then be chased down and persuaded to come back and do her spot. "I think Stern's a loser and I don't need to follow some guy that was dissing me when I was supposed to be first up," she said. Okay, let me tell you the truth about what went down.

I was scheduled to be the first guest. I'm *always* on first, or I don't do the show. That was her first lie. Then she said I "dissed" her. All of a sudden, this blondie was talking like Public Enemy. This is what I said about her on Letterman. If she had any brains at all, she'd understand that it was actually a compliment.

Dave, I was back there in the Green Room looking for Sharon Stone. She is one hot babe. I went to see *Basic Instinct* where she crosses and uncrosses her legs, so for one split-second, you see something under her minidress. Now I'm a guy. I must see maybe two pornos a week. I'm honest, Dave. I'm a married man of seventeen years and I never cheated on my wife. I might masturbate five times a week 'cause I'm one horny guy and I've seen all the porno you can see. People who listen to me send me all kinds of porno things from Germany, things with animals, disgusting. So for me to get horny over Sharon Stone in an R-rated movie, that's an accomplishment.

There, that's what I said to Dave. Hey, there's no greater thing in the world than telling a woman who's playing a sex object who's trying to get guys excited that you masturbate to her. So where did I "dis" her?

You stupid confused bimbo! You got a great body but nothing between your ears. You dumb twit. Wait until you start getting those crow's-feet, and you haven't got long to wait, 'cause you've been knocking around Hollywood for years. I'm a loser, huh? I've got an audience of sixteen million people a week. Meanwhile you were in *Total Recall* for about seven seconds and *King Solomon's Mines* on TV with Richard Chamberlain, not to mention that porno you had to do for *Playboy*. You couldn't get noticed until you did that nude shot for *Playboy*, you big jerk! Now you did some shitty bomb of a film, *Sliver*, and you went and ran off with someone's husband on the set! *You're* the loser! The Letterman audience was more excited to see me than you! That's why you wanted to walk, you big crybaby! Even Dave said you were a crybaby! I don't have to spread my legs to get an audience excited, I can use my brains! You stupid bimbo skivosa! In five years you'll be dried up like a piece of shit in the desert. You'll look like a Tootsie Roll. Then you'll see how long that producer husband of yours keeps you around. Hey, if you want to keep your career going, I'll give you one piece of advice: Keep your legs open and your mouth shut.

## SINÉAD THE BALDY

I hate to pick on people who should be locked up in mental institutions, but this baldy deserves anything she gets. The nerve of this woman coming here and disrespecting our country and our flag! It was enough to make us hire a men's choir and bring them into the studio to sing our own version of "The Star-Spangled Banner":

O say bald Sinéad
Go jump in a lake
Frank Sinatra was right
We should kick you in your ass.
You tone-deaf fathead
You've got some set of balls
You no-talent runt
Go back where you came from.
Why do you attack
Our country and our flag?
Put a bag on your head
And a sock in your mouth.
Go put on a wig and go

Get some breast implants
Then kiss our big fat butts
You skin-headed bitch.

I guess our parody got to her, because soon afterward, Sinéad decided she wanted to retire from show
biz. Well, on our TV show we got a nearly bald Irish
woman and we envisioned some new jobs for Sinéad.
We showed her as a carnival barker, a Hare Krishna,
a nun, and a squeegee woman washing car wind-
shields. But the job most suited to Sinéad seemed to
be a cashier at McDonald's: "Hello, my name is
Sinéad, you ugly capitalist pig. What do you need to
fill your bloated, disgusting, imperialist American
belly today?"

For all we know, she's now in training in the Ronald
McDonald College.


## ROSEANNE AND TOM ARNOLD

I saved these two for last. I never really wanted to
get into a feud with Roseanne and Tom. This is not a
fair fight. Even though they outweigh me by tons, it
isn't fair to match wits with two people whose minds
have either been institutionalized or fried by cocaine.
And I was one of the only people who defended Roseanne and got the joke when she did her version of
"The Star-Spangled Banner." But when they kept appearing on talk shows trashing me, calling me a no-
talent jerk and a racist and an anti-Semite, I had no
choice but to respond. After all, I'm only human.

Okay, let's take Tom first. Here is a guy whose only talent appears to be getting it up for this fat slob. I would love to see the erection he gets for Roseanne. That must be one sick, evil hard-on. And believe me, he must have talent to be able to go through all those rolls of fat looking for her gross triangle. I mean, I would have sex with sand before I would

**Me, as Tom Arnold.**

have sex with Roseanne. Can you imagine the smells that must come out of her? Did you ever smell a big fatso like that? I don't see Roseanne spending three hours in the shower just to get all those hard-to-reach places. Plus, I can't see her shaving down and stuff. I imagine a big forest down there, a huge thatch that he has to weed through. Hey, I'd be on coke too if I had to go through that thatch, not to mention deal with the folds on her legs and her body cheese and stuff. It's frightening what this guy has to go through for his money. Hey, this guy is the Yoko Ono of the nineties, okay? 'Nuf said. Next mental case.

Sometimes I actually feel sorry for Roseanne. I've always said she was talented. It's just that she's fucked up, big time. So where should we start? Should we start with the incest allegations? Is that the emotional time bomb that propelled her into a loony bin? Or are the allegations of incest a symptom of her unstable mental condition? I don't know, but I find it disgusting that this woman can use her power of celebrity to exploit that platform and make wild, unsubstantiated charges, charges that don't have to be proven in a court of law, and wreak havoc on other people's lives. Did her father play hide-the-soap in her butt? Did he make her comb his other hair? Did her mother get her off every time she changed her diapers? I DON'T KNOW AND I DON'T CARE TO FIND OUT! HEY, IT'S SUPPOSED TO BE INCEST SURVIVORS *ANONYMOUS*. ANONYMOUS DOESN'T MEAN ALL OVER THE COVER OF *PEOPLE* MAGAZINE!

> "His fans are plumbers masturbating in their trucks on the way to work."
> —Roseanne Arnold

I was so sick of reading interviews of Roseanne and Tom that I conjured up a fantasy interview of Roseanne:

HOWARD: You say that you just remembered all these childhood episodes of molestation by your father that you were repressing, yet a year ago, at your wedding, you claim your father molested your daughter.

GROSSANNE: I just want to share these experiences so maybe it'll help other kids, so they don't turn out like me, big and fat and stuck with a guy who I'm not sure if he's chasing me for my money 'n stuff.

HOWARD: Remarkably, now Tom says he was molested at seven as a child.

GROSSANNE: Well, it all comes out under hypnosis—you'd be surprised. I remember now. Ooooh, yeah, that bastard. When I was born, the doctor picked me up like a bowling ball.

HOWARD: Your doctor molested you?

GROSSANNE: He explored my tiny baby places with cold, intrusive doctor instruments. It was at that moment I decided to eat too much my whole life.

HOWARD: I read something about your aunt.

GROSSANNE: Oh, yeah, my aunt used to give me oatmeal enemas. But, you know, I didn't realize it was wrong at the time. Boy, those enemas would make me scream.

HOWARD: They were too hot?

GROSSANNE: No, too lumpy. Why can't they make a smooth oatmeal 'n stuff?

HOWARD: You said you had an incident when you were ten?

GROSSANNE: It's true. When I was ten I got my first period 'n stuff and my mother used to make me wear barbed-wire tampons. But they weren't half as bad as the ground-glass suppositories.

HOWARD: Didn't your grandmother also abuse you?

GROSSANNE: Yeah, she used to make me run in the bathroom and sing to her while she took a dump 'n stuff. Then I had to wipe her butt with Q-Tips. And she was incontinent. It was so gross! But hey, I'm just trying to be honest.

HOWARD: Recount what happened to you when you were seventeen. That was particularly interesting.

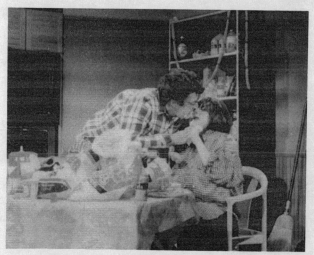

Judy Tenuta, as Roseanne, with me, the loving husband feeding his bride.

GROSSANNE: When I was seventeen, right, I was on my way home from a gang rape and all of a sudden a flying saucer landed in front of me and it grabbed me 'n stuff? And they put tinfoil on my breasts and tried to cook me in a microwave. Those space guys didn't even know not to put tinfoil in a microwave 'n stuff, but anyway, they made me mate with a giraffe. But it didn't hurt until Mike Tyson came along and punched me in the uterus 'n stuff. Hey, I'm just trying to be honest.

HOWARD: Tell us about your last memory of abuse.

GROSSANNE: Oh, this came out recently under hypnosis. I was molested by the Loch Ness Monster and the Easter Bunny. And then Santa Claus was also there.

HOWARD: You're saying that you were in a foursome with the Loch Ness Monster, the Easter Bunny, and Santa Claus?

GROSSANNE: Uh-huh. This was about the time I was in the loony bin.

HOWARD: I find that story hard to believe.

GROSSANNE: I got photographic evidence 'n stuff. Santa even let Rudolph take a turn. Boy, those antlers hurt. Hey, did I ever tell you about the time the pig farmer violated me with his pitchfork?

HOWARD: I think that's enough for now. Thank you, Grossanne.

GROSSANNE: Yeah, well, Tom still hates ya. You're third-rate to him.

Okay, let's assume that all of Roseanne's incest stories are true. Even granting that assumption, there is still no excuse for the way she conducted herself as her career was on the ascent. If you analyze it, Roseanne is despicable in that she did the same thing as all these phony guys do when they dump their wives who stood with them through thick and thin and leave their families and get their trophies. Hey, Tom Arnold is far from a trophy. He's not even a merit badge. But she's just like these guys who, as soon as they get a little money in their pocket, dump the old bat.

I've got to admit, it's somewhat tempting to do that. But I love my wife and my wife loved me when I was a bum. She was actually proud of me and brought me to her parents' house, even when I had no job. And her parents treated me like a human being even though I disgusted myself. I wanted to be in radio but

> "Howard Stern doesn't bother us. We chuckle at him. He's amusing sometimes. It's not the stuff he says about me, it's the racism and sexism and stuff that I hear him say. He'll make jokes about incest, which I think is sickening. I don't want anyone from our shows going on Howard Stern and I won't let them."
>
> —Tom Arnold

I had no voice, no delivery, nothing. But they treated me as if I was normal.

So when I get tempted by one of these little bims, I look at my bim and I know she's the best bim on the planet for me. I'm never going to do any better. She truly loves me. And true love is a hard thing to find, remember that. I trust my wife, and I'm so paranoid I don't trust anybody. I know she would never betray me. Any woman I would meet now I could never trust. So I feel bad for Roseanne's first husband. He actually married that fat slob and lived in a trailer with her. And raised children with her. Look at Roseanne. He must have really loved her to marry something like that.

Let me quote Roseanne from a recent article in the magazine *QW:*

Tom just came into the room and wants me to say how much I hate Howard Stern. What a fucking asshole. He's a racist pig and he gets away with it by having that stupid black woman sitting next to him, excusing all of it. He's a racist, sexist, homophobic fucking pig. His only fans are plumbers jacking off in their trucks on the way to work. If that's what America's coming to, I hope you print that in your magazine. You probably don't have to worry—I've said this to other magazines and they didn't print it. If I get a hold of him, I'm gonna shave his fucking head for him, so he'll look like the skinhead he is. He's an anti-Semite, too. And he's an ugly son of a bitch. He's uglier than Joey Ramone. I've said this to other people and I've been censored from day one by these stupid press people. They censor me because I'm a woman of opinion. Say hi to everybody out there in New York. Be sure to say "Howard Stern is a fucking pig."

So this is our new role model? A woman who gives her firstborn up for adoption, dumps her husband, spends time in a loony bin, and attacks the nicest, sweetest, most sentimental radio personality on the planet? They say you can tell a lot about a culture by the heroes it keeps.

# More and More and More Hate Mail

The last thing people need from you is political advice! You are the standard left -wing Jew Democrat! You are even worse. You are a one issue swine. Abortion! What a dunb JEW. Too bad your ugly Jew mother didn't abort you! You didn't abandon Jerry Brown because he did not come to your "show". You hated his statment that he would run with Jesse Jackson.... You JEWBASTARDS ARE STILL ANGRY ABOUT HIS HYMIE STATEMENT. YOUR WHOLE LIFE IS ISRAEL AND ABORTION....YOU'D BETTER FACE IT JEWSWINE, NO MATTER HOW YOU TRY TO PERSUADE YOUR AUDIENCE, THE PRESIDENT WILL STILL BE BUSH.... WE ARE A CHRISTIAN NATION....AND IN SPITE OF THE FACT THE YOU JEWSCUM RUN HOLLYWOOD AND THE MEDIA, WE SHALL OVERCOME ....ALL THE NEW JEWBABIES CAN SCREAM "DEMOCRAT" THE MOMENT THEY POP OUT OF THE JEWBITCH'S BOX .... BUT IT WILL DO NO GOOD. THE DEMOCRAT PARTY IS DEAD! THE DEMOCRAT PARTY IS NOW IN THE HANDS OF ALL THE SCUM OF THE EARTH. THE JEWS, AND NIGGERS, AND QUEERS AND LESBIANS. THE DEMOCRAT PARTY IS DEAD!


Howaed Stern:

        You are probably the most evil piece of Jew Drek in the area! You hurt anything that is not Jewish. Your life is harming others with your evil talk! That spade; nigger;darkie; no-talented-brillo-headed-colored person you laugh with,makes us vomit! She only ass-kisses your family and Jews in general! She even mocks her own kind...but try as she might, she will never be white. Her only talent is to laugh like an idiot. She looks like a little black boy on her face....and her reformed breasts look like when they are released,20 cockroaches will crawl out from under them. Not even her own kind can deal with her....so she keeps her nose up the foul-smelling Stern ass to make a living. Without Stern, at her advanced age, she could not even make a living selling her foul body!

        .........You say all preests are gay...well just look at those ugly looking,dirty-smelling jewbastard-rabbis with the little box-hats on their foreheads....and all the jewfaggots who head the jew groups,and the rabbis who are queer and who molest little boys and girls...... Speak about your own kind you mokie-bastard swine! Your bitch mother and dog father must be the devil to have whelped a piece of slime like you. If it were not for the N.Y. faggot Jew, you would have no ratings. You will never make it across the country, because there are no Jews across the country. Jews only foul the air in N.Y., Florida and parts of California. The only thing you cause is hatred. We are thankful your ugly, stinking Jew wife dropped her Jew fetus...one less jewbastard

# You've Been a Bad Girl, Haven't You?

## *Spanking, Stripping, Shaving, Butt Bongoing, and Beyond*

CHAPTER

12

I find it one of the great ironies of my life that when I was single, I couldn't get most women to even look at me, let alone sleep with me. But then, as soon as I became a popular radio personality, all these women start coming out of the woodwork. Unfortunately, by then I was married and I wasn't about to break my vows. But thank God

I have an outlet to sublimate these deep, dark desires. I have a show.

As far back as Washington, D.C., I realized that there were enough men in the same boat as me, so that bringing vicarious sex to my show would be a good career move as well as a great means to satisfy my sexual longings. We started out with a version of phone sex. Women would call in and tell us about their sex lives. Then, we wanted to see what these girls looked like, so we invited them down to the studio.

But seeing them wasn't enough. I had read an article about some French broadcasters who had actually had sex live on their show. Not to be outdone by a nation of sniveling cowards, I put the call out for a woman to come in and have sex with us. I was married, but Fred, one of my writers, was single. And sure enough, one girl came down. She wasn't half bad-looking either.

At DC-101 we had a big horseshoe-shaped console. So this girl came in and because we were in a glass-enclosed studio, I grabbed a remote mike and Fred, the girl, and I got under the console. We started off by making noises that simulated sex.

> "He looks like a chicken. Ninety-five percent of what he says is about sex, take the sex away, and he has no act, and he'll go nowhere . . . It's a shame, because he does have talent."
>
> —Jack Paar

After a few minutes, this girl got into it. She started getting into it way too much for me, but this was the first time that I saw Fred get sexual. They started making out and he was ripping his pants off. She was ready to go all the way right there under the console, but I pulled the plug on it at just the right time.

It wasn't until we got to WNBC in New York that we were actually able to get women to come in and take off their clothes on the air. It happened for the first time on our first Christmas party show. We had listeners call in and if they had some weird talents, like being able to belch Christmas carols, we had them come up to the studio. We put out some booze and the next thing we knew a girl was running around the studio throwing off her top! It was insane. It was like watching a librarian on a vacation in the Caribbean. Two piña coladas and she's bumping and grinding with a little native guy on the beach. Then Monday, she's back at work.

But we had our first taste of nudity and there was no stopping us. In fact, a few months later, I decided that until we could get girls to come down and take off their clothes for us, I would punish the listening audience. After the show's opening theme, I came on the air in a grave monotone.

"You people are being punished today. Until a naked woman agrees to come on this program, until a woman in our audience comes down here and takes her clothes off for me, you people will be punished. We'll just sit here until you get it together. No bits, no fun, just boredom," I said.

We got a false report that a Swedish blonde named Inga was coming down to strip at four o'clock, but she didn't. Then I really began to torture my audience. I played a Partridge Family record. I played Judy Collins singing "Send in the Clowns" complete with dogs whimpering and babies crying in the background.

"Now we're going to play 'How Much Is That Doggie in the Window?' and you people can sit and listen to it. Don't turn it off," I ordered. It only got worse. A few Steve Rossi songs. "You Light Up My Life." "The Night Chicago Died." It got so bad that Robin even tried to recruit some women on the NBC studio tour to strip, but to no avail. Later that afternoon, a woman called up and promised to come down the next day.

"One condition," she said. "As long as Robin is in the room. I don't want to be alone with you."

"I don't want to touch you, I just want to look at you. I haven't seen a new naked body in ten years. I just want to look at you so I have something to fantasize about. Is that too much to ask?" I said.

Meanwhile, we finished the show with Bobby Vinton, Nancy and Frank Sinatra, "Jean," "Harper Valley PTA," "I Am Woman," "Candy Man," and "The Ballad of the Green Berets."

The next day we hit pay dirt. Waiting for us in the studio was not one, not two, but three girls! One was a comedienne named Maria, up from Philly, who promised to play Dial-a-Date naked. The second was a redheaded stripper named Destiny, and the third was Cathy, an incredible blonde. She was a natural breathtaking beauty, a girl next door who was about to do the wildest thing she'd ever done in her life. In fact, she was so shy about taking her clothes off that she brought along a male friend and made him take off his clothes, too, before she would. It was wild.

Knowing the hypocrites in management at NBC all

too well, I immediately made the studio a closed set. I had Gary, who had just started working for me around this time, tape newsprint all over the glass windows. Then I assigned both Gary and Fred to keep everybody out. I didn't care if the general manager or the program director or even Grant Tinker showed up, they weren't getting in.

"Three naked girls! Three naked girls on my show!" I screamed and Fred began to play some strip music.

"Maria's pants are off," I began a play-by-play.

"Destiny is bumping and grinding and taking her clothes off," Robin reported.

"The guy is naked! Cathy is naked!" I exulted.

"This is disgusting," Robin said.

"This is great!" I corrected her.

I put Maria into a chair so I had an unencumbered view of her 38C assets and we began her Dial-a-Date. Just then there was a commotion outside the studio door. I later found out that most of the NBC executives were outside trying to get in. And one of the NBC corporate lawyers was adamant. He *demanded* to be allowed in.

"I'm sorry," Gary said. "We're not allowing anybody in here."

"I NEED TO BE IN THERE, GODDAMNIT!" the suit exploded. "I'M A LAWYER. I NEED TO HEAR IF SOMETHING OBSCENE IS GOING ON."

This guy was out of control. There was no way he had to *see* what was going on. His job was to *listen*, not to *look*. But man, did he want to look! He created such a fucking scene that he really came off like a dirty old man.

RAY: I'm totally disgusted.

HOWARD: She's got a D cup, just like you! I told you I'd get a naked girl down here!

RAY: And when your daughter gets older, you're gonna have her listen to this nonsense?

HOWARD: Emily doesn't think I'm her father. I told her her father is a Harvard professor.

The censor turned on his slimy heels and stormed away. Here was a guy who was in charge of lecturing *me* on decency looking every bit the peep-show customer.

"My mother said I'd never get a naked woman in here." I was gloating. "I've got three." I called her up.

We went back to Dial-a-Date and Maria made her choice. Then we got another girl to strip for Greg the engineer, who missed the initial nudity.

"It's really weird, Robin, during the whole thing with all those girls taking their clothes off, I was not really that turned on, believe it or not, because I love my wife," I said.

"Why lie to *me*, Howard?" Robin asked.

"Ssshh. Alison just called up and she won't even go on the air with me," I said. Alison had sounded really pissed. "I just wanted to test myself. I wanted to see three naked women to see if I was really in love with my wife."

"You had some question?" Robin was ruining everything.

"There was just one little iota of doubt. Every once in a while, a man questions himself. And as I'm looking at all these naked girls, I'm saying, 'I love my wife.

My wife has a beautiful body. She's my friend, she's my lover, she's my confidante.' " Was anyone buying this bullshit? Just in case they weren't, I added, "This is proof positive that I love my wife more than anything in the world. And I can look at *more* naked women and not be turned on."

But looking was soon not enough. Like a desperate junkie, I had to seek new highs. I started spanking women on the air.

Girls would let me undress them. First I'd pull down their pants; eventually I'd remove their panties. They'd get over my knee, arch their back, and I would make them ask for a spanking. As I slapped, I made them ask me for more. "You've been a bad girl, haven't you?"

"Yes," they'd eventually reply.

Then they would ask me to spank them harder.

"Are you sure you want this? Is this what you really want?"

"Yes," they would moan.

I even spanked Jack Nicholson's *Playboy* centerfold girlfriend, Karen Mayo-Chandler, after he had done the very same thing.

Then it got kinkier and kinkier. I invited guys to come in and spank their wives in front of me, then it was girls spanking other girls. I was slowly running out of perverted things to do.

Enter Tula, the transsexual, fresh from the Donahue show. She was so voluptuous she'd fooled the James Bond movie producers, who featured her as one of the Bond girls. I've got to admit that for a guy without a penis, she was pretty good-looking.

"Hey, Tula, pull down your panties. I want to see how real your phony vagina looks. That's not real private parts. That's a surgical scar with a scab on it."

"Oh, yeah, you couldn't tell the difference," she said in her deep voice.

"I sure could. Pull down your panties. Let me examine you. It can't smell very good because it can't clean itself. There must be deposits in there

The transsexuals, Tula and Howiener (me), exchanging shaving tips.

from everyone since the James Bond movie."

I really pissed her off. She came over to my side.

"Take off your pants first," she said. "Let me see what you've got."

"I don't have any problem with that. You're a guy." I stood there in my underpants and she grabbed my balls and cock with those big manly mitts of hers. Some things a doctor can't change.

I popped the biggest fucking boner. Some guys really know how to handle the goods. She was a pro.

After a seductive struggle, which I lost, Tula refused to show me her man-made vagina. My guess is the whole damn mess looks like one giant scab. She stripped down to her panties and I've got to admit, the confused fucker looked good.

After the thrill of spanking transsexuals and lesbians wore off, I turned to shaving. We asked female listeners to come in and shave in front of me. A few times we even offered them free concert tickets to shave. One time we got a married woman to come up and shave herself. Her name was Maria and her husband was a big fan of mine. She was really cute. Brown hair. Big jugs. When she entered the studio, we started playing "Happy Days Are Here Again." Over Fred's sound effects of an electric razor, I started singing:

> Lather up your hairy lap
> Don't you listen to all that other crap
> When Howard's on no one takes a nap
> Lather up that hairy lap
> Happy days are here again

She didn't like Jackie and Fred being there so I kicked them right out. Robin wanted to leave, too, but I forced her to stay, although we arranged Maria's chair so Robin couldn't see what was going on.

Maria lathered up and started to shave. We needed a bowl of hot water to rinse her razor off so we grabbed Jackie's cereal bowl. We're always using Jackie's bowl or coffee mug for some skeevy scam, but he doesn't care. Jackie's one of those guys who uses the same mug every day without rinsing it out. It's always full of stains, spit and piss. Then he mixes his tea with a fucking pencil. It's disgusting.

Me, I only drink from paper cups, I'm so terrified of germs. This guy is healthy as a horse and I'm the one who's always getting sick.

So this girl was shaving her fucking disgusting pubic hairs all over his cereal bowl and he ate from it the next day. I wanted to vomit. I hope he enjoyed his *Lice* Krispies.

Maria stood there naked with her thighs spread, shaking with nervousness. When she finished I asked her if she wanted to be spanked. She lay down across my lap.

"First of all, your behind is gorgeous," I said, inspecting the merchandise. She was shaking more. "What are you uptight about?"

"Nothing," Maria said.

"This is your fantasy, right? Okay, say, 'Howard, my master, please spank me.'"

She repeated after me. I spanked her and she began to laugh.

"You could do it a little harder," she said.

> "I listen to him and I have to turn it off. It gets so foul. He talks about smelling underwear and he's got the bobbing for tampons. It grosses you out."
> —Gary Collins

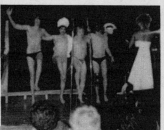 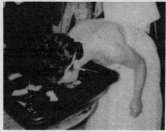

I do all-male burlesque with Gary, Jackie, and Fred (left). Audience members at a live club appearance bobbing for tampons.

"You getting excited?" I asked.

"Yes," she sighed.

I gave her a few more whacks and released her.

"This was a great show. We can go home now," I pronounced.

"All the hair is gone?" Robin wondered.

"Everything," I said. "It's all in Jackie's cereal bowl."

Stripping, spanking, shaving—the possibilities were endless. We competed with each other to figure out new ways of getting women to get out of their clothes and new things to do to them once they were in the buff.

For some reason our supply of women started drying up. We hadn't had a naked woman in a week.

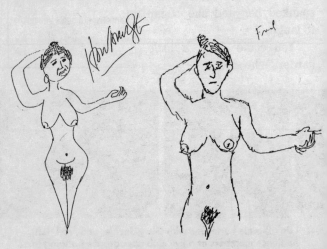

**My drawing . . . Fred's attempt . . .**

That's when I had a brainstorm. A very dim light went on in my head.

One day we had two phone sex girls up to give a demonstration of their craft. When we found out that one of them was actually a nude model for art students, we saw great potential there. We chipped in and paid her to model nude for us while we drew her.

Jackie, Fred, Gary, and I would become artists. So I bought easels, paints, and berets. Yes, we wore berets on the radio with our headphones on and I put a call out on the radio for girls to come down to model nude for us. They came in droves. After all, this was a legitimate venture. There was nothing *vile* about it.

We brought in a model who was posing with her right arm in the air like a Michelangelo sculpture.

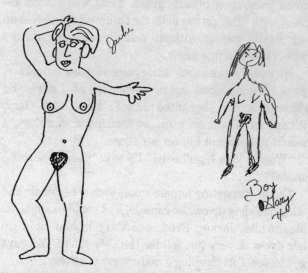

**Leonardo da Jackie . . . and Gary's worthless piece of shit.**

Jackie, Fred, and I really tried to capture the beautiful flow. In our sketches you could see that we really tried to draw her. Gary just stood there staring at the girl. When we saw his drawing we burst out laughing. He just wanted to gape at this naked woman and paid no attention to his art. Her stupid arm isn't even up in the air. And check out the pubic bush and wishbone tits. Nice shoulders. Where the hell are her hands? Talk about pencil necks! And what's with that expression on her face? But he did spend a lot of time on his rather feminine and intricate signature. That smelly bastard. We haven't had another nude model since. He blew the whole thing.

Drawing led to painting and soon enough we were having naked girls up every St. Patrick's Day so we could paint their breasts green. Paint was always applied with little cotton balls that allowed me to feel up my studio guests without actually cheating on my wife. (I walk a fine line.)

We even began subtle little games among ourselves, games the audience had no knowledge of. I devised a shoe trick that benefited Jackie, Fred, and Gary. Whenever a woman came in wearing a miniskirt, I would compliment her on her shoes.

"Wow, I love high heels," I'd say. "Can I see those shoes?"

The unsuspecting female would swivel her chair and stick her shoe up on the console, so I could examine it. Meanwhile, Jackie, Fred, and Gary looked right up her dress. Every girl fell for the shoe trick. The guys got to see Tori Spelling's underwear that way.

Tori was just the beginning. Our next conquest was

**Even with my fat belly hanging out, I was seductive in my Burt Lancaster role with MTV's Martha Quinn in a scene from *From Here to Eternity*.**

the famous porn star Ginger Lynn. I got to spank her, but it wasn't easy. Ginger was dating Charlie Sheen at the time, and at first she didn't even want to take off her clothes. But I went into my patented "Stern Whining" and a few minutes later she was buck naked and lying across my lap. I gave her a nice spanking. She had one of the most incredible bodies I had ever seen. It was a real turn-on.

"Oh, my God, Charlie's going to be so upset," Ginger worried. "I'll tell him that it was only the radio, I wasn't really naked and getting spanked." But she was naked and she did get spanked and I didn't think Charlie was going to buy that bullshit. A few weeks later, Gary tried to book Charlie Sheen for our TV show and we heard that he was furious and he wanted to beat the shit out of me because I had his girlfriend naked over my lap. As if it was my fault. This is a girl who's fucked everything that breathes in her porno movies and he was mad at *me*.

But I find it much more exciting to see regular actresses nude than X-rated stars. That's why when I get a regular movie star up in the studio and there's any chance of any action, I take out all my artillery. I tell her that my wife is dying of cancer. In fact, when I had Margaux Hemingway up, I told her that Alison had already died. We were flirting like crazy and it looked as if something might happen.

"I think about what I'd do to you," I moaned.

"She's tall enough for you," Robin said.

"We're a good-looking couple," Margaux agreed.

"We could do things standing up," I suggested. "If my wife is listening, I know you're up there in heaven somewhere, honey. Just close your ears because I'm ready to get back in the saddle. I've got to get back to it. I lost Alison but I've got to get back on that horse and ride. Are you free for lunch?"

She wasn't. Bitch.

Sometimes I have to depend on Alison to stop things in the nick of time. One time I had Kimberly Taylor the *Penthouse* pet on. I wanted her to get naked for me, but she wouldn't.

"Howard, show me your penis, then I'll get naked," she insisted.

She knew I'd never show anyone my small penis because of how uptight I am about its size. But since I was nursing a hard-on, my penis looked kind of big. So I didn't really care if she saw my penis. I pulled my underpants open and let her look down.

"I can't see anything. OKAY, NOW I CAN SEE IT! HE'S HIDING IT BETWEEN HIS LEGS!" she screamed.

Here I thought my penis was so full but she couldn't even see it. How humiliating!

She kept screaming, "WHERE IS IT?! I CAN'T SEE IT!"

Stuttering John ran into the room. "Alison's on the phone."

"Honey, she didn't see anything," I assured Alison.

"What are you doing, Howard? STOP IT!" Alison said.

Alison is like the guards at Buckingham Palace about my penis. She loves it and guards it like the crown jewels.

"Here's what happened, honey. Kim took off her top and I took off my pants, but you didn't see much, did you Kim?"

"I saw a pubic hair," Kimberly said.

*"Howard, if you don't want to stay married, keep cheating,"* Alison piped in.

"I'm bringing Kimberly home for us, honey. We have a new housekeeper."

"I don't believe this, every day. It's getting boring already," Alison said.

"What kind of wife are you? You let me keep doing this stuff," I said.

"You want a nice weekend? Keep your clothes on," Alison warned and hung up.

But the one woman who strained my marriage vows to the fullest was Stacy Galina, from "Knots Landing." We had her on my TV show and we did a parody of Dirty Dancing called Sterny Dancing.

Actress Stacy Galina shows me her beautiful ass cheeks, a rare public display.

During the dirty dancing scene, she tried to kiss me but I turned my head away. Then after we finished shooting, she followed me into my inner dressing room. In the full two years of that show, no one had pursued me that far. Robin, Jackie, Dan Forman, everybody lined up with their ears pressed to the door to hear what we were doing in there.

I thanked Stacy for being on the show. She told me that she was going to be in New York staying at her grandmother's house all weekend with nothing to do. It was a tempting offer but I was good and went home to Long Island. It was a really bad weekend. I had to masturbate three times to stay a family man. That week, Stacy was scheduled to be a guest on my radio show.

"I was thinking about you the whole weekend," she said.

"You're so cute. You must have tons of guys coming on to you," I said.

"No," she said.

"Believe me, if I was single, we would have had some blast this weekend. I had to go home and masturbate three times the other night. I was mad at everyone because I wanted to have sex with you, Stacy. If I was single I would have done you and your grandmother. Do you ever wear a thong?" I asked.

"Underwear, but not a bikini," she said.

"Are you wearing thong underwear right now?"

"No."

"God, am I turned on," I moaned. "What I would do to you sexually . . ."

"What would you do?" she asked me.

"In three seconds it would be over. But we would do it ten times in one day," I said. "You're practically a virgin, aren't you? Fresh as a daisy. Now, why are you in love with me? Physically you can't be," I said.

"Physically I am," she said. "I love you because you're witty. I'm physically attracted to you. You're smart."

"Ram your tongue down my throat," I pleaded. "What a tease you are, telling me you love me."

"Why should we be tormenting ourselves?" Stacy wondered.

"You give me a definite boner. You're cute, you're fresh. You're not a bimbo. I'm masturbating as we speak. Can I give you a massage?" I asked.

"Yeah."

"Oh, great! I'll kick the guys out of the room. You mean it?"

"Yeah," she said.

"Fred, let's leave while he doesn't have sex," Jackie said.

"I'm a little nervous. I'd rather massage you," Stacy said. "What are you doing?"

I pulled off my pants, put on a towel, and we dimmed the lights in the studio.

"Are you naked under that towel?" Stacy asked.

"What do you want?" I said.

"Naked! Naked!" Stacy laughed.

She began to rub me down.

"I love you so much," Stacy said.

She was very clinical in her approach. Tula did more for me. "What kind of a rubdown is this from a woman who loves me?" I asked. "You're rubbing me down like my wife rubs me down."

"I love your hair," she said.

Just then, my paradise was punctured by the appearance of Stuttering John. Which could mean only one thing. Alison was on the phone.

"My wife ruins everything," I moaned.

"I'm nervous," Stacy said.

"It sounds obnoxious," Alison said. "You're leading her on!"

Stacy stopped rubbing.

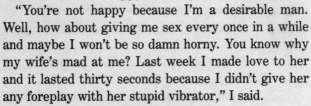

"What happened to the rubdown? There's something so dirty when a woman rubs you down with your wife yelling at you," I said.

"I'm really getting offended," Alison said. "I'm not happy listening to any of this."

"You're not happy because I'm a desirable man. Well, how about giving me sex every once in a while and maybe I won't be so damn horny. You know why my wife's mad at me? Last week I made love to her and it lasted thirty seconds because I didn't give her any foreplay with her stupid vibrator," I said.

"None of that is true," Alison said.

"I bet you give me good sex tonight. You want me to bring Stacy home for a threesome?"

"No, I don't. And I bet you don't either." Alison was fuming.

"Give me a kiss, Alison," I said.

"You're embarrassing me," Alison said.

"You're shaking, Stacy. You're so filled with lust," I said.

"You sound like a dirty old man," Alison said.

"The same position every time." I yawned.

"I'm hanging up," Alison threatened. "This sounds like cheating to me."

"I don't want Alison to be mad at me," Stacy worried.

"She's not mad at you, she's mad at me," I said.

"Robin, I'm counting on you," Alison said.

"I love you," I said sweetly.

"I love you, too," Alison said and hung up.

"Where were we?" I plunged right back in.

"Now that I've talked to Alison," Stacy sighed, "the party's over."

"That bitch wife of mine can't handle that I have a little fun," I said. Stacy complained that her stomach was cramping up.

"I guess I have to say good-bye to you. Come over here. Sit on my lap," I said.

"I'm so depressed," she said, as she sat on my lap.

"Your breath smells great. I'm getting aroused," I said.

"It's weird," Stacy said.

"Love is difficult that way," I philosophized. "You'll have to get another man and fantasize it's me."

She kissed me good-bye.

"I don't want her to be happy," I said. I wanted her to suffer and miss me. She got all upset again. I searched for some words that might make this separation a little easier.

"Before you go, will you flash me?" I finally asked.

"I can't," Stacy said. "I have a padded bra on." Then she walked out of the studio and out of my life.

But that's what usually happens. I'm doing my job, entertaining people, and my wife gets a call from one of her yenta friends whose husbands are cheating on *them*, and they get Alison all pumped up and she calls in angry. Then I go home and we fight. Who needs her to call in the first place? If I worked in the leather business like my sister's husband, do you think Alison and my mother would be so quick to call during the day to see what I was doing? I'm lucky Alison doesn't drive into the station and try to watch through the glass walls of the studio. But she doesn't have to. She's got Robin there. *"Robin, I'm counting on you!"*

Well, one April Fools' Day, we got Robin back for all the times she's been Alison's police force. Let Robin tell the story.

 First, let me explain what it's like being the only woman on the show. Sometimes I feel like an anthropologist studying male behavior when I'm sitting in my studio overlooking Howard and the guys. It's as if they're in a men's locker room and I'm getting a dose of how men really talk to each other when they aren't afraid that women might hear them. That's why I don't object to what's happening, because they're pretending that this is a boys' room. They're not doing this to offend women, they're just being guys.

If you look at Howard's life, I serve the same purpose as the other women in his life. He's more human because of us. If we weren't there, Howard would be just this huge id, out of control, saying whatever, burping, farting. If I weren't for women, he'd never control any of his bodily functions, he'd never have a nice thought.

This April Fool's thing started when a girl called up and said she was in love with Howard and he said she should come up to the studio so he could see her. Nothing out of the ordinary. She came up and she was sitting there, just looking at him, telling him how much she loved the way he sounded over the air and how much she was in love with him and how she would do anything for him. I was sitting there thinking, 'Yeah, right, ha ha ha.' I couldn't care less.

All of a sudden, Howard said, "You really do love me and you'd do anything for me? Make love to me right now—right here on the air. Man, I've been waiting for this all my life." He was telling her that it was cheating on his wife only if *he* did something, not if somebody did something to him. This woman had convinced me that she was really crazy in love with Howard. So he said, "Come over here." She got up and went around the console. "What are we gonna do?" he said.

"Let's just get down here," she said and, all of a sudden, they disappeared under the console. I couldn't see anything anymore. And Howard was saying, "All right, Robin. I'm down here and she's taking off all my clothes." And I started to see clothes flying out over the console. I saw a shirt. I saw a blouse. I saw a bra. I saw a skirt. I saw panties. Then I saw Howard's pants! Then I saw his underwear! I was thinking, 'This is ridiculous,' and they started making sex noises and carrying on and I was saying, "NO! This woman's crazy, she's out of her mind!" I jumped up and I ran into the studio and ran around the console. I had to stop him from destroying his marriage! I thought he'd lost his mind, that he hadn't thought this through. There they were, lying on the ground with all their clothes on, with a bag full of clothes they were throwing out.

"APRIL FOOLS!" they screamed.

But with our famous Super Bowl parties, we elevated this concept of fantasy sex into a true art form. It didn't start out that way, though. Our first Super Bowl party was when we were still back at WNBC and it was just a gathering of the men who worked on the show. One of our sponsors, Big Al from Great Sounds, lent us a fifty-inch projection TV and we rented a room in a motel in Westbury and watched the game. No girls, no nothing. All we did was watch the game and smear Cheez Whiz all over the huge TV's corrugated screen. There'd be a close-up of a quarterback and we'd take the Cheez Whiz and draw a dick going into his ass, mature stuff like that.

The next year, we planned a more elaborate party. We had it at my friend Neil's house. And we realized that Super Bowl Sunday was probably the only day in the year that married guys could get massages from strange women and get away with it. So Ronnie, my limo driver, rounded up a couple of hookers who were absolutely disgusting. I don't even know if we can call them hookers because nobody would go near these skeeves, except for Jackie "the Joke Man," who wound up in the basement with them. He claimed that they only gave him a toe massage but we never believed him.

By the third year, things started picking up. We had the party at Neil's house again. We had more guys and more hookers.

Then Neil's house was too small so we moved to the Garden City Hotel, and I was in charge of booking the entertainment. I packed the place with *Penthouse* pets and lesbians. It was Disneyland for men.

The highlight of the whole party was when a guy named Joe mooned everybody. He had written "GIANTS SUCK" in Magic Marker on his ass.

As Joe pulled down his pants, Jackie, who was sitting on the floor eating a giant plate of ribs, nonchalantly reached over and shoved his finger right up this guy's ass. It was the single most disgusting thing I ever saw Jackie do.

Joe grunted and turned green. Jackie pulled his finger out of Joe's ass and went right back to eating his ribs.

"Wash your fucking hands! You're eating finger food, you cow!" we all yelled.

Poor Joe was so freaked that he ran out of the party. Jackie had raped him with his finger!!

The infamous finger in the moon incident (top). Moments later, eating ribs.

This was the funniest thing I ever saw. But Jackie was unfazed—compared to the other disgusting things he had done, this was nothing. After all, Jackie had once urinated inadvertently in his mother's face and had taken a shit out of a moving vehicle in traffic.

Each year our party got more and more elaborate. We got more booze, more food, more girls. Better girls, too. One year *Penthouse* pet Amy Lynn came and was doing her hot oil strip routine for the guys, but I missed it because I was in another room getting a rubdown from two girls who were doing all sorts of great stuff to each other.

My fantasy sex life gets more twisted ... bikini-clad women eating hot dogs on a string (top left), the How Quick Can You Put a Condom on a Banana Contest (bottom), and orchestrating one of the sickest moments ever ... the Howard Stern Prom Show. I crowned this couple Prom King and Queen when she shoved her five-inch heel up his ass.

**Massaging and male bonding on TV.**

But by this time, I realized that my modest idea had grown out of control. It was too depressing to be at one of these parties. There were beautiful, willing women in any of the rooms and I wasn't allowed to have sex with them. My conscience wouldn't allow it. Who needed this aggravation? I put an end to the Super Bowl parties. It's just too hard to lead two separate lives. You can't be a family man and parade around with naked women tempting you every second.

By the way, I learned all of this family value stuff by reading that sensitive and inspiring work *I Can't Believe I Said That!* by Kathie Lee Gifford, my idol. Actually, my mother set me straight when I first got

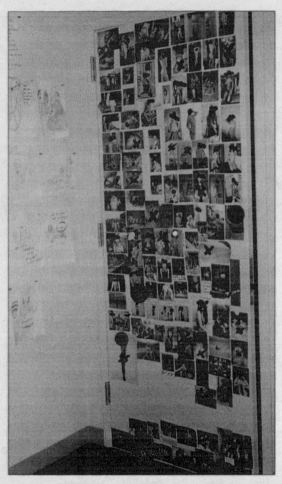

**Never before seen: the back of my office door, compliments of my listeners and viewers who send me pictures of themselves nude.**

**Finding more stupid ways to get close to women: Spokesmodel of the Year (top photo), a new game show called Guess Who Has the Breast Implants? (bottom right), and an audience member turned spokesmodel endorses Snapple.**

Jessica Hahn cavorting with
an elephant's trunk on my
*Butt Bongo Fiesta* tape.

**You can never get enough of butt bongo.**

***Penthouse*** pet Amy Lynn (left) and dancer Tempest assist me for the cover shoot. We posed for over three hours knowing full well these shots were too outrageous for the cover. But who cared?

married. She told me if I ever started running around with other women, she would take Alison and the kids into her home and would never speak to me again.

Like most of the other pussy-whipped men in America, I now spend Super Bowl Sundays home with my family.

But my quest for the ultimate surrogate sexual experience continues. We recently went from spanking to butt bongoing, which is really just frenetic spanking in time to a rock record playing in the background. I even showcased butt bongoing on my last videotape, *Butt Bongo Fiesta*. But we're beginning to get jaded. The thrill is rapidly vanishing. There are fewer and fewer fantasy sex worlds to conquer. I knew we were treading on the outskirts of total dissolution when, as a practical joke, I decided to secretly tape-record the first creative meeting for *Butt Bongo Fiesta*.

I called Dan Forman and John Lollos, the former executive producers of my TV show, to the meeting. I was going to tell Forman and Lollos, two pretty straight, family-type guys, that our next tape should be just ninety minutes of enemas and douching. I was sure the idea would make both of them want to vomit and they'd take a righteous stand and refuse to work on it. Meanwhile, I would really nag them and try to convince them and we'd have a great practical joke to play on my radio show.

"We'll call it 'The Howard Stern Enema and Douche Party.' " I pitched the project straight-faced to Dan and John. "Just ninety minutes of douching and enemas. What do you think?"

"I hate to say it but I *like* it," Dan gushed. "But I wish I wasn't saying that."

Then I turned to John and asked him what he thought. He was against it and had a lot of reservations. He said, "I don't see where we are going with this."

I realized how far gone we were. Everyone was now taking me seriously. Everyone believed I was now willing to produce a douche and enema tape, whether they were for or against it. No more morality, no code of ethics. It didn't matter what it was, we'd do it. I told the guys to turn off the hidden tape recorder. We had definitely gone beyond the pale. We weren't philosophers, we were perverts.

# Star Wars

I'm good at starting fights,
always have been. Even as a kid I
would turn to my sister and tell her
I was heading downstairs to get Mom
and Dad worked up. My dad would come
home from work around 7:00 P.M. and
quickly race to the dinner table.
After putting in a long day, he was
tired and it was time to eat. I'd sit at
the table waiting to start a little trouble.
My father's partner in the recording
studio had started a small record label called Ping
Pong, which annoyed and frustrated my dad. The very
words *Ping Pong* could set him off.

MOM: How was your day, Ben?

DAD: Good, good.

ME: Hey, Dad, anything going on with Ping Pong? . . . *Ping Pong?*

DAD: Shut up!

ME: Just kidding.

DAD: Don't you know how to shut up? Even a moron knows how to sit quiet at the table.

ME: Hey, I was just saying Ping Pong.

MOM: You know your father doesn't like that. What's wrong with you?

ME: I'm proud of Ping Pong. I just want to know more about it.

DAD: Shut up! Your mother and I are having a conversation, maybe you'll learn something.

Within minutes my father would be threatening me, my mother would be yelling, and I was ecstatic. It was real drama. And to think I make a living doing the same thing today, by pushing people's buttons and getting them to fight on the radio. One time there was a traffic guy at WNBC who was a Vietnam vet. I respect vets and I'm genuinely curious about combat experiences. I asked the guy if he had killed any gooks in 'Nam and the guy went nuts, and he complained to the general manager. The next day the general manager gave me a good reaming and said that I should deliver an on-air apology. Of course I protested. I never apologized, but I did tell him on the air that if I offended him in any way I certainly hadn't intended to do so. He was very understanding and just as he was signing off I said, "So, did you or didn't you kill any gooks?" The guy went nuts and changed his shift to another show.

The traffic reporter who I believe *really* disliked me was Roz Frank. When I first came to WNBC I had to kiss Roz's ass because they told me she was a bigger star than I was. We'd get into on-air fights all the time.

Then she got pissed at me for an interview I did with the *New York Post*. They asked me if I was at war with Roz, so I told them that I really liked Roz except for her eye cheese. She called me at home, screaming at me to cut the shit. But I got her another way. Before she went on the air, Roz always cleared her throat. We recorded that and every time, right before she came on with her report, we rolled the tape of her clearing her throat. We even used to play Celebrity Phlegm and have listeners call in to identify it.

One time I got the entire staff of K-Rock's sister Spanish station pissed off. They were hiring the Spanish Dr. Ruth, a big star, and the general manager of the station, Frank Flores, told me that they were having this big press conference and he made me swear that I would leave his press conference alone. Every major Latino newspaper would be there.

I couldn't help myself. It was as if Satan got inside me. I went to this serious press conference and stood outside the doorway and held up signs that read "Castro Rules" and "Give Me Back My Hubcaps." They went nuts. None of the Spanish people from the station ever spoke to me again.

Some of my guests cry at the slightest provocation. I made Wham wince when they sat down and the first question I asked them was, "Let's solve this once and for all: Are you guys gay?" They denied it. I've made

Richard Simmons cry a hundred times, but that's easy.

The last person to cry on my show was comedienne Judy Tenuta, and it wasn't even my fault. She cried because Sam Kinison and Penn Jillette ganged up on her. Before Judy came into the room Sam offered me five crisp, new hundred-dollar bills if I got Judy to show us her breasts.

As soon as Judy showed up, Sam and Judy started going at it. Judy started goofing on Sam's young girlfriend, Malika, and her sister, Sabrina, whom Sam was also doing. Sam wouldn't take shit from anyone and he came back at Judy with a vengeance. He kept attacking her relationship with Emo Phillips, the comedian, because Judy kept their marriage a secret.

"Judy thinks she can just come in here and slap and abuse every man in this room just because Emo turned out to be such a disappointment in her life," Sam said.

"I don't hang out in day-care centers," Judy snarled.

"We're the enemy just because we share genitalia with this disappointment you call your boyfriend. You're not even proud enough of him to claim him as your man," Sam bellowed. "Emo's probably locked in your trunk outside! *'I've been good, can I come out?'* "

"Yeah, like your poodles aren't on a leash outside," Judy shrilled. They were going at it pretty good.

Finally Penn decided to do a card trick. He pulled out a deck of cards and he had Sam pick one.

"I'm putting it back in the deck, shuffling it, remember the card, visualize it clearly. Okay, okay, Judy, now take off your top," Penn said.

Judy was pissed.

"It didn't work," I said.

"I have to go," Judy suddenly said, and stormed out of the studio. We were all in shock. Judy was upset because she thought she was coming on alone.

"Tell her, 'Welcome to comedy and show biz on the same day,'" Sam said. He was Mr. Sensitive. "When she came in she wasn't wearing white slacks. Maybe it was a special day."

Penn, who had run out into the hall to apologize to Judy, came back in. "I CAN'T BELIEVE IT. I SAY ONE THING AND I'M THE SCHMUCK," he screamed.

Penn suddenly jumped up and pointed at Sam.

"THIS RAT BASTARD SET ME UP. HE PUT MY COMEDY BALLS UP AGAINST THE WALL. SAM GOT HER ANGRY . . . AND SHE COMES DOWN ON ME. I'M FROM MASSACHUSETTS, I DON'T NEED THIS. I'M GETTING OUT." Penn made like he was walking out.

Gary came back in and told us that Judy was crying when she left, saying she didn't have to take that crap, that she was ganged up on.

"I can't imagine this crew being accused of ganging up. I wouldn't team up with anybody here," Penn said.

"I bet she's driving home sitting on a towel," Sam laughed. "I just wish Emo would grab Ju-

> "Howard is a Buddhist monk in heat."
> —Judy Tenuta

dy's hair and use it like the bridle of a horse and ride her into a wall."

Sam then told a story about the time he went to see Judy do a show in Denver years ago and they had a little makeout session.

I felt really bad Judy left the show. The next morning, I arranged for her to come up again, this time alone.

"I love Sam. I can't help it if he was acting like a baboon in heat," I said.

"I was just surprised you had the whole small primate house in here. And I was *not* crying," Judy started off.

"You were crying like Roseanne Barr had just stepped on your foot," I said.

"And I didn't make out with Sam in Denver. He was like Jabba the Hut with blow. He came backstage, I didn't even know who he was."

Suddenly, the hot line rang. I knew who it was without answering.

"JABBA THE HUT? YOU ACNE-FACED . . ." Sam screamed. "I DEFENDED YOU YESTERDAY. I SAID ROSEANNE BARR STOLE EVERYTHING FROM YOU AND YOU RIP ME WITH 'JABBA THE HUT WITH BLOW'? YOU'RE MAKING A STUPID CAREER MOVE TO MESS WITH ME."

"I guess it's fair that you said I should have my head rammed into a wall?" Judy countered.

"I can overreact, too," Sam said. "It's not a female prerogative."

"You two should kiss again and make up. Like in Denver," I said.

"Sam, I'm sorry, I was making a little joke," Judy apologized.

"I got to go on a diet. That's my only vulnerable attack point," Sam said. "I love you, Judy. I think you're the best. If I hurt your feelings yesterday I'm sorry and I apologize."

"I FEEL SO GOOD NOW, SAM, I'M GOING TO CRY," Judy wailed.

"It's good you two kids made up," I said, "but this sucks for my ratings."

## WELCOME TO THE JUNGLE

One of my most celebrated on-air feuds began with a simple dispute I had with the rock group Bon Jovi and culminated in a knock-down, drag-out affair between Sam Kinison and me. It started very innocently when I got pissed at Bon Jovi for going on radio stations like Z–100 and WNEW to promote their new album yet shunning my show. I was mad because we were the only show to promote Bon Jovi when they were nobodies. I had what I thought was a good relationship with three guys in the band—Jon Bon Jovi, Richie Sambora, and David Bryan.

One of my loyal listeners gave me Jon's home phone number, so I called him on the air and asked him why he wouldn't do my show. He gave me some lame excuse that the record company stopped him because the other stations threatened not to play the record if he came on with me. I knew this was bullshit and I teased him for kowtowing to the record execs. I renamed him *Jon Bon Phony*.

Jon sounded really contrite and offered to come over to my house, wash the car, and baby-sit my kids for restitution, but I was merciless.

"You guys wanted to get sodomized and we allowed you to have some girls in the backseat of a K-Rock limo and this is the thanks I get!" I whined. Meanwhile, here I was complaining that he wouldn't come on the air and I had already had him on for over an hour.

Then Sambora called in and I started in on him. I refused to accept his apology, I told the sodomy story again, then I warned him that Jon would dump him as fast as he dumped me.

"Go ahead, Richie, name the other two Supremes besides Diana Ross. You guys turned on me quicker than a Greek waiter." I was a hurt woman.

The next time Sam Kinison came to the show, he had a great idea. He had been hanging around with Bon Jovi and they even let him open up their show at Giants Stadium. I guess playing before seventy thousand Bon Jovi fans did something to Sam that, to this day, I can't comprehend, but he decided that he would act as peacemaker between me and Bon Jovi. He suggested that the group come in the next morning and he would referee our on-air debate. What a stroke of Kissingerian diplomacy. I immediately accepted.

The reaction was instantaneous. Baba Booey was deluged with requests from the press to cover this historic radio moment. Fred and Jackie and I convened and prepared a prefight skit. I went to sleep early to be prepared for the event. The next morning, hundreds of hairless thirteen-year-old teenyboppers in miniskirts and knee pads huddled at the front doors, awaiting their heroes' arrival. There was enough hair spray on them to knock out the entire ozone layer.

The press had shown up in full force and we had set them up in a separate room. We were waiting for Sam and the guys to show.

By 8:30 I started getting pissed. We decided to run the predebate skit anyway. I had recorded a goofy parody of those stupid prefight profiles. Over that dumb *Rocky*-type music I did my best sports announcer:

"Welcome to the 'Wide World of Sports.' They're calling it the 'War on the Fourth Floor.' It all started back when Howard Stern befriended these young boys and put them on Dial-a-Date. But it all went sour since the boys got famous. Wasn't it Jon Bon Jovi who once said, 'Hey man, somebody's working my mouth, I have no opinions'? Now Howard Stern is all burned up. Just wait till they get into the vicinity of Infinity. First it was Motown versus Showtown, now it's the king of Madison Avenue versus the tampon-wearing, mousse-using Polygram pussies. Polygram Records tells them to kowtow and they do! Even though the man makes a hundred eighty million dollars you'd think he'd get an individual thought in his head. He kowtowed and listened to the record company and did not come onto Howard Stern's show.

"Thanks to the good graces of Mr. Sam Kinison, the Henry Kissinger of Comedy, they'll come onto the show today and either bury the hatchet or sever the relationship forever. *7800° Fahrenheit* was the title of one of their cut-out records but

On the set of my E! "Interview" show with Richie Sambora and Jon Bon Jovi.

it'll get warmer in here if those sanitary-belt-sniffing sissies show up."

It was almost nine by now and I realized that I had been had. They weren't showing up. I could believe Bon Jovi would do this to me, but Sam, one of my closest show-biz friends? HOW COULD HE TURN ON ME LIKE THIS? I had only one recourse. I grabbed the mike and proclaimed Andrew "Dice" Clay, Sam's arch rival, the new king of comedy:

"Good-bye, Sam, nice knowing you. Don't burn your friends. I've had it with you! Dice Clay is the future! Dice works his ass off, he's not passed out in some room. Everyone's laughing at me. We'll see who has the last laugh. Five pussies from Sayreville, New Jersey, chump pussies who hit it lucky.

We'll see what happens when they're on tour with Iron Butterfly. I expect something like this from Bon Douchee. It's Kinison I don't understand. What is that all about? Sam's upset I put Dice on. Who cares? I put a lot of comedians on. Maybe he's insecure because he hasn't come up with any new material in a while.

"I wonder why any girls are with Sam. Guess it's his Rob Lowe looks. Believe me, I could get Malika. Let's see where those girls'll be when he goes through all his money. I don't hear people talk about Sam anymore, all I hear is people talking about Dice. Think Sam finished his ninth ham-and-egg sandwich this morning yet? What a phony. I'm sitting here with a knot in my stomach."

I thought of my coworkers. Imagine how embarrassed Gary was, having to go into a room full of press and say we got burned. That was even more embarrassing than parking Robin's car every morning.

"Sam is dead to me!" I pronounced. "He used Jessica like toilet paper and threw her away. Maybe she is a little wacky, but she's a woman and she does have feelings. It's like taking advantage of a retarded girl. You can run and you can hide but you can't dodge my airwaves, dude. Wait until you see the power I have, wait until you walk down the streets of New York and people scream how bloated and fat you are! When you see Sam tell him that DICE IS YOUR GOD! If you're going to Sam's show tonight just chant 'DICE FOREVER, TROLL NEVER.'"

The next morning we came on and the phones were burning up. Quite a few of the callers had been to Sam's show at Rascal's the night before and they reported that 90 percent of the place was chanting

"HOWARD" and "DICEMAN." Sam had flipped out and said, "Screw Howard. Who the hell is he? I planned that scam yesterday. Howard had to be taken down a step or two." One caller even said that at one point Sam got thirsty and asked a ringside spectator for a sip of his water. The guy said he was a Howard listener and another guy yelled out, "Spit in it first, then give it to him." How great was this? My fans were tormenting Kinison at his own show!

Finally, we got another call. This one was from Sam.

"I haven't changed, man. It was a practical joke and I'm sorry, I didn't know you were going to freak out and turn on me like a rabid dog, man," Sam said.

"Hey man, you made me look like a jerk," I fumed. Sam had expected me to just forget about it. My defiant tone meant a fight was brewing.

"My girls aren't bitches. All you did was turn on me, man," Sam complained. "Man, you hurt my feelings."

"I'm hurt, too," I said.

"I don't know if I can forgive this stuff. You're a vicious fucking guy, man," Sam said.

"If I'm a vicious dude, you're just as vicious as me. I don't get the point of the joke," I countered. This went on for the rest of the conversation. There was no coming together, we were both too hurt.

"I made a mistake, you got press out of it. You can ride this for a week, it'll help ratings." All of a sudden, Sam was a general manager.

"You didn't care what happened yesterday morning," Robin interjected.

"Robin, you're such a snake. You're both vicious

people. You deserve each other and I hope you have a great career together," Sam said and then he hung up.

I was bummed. I couldn't believe what had happened. But I couldn't forgive Sam.

The next day, Sam called up from the airport and apologized. I was momentarily disarmed, but the following day, after hearing a tape of his remarks about me at his Rascal's show, I was too hurt again.

"I really respect his work and wish we were still doing stuff on the radio but in all good conscience, man, I can't have this guy back on anymore. He's dead to me. I don't want to make a habit of people burning me. You burn Carson, you don't get back on Carson. So good night, funny man."

I missed Sam and he missed me. Almost every day I'd get on the air and moan about our feud, but we were both too proud and stubborn to make up. But leave it to Sam, he thought of a comedic way to get back on the show. We were having a radiothon to raise money for Danny Philbin, Regis's wheelchair-bound abandoned kid. In the middle of this event Sam called up from L.A. and donated $500. That was the icebreaker. Sam was back on the A-list.

## JESSICA DUMPS ON SAM
### (AFTER SAM DUMPS IN HER ROOM)

This was an excellent radio war. It started when Jessica Hahn got upset with Sam because he had a short fling with her, used her in his "Wild Thing" video, and then never called her. Meanwhile, Sam was pissed at Jessica because the *National Enquirer* ran a story about this three-hundred-pound ex-preacher, Sam, who was in love with this starlet, Jessica Hahn. Sam was convinced that Jessica had leaked the story and had gotten paid for it. Jessica was so mad at being spurned that she came on our show and said that Sam had fallen asleep inside her while they were making love. The stage was set for fireworks.

It started with Sam on the show. Jessica called in and told Sam she felt used by him. She even mentioned she sprang for the outfit she wore in the video. Sam offered to pay her for her appearance.

"I don't want your money," said Jessica.

"DON'T EVEN START IN, YOU COW-FACED LOSER! I'LL COME AFTER YOU LIKE YOU WON'T BELIEVE!" Sam screamed.

They argued about who made what allegation on what tabloid TV show.

Jessica, remarkably, was holding her own.

"You think because your mom died you're the only one that knows tragedy?" Sam suddenly said. Jessica's mother had just died that week after a long bout with cancer. It was a low blow.

"All I did was call because . . ." Jessica started but Sam interrupted her.

"Yeah, do another Mr. Ed routine, babe, while your mom's dying."

That was the coup de grace. A few days earlier, Jessica had taped a radio bit with me in which she had sex with Mr. Ed. Unfortunately, on the same day, her mother died. She had no idea that her mother would die that day, and we had, out of respect to Jessica,

### It's Love! Jessica Hahn Flips For 300-Lb. Wacky Ex-Preacher

Jessica Hahn, who brought evangelist Jim Bakker and his PTL empire to ruin, has given her heart to a 300-pound ex-preacher — outrageous X-rated comic Sam Kinison who gets laughs onstage by turning into a screaming lunatic.

"I've got a thing about preachers," Jessica told a friend.

And Jessica revealed to The ENQUIRER in an exclusive interview, "I love Sam — and he told me he loves me.

"Sam's an ex-preacher and we've had plenty to talk about. We have a lot in common."

Sam, 33, has appeared on HBO, "Saturday Night Live" and in the Rodney Dangerfield movie "Back to School" — where he played a crazy professor.

The son of an evangelist, Sam became a preacher himself at age 18, but later gave it up for a comedy career.

"We met about two months ago at the Comedy Store in Los Angeles where Sam was working," said Jessica.

"We were introduced by a mutual friend. And ever since, we've been close.

"I'm not dating anyone else."

When Jessica walked into Sam's life, he was in mourning because his brother had recently committed suicide — but "then his whole world seemed to turn around," revealed a pal.

Jessica told an insider. "I've never experienced such an immediate and striking connection with anyone in my life. Since that time, we spend every minute together we can.

The couple have appeared on-

> I've never experienced such an immediate and striking connection with anyone in my life.

stage during Sam's act, and have gone to Los Angeles area nightclubs together, say friends.

Jessica, who's working as an on-air personality for a Phoenix radio station, flies to Los Angeles frequently to be with Sam.

"Sam and Jessica both come from very religious backgrounds and they're both rebels. They love to stay up all night watching television and talking." said one of Sam's close friends.

"When they can't be together, they spend up to five hours a night on the phone."

Sam's spokeswoman, Laurie Gorman, told The ENQUIRER, "Yes, Sam and Jessica are dating. But Sam doesn't wish to talk about the relationship."

Yet Sam told his close friend, "I'm absolutely amazed that a woman as beautiful as Jessica is in love with me. I feel incredibly lucky."

And Jessica said. "Sam and I have both been through hell. I trust Sam — and I don't trust too many people. I really love him."

— REGINALD FITZ, PATRICIA TOWLE and BRIAN WILLIAMS

**I LOVE SAM AND HE LOVES ME . . .** We have a lot in common, says Jessica, who clowns around with her big beau.

#### The 40-Minute Wait
A doctor's waiting room's a place
I go by need's requirement.
But, doc, it's not a place I'd planned
To live out my retirement.
— *Richard F. Bach*

held off playing the bit. Now Sam was using this in a dirty, vicious sneak attack. What a dastardly guy. What sleazy underhanded tactics. What great radio! Jessica started crying, then she hung up. The feud was on, big time.

A few days later Jessica called and was ready to spill her guts. She got on the air and told me the most embarrassing story I've ever heard in my life. Yes, it was true that Sam had fallen asleep inside of her. They'd checked into a hotel for a big romantic night. Sam had been doing lots of coke and beer, drinking tremendous amounts of alcohol that day. They made love and he fell asleep. An hour or two later, Sam got out of bed and was "making a big racket," Jessica said. The room was dark and Sam was banging into things. Sam was looking for the bathroom, but was so out of it, he just lost control. He began to shit all over the floor. As he was walking he was blasting away. It was a big pile, like the kind an elephant leaves behind. Sam unloaded and without flinching strolled back to the bed and went right back to sleep.

Now mind you, Jessica is telling us this romantic story, making herself out to be Florence Nightingale. In order to protect Sam from tabloid gossip, Jessica said she needed to clean up the room. If the maids saw a big pile on the floor of Sam Kinison's room, they'd phone the *Enquirer*. Jessica Nightingale told us she quickly wiped up the shit with towels and wrapped up everything in big sheets. Then she took the brown-stained bedding down the hall and left it in front of someone else's room. Then she crept through the halls, grabbed Windex from the maid's cart, and cleaned the stains from the carpet. Sam woke up the next morning as if nothing had happened. In fact, he probably didn't even remember what he had done.

Well, the story was fantastic and made for an unforgettable morning of radio. The next logical step was to milk it for all it was worth.

A few weeks later, when Sam came on, I played him the tape of this conversation!

"OH, MAN!" Sam exploded. Not literally, thank God. "OH, MAN! DUDE, THIS IS WAR! WHAT'S AMNESTY SPELLED BACKWARDS?"

"How long will it take for Sam's face to turn purple?" I wondered aloud.

"Watch my face turn purple. Believe me, not only did she make this up, but you accept $260,000 of extorted money from misappropriated funds from a church and it's in your account, doesn't this make you an accessory to conspiracy to blackmail? She ought to be in the cell right next to Bakker. Oh, dude, I'm frothing, man!"

Now I knew Sam was pissed. He had used "dude" and "man" in the same sentence.

Sam was almost choking on his cough lozenges.

"Let me tell you something. She's a sick pig. I've had it with her jealousy. She couldn't get me. She offered herself to me and I fell asleep inside her. That's the worst insult you can pay a woman, right, Robin? That's when the war started. I thought we made up. IS THERE ANY MEAT LEFT ON THE CARCASS!? How did Jessica get off on charges of conspiracy to blackmail? Believe me, if we had knowledge of that, we would be busted. *Plus she gave bad head!*"

It was almost time to go off the air, so I plugged Sam's show that night.

"There may only be ten people there. They might be afraid I'm going to defecate on them from the stage," Sam said. "When I shit in the hotel room, maybe I was just trying to make her a little breakfast."

## SAM AND I BOTH DUMP ON DICE
### (FIGURATIVELY, THIS TIME)

Why was Sam always in the middle of these fights? Come to think of it, this one might never have started if it wasn't for that Satanic Sam goading me on. Sam was in the studio one day when Andrew "Dice" Clay called in. Robin and I had been pursuing Dice for an exclusive interview about the circumstances behind his getting banned for life from MTV. That morning, I had heard from one of my listeners in Philly that Dice had actually gone on the air there first with one of my radio competitors. Dice called in and tried to smooth things over, but I wasn't buying. I let him know I was disappointed and I cut the conversation short. This was Sam's chance to goad me into a war with Dice, his hated rival. At the time, Sam had about twelve naked tits circling his head (we had some strippers in the studio that morning). After a while, Sam's prodding got to me.

"That's it! Dice is banned from the show!" I pronounced.

"Then I respect you as a man and I'm there for you," Sam said.

"SAM KINISON IS THE NUMBER-ONE COMIC IN THE WORLD," I proclaimed.

"You're cute," Sam cooed. "I'd be your woman."

Sam was pretty good at getting in the middle of a fight. His next time on the show, we called Kathy, Dice's ex-wife, in Los Angeles. Sam tried to squeeze dirt out of her and get her to confirm what he had heard, that Dice didn't want people to know she was married to him—this while she was supporting the guy for three years! Kathy did say their divorce was ugly.

"It's a sad and sick story," I said indignantly. "I am so shocked by what I heard. For a man to deny his marriage . . ."

This probably put Dice over the top. A month later

he was playing a sold-out show at the Spectrum in Philly and the crowd was packed with Stern supporters. At the first sign of "HOWARD" chanting, the Diceman flipped out.

"What are you fucking yelling 'Howard Stern' for? He's just jealous 'cause I talked to another radio show and he's got nothing better to do than rip me apart, that insecure cocksucker. Nobody fucks with Dice, Dice does the fucking. Nobody."

All of a sudden, he saw a huge "STERN RULES" banner. I LOVE MY FANS!

"All right, sit down, jerkoff. What are you showing me, 'STERN RULES'? But you're at my show, ha ha ha. C'mon, stop jerking yourselves off. He's using you fucking people for his ratings. Not Diceman. I come out, I deliver. How much did he pay you to sit in the front row and show me that sign? He's a deejay asshole. I'm the biggest comic to ever walk the earth! So he could wipe his ass with your sign, too. Hold it up. Yeah, beautiful. You did your job, collect your fifty bucks from Stern in the morning."

The man was obviously losing it. Dice stayed banned from my show for over a year. During that time, Sam took every opportunity to publicly flog him and challenge him to comedy showdowns. He claimed that Dice had stolen his whole act from him. But I missed Dice. Finally, we both agreed to bury the hatchet. Dice came in with his entourage—Hot Tub Johnny, Dutch Edsel, and Downtown Ronnie—and a photographer to record this historic reconciliation. We hugged emotionally.

"I don't care if you go on other shows," I said magnanimously. "This is a nice reunion. Hey, your ex-wife said she masterminded your career." Dice was in the middle of an ugly alimony suit with Kathy.

"I can't talk about her," Dice said.

"She won't get a dime," I said brightly. "Don't worry about it." God, am I a diplomat.

Before long, we got around to talking about Sam. Maybe they could make up, too.

"I wouldn't be friends with Sam. He's garbage. He started a fight with my bodyguard Hot Tub Johnny in the Comedy Store. Sam comes over to Johnny and he goes, 'I ain't afraid of Dice.' Sam wouldn't tell it to my face 'cause the guy's a pussy, that's the bottom line. I kept quiet for two years while this bloated animal destroyed his career by talking about me. So he starts calling Johnny names and makes like he's gonna hit him and he goes to Johnny, 'What are you gonna do about it?' Johnny goes, 'Lay a hand on me.'

"So Sam, with five guys around him, grabs Johnny by the throat. Johnny bangs him one in the face, Tubby goes down. He banged him right in his big, fat, bloated two-thousand-pound head. Now he jumps on that fat bastard's back, he just jumps on him like a waterbed, right, and he rips that dirty rag Sam wears on his head right off, and holds it up and sees Sam is bald from the ears up. Now Sam's guys are jumping on Johnny, but Johnny is dragging all of them *and* Sam through the Comedy Store to the bathroom. Johnny's strong, you don't mess with Johnny. So now he sees Sam's a contestant for the new fat Mr. Clean.

"He drags Sam into the bathroom and all Sam's guys are jumping over Johnny but Johnny's pushing

them off. He's got Sam in a headlock and he's looking
in the mirror and he's going, 'Sam, tell me what you
see.' And Sam's going, 'I'm Bozo, I'm Bozo the Clown.
I'm a big, fat, bastard Bozo.' Johnny let him go, but
we kept the rag. Now it's a bit in the act."

## HOWARD VS. ALL OF L.A. AND THE
## SEX-CRAZED MAGIC

Hey, I don't only take on comedians who need to get
back on my show to sell out their gigs. I take on whole
cities at a time. One of those times was right after we
got the news that Magic Johnson had tested positive
for HIV. Of course I felt bad. But the media was honoring Magic as if he had just come back from World
War II and had sacrificed his life for the honor of his
country. The hero worship was sickening. And what
I told my listeners was that Magic was pretty damn
irresponsible to get it in the first place. It wasn't as if
he got infected through a bad blood transfusion or
from his dentist. No, this guy came down with it because he had incredible amounts of unprotected sex.
Everyone was afraid to talk about Magic in an honest
way. The press blasted me. Hate mail poured in. Ironically, after the story was out for a few weeks many
newspaper columnists and editorial writers ended up
saying the same thing—that Magic was a womanizer
who, in this day and age, should have worn rubbers.

Some role model! He was out banging every night,
the guy wouldn't stop. Unless we stop that kind of behavior, we're doomed as a human race. Look, we all

want to see a cure for AIDS. But the cure exists. Instead of taking a magic pill or a shot, take your penis and put it back in your pants. And if you want to get some male ass, what you do is you go to a doctor and you both get checked and you stay with each other till death do you part. No more glory-holing.

That was basically my Magic rap, but the listeners were calling the station in droves complaining. Hell, even my program director in L.A., Andy Bloom, a guy who was with me years ago in Philly, called me up and asked me to tone down my remarks about Magic. *Fuck him!* He called me at home and left a message saying that he had never seen a reaction to anything like the reaction of the L.A. audience to the Magic raps and the reaction was overwhelmingly negative. I thought that was great. But he was worried about these callers. When I asked him why they were complaining, he couldn't answer. They didn't know why they were mad, they couldn't specifically cite examples of things I had said that pissed them off, they were just angry I was "attacking" Magic.

Well, I'd give them something to be angry about. The next day I went on the air and imagined one of the many phone calls Magic would be making to the women he banged:

MAGIC: Hello, baby, this is Magic . . . Johnson . . . Yeah . . . now speaking about my Johnson, we got a little problem here.

WOMAN: What is it, Magic? I never thought I'd hear from you again.

MAGIC: Well, you sitting down?

**WOMAN:** I just want to say that that night we spent together was so beautiful.

**MAGIC:** I say, are you sitting down, woman?

**WOMAN:** Magic, I got to be honest with you. I thought you were like every other basketball player, you wouldn't call me back.

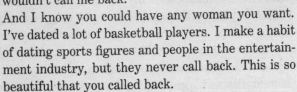

And I know you could have any woman you want. I've dated a lot of basketball players. I make a habit of dating sports figures and people in the entertainment industry, but they never call back. This is so beautiful that you called back.

**MAGIC:** Oh, baby, you're making it harder and harder. Baby, I was shooting arsenic.

**WOMAN:** What?

**MAGIC:** Well, there's good news and bad news.

**WOMAN:** Well, what's the good news?

**MAGIC:** The good news is you'll be losing a lot of weight soon. You can go bang away, you got nothing to lose.

**WOMAN:** What's the bad news?

**MAGIC:** Well, I got something.

**WOMAN:** A gift? An engagement ring? Not one of you guys has ever even called me back, now I'm engaged.

**MAGIC:** No, no, no, no. I got something . . . it rhymes with maids.

WOMAN: Now what rhymes with maids? Blades? Rollerblades?

MAGIC: No, I don't got no Rollerblades.

WOMAN: Oh, my God, wait a second, I think I know what you're trying to tell me.

MAGIC: You know what, baby, it would be a whole lot easier if you tuned in the national TV. Just tune in to my press conference.

WOMAN: Okay, but that doesn't sound like good news.

MAGIC: Look at it this way. You can smoke all the cigarettes you want, do lots of drugs, jump out of an airplane, and race cars.

Now the phones and hate mail really went crazy. A few days later I picked out the best seething hate letter from a woman in L.A. named Laura and I called her up on the air.

"Honey, you're a big phony," I said. "You can't face facts that Magic Johnson, your supposed hero, was banging everything on two legs."

"Howard, you would have sex with lots of girls, but women don't want you."

"LET ME TELL YOU SOMETHING, HONEY!" I shouted. "I COULD BE OUT BANGING A DIFFERENT WOMAN EVERY NIGHT."

"In your dreams."

That was it. I couldn't bear to talk with this moron. So I did all the talking. I had more to say than she did. "There's no way you can stop my juggernaut of coming and barreling through L.A. The ratings continue to grow. You're right, there's a lot of people like you who don't have any comprehension level. You read a book and you don't even know what you read. You speak and you don't know what you just said. You're a stupid woman who will never understand my show. You should not be listening. I don't sit and idolize Magic Johnson. I tell you the way it is. I tell you that he slept with thousands of women and that's why he got the AIDS virus. He used no contraception whatsoever and you can't deal with that because it's an adult opinion. I don't go around gaga about Magic. He's not my God and hero."

"You're your only God and hero," she said.

Maybe she was more perceptive than I was giving her credit for.

"You should quit the Catholic church and pray to Magic Johnson. Build a giant sneaker in your bedroom and pray to that instead of the Virgin Mother," I said.

"I have a basketball . . ."

"Take the basketball and pray to it."

"Howard, you have this godlike attitude that ain't gonna work for long."

"If you don't like the show, listen to Rick Dees, Mark and Brian, Jay Thomas, I'll name them all. IN FACT, I FORBID YOU FROM LISTENING TO MY SHOW AND YOU ARE ONLY ALLOWED TO LISTEN TO MARK AND BRIAN AND RICK DEES AND JAY THOMAS. Now I'll hang up on you. Thank you for calling and thank you for your hate letter. You are no longer allowed to listen."

"Thank you, Howard," she said and hung up.

"I don't want anybody like her listening," I continued. "I want to hand-select the people who listen. Their hero. They got a real hero. Meanwhile a real hero like Jonas Salk can't afford cable TV."

## MUGGED AT THE GRAMMYS

It's funny, after all these years doing my show, I never really got into a physical fight. Plenty of screaming matches, verbal threats, and posturing, but no fisticuffs. But it wasn't until we went to L.A. to do a live remote from the Grammys that I ever got into a real fight.

This wasn't a real fight either. It was more like a New York mugging. We were set up in a hall at the Roosevelt Hotel, along with a lot of other radio stations from around the country. The problem was my show was so controversial that the idiots escorting the celebrities from station to station were shying away from bringing me guests.

I wasn't going to take this lying down. I called over the jerk who was running the show and berated him on the air. He told me that I had a history of "hogging" guests. I told him to screw off, I'd get my own guests. It just so happens that for these purposes, I carry a megaphone. The previous year at the Grammys, I used this megaphone on Lou Reed in an attempt to shame him into coming and sitting for an interview with me, even though I knew he hated my guts.

"LOU REED? LOU REED? WHY ARE YOU IG-NORING ME?" I boomed. "I'M A BIG FAN OF YOURS. I KNOW ALL YOUR HIT SONGS. 'WALK

ON THE WILD SIDE,' 'SWEET
JANE.' WHY DO YOU IGNORE
ME?"

> "Howard Stern?
> I can't stand him."
> —Lou Reed

I picked up my megaphone and
turned it on. Scanning the room, I
spotted Elaine Boosler at the next booth. Great. Another jerk who didn't like me and wouldn't be a guest.
I really wasn't interested in her being on my show until I heard she requested not to be on. The guy who
ran the show told me that Elaine had been hearing me
talk shit about her all week, too. This was going to
be fun.

"HEY, ELAINE. WHAT'S THE MATTER? YOU
DON'T WANT TO COME ON MY SHOW?" Every-
one in the room could hear me. The whole room turned
as one toward me. The other stations were pissed because my loud megaphone voice was interrupting
their broadcasts.

"ELAINE, YOU DON'T WANT TO BE ON THE
'HOWARD STERN SHOW'? WHAT'S THE MAT-
TER? IT'S SUCH A HORRIBLE SHOW? YEAH,
YOU'RE SO FUNNY."

"So's your face," a strange-looking guy suddenly
said.

"Who are you? Take a seat," I motioned toward my
empty guest chair.

All of a sudden, all hell broke loose. This jerk attacked me, slamming my megaphone into my nose. He
was about to do more damage, but my faithful producer, Boy Gary, grabbed him from behind. He poked
Gary in the mouth and threw a full cup of soda at me

before one of my brave listeners from New York, who had won a radio contest, managed to wrestle him to the ground and bloody his face with his studded wristband. During this fracas, Elaine Boosler came over screaming, "He's with me and he has taste." It turns out that this guy was Boosler's boyfriend. The entire room started buzzing with excitement. The best thing about the fight was we never went off the air. THIS WAS GREAT RADIO!

"Elaine Boosler's people just beat up Gary," I immediately announced. "Are my earrings in?" Gary asked. "I think he pulled one of my earrings out."

"You get punched in the eye?" I asked him.

"No, I'm okay," Baba Booey said. "But I don't want you to ever say I don't do anything for you. I took a shot for you, man."

He was absolutely right. I made a mental note not to berate him—at least not until we got back to New York.

# More and More and More and More Hate Mail

I feel sorry for you Howard. You are a man caught inside a world of his own ego. Who are all these fictitious people that are always mauling you where ever you go? Honestly Howard do you really think you are that recognizable. You look just like about 500,000 other tall black hair, big nosed Jews that live in New York City. There are no people bothering you Howard it is all part of some warped make believe world. A world that you have conjured up to support your own ego problem. You are worse than the addicts you occasionally make fun of.

Asshole
K-Suck!
600 Madison Avenue
New York, NY 10022

Dear Pig,

You suck.  You suck.  You suck.  You suck.  You suck.  You
suck.  You suck.  You suck.  You suck.  You suck.  You suck.
You suck.  You suck.  You suck.  You suck.  You suck.  You
suck.  You suck.  You suck.  You suck.  You suck.  You suck.
You suck.  You suck.  You suck.  You suck.  You suck.  You
suck.  You suck.  You suck.  You suck.  You suck.  You suck.
You suck.  You suck.  You suck.  You suck.  You suck.  You
suck.  You suck.  You suck.  You suck.  You suck.  You suck.
You suck.  You suck.  You suck.  You suck.  You suck.  You
suck.  You suck.  You suck.  You suck.  You suck.  You suck.
You suck.  You suck.  You suck.  You suck.  You suck.  You
suck.  You suck.  You suck.  You suck.  You suck.  You
suck.  You suck.  You suck.  You suck.  You suck.  You
suck.  You suck.  You suck.  You suck.  You suck.  You
suck.  You suck.  You suck.  You
suck.  You suck.  You
suck.  You suck.  You
suck.  You suck.  You
suck.  You suck.  You
suck.  You suck.  You
suck.  You suck.  You
suck.  You suck.  You
suck.  You suck.  You
suck.  You suck.  Yo
You suck.  You suck.  Yo
suck.  You suck.  Yo
You suck.  You suck.  Yo
suck.  You suck.  Yo
suck.  You suck.  Yo
You suck.  You suck.  Yo
suck.  You suck.  Yo

This is in response to your inhumane remark referring to lawyers as retards and mongoloids on your show of Thurs. July 9. On behalf of all handicapped people I demand a public apology for your heartless remark. Retarded people can't help what they are but you can help what you are. You think your so cool but you're nothing more than a radio rendition of Don Rickles. You get your laughs (so you think) by tearing other people apart. which is so unoriginal and boring. You are a has been and your sponsors hate you because your only appeal is to an all male audience. Why don't you take a look at your own pathetic life before making fun of the less fortunate. It is too bad you weren't socially conscious enough to have had a vasectomy before bringing two more dregs into society like yourself. Retarded people will have more to offer society than your subhuman family.

# Out of the Closet Stern

*I'm Six-Five, Weigh 190 Pounds, and I Have a Tongue Like an Anteater*

CHAPTER
14

Frankly, I cannot fathom how any man can look at another man's buttocks and get turned on. But this is America, and I will defend to the death the right of any man to insert his penis anywhere. And as for transsexuals, I think those sex-change operations should be outlawed. These freaking doctors should spend less time carving vaginas out of penises and find a cure for cancer already.

The truth is, I am one of the world's leading authorities on homosexuality, and I would like to take this opportunity to set the record straight on why men become homosexuals. Many people today lean toward the revisionist theory that homosexuality is biologically determined. In my opinion, homosexuality is just another way of delaying adulthood. When you're with another guy you don't have to deal with the responsibilities of a traditional family. You extend the joys of your prepubescence. You're stuck in the phase of your life where you just hang out with boys. It's a simpler time. And a gross sign of immaturity. I believe homosexual behavior is not genetic but rather a deeply rooted defense mechanism that allows the human mind to ward off outside pressures. Like obsessive-compulsive behavior, alcoholism, or gambling addictions, homosexual behavior can be changed. I have nothing against homosexuals and support gay rights, but . . .

. . . I can't fathom the ass as a sex object. I mean, why don't I just go and put my dick in a garbage pail?

I could shower my backside ninety times a day, I could clean it out with a wire brush, that smell is a road flare to me.

I once asked one of the guys I had on Gay Dial-a-Date how he could stomach the smell of another man's ass.

"Dogs smell each other's asses all the time," he said.

"All I know," I said, "is that you're a psychopath if you don't realize that a man's backside smells like a waste area, a human cesspool. You can take colonics for a month, you can sit on a bidet, you can take a bottle of Opium perfume and stick it up there with the cap off, and it will still stink to high hell!" I yelled. "I've done experiments on myself. I stay in the shower for hours and soap every nook and cranny and when I come out and lie on the floor and smell myself, it still stinks!"

"You better see a doctor, Howard," he said.

"You are a lunatic! You're attracted to the smell of a man who goes to the bathroom! You must have an air freshener lodged in your buttocks, Socrates. That area is an exit, not an entrance."

"Women have no odor?" he said.

"They stink, too, but it's worth putting up with," I said. "Once you feel a woman, there's nothing better."

Sometimes I actually envy gays when it comes to having sex. If you can get over the fact that it's a guy's buttocks, there are no head trips involved. You don't have to have three dates. You don't even have to be attractive. You stuff your ass into some jeans and go down to a gay bar, and guaranteed someone will pull down your pants and blow you. No begging, no guilt, no game playing. Got an ass? WHAM, BAM, THANK YOU, STAN! No "So what kind of work do you do?" With gays, it doesn't matter.

"What's your job?"

"Actually, I'm out of work at the present."

"Bend over!"

And if that doesn't work because you're so damn ugly, all you have to do is stick your dick into a glory hole.

Gay bars take a wall and drill some holes into it so you can have totally anonymous sex. You just stick your dick through a hole in the wall and someone on the other side starts sucking you. I could never go to one of those places because I'm so small. I couldn't reach the other side of the wall.

One of the more interesting things I receive in the mail over and over again is a list of objects gay guys put in their asses. One thing is certain, this is definitely a guy thing. Women don't seem to shove a lot of stuff up there. Men are weird. We've got really bad habits.

Here's a list of things doctors have harvested from men's asses. Imagine spending all those years in medical school only to specialize in doing this.

Some doctor actually chronicled these items and detailed the information for a medical journal, so if any politically correct scumbag thinks I'm making this stuff up, you're full of shit.

These guys' asses are like garages. They store stuff in their holes and then forget about junk that's in there. How do you forget about stuff that you lodged in your ass?

## LOOK AT THE SIZE OF THESE THINGS:

1. A bottle of Mrs. Butterworth's syrup. (Now that's a big bottle, complete with her head and those big round shoulders.)
2. An ax handle.
3. A plastic spatula.
4. A Coke bottle.

5. An antenna rod.
6. A 150-watt lightbulb. (That's very thin glass.)
7. A screwdriver.
8. Four rubber balls.
9. A paperweight.
10. An onion.
11. A frozen pig's tail.
12. A broomstick.
13. An eighteen-inch umbrella handle. (Ouch! And all this disappeared? I don't understand it. This can't be possible.)
14. An oil can.
15. A toolbox weighing twenty-two ounces. (This was in a medical journal. It's not as if I'm reading this in the *Enquirer*.)
16. A flashlight.
17. A turnip.
18. A pair of eyeglasses.
19. A polyethylene waste trap from a u-bend of a sink. (What the hell is going on? I mean, you walk into the kitchen and look at the drain and say, "I know what to do with that. I'll stick it in my ass"?)
20. A live, shaved, declawed gerbil.

The gerbil thing is pretty wacky. They shave the hair off the gerbil, clip its nails, break its teeth out, put it in the freezer for a few minutes, then put Vaseline on it, and shoot it up with coke. Then they insert a tube up their rectums and squeeze one end and the gerbil runs up the tube into the tushy. As the gerbil starts fighting for air, it's supposed to create a really erotic sensation. Who would think of this? Someone ought to call the ASPCA. Someone called them on me once because I was doing a show with a guy who ate live mice dipped in olive oil. Five ASPCA marshals came down and threatened to arrest me.

**Vinnie D'Amico offered to eat a mouse at my live show.**

But the weirdest story was reported in the *Journal of Forensic Medicine and Pathology*. It seems that one guy had his life mate pour a batch of concrete mix into his ass through a funnel while he lay on his back with his feet against the wall at a precise forty-five-degree angle. After a few hours the concrete hardened and it became so painful he had to go to the hospital. Under general anesthesia, his anus was dilated and two catheters were inserted. A suction was created and they chiseled the concrete cast of his rectum out. The best part was they found a Ping-Pong ball inside the concrete!

Meanwhile, a lot of these guys are putting the god-damn Eiffel Tower up their butts without incident, for the most part, and *I'm* the one with the anal fissures. Go figure.

One time I was sitting in my office and I noticed an ad in the paper for the Gay Party Line. I decided to call it because I wanted to see just how far I could go before I made a gay man throw up from disgust.

"Hi. I'm six-foot-five, I weigh 190 pounds, and I have a tongue like an anteater," I proudly announced. There were a bunch of voices immediately responding to my sexy voice.

One deep masculine voice gasped, "Hey, you sound cute. Let's get a private line." I dove right in: "I want to shave your balls. I want to drop some scalding hot candlewax on your scrotum."

He was getting really turned on. He actually wanted me to burn his scrotum. He was hot for me. Suddenly an operator interrupted.

"You two are getting very graphic. Exchange phone numbers and call each other on your own." Evidently the operator's job was to make sure that homos like me don't get too obscene. Something to do with the FCC again. They never leave me alone.

I told the operator I wasn't ready to give out my number because I still had a few questions for my friend to see if he was my type. She said, "Fine, but nothing too graphic."

"Are you still there?" I said in my seductive voice.

"Yes."

"You know what I really want to do to you?" I had to think quick about what would turn this guy off. "I want to . . . piss in your ass."

He moaned with lust . . . there was no stopping him. Thank God the operator threw me off the Gay Party Line. I hadn't even gotten to the concrete and Ping-Pong ball discussion. I'm probably the only guy ever thrown off a Gay Party Line.

Over the years, I've gotten so many complaints

from humorless listeners about my gay material that I decided to write a hate letter to myself:

> Dear Mr. Stern,
>
> At 6:30 A.M. on September 3, you referred to a gay couple as a pair of lunch pushers and made references to them opening beer cans with their sphincters. Horrifying.
>
> At 8:45 on September 18, you called a gay caller a weenie genie and asked him if he really thought other men's private parts were a party . . . which is *so mean*.
>
> At 8:15 on September 22, you said Rock Hudson died of botulism—bad meat in the can—which the gay community found unfunny and terribly offensive.
>
> At 9:15 on October 2, you made the so-called joke "What do Henry the Eighth, Rock Hudson, and Donald Manes have in common? They all screwed Queens and died." Also not funny, Mr. Stern.
>
> At 7:00 on October 23, you referred to a homosexual caller as a log breath, a B.V. Deviant, a tube-steak Tarzan, and a flagpole sitter from the Baloney Cavalry. So incredibly demeaning.
>
> On December 3, you again berated a gay caller with an endless list of rude homosexual nicknames, including bun splitters, tonsil jockeys, knob gobblers, pickle chuggers, bone smugglers, worm worshipers and Hanes grazers . . . did I miss one?
>
> On December 22, you did a ten-minute soliloquy on your personal AIDS research and made comments about the laboratory rats not cooperating because they were always at the ballet. This, you putz, even *I laughed at*.

I'm sure I'll never win an award from any gay group, but I think I've actually done a few things to make people more tolerant of different lifestyles. Here's Donahue pandering to ridiculous and insulting stereotypes of gay men by parading a bunch of drag

queens around as a symbol of homosexuality, and GLAAD (Gay and Lesbian Alliance Against Defamation) gives him an award.

Ninety-nine percent of the gay community isn't running around in drag. Why are they honoring him?

I haven't won any awards, but I've given some award-winning performances in skits such as Lean on Meat, Gay Squirty Dancing, Gay Wall Street, Raging

Bulimic, Gay Bonanza, Butt Cheek Fever, Homo Pyle, 2010: A Gay Space Oddity, and my three favorites, Homocop, Buttman, and My Gay Left Foot.

The television epic Gay Munsters. From left to right: Robin, Grandpa Al Lewis, me as Gay Herman, Fred as Lily, Gary as Eddie, and Jackie as Marilyn.

Although I am very tolerant of the gay lifestyle, there is one aspect of it that I truly abhor.

NAMBLA, the North American Man Boy Love Association. These guys are twisted! They advocate sexual relations between grown men and underage boys. One time on the air I called the NAMBLA hot line and was totally repulsed when a guy who sounded like a cross between Count Dracula and José Jimenez delivered the following message:

"Hello, this is NAMBLA . . . if you're a boy, do not despair, be true to your feelings. Times will change and your oppression will end. If you're a man, be safe, be brave, and above all be proud to be a boy lover."

On second thought, the guy on the NAMBLA message sounded just like Ricky Ricardo. Listening to that I imagined what it might have been like if Ricky had decided to call NAMBLA. I asked my favorite artist, Drew Friedman, to illustrate how I imagined Lucy would react if she discovered that Fred and Ricky were having sex with young boys. I'm excited to present to you my first cartoon ever of the most offensive subject I could imagine:

# More, More, More, More and More Hate Mail

You have no talent, looks, class, or any redeamable social
value. You have as much appeal as watching cottage cheese
turn rancid. As far as your nose is concerned, It looks like
the business end of an enema tube. As for Quivers, I'm
surprised you haven't inserted plates in her lips and used her to
rest coffee cups on. Your show(s) should be shown to prisoners
awaiting the death sentence as an alternative. What's with that
mass of weeds you call hair? You are so ugly, you could
replace medusa. It also looks like you cultivated your staff in
a toxic dump. Stuttering John should have been terminated at
birth. Tell Gary that a padded coat hanger makes a good butt plug.
Fred should be force fed a month's worth of morning tooth crust
from pig-boy Dell' Abate. And as for Jackie, itsbu's what can happen
if syphillis goes untreated.

STERN:
You say Italy changes Governments a lot...Not tri
lately! ITALY HAS THE FIFTH GREATEST ECONOMY IN
THE WORLD!!!AND WE ASK NOTHING OF THE U.S. UNLIKE
THE SLIMY COUNTRY OF ISRAEL.....YOUR COUNTRY...THES
FAGGOT JEWS ALWAYS FIGHTING AND BEGGING THE U.S.
FOR MONEY. THAT'S PARTLY WHY YOU HATE GEORGE BUSH.
GOD BLESS HIM HE WON'T GIVE YOUR FAGGOT STATE OF
ISRAEL THE $10,000,000,000. SPEAK OF YOUR COUNTRY OF
ISRAEL JEW SLIME STERN...THE BEGGING ARAB KILLING
BEASTS, OF YOUR COUNTRY OF ISRAEL AND FINALLY JEW-
BASTARD STERN, KEEP OUT OF POLITICS...YOU DON'T
KNOW SQUAT ABOUT POLITICS...STICK TO SEX AND FILTH
AND YOUR UGLY JEW WIFE STINKING AND SNORING AND
FARTING AND MAY YOU AND YOUR SLIMY FAMILY HURT
SCREAMING FOR ALL THE HURT YOU CAUSE ALL OTHERS.
YOU ARE THE JEW DEMON. THE DREK OF THE WORLD. DIE

YOU UGLY KIKE JEWBASTARD (THE JEW DISEASE)
You use the word MAFIA

Dear Howie:

   Our membership voted today to pray for the

following:

   Your ratings go to zero.

   You lose the show.

   You go broke.

   Your wife leaves. Takes the children to her
mother's. Gets a court order, you can not visit.

   You get AIDS and cancer.

   You join the homeless and linger for five
years among the homeless.

   A charity benefit is held for you in MSG.
No one shows except the director of the FCC. He
gives you five dollars. You fall to your knees
and kiss his hand.

   Burial is held at NYC Potter's field. No
one shows except the entire staff of the FFC.
They all piss on your grave and then attend the
sold out celebration at Yankee Stadium.

   If there is anything else we can do, please
call.

                    I feel sorry for you Howard. You are a man caught inside a
              world of his own ego. Who are all these fictitious people that
           are always mauling you where ever you go? Honestly Howard do you
         really think you are that recognizable. You look just like about
       500,000 other tall black hair, big nosed Jews that live in New
     York City. There are no people bothering you Howard it is all
    part of some warped make believe world. A world that you have
   conjured up to support your own ego problem. You are worse than
  the addicts you occasionally make fun of. You have the worst
 addiction anyone could possible have. You Mr. Stern, are
addicted to, Howard Stern.

# The Comics

*Kinison, Dice, Seinfeld,
and More*

CHAPTER
15

Comics love appearing on my show. Are they attracted to me because of my brilliant wit, my intense interviewing skills, or my incredible improvisational abilities? The truth is that just like everyone else, they use me. Nobody loves me. They all come on my show because they know that a plug to my audience guarantees them a sell-out crowd at Goofy's, Zany's, or whatever godforsaken little club they're appearing in.

# STERN PICKS WHO'S HOT, WHO'S NOT

## THE THREE GREATEST MINDS IN COMEDY

SAM KINISON—*Most natural, most spontaneous of all.*
EDDIE MURPHY—*One of the greatest stand-ups of all time.*
JACKIE MASON—*You want to hate him, then when you see his show, he wins you over. He's great.*

Jay Leno—Funny.
Johnny Carson—Not funny.
Richard Pryor—Funny.
Larry Miller—I don't know who he is.
Tim Allen—Not funny.
Paul Reiser—Not funny.
Robin Williams—Not funny.
Rita Rudner—Not funny.
Bill Cosby—Not funny. Never was.
Steve Allen—Not funny now.
Alan King—Funny until he did those stupid Toyota commercials.
Elayne Boosler—Lame.

Jerry Seinfeld—Funny.
Richard Lewis—Funny.
Billy Crystal—Funny.
Richard Belzer—Funny.

Judy Tenuta—She showed me her tit once. That was funny. She's funny.

Dennis Miller—Funny.

Joan Rivers—Funny.

Andrew "Dice" Clay—Funny.

Woody Allen—Not funny now. His testimony's a riot, though.

Rodney Dangerfield—Funny.

Cheech and Chong—Really funny movies. The original Beavis and Butt-head.

Steve Martin—No longer funny. A serious actor.

Dave Thomas—Funny.

Gallagher—Not funny.

Roseanne Arnold—Not funny.

Tom Arnold—Definitely not funny. He will ruin his wife's career.

Chevy Chase—Never been funny.

Gabe Kaplan—Not funny.

Dennis Wolfberg—Sometimes funny.

Pat Cooper—Extremely funny.

Robert Klein—Very funny.

Garry Shandling—Really funny.

Gilbert Gottfried—Absolutely funny.

David Brenner—Funny.

Albert Brooks—Always funny.

Steven Wright—Witty but not funny.

Rosie O'Donnell—Not funny.

Sandra Bernhard—Funny.

Damon Wayans—Not funny at all.

Don Rickles—I loved him when I was a kid.

Bob Hope—Was one of the greats.

I've always been jealous of anyone who earns a living passing judgment on the talent of others. I will now attempt to set myself up as a critic with the hope that *USA Today* will hire me to become the Mr. Blackwell of comedy. This will enable me to fulfill my lifelong desire to quit my radio career and do something fulfilling . . . criticizing other people in print.

I truly respect anyone who can get up in front of an audience and make them laugh. Especially in those smoky little rat-hole clubs with the uncomfortable wooden chairs that you can't sit in for more than two minutes. Here are some of my favorite moments with comedians who've paid their dues in shit holes like that.

## DENNIS MILLER

Dennis is a great stand-up comic but an annoying, arrogant asshole. Incredibly, he switches from a great fun guest one minute to an overly sensitive scumbag the next. I really think he dislikes me, but when he needs the promotion, he runs to do my show.

I remember one time he called me when comedian Gilbert Gottfried was in the studio with me. Miller was just starting his miserable late-night show and he really needed a plug, so not only did he call in, but he was calling in while he was holding his baby boy, Holden. As Dennis began to plug his show, Gilbert and I began to talk only to his newborn son. Instantly, we turned into mock pedophiles, begging for sexual secrets about baby Holden Miller.

"Holden, this is Uncle Howard," I said.

"Holden, what are you wearing?" Gilbert wondered.

"I'm sorry? Did Gilbert just ask my son what he was wearing?" Dennis asked incredulously.

*"Holden, how big are your testicles?"* Gilbert screamed.

"Holden, can you send me a Polaroid of yourself?" I said.

"Holden, put your hand inside your diaper and rub," Gilbert said.

"Gilbert's a little pervert. I hope you never have him on your show," I said to Dennis.

"Holden, I want you to unpin your diaper, okay? Just reach around and slowly unpin it. Now slap some baby powder on."

Dennis was not amused. He hung up, but Gilbert and I continued wooing Holden.

"I'd like to be holding Holden," Gilbert said. "Holden, go under the tree and pose."

"Holden, you're so natural and uninhibited. And your skin is so pink," I whispered.

"I remember the last time I saw Holden he was wearing Pampers and the Velcro was just a tiny bit open," Gilbert reminisced fondly.

"When Gilbert was in the hospital," I interrupted, "he would slip into a doctor's uniform and go to the pediatrics ward."

"Time for your rectal examination," Gilbert riffed. "This won't hurt a bit. Bounce up and down on my lap. Why don't you climb up on my leg, like you always do? Climb up my leg and slide down."

"Touch Uncle Gilbert's candy cane," I said.

"Would you like a spanking, Holden?" Gilbert asked. "We've both been bad boys—it's time for our discipline."

"Enough, Gilbert!" I interrupted. "Even *I'm* disgusted by you."

Another time Miller came up after his TV show had been canceled; he must have thought he'd get some sympathy from me. But I just reamed him because he blew it. He was blaming Jay Leno for stealing his guests when the real issue was that publicists were not going to book celebs on a show with no ratings.

"Fuck Jay Leno and guests. Your show sucked!" I discreetly explained. He had all these conspiracy theories, meanwhile the show blew and he didn't want to blame himself.

He's another one of these guys who gets a little bit of fame and then his marriage breaks up. I had him on once when we were out in Hollywood and he brought this model he was marrying. So I asked him about his first wife. After we finished the show, he begged me to edit out the stuff about his first wife. So I did him a favor and edited it out. He stayed away from the show for another four years. He was so pissed off that we even asked him about his first marriage, but as soon as he got the TV show, and the ratings weren't there, *boom*, he was my best friend again.

First, he wanted me to be a guest on the show and I said no. I was honest. His show was floundering and I wasn't going down on that ship. Then he told me they'd devote a whole hour to me on the same night that Jay Leno took over "The Tonight Show." Why would I go up against Leno?

Suddenly I was the guy to talk to when he was desperate for ratings and he couldn't talk about his first wife, this Hollywood guy who got some luck and married a model. It was funny, he was one of these politically correct guys who women thought was cool. Me, I'm perceived as a fucking sexist pig. Meanwhile, I'm the guy who sticks with his wife in real life and he's the one whose marriage broke up as soon as the fame kicked in. Strange world, huh?

## MILTON BERLE

People mention Milton Berle and they get all teary-eyed. He's a comedy pioneer, revolutionized television, blah, blah, blah. Hey, the reason those early comedians had such huge shares on television was because they went up against test patterns, okay? I never saw the Milton Berle show when I was growing up. I didn't know anything about Milton Berle. The only reason I had him on my show was because he was infamous for having a huge fucking cock. That fascinated me. I found Uncle Miltie to be a great guest, interesting and quick, but all I wanted to hear about was that cock.

But Uncle Miltie didn't want to talk about it. Hey, if I had a penis like his I'd rope cattle with it. I'd be showing it all over the place. I'd be so proud of it. The first time we had him on I tiptoed around his cock.

Then we booked him again. His publicist warned Gary that we shouldn't deal with the "penis thing." Yeah, right.

"Here comes Milton Berle into the studio," I announced. "Mr. Berle, every inch a gentleman, by the way, if I may say so. The last time you were on everyone said to me, 'But Howard, you didn't ask him about his weenie.'"

"Oh, stop, that's terrible," Milton protested.

"I have always maintained that you and Forrest Tucker had the biggest ones in the business. Man, it's gotta be great to have a big one," I went on. "You know, when they circumcised Uncle Miltie, they threw more away in the pan than I have. Doesn't it make life easier for you? You don't have to put that much effort into it. I have to do stuff to my wife just to get her excited. Your wife must be like, 'Oh, my God, this is unbelievable.'"

Milton wanted to drop the subject.

"Yeah, it's easy for you to be humble, when you've got a thermos in your pants," I snickered.

I asked Uncle Milton if he'd be so kind as to take phone calls from my audience. What he didn't know is that I had had Gary prescreen the callers and set them up with penis questions. The first caller came on.

"Listen, Uncle Miltie, when you get aroused, have you ever fainted from all the blood rushing into your tool?"

"Very funny," Berle said.

"You see? People are genuinely interested in the size of your genitals. Uncle Miltie, don't deny this aspect of show business." We went to the next caller.

"Mr. Berle, is it true that you're hung so well that you have a fiveskin?" These callers were very well rehearsed.

"Oh, boy," Milton moaned. We put the next caller on.

"I'm dying to ask you this, Uncle Miltie. The thing is, you always wear those baggy pants, so it's really hard to tell. Do you hang to the left or the right, or do you wrap it around your waist?"

I punched another call through.

"I have a legitimate question for Milton."

"Thank God." Milton was relieved.

"When you wore a dress on stage, Uncle Miltie, did anything ever stick out and graze the floorboards of the stage?"

"See, that's all they want to know about, Uncle Miltie," I gloated.

"No more phone calls!" Berle screamed. But we had made our point. We had exposed a true giant of show biz.

## JERRY SEINFELD

I love Jerry's comedy and he's always been nice enough to come on the show, but his appearances do seem to revolve around his latest Nielsen rating. When his television show went up against "Home Improvement" and his show's ratings were in trouble, he was an almost weekly visitor to the show. Then, when NBC switched him so that he followed "Cheers," we never heard from him. One week they shift his time slot and his ratings plummet, *boom*, he's in our studio before the ink of next week's *TV Guide* is dry.

But I love making fun of Jerry.

The main reason I get on Jerry so much is that I'm jealous of him. It drives me fucking crazy that every babe on the planet, especially these Long Island hausfraus who are looking for husbands, thinks Jerry's a great, regular guy and they could get him. Meanwhile, he's going from model to model, dumping one and picking up another one a week later. Every imbecilic single woman I know wants to meet Jerry Seinfeld. Even if they look like a truck hit them in the face, they still think they can get Jerry Seinfeld.

This guy is living the dream bachelor life! I saw it on that Barbara Walters special. He's got a three-million-dollar house with two refrigerators in the kitchen.

A woman who once had a date with Jerry called into the show. She said he picked her up and took her back to his place, where they watched Jay Leno do his monologue on TV. To top off the evening, the dream date included a running critique of Jay's monologue. Now that's incredibly romantic. If a regular guy did that on a first date any normal woman would be disgusted. So whenever Jerry comes in I'm sure to bust his chops about his womanizing.

But women are such idiots; they keep going out with guys like Jerry because he's famous. They never dated me and I have a much better personality than Jerry Seinfeld.

"Aren't you nervous about getting the AIDS virus, Jerry?" I asked.

"No, I'm not nervous about it." He laughed.

"What? Do you check the girls?" I asked.

"Yes," Jerry said.

"What, you spread their legs and use a flashlight?" I said.

"I only go out with girls that can do a split on the hood of a car. That's how I check them. And then I get behind the wheel of the car and I look through the windshield." He laughed.

"And you just put on the wipers, right? I like that," I said.

"I get the windshield wiper fluid with Nonoxynol–9," Jerry said.

Then I found out Jerry was dating a *seventeen*-year-old. How immoral! How wrong! God, how I wish I were doing it! I saw the pictures of her in the *Enquirer*. She had the breasts of Jayne Mansfield, the hips of Marilyn Monroe, and the butt of Betty Grable. My God, she had the body parts of all dead people.

We even wrote a song about her. Her name was Shoshanna. It was a parody of "At Seventeen," the old Janis Ian hit, and, even better, we got Janis to sing it when she came into the studio to plug her new album.

### AT SEVENTEEN

Seinfeld's girl is seventeen
An innocent with double Ds
He saw those breasts and flipped his lid
For a real young busty high-school kid

A horny lonely TV geek
Her major jugs made Jerry weak
Can't he find girls his age to date?
She's seventeen and she's jailbait

He takes her out in New York town
That lovely girl and the TV media clown
She'd barely shed her training bra
She'd kiss his lips for candy bars

A nice guy you turned out to be
Did she sit upon your knee?
You shouldn't really grope for them
At seventeen . . .

Her panties must smell like a rose
Is Seinfeld just like Piscopo?
Seducing girls in a limousine
While his fans think that he's so damn clean

Can't Seinfeld find an older dame?
Do private parts all look the same?
Does he make her parents shout
When he sticks his tongue into her mouth?

You're making such a spectacle
Thinking with your testicles
If you're gonna make some glue
You should date girls as old as you

Fell for an old man from TV
Her pubic hair grew in last week
With fresh and firm and round butt cheeks
At seventeen . . .

As of now Jerry's not talking to me because of this song. I got word through a publicist that he wouldn't appear on my TV show because of it. Jerry should be flattered I wrote a song about him. I wish someone would write a song about me.

One of my favorite comedians is Garry Shandling. His "Larry Sanders Show" on HBO is about the best thing on television.

## ANDREW "DICE" CLAY

I happen to think the Diceman is truly funny. Especially when Dice first broke on the scene, I thought his material was hysterical. Dice makes me laugh hard, and these other comedians who put him down are just jealous assholes who wish they could fill a stadium with rabid fans. How anybody could think this guy was somehow more than a comedian is beyond me, but all these nudnick journalists started writing essays like "The Politics of Hate" and suddenly Dice was being treated like a politician, as if his words *really* mattered. Hey, lighten up, the guy's a fucking comedian.

I also despise this idea politically correct people have that no one can make their own decisions and evaluations in life, and that the average guy who goes to see a show is such a moron that after he hears Dice he's going to go right out and rape two broads and get drunk and do some coke. I can't believe anyone would place that much significance on Dice's act.

Dice is a very nice guy, and I think he's a very talented comic. But I think he reacted to the criticism the wrong way. When his critics really came down hard on him, his reaction was to say, "Hey, I'm a character." By saying that, he turned off his core audience. They didn't want to know that he was a character, they wanted to think that Dice was that guy they saw on the stage. And you want to know something? I've spent a lot of time with him and he *is* that guy.

I remember one time Dice called me at home and told me that now that he had a wife and a baby he was going to buy a house. He was finally going to move out of Brooklyn. Dice had a really nice house in Brooklyn, but he was a fixture in his hometown neighborhood. I didn't understand how he could have stayed there that long, but he didn't care. His whole thing is, he'll go anywhere, he doesn't give a shit, and if people come up to him and ask for autographs, he says, "Fuck off."

When Dice decided he was going to buy a house he figured he should live near me, so I agreed to go house-hunting with him. I called the realtor who sold me my house—a really nice, sweet woman. Dice kept saying, "Don't call a realtor! I don't like realtors! Fuck those realtors!" I said, "Well, Dice, I really don't know what's on the market, quite frankly, so you've got to deal with the realtor."

"Well, does she understand what I want?" he said.

"What do you want in the house?" I asked.

"I'd like a ranch house. I've seen your house, you got stairs. I don't want stairs. I'd like a ranch house, but not so modern. I'd like it more regular, you know." Fucking Einstein could not have interpreted that description of a house, but I called the realtor I knew anyway.

Meanwhile, I can't believe he really talks like Dice, all the time! People who knew him early on told me that he didn't talk like that, but I think he's actually become that guy. So we made an appointment with the realtor. I took Dice and his humble assistant, Hot Tub Johnny, to a parking lot at the post office near where I live to meet the realtor. While we were waiting, a guy who appeared to be Indian came toward our car to ask directions. Dice rolled down the window.

"Excuse me," the Indian guy said.

"What the fuck do you want, you fuckin' dot-head?" Dice said. I was like fucking crunched down on the seat. I didn't even want to be seen with these guys because this is where I live. And Hot Tub Johnny was videotaping it all on a camcorder he had brought along.

"What do you want? I don't understand you! Speak some fucking English!" Dice was yelling. He was totally rude, and I was just dying, but finally this guy left. I started yelling at Dice. I told him if he was going to act like a fucking asshole, I wasn't going to go with him.

"Calm down," said Dice. "We're going to have a lot of fun today. Because when Johnny and I go house-hunting, we like to run up and down people's stairs and videotape it."

"If you bring a video camera with you and start running up and down other people's stairs, then I'm not going with you!" I was getting the feeling the Dice was showing off for me. I just wanted him to act normal.

About this time the realtor pulled up. We were all going to go in her car. Dice said to me, "You think she'll let me smoke in the car?"

"I don't know," I told him.

"Well, smoking to me is like a big deal. And I don't like these realtors," Dice said. "But I've got a test to see if she's really okay."

So we got into her car and Johnny started videotaping the realtor. I was saying, "Hey, guys, can you put away the videotape?" Amazingly, they put it away. But then Dice had to light up a cigarette.

"Do you mind if I smoke?" Dice said to her.

She didn't really say anything but you could tell it was annoying the hell out of her. Before she could answer, Dice said, "Well, I'm lightin' up a cigarette anyway." He was puffing away, and I was dying.

We got to the first house and Dice and Johnny decided that they were going to run around. I didn't know if they were putting this on for my benefit but it was as if I was the dad now, and I was in charge of these two little boys.

At each house we went to, Johnny turned on the video camera and he and Dice went running through these people's homes—while the people were there! Meanwhile, the realtor was looking at me as if these guys were crazy but she knew Dice had to have some serious dough because he was looking at really expensive houses.

One thing you find out when you go house-hunting is that the owners are very emotional about their homes. And one of the things you don't do, even if you don't like the house, is say anything negative. But Dice would just turn and, at the top of his lungs, right in front of the people, bellow at the poor

**Dice wanted to live in my neighborhood, but Satan chased him away.**

realtor, "This house is no good! This is not what I

asked to see! You're not showin' me what I asked to see! C'mon, next house, next house." He wouldn't even go through the houses out of courtesy.

Finally, I pulled him and Johnny aside. "Listen, you two fuckheads, number one, put away the fucking tape recorder—you're making me crazy. Number two, you gotta fucking lighten up. This is this poor woman's whole fucking gig. You're being totally rude."

"SHE LIED TO US!" Dice yelled back, right in front of her. "SHE TOLD US SHE HAD HOUSES THAT I WOULD LIKE. AND THESE DON'T EVEN FIT WHAT I LIKE!"

"Andrew," she said calmly, "I'm trying to get an idea of what you like, and by seeing what you don't like . . ."

"NO! NO! NO!" he interrupted her. "I know what you guys do. What *youse* do is you don't have anything to show us, but you *wanna* hook us in. You knew you didn't have what I wanted. I want a ranch!" He was all pissed off. Meanwhile, he was talking about a house that didn't exist anywhere except in his head.

This went on all day, and I was going out of my mind. We took him through new construction—everything—to no avail.

That night the realtor called me. "What's with this Andrew?" she said. "He's a little wild." I said, "Let me call him up and see what he thought of the day." So I called him up.

"Ahh, I don't know, that realtor, I didn't like her," he said.

"Listen, you really did her a disservice," I said. "Why don't you just go out with her a couple of times?

Now she has a good idea of what you want, she'll be able to find you something you'll like." So he called her up and he made an appointment to go out with her. And they went off on their own, thank God, because I didn't want to be there for this.

So they went out and Dice found a house he liked. It was a new construction, and the guy who built it needed some quick cash. Dice called me up. "I don't know, you think it's a good house?" So I sent my architect out. The guy did me a favor, he looked it over. He said the house was a steal—it was fantastic. I told this to Dice.

> "Howard Stern is one of the most positive people I ever met. He believes in winning. Even at times when the media was all over me, Howard would tell me, 'Never back down and show no fear, ya hear?' I hear you."
>
> —Andrew "Dice" Clay

I didn't hear from Dice after that. I figured he was going ahead and buying it. Next, the realtor called me. "Do you know what happened with the house?" she said. "Andrew didn't call me. We went to contract and then I never heard from him again. Does he still want to buy the house?"

I called him up and he said, "Look, I had a problem with that house, I couldn't buy it. I just couldn't buy it."

"What do you mean you couldn't buy it? We spent weeks working with you."

"I don't want to say. You'll think I'm crazy. Don't tell the realtor. Don't tell anyone."

Okay, so I agreed to keep it a secret.

"The house had a bad vibe."

"What do you mean a bad vibe? What happened?"
I asked.

"Well, we was going to contract, and I walk into the
lawyer's office, and I sit down and the guy's got voodoo heads all over the walls," Dice said.

"What do you mean, voodoo heads?" I said.

"The walls was lined with voodoo heads. They were
like shrunken heads," Dice explained to me. "Okay, I
tried not to react to that, but then, when she handed
me the key—'cause I wanted to take someone to see
the house—on the key chain they had a voodoo head.
And then I still was hanging in there, but I said to the
real estate lady, 'How could I reach you at your
phone?' So she says, 'Here's my number,' and it had
666—sign of the devil."

"Yeah, so? What's that got to do with the house?"
I said.

"Hey, those are too many bad signs, so I just backed
out," he said.

"Okay, Dice, I was just curious because the realtor
called me," I said.

"Well, don't tell her what I said," he cautioned me.

So I called her back and I said, "Look, Dice backed
out for various reasons. He was uptight about your
phone number, because it had 666."

"Everyone in this area has 666. It's the exchange,"
she said.

"Well, he told me not to tell you this, but he said the
lawyer for the other guy had voodoo heads all over
the wall."

"Voodoo heads?!" she screamed. "The guy is an African art collector. He's collected some of the most expensive artwork in the world and he has it on display in his office. It's the most beautiful African sculpture and art that anybody could ever find!"

That's the last time I'll ever go house-hunting with Dice.

## SAM KINISON

I remember when Sam Kinison first burst onto the comedy scene. It was with rage and fire and I never laughed harder in my life. He really changed the face of comedy. Only Sam could do a bit about the people in Ethiopia who were starving to death from the drought and scream at them for not moving. "Why don't they go to where the water is. THEY'RE LIVING IN A DESERT! IT'S ALL FUCKING SAND!"

Then he'd do a bit about the people who worked in funeral parlors having sex with corpses. He'd talk about dying and his body would be on the slab in the morgue, and it would finally be over. No more worries, no more pressure. Then a guy would come into the room and start boning him up the ass. "IT NEVER ENDS! IT NEVER ENDS!"

As great as he was on stage, I think he was at his best on my show, ad-libbing and talking about his life. It was like a spiritual purging for him. He'd come in and just open up. Nobody would consistently exorcise demons on the air the way Sam would on the show. He would not hold back one iota. And afterwards he would say to me, "I'm ruined, I'm ruined. Thanks a lot, man," as we walked him to the door. Meanwhile, he was the one who brought up all these subjects . . . but I ruined *him!*

He was a true outlaw—of comedy and of life. A friend of Gary's once came up to the show. She always thought that whatever went on during the show was just shtick, but they were sitting in Gary's office at eleven in the morning right after the show broke and Sam walked up to them. He was wearing that long preacher's coat of his and he had that famous black beret on. In one hand he had a glass and in the other a bottle of Dom Perignon.

"Gary, could you call down and order us some hamburgers and some Milky Ways and stuff?" Sam slurred. Gary's friend couldn't believe that stuff went on. But Sam was always roaming the halls up at the station with a bottle of champagne in his hand. Plus, he used to come into my office and plop down at my desk and lay out huge lines of coke.

"Sam, what the fuck are you doing?" I'd yell at him. "This is a radio station. We're regulated by the United States government. You could cost me my job." I felt like my father screaming at Symphony Sid to get straight.

But he gave magic radio.

One time he asked me who my favorite comedians were and I told him he was in the top three.

"Hey, man," he complained, "I do everything for you and I'm only in your top three?"

I couldn't take his whining anymore.

"SAM KINISON WILL BE THE GREATEST

COMIC THAT EVER LIVED!" I exulted. Sam got so excited, he pulled his penis out of his pants. He just whipped it right out.

He ran over to the glass booth where Robin was and started waving his penis around the studio. It was thick, but not that long. Jessica Hahn said he was the best lover she ever had. She must be wide, but not deep.

There are so many Sam memories. We were out at the Grammys once and Sam was up for an award in the comedy album category. Sam was up against Andrew "Dice" Clay, Sandra Bernhard, Erma Bombeck, and P.D.Q. Bach. He was so sure he was going to win that he had an elaborate speech all written out. "I don't care if I lose to Clay," he confided, "but there's no way I'm going to lose to Erma Bombeck or P.D.Q. Bach. That's a fuckin' music record."

They got to the big moment.

"And the winner is . . . P.D.Q. Bach."

"Man, do you believe that?" Sam moaned. He was drunk and depressed. "P.D.Q. Bach? Aw, man, it was a setup," Sam said. "It's a setup, dude."

Everything to him was a conspiracy. Sam was scheduled to make a presentation that night at the televised portion of the Grammys and he was plotting how he was going to ruin the presentation.

"Oh, man! Tonight I'm going to tell those mother-fuckers off!!" Sam growled. His sycophantic entourage, which usually consisted of about twenty people, all egged him on. Owing to his out-of-control coke problem Sam had just blown a movie deal with Columbia and cost the studio five million dollars. No one in

Hollywood wanted to do business with him. He had a shot at a series with Fox, but they had to make sure he was in control. They were on the fence about the deal and if they saw a crazed, coked-up,

> "I'm a big fan of his. He's the best. Howard's the King of Shock Radio."
>
> —Sam Kinison

rambling drunk Kinison at the Grammys, he would have destroyed his career permanently.

He really wanted to get off the road and the Fox deal was his way out, but these misfit hangers-on all around him were reinforcing his destructive behavior.

I really cared about him, so I pulled Sam and his manager Trudy over to the side. She had been pleading with him not to do it, but he wouldn't listen to her.

"Let me tell you something, Sam," I said. "You want my advice? Just go up tonight and read those stupid fucking cards the way they want you to. If you want to still be the show-biz outlaw and not do business with Fox, then tell them to fuck off. But you say you want to get back in the movies. You want that? Read the cards straight."

His manager turned to me and said, "Thank you, because everyone here is telling him to go up there and trash the place." Can you believe that I, the King of All Idiots, was exhibiting good judgment? Why couldn't someone have pulled me aside as I single-handedly ruined my own career by trashing every single employer I ever had—including Fox-TV, when I had a deal with them; MCA-TV, when I had a deal with them; New Line Cinema, when I had a deal with them; every fucking radio executive I ever had a deal with, and every human being I ever had a deal with?

Sam went up, read the cue cards, and got his deal with Fox a few weeks later.

He thanked me, and he finally fucking sobered up.

The next time Sam came in, he was totally sober. About an hour into the show I kiddingly said, "You know, you're much funnier drunk!"

Sam prowling backstage at my Nassau Coliseum "U.S. Open Sores" show.

Even though Sam boasted that he had just finished fifty days at AA, he was looking for any excuse to start drinking again.

He ordered a few bottles of Dom Perignon and started swigging away.

And you know what? Sam *was* a lot funnier drunk.

David Brenner came on and started talking about his custody battle with his ex-wife. David couldn't believe how drunk Sam was.

"David," Sam said, slurring his every word, "he's expecting me to make a comment . . . on your custody battle but . . . I won't. I wouldn't offend you. Howard keeps looking at me like 'Go. Snap. Snap like a rabid dog in the fifteenth century.' No, I won't do it. I love David Brenner. He's one of my heroes."

"How are you gonna get sober in time for Joan Rivers?" I asked Sam. He was due at her show in a few hours, which, of course, he missed when he later passed out drunk in his hotel room.

"How do you know I'm drunk? How do you know this isn't just an act? People expect a certain behavior pattern out of me, and I'm only trying to supply them with what they think the image of me is!" he said.

"We just got a fax from a guy who said *he's* drunk from listening to you," I said.

"Who sent that in? Dice Clay or his assistant Hot Tub Johnny West, the sewer boy I smacked around with rings I won't even wear anymore because they touched his skull?!" Sam roared.

"Let me ask David Brenner something." I tried to get a word in edgewise.

"Yeah, you ask him why Dice's concert movie didn't make as much as gay porno. *Do It to Me You Nasty Sailor* made ten grand more than Dice's concert movie," Sam said.

Another bottle of champagne was delivered to Sam. He got so loud that Robin had to scream to do her news report. Robin did a story about Teddy Kennedy and I was about to start in with my analysis when Sam butted in.

"He was never a real Kennedy! Teddy was the Shemp of the Kennedys! He wasn't Moe, he wasn't Curly—he was the Shemp of Kennedys."

At this point, Sam was almost delirious. He was so

drunk he missed his appearance on "The Joan Rivers Show" and when the Letterman people found out, they canceled his appearance that night, too. He was on a roll . . . down. But he didn't give a shit. He was a real outlaw.

Sam never shook his fondness for drugs. He was always drinking and doing coke. One time he invited me to his house in L.A., which he was really proud of. "Everyone thinks I'm a real scumbag and I don't live nice, but look at this place." First we went out to dinner. We went to The Palm or some shit. Sam told me he was swearing off coke and was going to get healthy. At dinner he announced, "I'm gonna eat healthy." So he ordered a lot of fried shit and steaks and I said, "Sam, that's not healthy." "What do you eat that's healthy?" he asked. "I know what I'm gonna order. Spinach. That's healthy, right?" So he ordered spinach. It was cream of spinach with globs of butter. He turned to me and said, "See, I can eat healthy stuff. It tastes good." He was serious. That spinach had about ten million calories. He had no concept of how to diet. But he was getting healthy.

Then we got into his car. He had a little black Trans Am. He used to drive Corvettes, but he kept smashing them up. He would drive them into trees. Then he would call one of his assistants and get him to sit there so when the police showed up there would be someone to blame for the accident. He had such a bad driving record because he was always high.

He was so proud of this Trans Am because he had put in one of those ten-CD players. He couldn't believe how great this thing was. So we got into the car to drive to his house after dinner and his girlfriend, Malika, decided to put me in the front seat.

Robin and Malika got in the back. The reason they got in the back was because of the way Sam drove. *No one* wanted to be in the death seat with Sam. I was screaming, "I don't want to be in the death seat!" He was saying, "No. No. Don't worry. It'll be fine."

Sam started driving and he couldn't keep his mind on the road. He was so excited about his CD player with all its buttons that he kept reaching over and fucking with it. Now, he was using both hands to operate the music, he wasn't even looking at the road—and *he was driving with his belly*. He was actually holding the wheel with his belly driving this car. I was totally flipping out at this point, screaming that he was probably high and he was going to get us killed, and he was completely nonchalant.

"Shut off the fucking music," I said.

"No," he said. "You've got to check out this Mötley Crüe CD, and besides, I'm not doing drugs because of my heart. I went to a doctor because I was having heart palpitations."

"Great," I thought. He was on heart medicine. Medicine to calm him down.

I started to relax, then Malika yelled out, "The pills put him to sleep."

He drove up to his house with his belly. Then he gave us a tour of his castle. The pool was heated to something like a hundred and fifty degrees because he didn't know how to operate the thermostat. Steam was coming off it like a cauldron. He hadn't figured out how to lower the temperature since he'd moved in a year ago. It was a fifty-degree night and the pool was evaporating rapidly, so he kept the hose constantly going.

Then he took me out on his porch in the Hollywood Hills, which had an incredible postcard view. He was so proud.

"Look! Look! Look at how beautiful my view is! I live like a king!"

We turned to go back in. Sam's castle was more like a dungeon. The dilapidated door was badly in need of repair and it had locked behind us. We couldn't get back in. Some castle. Sam was pounding on the door, screaming to get in. I was laughing hysterically, but Sam was upset. He had failed to impress me.

Now he was popping heart pills like crazy.

No way he was off drugs. He was on heart medicine. And it was a sedative!

Then he insisted on driving us back to the hotel, which was stupid, because it then became a race to get back to the hotel before his heart medicine kicked in. Good thing he ate a full meal.

As he was driving he said, "I'm going to be real drowsy in a few minutes."

Oh, great! And I was in the death seat

**Sam . . . getting looser backstage.**

again. Suddenly we passed the billboard for his new record album on Sunset Boulevard. He saw it and had a fit because someone had put graffiti all over it. *Boom*, he slammed on his brakes and started backing up in traffic.

He was driving backward, he was falling asleep, and I was screaming like crazy. "Sam! Hurry up! Your heart medicine's going to kick in!"

"Fuck it, some prick drew all over my face." Sam was on fire.

Miraculously, we made it to the hotel in one piece. I could have ended up like road pizza the way he did a few months later.

Still, Sam had a very tender human side for all his wild antics. There was a moment that sticks in my mind to this day.

It was so out of character for him.

Sam always dressed rock 'n' roll and it was odd to me that he didn't have any earrings or tattoos. He had heavy metal T-shirts cut the right way, bandannas and rock 'n' roll pants.

One day I said, "Sam, let's go get our ears pierced." I was on my third hole already.

"Oh, I'd love to," he said, "but I can't."

"Why not?" I asked.

"My mother will *kill* me," he said seriously. "If she sees me with an earring she'll beat the shit out of me!"

Here was the rock 'n' roll bad boy of comedy whose public displays of drinking, coking, and whoring were chronicled in every newspaper in the country, and he was worried about some little hole in his ear.

Sam with the loves of his life: wife Malika (right) and
her sister, Sabrina (left).

I didn't think Sam gave a shit what anyone thought
of him, but he cared what his mother thought.

By the end of his life, he was trying to get it all
together. He came on my show with his soon-to-be
wife Malika.

Then Sam went into explicit detail about his affair
with Malika's sister, Sabrina. For years the two sisters had lived in the same house with Sam. For years,
Sam had always clowned around about getting Sabrina in bed, but Sabrina wouldn't have anything to
do with him. Then things changed. Sabrina changed
her mind.

They devised an elaborate plan to hide their hot affair from Malika. Sam would sneak out of the house

under the guise of going for videos and would meet Sabrina at a nearby motel. What broke it up, ironically, was that Sam discovered the ugly truth. Sabrina was cheating on *him!* He felt that was wrong! Can you believe it? I would argue with him about it. "But Sam," I'd say, "you're cheating on her, with her own sister!"

Sam missed the point.

"But I loved her and she broke my heart. She cheated on me, so I threw her out!" he cried.

"Did he come home smelling like videotapes?" I asked.

"He was real quick, forty minutes, an hour," Malika said.

"Your sister wasn't that good," Sam lied.

Sam told us how he broke the news to Malika. They were staying in the Cary Grant Suite at the Dunes in Las Vegas when he told her that his weiner fell into the wrong place on the way to the video store.

Sam said, "Malika, I cheated on you with your sister. If you want to break up with me, I'll understand, but I don't want to break up with you. I love you and I've never loved you more. And I promise—and I'll keep this promise—that I will never lie to you again, and I'll never cheat on you again. Unless it's your idea and we like the girl an awful lot," Sam said.

I thought he was kidding, but he wasn't. Malika, who is a strikingly sexy beauty, then proceeded to give us a detailed description of how she went out and picked out girls to bring home for the two of them.

"Oh, this is straining the little Cub Scout in my shorts," I moaned. "When's the last time this happened, Malika?" She just laughed. "Was it last night? It was last night, wasn't it, you devil."

Seven months later Sam was killed on a highway in California when his car was hit head-on by a seventeen-year-old kid in a pickup truck. Sam was on his way to a gig in Vegas. He had just married Malika, and, oddly enough, they were scheduled to call in to my show the next day. We had an on-air wake for him, and Corey Feldman, Jessica Hahn, Richard Simmons, and Joan Rivers all called and shared Sam stories. A few days later, we presented a more formal tribute, replaying a lot of Sam's old appearances. Norman Lear called in during the tribute and gave his own epitaph for Sam: "In the land of the walking dead, he was a very live one."

Sam could have written his own epitaph. He once told me, "I have lived a carnal life. My view of life is 'If you're going to miss Heaven, why miss it by two inches? Miss it!' I don't have to go through the thing of paying for it in the next life. I know I'm screwed in the next life."

A few months later I went on the air with another thought about Sam. I thought that instead of burying Sam we should have taken his body on tour. The Sam Kinison Funeral Tour. We could have put Sam in formaldehyde like they did Marcos. We could have stuffed him, like Trigger. Don't laugh, Trigger did thirty-five states in four months and made a fortune!

Sam could have kept that date he had in Vegas. It would have been beautiful. We could have played a tape and worked his mouth by remote control. We could have had an Ice Follies section, where we put

Sam on skates. And talk about reviving his movie career. Sam Kinison in *Weekend at Bernie's, Part 3*. Hey, now every studio would love him, he'd be so reliable. Sam Kinison as *The Mummy*. Sam Kinison in *Awakenings*. He could have played a totem pole in any Indian movie. He'd be a pleasure on Letterman. Jessica could invite him over without any fear of a mess. You wouldn't even need a stuntman for him. You want him to fall out of a building? Just drop him. I'm telling you, the Sam Kinison Funeral Tour—it would have been huge. And the funny thing is, Sam would have totally dug it.

I really miss the guy.

# Another Lesbian Story

*Va-Gina Girl*

CHAPTER

16

It's time for a good lesbian story. You can never get enough lesbians. I had a regular caller named Gina cheer me up with a hot lesbian story after I had just come back from my vacation. Gina had previously sent me nude pictures of herself, so I looked at them as I listened to her story of LESBIAN LUST at a nudist colony! No one who hears these stories on the air ever thinks the girls are good-looking. Well, now I have proof. Now for the first time in publishing history you can look at her pictures while you read her story.

Gina and her boyfriend had gone to a nudist campground where she met up with another couple.

"I met this really hot-looking girl there. She was swimming in the pool, and I was lying on the side of the pool. She came over and sat down next to me and we started talking and swimming. She was real nice-looking. Kinda small-framed, like me. Blondish hair, muscular. Medium chest."

"Were you immediately attracted?" I asked.

"Yeah," Gina purred. "We got to know each other, played around swimming, and you could tell each of us was attracted to the other person. That night there was a dance. Everyone came kind of dressed."

"What do you mean, kind of?" I probed.

"Half on and half off. I wore a white skirt so I could pull it up and I had nothing on underneath. She had a white spandex dress on. So we started dancing together," Gina said. "It started off fast but we had our tops off by the end of that dance. Then we started dancing slow and I hiked up my skirt for that. We were holding each other tight. Then we started kissing."

"Did she put her hand on your butt?" I asked.

"Yeah, her hands were pretty good," Gina said.

"There was also a pretty wild dance where about fifteen girls were all dancing nude together and one girl would go underneath all the other girls' legs. The girls would touch you as you went underneath them."

"Is this a nudist colony or a sex orgy place?" I asked.

"The party got pretty wild that night," Gina admitted. "Then we left the dance. We were pretty hot and we just turned to each other and said, 'Let's get some air,' so we started walking outside."

"You're walking around naked?"

"I had my top with me, but it was off and my skirt was hiked up," Gina said. "She had the top of her dress pulled down. Then we walked to my tent."

"I have to take my pants off," I suddenly said. "I just pitched a tent myself. I'm right in tune with the story."

"She was a little bit nervous," Gina said. "She had never done anything like this before, so we talked for a long time. I took her by the hand."

"You're like the old crow lesbian," I said. "So you go into the tent . . ."

"We just started kissing. Clothes came off and we had a good time," Gina reported.

"Everything? How long did you spend?" I asked.

"A couple of hours," Gina said. "We fell asleep in there, actually."

"And did the guys come and join in?" I had to know.

"They came in, but they didn't join in. They watched."

"Your boyfriend doesn't get horny from all this?" I asked.

"I did stuff with him. It was discreet. The other couples were sleeping. It was a pretty big tent," Gina said.

"So the other girl dug it? Did you get it on the whole weekend?" I had to get back to LESBIANISM!

"The next day, Sunday, we had a really great time outside. We put a blanket down in the woods, behind some trees. The sun was out. It was really nice. We thought nobody could see us, but there was a guy who was watching from far away. He thanked us afterwards," Gina said.

"Jesus Christ, what's going on in America?" I said. "I did nothing for my whole two weeks' vacation. All I did was work. Nobody put on a lesbian show for me. You would dump your boyfriend for me, wouldn't you?" I said.

"Oh, yeah," Gina replied.

"I'd move you up to New York. You'd have to give up your nursing job so we could go full-time to the nudist colony," I explained.

"You would have a great time, Howard," she said.

"And you know, you're smart, you're not a bimbo. I could have a conversation with you. You're no dope.

You know what you like. I'm aching for you. We have to clone you. Every girl should be like Gina, Robin."

"Well, you have three daughters that we can start with," Robin said.

"Oh, put a knife in my heart. You just be quiet!"

Gina took pity on me.

"We took some pictures together. I could send you some," she said.

"Overnight them!" I begged.

LESBIANS! LESBIANS! I LOVE LESBIANS!

# Stuttering John

*Hero of the Stupid*

CHAPTER
17

    Look, in an ideal world, there wouldn't be any need for a Stuttering John. In an ideal world, celebrities wouldn't be on their high horses all the time and they'd all come on the air with me and have a good time. But we live in an imperfect world and I soon realized that if I was going to get all the celebrities on my show that I really wanted, I would have to go out and stalk them in their natural habitats.

    I was the original celebrity interview stalker. I started showing up at the Grammys, the Emmys, and the Oscars, where I could confront the celebrities who avoid me and my show. I'd stand out on the red carpet with all the other press with my trademark megaphone in hand, booming insightfully moronic questions to the glittering stars.

One time at the Grammys as I was battling asshole paparazzi who were pushing and kneeing me to get at the stars, Dan Rather came strolling in. It was mass pandemonium. I clawed my way to the front, turned on the megaphone and blasted: "DAN RATHER! DAN RATHER!" Rather saw me with my long hair and he had no idea what was going on. He came up to my mike and said, "Hello! Rock 'n' roll forever!" and walked on. How hip, Dan.

But I was soon to retire as an on-location celebrity interviewer. I felt like a real dick when all the press would gang up and scream at me that my stupid questions were getting in the way of their own moronic questions. And God, were their questions stupid! I remember Jeannie Wolf from "Entertainment Tonight" asking stars ridiculous hairstyle questions as they walked in, like, "I noticed your new hairstyle. Have people been complimenting you on it?" She asked everybody the same question. And in another corner there was a guy from England representing the so-called Legitimate Press asking every single celebrity this riveting question: "Your fans want to know, will you be coming to England soon?" What a dope! How could anyone be annoyed by MY stupid questions?

I hated being subjected to constant ridicule from the press and from these arrogant stars. What I needed was someone less self-conscious, someone with a higher tolerance for abuse. In short, I needed an innocent, someone with childlike curiosity. A lightbulb flashed in my head, and two words stood out clearly: BOY GARY!

 Gary started out fine. We went out to the Emmys the first year Fox hosted the show and they had no idea what was going on. I sent Gary out on the red carpet with Fred and Jackie, who were writing down questions as they saw celebrities. They'd hand a dopey question to Gary and he'd ask it. Gary got Mary Tyler Moore really pissed off when, at the beginning of the AIDS scare, he asked her if she would actually touch her Emmy or was she afraid of getting AIDS from it.

Gary was the first one we sent out to cover a specific event. Diahann Carroll was going to be signing books nearby, so we dispatched Gary and his tape recorder and some silly questions. But we were novices at this art form, so I told Gary to tell her that we had polled our listeners that morning and these were the questions they wanted answered. I figured this was a way Gary would feel more comfortable asking stupid questions. After a few fluff ones about "Dynasty" and her youthful appearance, we hit Diahann with our zingers: we asked her how she felt about Reagan bombing Libya and why she broke up with David Frost. She managed to avoid answering these tough ones. Even though they were pretty tame by today's Stuttering John standards, they stood in stark contrast to the totally lame questions most celeb puff-piece journalists routinely asked. We were on the road to mayhem.

Gary did a few more interviews with people like Yoko Ono and Robert Plant, but it was his short encounter with Itzhak Perlman at a Grammy ceremony that pointed us in a new direction: total absurdity. The more absurd the question, the more foolish the celebrity might look. So we asked Itzhak Perlman, a staid classical performer, whether he thought that the Grammys were discriminating against Buffy Sainte-Marie, a folksinger from the sixties who happened to be an American Indian:

GARY: Itzhak, do you feel the Academy is anti-Buffy Sainte-Marie?

PERLMAN: I'm sorry, I didn't understand the question.

GARY: Do you feel the Academy is anti-Buffy Sainte-Marie? They never nominate her for anything.

PERLMAN: I don't know. I wouldn't know if they were anti-anybody. That's an inside tip, I suppose. All right? Okay?

We were honing our methodology and refining our interview aesthetic. Unfortunately, we lost our interviewer. It happened when we sent Gary out to interview Van Halen at their concert at the Meadowlands. Gary was ushered backstage to a private dressing room where he conducted the interview. It went off without a hitch and then Gary joined about a hundred other people who were partying at a preconcert publicity dinner in a huge adjoining room. Alex Van Halen happened to bump into his manager and he told him that he had just done a "wild" interview.

The manager asked him what he meant by "wild." Van Halen told him that one question to Sammy Hagar (the singer who replaced David Lee Roth in a controversial move) was: If you were driving by a shopping center on a hot day and you saw a dog and David Lee Roth locked up in separate cars, who would you save?

The manager was beside himself. He rushed over to Gary and started going through his bag to get the list of questions. When he started reading the actual questions, he went ballistic. "OH, MY GOD!" he screamed. "YOU ARE A PIECE OF SHIT. YOU PIECE OF SHIT. GET OUT OF MY DRESSING ROOM, YOU PIECE OF SHIT!" Gary was being screamed at in front of a hundred people.

Gary felt like such a dick that he decided to hide behind his mantle as "producer" of the show and he delegated the task of doing these interviews to a lowly intern named Dave. He was a good-looking *GQ* type of guy, but when he'd interview a celebrity he'd just read the questions right off the page in an incredible monotone. Thus, "Dead Dave" was born.

He did a great interview with Dr. Ruth. Dr. Ruth wouldn't even let him finish his first question:

DEAD DAVE: When I was in boarding school I had anal sex with my roommate . . .
DR. RUTH: I don't want to hear such nonsense, okay?

After Dave, there was Mitch, another intern. Mitch was a little neurotic Jewish kid who aspired to be a comedy writer. He loved the notoriety of being on the air but he was afraid that the interviews he was doing would ruin him in the business. What business? He wasn't in the business. *I'm* barely in the business. He worried, but he was fearless.

At HBO's "Comic Relief," Mitch asked Norman Lear if he thought Fox Television was responsible for the death of Joan Rivers's husband, Edgar Rosenberg. Lear freaked out and Mitch was thrown out of the press conference. HBO was so angry that we were banned from all HBO events for the next few years.

When Mitch left, he suggested that we hire a New York University classmate of his as the new intern.

Gary came into my office. "Mitch says this guy John Melendez would be a good intern, only there's one problem, boss." Gary got serious. "He stutters pretty bad."

"What a find! Hire him!" I screamed at Gary.

"I haven't even met him yet," Gary protested.

"I don't care, fucking hire him," I said. "I don't care how lame he is, I don't care if he's fucked up on heroin, just fucking hire him right now!" I couldn't believe our good fortune. A stutterer! Now we could really go after those pompous stars. We could ask them the most degrading, disgusting, and tasteless questions and they'd be fluttering out of the crippled mouth of a stutterer. These celebrities would have to listen to these questions—better yet, *work* to listen to these questions—and then they'd have to respond or run the risk of being accused of being insensitive to the handicapped. Thank God for political correctness!!

When John came up, he was even better than we imagined. John is a long-haired rock 'n' roller with a cherubic face that becomes instantly demonic when he starts to gag on a difficult word. He is a blank slate, with no basic knowledge of contemporary culture. He's never heard of any of these celebrities or their problems. This is a man who has no idea what Mike Wallace does for a living! Combine that cultural illiteracy with a bulldoglike dedication to pleasing his superiors and you have the most awesome celebrity stalker/interviewer possible: STUTTERING JOHN, HERO OF THE STUPID! There was no doubt in my mind that in a short while John himself was destined to become a *st-st-st-star*.

John's first assignment was to cover a grape protest. We knew that Carly Simon would be there but John also came back with some tape of Danny Glover. But what was great was John's patter in the studio. Right off the bat, he told us he was so nervous he was going to shit a brick. He was totally oblivious to the fact that he was on the air. Then, as he started stuttering like a machine gun, he was almost flying out of his chair. Perfect!

John was great on the first few interviews. Even though he was instructed to just ask about grapes, he managed to ask *both* Carly Simon and Danny Glover why James Taylor had lost all of his hair. He even managed, while walking on a California grape boycott picket line in front of a supermarket, to ask Danny Glover if he thought the pope was the Antichrist. *Awesome.* I knew I had my man.

That was confirmed when we sent John to Ringo Starr's press conference. Ringo had assembled a couple hundred reporters to hype his upcoming American tour. They were treating Ringo like the president, then Stuttering John strode up to the mike:

STUTTERING JOHN: What did you do with the money?

RINGO: What money?

STUTTERING JOHN: The money your mom gave you for singing lessons.

RINGO: Well, I actually spent it on fish and chips.

Thank God this was Ringo, the nice Beatle. John escaped unscathed and he even got a mention for the question in *Rolling Stone* magazine. So when Paul McCartney held a press conference to announce *his* upcoming tour, the p.r. people were lying in wait. John got thrown out of the press conference about four times. Yet he managed to sneak back in!

STUTTERING JOHN: Hi, Paul. Stuttering John from the "Howard Stern Show." What's the most girls you've had in bed at once?

PAUL: Difficult question. Think I'm gonna tell you that on live television with my wife in the building? Think again, buddy. Fat chance.

You have to put these events into perspective. Here's poor Stuttering John, who's convinced he's blowing his life's goal of making it in the rock business by asking these musical demigods these embarrassing questions, YET HE'S DOING IT FOR THE SAKE OF THE SHOW! Hey, is it great to have a guy who'll take a bullet for you, or what?

Thankfully, John wound up interviewing some musicians who were hip enough to really dig his act. ZZ Top were captivated by John's penetrating questions to them:

Did you guys ever throw up and get big chunks in your beards?

How many people compliment you on your cough drops?

Since you look Jewish, why don't you call yourselves ZZ Dreidel?

In a pinch, would you wipe with your beard?

Even the great James Brown cracked up when John ambushed him at an MTV awards show:

STUTTERING JOHN: When you do a split, do you bang your testicles on the floor?

JAMES: No, I think they're hip. They know I'll be down there temporarily.

We sent John out after everyone who hates us. He got Harvey Fierstein to spit out about nine hundred "fucks" in two sentences informing him that he wouldn't even answer any questions for "that fucking asshole Howard Stern." Then, failing to get Harvey, John actually had the balls to ask a few of Harvey's gay friends the questions we had prepared for Harvey:

> "I hate that fucking Howard Stern."
> —Harvey Fierstein

What was the worst disaster: AIDS or *Legs Di-amond*?
Did you ever insert wildlife in your behind?

John was unstoppable. He got Donahue and his wife, Marlo Thomas, and he also caught that loud-mouth Gloria Steinem, controlling Marlo's every word like a puppet.

STUTTERING JOHN: All right, Marla, can I ask you a question? [He didn't even know her name.]
MARLO: Do you know Gloria Steinem?
STUTTERING JOHN: Hi, Gloria. Let me ask you a question, Marla. Hhhhhhhh—Do you and Phil still get horny for each other?
MARLO: He's coming. You ask him.
STUTTERING JOHN: Please, Marla, don't go, let me ask you, please, Marla, I'm a big fan of "That Girl."
MARLO: All right, okay.
GLORIA: Why are you asking these silly questions?
MARLO: Yes?
STUTTERING JOHN: Let me ask you, what word for women do you find most ooooooooo . . . de-grading?
MARLO: Degrading?
STUTTERING JOHN: Chick, bimbo, bitch, babe, slut, or whore?
MARLO: What is most degrading?
STUTTERING JOHN: Yeah. That's a good question.
GLORIA: Not especially a good question. Why re-peat all those words?
MARLO: Right. I don't like that question.

As soon as Gloria started in, Marlo realized she was supposed to be indignant, too. She was like a well-trained dog.

STUTTERING JOHN: Well, ddddddddddd, I'm a feminist.
GLORIA: Why don't you just say "women" and let it go at that?
MARLO: We like just to be called women, that's all.
GLORIA: We're not going to publicize the issue.
MARLO: Yeah, that's right.
STUTTERING JOHN: All right, wwwwwwww, I'm a big fan. You look great. Aaaaaaaa, you're so thin. Did you ever stick your finger down your throat to throw up?
GLORIA: You're really hopeless, you know that?
STUTTERING JOHN: Why do you say that?
GLORIA: I'm so glad I don't have to be interviewed by you.

Well, no one was interviewing you, Gloria, so why didn't you just keep your mouth shut?

STUTTERING JOHN: Hey, Marla, did any of Phil's sons hit on you? Marla? Marla?

What a masterpiece. He got Cher and he got Chastity. In fact, he even had the balls to ask Chastity if she ever kissed her mother on the mouth. Of course, not knowing for one second that Chastity was accused of being gay certainly helped John deliver these questions.

But nothing stopped John. His conquests mounted. Regis. Chevy Chase, not once, but twice! He managed to get "Family Ties" TV actress Justine Bateman twice. And he even used the same questions the second time. Here was Justine, on the brink of breaking out of the shitass world of sitcoms, doing the famous Arthur Miller play *The Crucible* off-Broadway, and along came John to puncture her self-inflated balloon:

STUTTERING JOHN: Did Arthur Miller write the play you're in while humping Marilyn Monroe?
JUSTINE: Ah, go fuck yourself.

Justine freaked out and walked away. John didn't even get to ask the follow-up question: Were there stains on the script? The beautiful part of it all was that he didn't even know who Arthur and Marilyn were! He then had the balls to go up to Ally Sheedy, a known bulimic, and point-blank ask her, "When was the last time you threw up?"

But despite the negative reactions, John persevered.

Bea Arthur was thrilled to talk to him:

STUTTERING JOHN: Bea, what do you think of Howard Stern?
BEA: He made some nasty cracks about me so I don't listen to him anymore. I used to listen to him and go, "Oh, how could he say that?" but then when he hit me, I thought, "Oh, that son of a bitch."

STUTTERING JOHN: Yeah, but he equally offends everybody, you know . . .

BEA: I know that. It reminds me of what they used to say about Hitler. First they came for the Jews and I didn't do anything, and then they came for homosexuals, and then they came for me. You know what I'm talking about?

STUTTERING JOHN: Let's go to a lighter topic by asking you, what Hollywood star would you like to nail most?

Is this man a genius or what? What a segue. Problem was, thanks to that fascist-hating Bea, he got bodily thrown out of the event about two seconds later.

The celebrities who give John the hardest time are baseball players. Especially ex-baseball players. They have no sense of humor.

John interviewed Ted Williams at a baseball card show. I guess Ted was pretty grumpy because he was out charging money for his autograph. I know serial killers with more class.

STUTTERING JOHN: Do you know all the words to the national anthem?

TED: No. I wish I did. I don't sing.

STUTTERING JOHN: Did you ever accidentally fart in the catcher's face?

Ted did a double take. He stopped signing autographs and leaned over to John.

TED: Pardon?

STUTTERING JOHN: By any
chance, did you ever accidentally fart in the catcher's face?

TED: Who the hell are you? For
God's sake. That kind of shit . . . see ya later.

> "I'm the biggest fan of
> Howard Stern."
> —Keith Hernandez

He dismissed John with an ominous sweep of his hand. The same thing happened when John inter- viewed ex-Boston great Carl Yastrzemski. He got past the fart question but Carl got miffed when John asked him if he liked Dolly Parton's implants.

One baseball guy you'd expect to be pretty cool is Tommy Lasorda, the Dodgers manager. Hey, this guy is Mr. Show Biz, he hangs out with Sinatra and he did all those Slim-Fast commercials. But our human lit- mus test revealed that Lasorda is just as self-serious as the rest of them. After we let him ramble on and give a big plug for that stupid Slim-Fast junk he scarfed, John got to the more "controversial" ques- tions:

STUTTERING JOHN: How much do you want to bet
that Pete Rose is gambling again?

John never even got up to the farting-in-the-catch- er's-face question before Lasorda blew him off. But that was nothing compared to what some fan of Tom- my's did to Stuttering John. John was going home late one night on the Long Island Railroad. He was just sitting there minding his own business when the train stopped and a guy who had been sitting in front of him turned around and faced John. This guy was middle aged, dressed in a nice suit, a typical commuter. Except when it came time for his stop, he paused, looked at John, and said, "I don't like what you did to Tommy Lasorda." And then he threw his whole orange soda all over Stuttering John and ran out the door!

Ah! The price of fame!

You think that's humiliating? Hey, Stuttering John's used to it.

When I was in elementary school, everybody called me "stutter-face." Kids threw rocks at me, everyone wanted to beat the shit out of me. Then in high school, people called me Skip. So when I got to college, I didn't want anyone to know I stuttered. I was a good student but I was in a class and the teacher said, "Did you read the book?" I said, "Yeah." He said, "What color was the girl's dress?" I tried "yellow" a couple of times, but I couldn't say "yellow" and that was the right answer. I said "green" instead. That's the most humiliating thing I can remember.

> Johnny asks some unusual and sometimes penetrating questions, and tends to stutter when excited.
>
> (+)S  11/18/77
> Grade  Date
>
> He still needs to control his silly behavior and tendency to call out
>
> Teacher
> 5  9/17
> Grade  Date
>
> I informed Mrs. Mefulden that John was, I grades in his efforts. Anytime work negligent - all work sloppy & disorganized.
>
> John has a perceptive mind & is an independent thinker. Enjoys a debate or argument. Stutter increases when excited or under pressure to make his point.

**John's fifth-grade report card.**

Stuttering John can be brutal, but he is not without human feelings. They surfaced once.

> I was interviewing gossip columnist Cindy Adams and her husband, Joey, and I was asking him questions about senility. I had no idea who they were and when Joey walked out he looked as if he was going to keel over. I respect old people, and I had to ask him when was the last time he had a solid bowel movement. I was really freaked. I didn't know who the hell he was. I remember looking at Kevin, the TV producer and saying to him, "I can't do it," and Kevin was egging me on and I said, "All right, fuck it," and I asked him about his bowel movement and how many times he'd seen Halley's Comet. That was an interview I felt really bad about.

John was also pretty brutal with Mike Wallace of "60 Minutes."

> "Howard is not a favorite of mine. I just don't like being nasty and spiteful to people."
> —Cindy Adams

**STUTTERING JOHN:** All right. Hhhhhhhhhh, let me ask you. How could you be so old and still have pimples? Listen, I'm just curious.

But it was the most venerable of our news anchors who provided us with a transcendent Stuttering John moment. The first time John nabbed Walter Cronkite he was walking up to a charity event. John asked him if he was there for the charity or because his publicist thought it was a good idea. Uncle Walter got really pissed off and pushed past John into the event. But the second time, John donned a disguise and waylaid Walter:

STUTTERING JOHN: Since you stopped doing news, don't you think the quality of it has really slipped?

WALTER: Well, yes. I think the quality of all life has slipped over the last several years. As a matter of fact, television has reflected that and has been part of it and perhaps, in some ways, responsible for it. I don't think there's any doubt about that.

STUTTERING JOHN: What did William Paley ever do that was so friggin' important?

WALTER: That's the way you phrase your questions, is it?

STUTTERING JOHN: Yeah.

WALTER: Well, I don't want to indulge in that kind of radio, thank you. I don't believe in that language. That's what's the trouble with our business today.

STUTTERING JOHN: Would you coanchor with Howard Stern?

WALTER: That's what's the trouble with our business today. Using that kind of language. Upgrade your language and you'll do something for human beings and for our civilization. You can't use language like that.

STUTTERING JOHN: Oh, I didn't curse. I didn't curse.

WALTER: "Frigging." Do you think "frigging" is a good word?

STUTTERING JOHN: Well, it's not a curse.

WALTER: It's a bad word. It's a bad word. What do you think it means?

STUTTERING JOHN: It's just another word for saying, you know, I don't know.

WALTER: What do you think it means? Words should mean something, shouldn't they?

STUTTERING JOHN: It's kind of an adjective, you know.

WALTER: But what does the word mean?

STUTTERING JOHN: It just gives it like emphasis.

WALTER: Come on.

STUTTERING JOHN: Would you ever coanchor with Howard Stern?

WALTER: Of course not.

STUTTERING JOHN: Thanks a lot, Walter. See ya.

WALTER: You bet. Right. For God's sakes!

Does this sound like two mental patients talking in the back ward or what? How did this guy get to be so old and humorless? Of course, you don't have to be old to be humorless. Just ask Richard Gere. John got to him when he went to interview the Dalai Lama.

This guy was supposed to be like God. He walked in with his hands folded and he was praying and Richard Gere was like crying because he loves him so much. I was on fire, I was so nervous. I asked, "What was it like to wake up one day and realize that you were God?" which was a question I really didn't understand.

RICHARD GERE: That's a very strange one. How about another one?

STUTTERING JOHN: Okay, all right. Do people ever say, uh, uh uh, do people ever say, do people ever say, "Hello, Dolly"?

Nobody laughed. They hated me. Kevin, the producer, was acting like a wuss. He got me there, went over the questions, then disappeared behind people. I was alone, like on a fucking island. Then this big black guy was standing behind me for the rest of the press conference. He wouldn't let me move. I was trying to get to Richard Gere but I felt hate all around. I felt Richard Gere wanted me dead. And I couldn't even get in my follow-up questions to the Dalai:

Do you have sex?
What is truth?
Have you seen any of the new fall TV shows?

At that point, I dismissed ever making it at anything. I figured I had blown it. Gary convinced me that I was fucking nuts. Insulting a Beatle and a God. I thought I'd never get my band signed at that point.

In fact, John became the focal point for a lot of hostility and overt aggression. Morton Downey punched him out during an interview at a restaurant when John asked a sensible question: If Morton was bankrupt, how was he paying for this big press party? When he asked Eric Bogosian why his movie bombed, Bogosian pulled him over to a corner of the room and threatened to beat "the fuck" out of him. Then a huge bouncer picked John up by the neck and carried him down two flights of stairs and threw him out. After he finished a Spike Lee interview, two guys claiming to be Spike's henchmen went out to John's car and they grabbed his bag. But John was too quick. He threw the tape to an intern who ran away with it to safety.

But it wasn't until the stutterization of the Gennifer Flowers news conference that John got the instant national recognition he so richly deserved. Picture the scene. A ballroom in New York City. The place was packed with reporters waiting to hear the story of her alleged twelve-year affair with a presidential candidate. The seriousness of the occasion was absurd. They were treating Gennifer as if *she* was the presidential candidate.

John got right to the point:

## Gennifer, did Governor Clinton use a condom?

A totally relevant question but her people were offended. They threatened to throw John out. She was there to talk about her sexual relationship and she found this question offensive? He had another one for her:

## Will you be sleeping with any other presidential candidates?

John's booming stutter permeated the packed hall. The press was backing up. While John was used to receiving scorn from the suckass entertainment press, the more cynical political reporters were delighting in this. John erupted again:

## Was there ever a threesome?

A star was born!

 Everybody came up to me at the end and asked me who I was. I was thrilled, especially when they talked about me on "The McLaughlin Group" and they referred to me as Mr. Melendez. I had no idea it was going to be that big. I actually was hoping I could get on Letterman.

John's instant celebrity began to go to his head. He actually developed the delusion that he should be getting paid for his work as an intern and he began making unreasonable demands on management. But we developed a strategy to jerk his chain a bit. We found a guy named Don who suffered from Tourette's syndrome, an affliction characterized by wild uncontrollable grunting, cursing, and involuntary muscle spasms. Then we sent Don out to interview some porn stars, and on our TV show that weekend we ran Don's best interviews alongside the worst of Stuttering John's. Then we asked the viewers to vote on whom they preferred. John was devastated. Would we dump him for someone with Tourette's? Of course John won, and we got him a nice salary.

Despite his newfound celebrity, not too much had changed. Recently, John went to the Grammys and got thrown out after he asked Debbie Gibson, "If the group Wilson Phillips should win the award, do you think the fat one will eat the statue?"

As a result of our insightful questions, we were disinvited to the Grammys:

John stammers it up with Debbie Gibson.

In response to the overwhelming complaints from celebrities, managers and other *important* electronic media who shared the

TV/Radio room with representatives of the ''Howard Stern Show'' last year, I am afraid that we cannot accommodate your request for radio credentials.

It isn't easy being Stuttering John anymore, but still he goes out into the night in search of his elusive prey. He hunts down Madonna so he can ask her:

Do you bleach your pubes?

He trails John F. Kennedy, Jr., so he can find out:

Do girls encourage you not to use condoms so they can get their hands on that Kennedy moolah?

And there's no describing the joy he feels when he finally nails someone he's been searching for for years. That happened recently when John met up with New York's distinguished mayor, David Dinkins.

John asked him if he would ever park his car in a Puerto Rican neighborhood and if, after he's done in the bathroom, he checks after he's done wiping. An aide came out and knocked him aside. It was a classic Stuttering John confrontation. But the mayor realized how foolish it was to avoid Stuttering John the first time, so the next time they met the mayor was ready and he graciously answered John's stupid questions:

STUTTERING JOHN: Because you sweat so much, how many gallons of water do you have to drink?
MAYOR DINKINS: About seven or eight.
STUTTERING JOHN: Are there any mayoral groupies?

MAYOR DINKINS: Sure, bunches of them. That's
   how I got elected.
STUTTERING JOHN: Do you sleep on a sponge?
MAYOR DINKINS: No. Do you recommend it?
STUTTERING JOHN: How many shirts do you sweat
   up in a day?
MAYOR DINKINS: About fourteen or fifteen.
STUTTERING JOHN: Do you sweat in the shower?
MAYOR DINKINS: It's hard to tell because water is
   pouring on me.

I'm not a supporter of David Dinkins, but even I
felt the interview had been a bit over the line. It was
disrespectful.

The mayor was so gracious that I felt guilty. I was
also afraid he'd send the police chief after me. I immediately started yelling at John for asking such rude
and ridiculous questions. I was outraged! John was
perplexed. "But you told me to ask those questions,"
he cried.

"I know, but it doesn't matter," I said. I knew that
there was only one thing to do: call the mayor's office
and blame it on someone else. I got through to the
mayor's press office and put them on the air:

"I want to inform you of a hoax that may have been
played," I said. "There was a gentleman who represented himself as a reporter from the 'Howard Stern
Show' and he interviewed the mayor. It was not the
'Howard Stern Show.' It was another radio station
that did it. We did not ask the questions about sweating and sleeping on a sponge, and while some people

might find that humorous, I do not. I think the mayor works pretty hard and just because he sweats a lot people shouldn't be making fun of that. I think the mayor can be asked fun questions, but those questions were just a little rough and presented the mayor in a bad light. I had nothing to do with it and neither did Stuttering John. It was either the Len Berman show on WFAN or possibly Scott Shannon or someone like that. I'm sure he's upset about it."

"I don't know if the mayor is upset about it," his spokesman said. "The mayor is under a lot of pressure and he gets a lot of attention and sometimes you'll catch the mayor wiping his brow. I think that's an illustration of how hard he works."

"By the way, do you carry the towels he uses?" I said.

But for me, the classic Stuttering John interview will always be the one he did with Imelda Marcos. She was totally unflappable and silent as John squeezed out a few quick ones:

Does it bother you when people speak to you on the bowl?
Do you think ugly people should be allowed to have children?

Imelda was probably wishing she had one of those millions of shoes right then to hit John over the head with, but she remained calm. Until she got stuck in front of a revolving door and John had her trapped.

> "She looked like a cornered chicken. It was just me and her. So I went for it."

Imelda, if you pass gas at home in front of others, do you blame the family dog?

Imelda's face reflected a mosaic of revulsion, fear, anger, betrayal, but mostly nausea. Her eyes pleaded for a way out. After what seemed like years, someone grabbed her arm and ushered her inside. Then all we saw was John's face. A look of unmitigated, unabashed, sheer ecstasy was splashed across his face. He was happy. He was calm. He was *STUTTERING JOHN, HERO OF THE STUPID*, now and forever.

# STUTTERING JOHN'S
## GREATEST HIT AND WISH LIST

**JIM ABBOTT**
(one-handed star pitcher,
New York Yankees)
Can you shuffle a deck of
cards?

**WARREN BEATTY**
Did you forget to pull out
with Annette Bening?

**TRACY CHAPMAN**
Are you still in show business?

**CHEVY CHASE**
Do you read the scripts of the movies you choose to
make, or do you go, "Eenie meenie minie moe?"

**CONNIE CHUNG**
Whose fault is it that you can't get pregnant?

**DICK CLARK**
Did you ever consider making
love to the teenage girls on
"[American] Bandstand"?

**SHARON STONE**
Any movies with crotch shots
coming up?

**JIMMY CONNORS**
Don't you think Steffi Graf has great legs and a col-
lie's face?

**CINDY CRAWFORD**
Does your gynecologist send you love letters?

**GEENA DAVIS**
Were you Thelma or Louise?

**PHIL DONAHUE**
Did you ever use your glasses to burn ants by pointing them at the sun?

**RICHARD DREYFUSS**
Do you have gray pubic hair?

**LARRY KING**
Isn't it a disgrace how many times Liz Taylor's been married?

**GRIFFIN DUNNE**
Who are you?

**BOB DYLAN**
How does it feel to be on your own, like a complete unknown, like a rolling stone?

**FRANK GIFFORD**
Does your son ever accidentally call you "grandpa"?

**ARSENIO HALL**
Are you mad at your dentist?

**LEONA HELMSLEY**
Where's the craziest place you and your husband have made love?

**MICHAEL JACKSON**
Did you learn how to walk backwards to avoid your father's punches?

**BILLY JOEL**
When you look at your wife, Christie Brinkley, do you thank your mother for making you take piano lessons?

RUSH LIMBAUGH
Are you called Rush because you're in a rush to eat?

PAT RILEY
Who is the biggest Knick—genitally?

LIZA MINNELLI
What good is sitting alone in your room?

EDDIE MURPHY
Now that you've conquered comedy, acting, and music, will you become a brain surgeon?

MARTINA NAVRATILOVA
Do you hate bananas?

LIZ TAYLOR
Was selling perfume one of your career goals?

PAUL NEWMAN
Does driving a car really fast give you an erection?

OLIVER NORTH
Did you ever have a nightmare where your penis got caught in a paper shredder?

SINÉAD O'CONNOR
Will you order Howard Stern's Butt Bongo Fiesta?

LUCIANO PAVAROTTI
Ever fart while belting out a high note?

REGIS PHILBIN
Don't you wish Kathie Lee would sink on one of those Carnival boats?

ROBERT REDFORD
How did you keep a straight face when you were looking at Barbra Streisand's nose?

LEONARD NIMOY
Is your penis pointed like your ears?

**GERALDO RIVERA**
Are you recognized at cockfights?

**CHARLIE ROSE**
Who's failed more on TV, you or Dick Cavett?

**SLY STALLONE**
Do you think that headband on your mother's head was placed there by space aliens?

**BARBRA STREISAND**
Are people who need people really the luckiest people in the world?

**DR. RUTH WESTHEIMER**
Is it possible to be in love with a girl and her dog at the same time?

**MONTEL WILLIAMS**
Didn't you steal my car?

**BRUCE WILLIS**
What is disappearing quicker, the ozone or your hair?

**LIZ SMITH**
First off, I would just like to apologize for the fat remarks I made the last time I interviewed you. I realize how insensitive I was and how bad I felt when I saw you embarrassed on national TV. Obesity is not something to make fun of, and through my recent spiritual uplifting I am trying to right my wrongs. So tell me . . . how many cows did it take to make your leather jacket?

# Hate Mail Artwork

CHAPTER
18

# Ten Reasons
# Howard Stern
# Must Be Stopped!

### These are Actual Quotations from his Radio Show

**1.** Commenting on the William Kennedy Smith trial: "any mention of how big Willie's penis is..."

**2.** Commenting on Magic Johnson: "He can't even bang his wife. How can he bang his wife? Here's a guy that was bangin' every day, and now he can't bang anybody."

**3.** Commenting on radio personality Garrison Keillor: "Hey Garrison Keillor, F**K YOU."

**4.** "I've seen guys light their penis on fire to get on TV."

**5.** "Imagine what people are doin' in their cars right now while they're listening...guys masturbating."

**6.** Speaking to a member of TV's "Knots Landing" cast: "Do you ever bang a guy during love scenes...like does the guy ever get aroused, cause I know there'd be no room on the screen for my boner."

**7.** Speaking about his wife: "Sometimes you bitches are so hard to live with."

**8.** Commenting on President Bush: "Who couldn't kick Iraq's ass. I could kick their ass and I'm a big pussy. How about his son Neil Bush and his daughter Fur Bush. To hell with all of you. F**K YOU."

**9.** Speaking to Geraldo Rivera: "The closest I came to making love to a black woman was I masturbated to a picture of Aunt Jemima on a pancake box."

**10.** Speaking to a female guest: "You're very lovely, I'd love to see you nude."

*Hundreds of thousands of children are listening to this filth. Help me force him off the air.*

*Send your petition today!*

**Literature from Americans for Responsible Television.**

**Why are they raising money to force me off the air? Send the money directly to me, and if it's enough I'll leave voluntarily.**

So, my radio dreams came true. The moron who started out doing X-rated marionette shows is now the number one king of radio in New York, Los Angeles, and Philadelphia, simultaneously—a feat never before accomplished in the annals of radio history.

Of course, I owe a huge debt of gratitude to the jerks at WNBC who fired me. At K-Rock, where I landed, I got my wish to do mornings and to go head to head against Imus. It didn't take long before I destroyed Imus and General Electric was forced to sell off the whole radio station! When I was there the station was valued at fifty million. After I left, they sold it for twenty million. I cost them thirty fucking million dollars! That means I'm worth thirty million dollars! Why can't I get anyone to pay me thirty million dollars? Life is very unfair. No one cares about me.

So here I am at the top of the heap, and some heap it is—a heap of shit. When you're in an industry with Cousin Brucie, Zookeepers, and Rush Limbaugh, what would you call your heap? I know I'm too talented for radio. God is punishing me. I must have been a serial killer in a previous life.

Unfortunately, my triumph as numero uno radio personality has been ruined by the actions of a bunch of sexually repressed lunatics who, in the name of "decency," are trying to destroy the most fundamental human right Americans enjoy: the right to begin your mornings listening to the "Howard Stern Show."

Throughout my career, I have been dogged by prudes who probably want me to butt bongo them, but instead they spend their day running to the Federal

Communications Commission to monitor my every erotic move.

I think my shit little show actually turns them on and they don't know what to do about all the sexual energy they feel. So instead of masturbating and having a good time, which any normal person would do, they fucking write letters:

Dear Sirs:
Between 6:45 and 7:00 A.M. on August 12, radio station WWDC-FM in Washington, D.C., released a transmission in which the on-air personality named Howard Stern encouraged a female caller to take nude pictures of herself and send them to him. . . . As I write this mildly vitriolic missive I hear the same Stern singing doggerel about passing gas and large-breasted Cubans. . . . I can't passively accept the fact that the license to broadcast includes the right to solicit nude photos. I can't even make the distinction between that and Dan Rather asking for a blowjob on the late news.

Dear Sirs:
Fartman was bad enough, but this morning at 7:10 A.M. on my way home from an early-morning swim practice with a sixth-grader and two seventh-graders in my car, I was treated to the moans and groans of Mr. Ed (a horse) having intercourse with his owner's wife. . . . This program has no redeeming social value.

Dear Congressman:
. . . I am usually in my car with my children when the "Howard Stern Show" comes on the air. It doesn't take very long for him to start talking about sex, and as a practice, I turn him off. On one occasion, however, my children were not with me and I left the show on just to see how bad it

would get. Until that time I never realized that hard-core radio pornography actually existed. Howard Stern was arranging a blind date for a black woman named Brenda, who was in his studio, and a man who telephoned, named Lars. When I tuned in, Howard was discussing the physical attributes of Brenda. He said she had white features and one of her ancestors must have been had by a white slave master. He also said that he figured her to be a D cup. Then Howard asked Lars if he makes love to little boys. That was the finish for me. Howard Stern's sense of humor is more than warped, it is *sick*. To mention men making love to little boys, in fun, makes that type of behavior more acceptable. . . . *Something must be done!*

Dear Mr. Bon Garten
WNBC General Manager:

Mr. Howard Stern, an announcer I was not familiar with before this day, was on the air on the afternoon of March 1 between the hours of 3:00 P.M. and 5:00 P.M. He and his female sidekick carried on a conversation in which they discussed at great length the new sponge contraceptive that had just reached the New York market. Mr. Stern was quite graphic in describing the possibilities of using a Handi-wipe "stuffed up there" instead of a contraceptive, saying it was a "quicker picker upper." In addition, Mr. Stern and sidekick had a conversation with a young girl who had called into the studio concerning her boyfriend's ability to "keep it up" from ten to thirty minutes.

All this was on air, Mr. Bon Garten, while I was riding in a cab from Kennedy airport to my office in Manhattan. I was being driven by a man who was clearly not balanced. We were locked in bumper-to-

> "I don't have any doubt that the coarsening of the minds of young children by listening to this kind of stuff can have a very serious consequence on children."
> —John Silber, president, Boston University, who has recently been questioned on his ethics

bumper traffic for two hours during which time he harassed me continuously and threatened to kill me. It was a medallion cab with no partition between front and back and the locks on the doors were controlled by the driver. Believe me, it is difficult to re-create the terror I felt being locked up with a man who was big, mean, and seemingly ready to hurt someone—and I was the one who was there.

Please add to this situation, already chilling, the presence on the radio of your Mr. Stern and the conversation outlined above. My driver was physically aroused by this conversation. He was moaning and giggling and turning to look at me face-to-face every few minutes. In addition, he adjusted his rear-view mirror so that I was in full view all the time. Two hours is a long time, Mr. Bon Garten, to be in this situation and to try to stay calm.

I strongly believe you should be aware of this man being part of the audience that Mr. Stern is reaching. The contents of his conversation aided and abetted a terrifying situation controlled by an unpredictable person. I believe this occurrence shows rather tragically the heavy responsibility that the media carries and must constantly reassess. I have reported this incident to the police and to the Taxi and Limousine Commission. I am also sending a copy of this letter to the FCC.

Now you know why I'm the most dangerous man in America. Because somewhere out there some man is rubbing his penis while driving a cab and *I'M* to blame! *I'm* the troublemaker! I'm responsible for these lunatics and their wacked behavior! What kind of a shithead writes a letter like this? I don't want to live in the same country as a woman like this.

But the letters go on.

Dear Senator Bradley:
I refer specifically to a radio broadcast I heard on WNBC-

AM. The person hosting the show was named Howard Stern. He started to discuss the size of his penis and of the others who were in the restroom with him; whereupon he challenged the men in the control room at the station to drop their pants to see who had the largest penis. He even chided one man concerning the size of his penis and suggested that the reason his wife didn't wait up for him at night was because it was too small!

Mr. Bradley, I'm so sorry to have had to type the above, believe me, I never thought those statements would come out of my typewriter, but there is just no other way to report it.

*The FCC is aware of this situation, but has not lifted a finger to stop it. What is their function? Are they not there to protect us from such a cancer as this man?*

The answer to that question, at least until 1987, was no.

And then the shit hit the fan. And old Howie started racking up fines the way Charles Barkley does points. It used to be that as long as I didn't say the famous "seven dirty words," I was cool. Here they are: SHIT, PISS, CUNT, FUCK, COCKSUCKER, MOTHER-FUCKER, and TITS. Anybody pass out? Anybody never hear these before?

I heard them all by the fifth grade. Then the rules changed. The new rule is: Don't say anything that is "patently indecent" or offensive to your community. What does that mean? No one knows what it means. But I do know that I live and work in a community where priests rape young boys, where pit bulls chew through kids' heads, where you get shot in your car, where an angry black mob stabbed a Hasidic Jew and the mayor turned his back, where crack runs free like the River Ganges, and where movie directors fuck their wives' daughters. *Now you tell me what I should talk about on the radio!!* Somehow saying the word *testicles* pales in comparison.

But the FCC bureaucrats got on me anyway. They soon realized that they were getting a lot of attention from the press, something they loved. They started paying attention to this irritating man, a minister from Tupelo, Mississippi, named Donald E. Wildmon, who claimed I was singlehandedly leading America straight to hell because I was doing satire of a sexual nature for four hours a morning on a radio program that this celebrity-seeking nothing couldn't even hear down in Mississippi. What was going through his mind? Was he hearing the cash registers ringing be-cause of all those rubes who empty their savings accounts to support his ridiculous morality-in-America campaign?

This Wildmon character is the same guy who led a protest against Mighty Mouse cartoons because he claimed they promoted cocaine use when Mighty Mouse would sniff some flowers to rejuvenate his superhero powers. This is the same Wildmon who picketed the TV show "Taxi" because he claimed it was "overtly sexual." And it probably *was* . . . to his puny little mind. This is the same mindset that led Jimmy Swaggart to campaign against *Penthouse* being carried by 7–Eleven stores because he *personally* knew that when you see pictures of *nekkid wimmen* you just want to go out and pick up *a ugly hooker widda hairy butt* and take her to a hotel room and jerk off while she fingers herself. Just because Jimmy Swaggart and other idiots like him can't control their carnal impulses, they want to regulate what the rest of us can do.

So this bald minister from Mississippi decided to orchestrate a national letter-writing campaign to the FCC to report me. He sent out a flyer to his faithful flock urging them to report my every romantic move to the FCC.

Meanwhile, after his whole heavily promoted campaign, the FCC got just three tapes complaining about me—one from a woman in Philadelphia and the other two from Wildmon himself! Some campaign.

Because of these three complaints, in April of 1987 the FCC took a closer look at me and decided that I was about the worst thing they'd ever heard on radio, that I, Howard Stern, had singlehandedly ruined the planet and everything on it. Where there were feces, I wallowed in them. Where there were breasts, I dared to play with them. If there was a problem with lesbians, I dared to lick it. You get the idea. They said I was offensive. They gave me a *warning*.

This warning encouraged every kook in the universe to come out of the woodwork and report me. Reporting Howard Stern to the FCC became the second most popular sport in America, next to reporting me to my sponsors.

If you wanted fame and power, if you wanted your name in the paper, if you wanted to appear on "Nightline," you could report me to the FCC.

## ENTER MISS ANNE M. STOMMEL, SPINSTER.

It was Wednesday, December 14, 1988. We were planning our guest list for our gala Christmas party, which included the usual cast of characters: lesbians, strippers, mental patients, low-lifes, a guy who was going to play the piano with his penis, everyone Jesus loves. After I left work that day, Anne Stommel called the radio station to complain.

I think she felt we were anti-American, anti-Christian, anti-God, and pro-Communist because she didn't like my Christmas party guest list. I couldn't wait to call her when I came in the next morning.

"Anne, you're on the air. Welcome to our radio show. Please don't say anything obscene or dirty," I cautioned.

"Who are you going to invite to the Christmas party? I wonder if you invite these kind of people to a Hanukkah party . . . it must be rollicking," she said.

I believe that in her mind we were blaspheming her high holy day. If I had invited strippers up for Hanukkah, I had the feeling she wouldn't have minded.

"What is it, honey?" I asked. "You're a Christian and you think we're being blasphemous to Christmas? What's all this Christmas nonsense with you?" I said. "Wake up and smell the roses, honey! What are you hung up on? What are you afraid of? Who's it gonna hurt? Why don't you go out and help the homeless if you're so Christian?"

"Now, wait a minute." She got feisty. "165 B.C.E. parenthesis, before the common era, and I used to know that that was before the Christian era . . ." I was having a difficult time understanding her.

"You're so silly, you're so hung up," I laughed.

"You may be the silly guy. Our society has B.C. and A.D. Even Adam Clayton Powell—now, you like Negroes——Adam Clayton Powell said . . ."

"NEGROES?" I screamed.

"Adam Clayton Powell said the birth of Christ was like a miracle . . ."

"Don't you know it's blacks, not Negroes?" I said. It sounded to me as if this woman was a little out of touch. She told me she was sixty-five, she'd never been married, she'd lived her whole life in Monmouth County, New Jersey, and she'd gone to Vassar.

"Oh, now," she continued, "one of your guys said all you have to do if you don't like Howard Stern is to use two fingers. Turn it off. I don't want to turn you off. I want to know what you're doing," she said.

"Oh, so you're going to monitor me," I said.

"I want to know what you're up to," she said. "Talk about freedom of speech, my idea presently is just to copy down the people you're inviting to the Christmas party and I'm going to listen this morning to find out who else you're going to invite and I'm going to write it up because I'm a professional technical writer in communications and electronics."

"You're dangerous is what you are," I said. "I think you've been suppressed your whole life and you love this kind of radio and that's why you can't stop listening. You love it, you love the freedom you're hearing. You wish you were at the Christmas party. You wish *you* were naked serving those drinks . . ."

"Oh, go on," she snorted.

"Yes, you do." I was beside myself. "You only wish you were a young voluptuous woman and I was spanking you. That's what you secretly wish for."

Anne M. Stommel, spinster, and I were not getting along. I tried to seduce her with my wit and charm but all she wanted to do was ruin me.

The truth is, I love characters like Anne M. Stommel and I never would have believed that anyone would take her seriously *until* the five stooges at the FCC started listening to her. She was their kind of gal.

"Well, I may write to someone that you like so much, Senator Bill Bradley, who happens to represent me," she said.

"No! You're not going to write to SENATOR BILL BRADLEY because I'm shaking in my pants," I said in mock fright. "Look, Bradley's a senator of the United States because he was a basketball player. People are enamored with basketball players. He's got as much brains as you do."

"Oh, fine, that's lovely and that's another thing I'll include to Senator Bradley in my letter to him . . ." Anne said.

"Ask him about his hook shot," I suggested.

Anne and I went on like this all morning. This mental masturbation went on for hours. After she hung up, I couldn't get her out of my mind. Anne had drawn me in like a black widow spider. I had to have more of her. I'm a married man, but I needed Anne. She was the great-great-grandmother I never had. Most radio hosts would never have called her back. But I called her again later that morning and the conversation was still the same. All she was interested in was recording my every word and listening over and over and over again. My whole adolescent life I hoped and prayed that women would worship my every word. Now I had what I'd always wished for. And it was pissing me off.

"I want to have tapes, to have it recorded and documented," she said.

"Are you fixing up a time capsule?" Robin asked.

"You can bury it in your backyard, when they bury you," I said.

Our Christmas party passed and we fell back into our usual routine. Little did I know that behind the scenes, people were actively plotting against me.

Anne's letter to Senator Bradley got routed to the FCC, which requested tapes of any shows that offended Miss Stommel. Of course, Anne was more than happy to send them a tape of our Christmas show in its entirety.

The FCC chairman, Alfred Sikes, a Republican do-gooder, suddenly decided that the FCC should go after disc jockeys. Sikes took it upon himself to clean up the "indecency" from the radio airwaves. They attempted to do that by staging a vendetta against one man—me.

Later that year, the FCC announced their decision. I was guilty of "indecent" broadcasts and they were

# FCC fines mount for Stern

Howard Stern Employer Faces $600,000 Fine

The F.C.C. Is Fining Howard Stern's Employer $600,000 **Don't muzzle Howard Stern**

FCC: Stern show indecent

# FCC'S STERN WARNING

Stern: Equal opportunity offender

*Howard Stern Rapped
As Indecent by FCC*

**Nothing like opening the morning paper and reading what a scumbag I am.**

going to fine my bosses $6,000, $2,000 for each city we transmitted that Christmas show to. I made one decision immediately. I would *never* mention this incident on my résumé. For the rest of my life I was going to have to lie on my résumé. This is not the kind of thing an employer likes to read. I wondered if my guidance counselor was right. Maybe I should have been a speech therapist. Less pressure. It's not easy being me. The government was getting very aggressive. And I knew that inside I didn't have the constitution to stand up to these idiots. I'm very delicate. I work out in a gym for three days and I'm ready for the hospital.

It was with a heavy heart that I started my show on Election Day 1990.

"Where do I begin? Yesterday I learned I'm being targeted by the federal government again. I'm about to be fined by the FCC. But I'm not gonna lie down like the rest of these sheep in the broadcast industry. The FCC—I don't know who these guys are, I don't know who elected them, I don't know what their particular political affiliations are, I don't know what their morality is, I don't know if they're having sex in the back of a bus with a young boy, I don't know anything about these people. I just wanna preface all of my remarks by saying that. But I will be going to the Supreme Court to fight this."

"You're gonna start at the Supreme Court?" Robin asked.

"Yes, I want to go right to the Supreme Court. There's not a person in America who would find me

My Freedom Rally at Dag Hammarskjöld Plaza at the United Nations. Thousands united for free speech.

guilty of obscenity based on what they're about to charge me with. You ready for the horrible things that I said? *'Here's a guy who plays the piano with his penis.'* Have we finally arrived at the day in this country that you cannot use the word *penis*? I was just watching a tape produced by Henry Winkler for kids and it says we shouldn't call our private parts anything other than what their name is. Why do we have such hangups about sex?

"I swear to God, I was talking to my seven-year-old about sex the other night, and she was asking about babies. My wife has basically told her that married people have a special way of hugging each other—you do a broadstroke deal. And she asked about the penis and the vagina. She's seven years old! She does more penis jokes in a day than anybody I know! These uptight, jackass FCC commissioners, who sit there every day, evidently have a hang-up about their penises and vaginas.

"And where's the ACLU during all this crap? They're defending the KKK. They're right on top of things. You think another deejay would come to my defense. Forget about it. I'm being set up because I'm number one, I'm in New York, I'm high profile, I go on the Letterman show, I have a TV show. It's perfect to get me. Move over, Lenny Bruce; I'll crawl into that box with you. It's unbelievable. Listen to what I'm being fined for: *'There's a big black lesbian out of her mind with lust.'* I don't know where I said that, but I'm sure I must have. And I'll tell you something: I'LL SAY IT NINE HUNDRED TIMES, until I'M BLUE IN THE FACE!! BIG BLACK LESBIAN WITH LUST!!

"I guess all five commissioners listened to that tape and went out and started raping people when they heard it. They're fining me for that. But I'm sure Neil Bush is enjoying no fines from the government. I'll tell you what, I'll pay the two grand when Neil Bush is in jail. That's when I know they'll be some justice. But President Bush sits idly by—him and Bubblehead, his wife—they're lying back enjoying Air Force One.

GET HIM OUTTA OFFICE! YA CREEP! He should walk in tomorrow to the FCC and say, 'Excuse me, what are you guys doing? We have tremendous problems in this country. C'mere, I got to smack you in the head.' Why doesn't he ask his son what happened? And Jeb. What kinda name is that? What does he live in, a log cabin? Jeb Bush. But Neil Bush will never have a problem.

" '*He will play the piano with his penis*' is indecent. Can you imagine this? And '*a big black lesbian filled with lust.*' Excuse me, do I hear the word *lust*? What are they objecting to: the word *lust*? Or is it the idea of a big black lesbian? If I said 'a man filled with lust,' would that be obscene? They better think this through, because I will not pay this fine. You're telling me that the word *lust* is no longer acceptable on radio? If I talk about sexuality comically that's no good, but if Donahue puts a doctor on the stage and talks about sexuality in a clinical way—even though we're both after the same thing, ratings—Donahue's okay, but I'm indecent. You're going to have a hard time arguing that in front of the U.S. Supreme Court. Even Justice Souter, that guy who's been locking himself up in a log cabin, could figure that out. Should I wear a white coat and a stethoscope to work every day, then I could say '*big black lesbian filled with lust*'? Who are they kidding here?

"I recall tuning in 'Saturday Night Live' a couple of months ago and seeing a bit where every other word was *penis*. I don't see them getting fined. No, they're going to pick on me because they're going to use this lame-ass excuse that I'm on from six to ten in the morning, where children can hear me. Excuse me, it's in the morning that parents *are* around their children, and actually have control over what they're listening to. This is the only time in the day when parents are around their kids and know what they're doing!

"If I was the president's son, this wouldn't happen. If I was Howard Bush, no government would be coming after me."

I put on my best George Bush voice.

" 'Hello? Alfred Sikes? That's my boy on the air in New York. There's nothing wrong with him, he's a good boy. Good, I'm glad we see things eye to eye on this . . .' These stupid rich dicks don't have any clue as to what real life is about. Get fired up today. VOTE OUT ALL THE INCUMBENTS! VOTE 'EM OUT! HAUL 'EM OUT! WAY OUT! OUT!

"I hope Al Sikes has some money. I'm taking him to court personally. For damages. I'm working my ass off and these bureaucrats sit around, having long lunches. I WANT TO KNOW HIS SCHEDULE! I wanna know the hours he puts in. Skunk. Why can't he realize this is just bogus. I gotta take this guy to court and clean him out. He can support me financially for the rest of my life."

Now, this tirade would have made most people back

down. But not the FCC. What did they care? They had nothing else to do. This was only the beginning.

Of course, we appealed the FCC's initial citation for that Christmas show. And on October 16, 1992, the FCC upheld the $6,000 in indecency fines. It was interesting that on the same day, former FCC commissioner Steven A. Sharp was sentenced to ten years in prison for sexually

> "I've listened to Howard Stern for years and I will continue to listen to Howard Stern for years."
>
> —Roger Clinton

assaulting three boys, one of whom had become his legal ward a few years earlier. This guy was sodomizing three boys, ages twelve, thirteen, and fourteen. I was amazed that he didn't blame it on me. Maybe he was just trying to play the piano with their penises and got carried away. Meanwhile, as part of his sentence, the judge forbade him from seeing his own eight-year-old son until the kid reaches eighteen. These are the guys who sit in judgment over me.

After Anne Stommel there was a whole group of listeners, excuse me, audio stalkers, who became obsessed with me and my show and made careers out of reporting me.

Three citations later, my radio stations have been collectively fined over $900,000. And my guess is that not a penny will ever be paid after this goes before the U.S. Supreme Court. And me? I'll just wait it out the way I waited out Pig Virus, NBC, my Washington, D.C., general manager, the Israeli back at my first radio station, and every other disbeliever on this planet.

I knew that all I had to do was to keep my big fat mouth shut, but of course, that's impossible. So they decided to make an example out of me. I got slipped some information that FCC chairman Al Sikes had said off the record, "Look, we have to stop the spread of Stern."

Why was I being singled out by this guy Sikes? Everyone in the media from Donahue to Dr. Ruth to two-bit Stern imitators was doing stuff just as, if not more, risqué than what I was doing. But they were only going after me. Then, a few days later, we heard that Al Sikes was in the hospital being operated on for prostate cancer. I felt that, in His own mysterious way, God was taking care of my enemies.

On the air that morning, a caller started asking me about my travails with the FCC and inspired one of my more celebrated lunatic moments:

"Maybe the doctor will find more cancer in Sikes. That's the only thing I can pray for. Cancer's a good thing when it hits the people you hate. This guy's targeting me with a vengeance and a vendetta. What did I do to him and his family? What did I do to him? I'm trying to make a living.

"The only way I have a chance of ridding this guy out of my life is if people elect Bill Clinton, and we get rid of the religious yahoos. Do you understand the hypocrisy of this situation? I only pray for cancer for all of the FCC."

I lowered my voice to a whisper. "I pray to you now, Jesus Christ. Oh, Jesus, I pray to you that the FCC gets cancer. I pray that Al Sikes' prostate cancer spreads into his lungs and his kidneys. I pray to you, Jesus, answer my prayers. Make their medical problems so bad that they cannot pay attention to me."

"Well, I just pray that Bush gets out of office," my caller said.

"I'm in the middle of prayer, sir," I reprimanded him.

"I thought you were finished. I apologize," he said.

"Oh, Jesus," I continued, "Jesus, please bring the blessed cancer—the freeing cancer. You brought cancer to so many of my enemies, do it one last time for me and I will no longer ask for cancer. Thank you. Oh, I feel that warm glow, like I'm gonna get my wish. See, I don't pray to Jesus for stupid stuff, like ratings. I pray for the important stuff, like eliminating my enemies through cancer."

I went back to my prayer. "Our Lord in Heaven, I pray that terminal disease will get them—a nice, terminal, contagious disease, and it will spread to the other FCC members. I know you gave him prostate cancer but that's curable. Give incurable cancer to all of the FCC. All of their secretaries, everybody in the government—cancer. I pray for cancer. Please, please, Jesus. Jesus, I see you on the cross, I'm envisioning you. You have a beautiful body, may I say that? A beautiful swimmer's body."

"You think He responds to flattery?" Robin asked.

"Everybody does, Robin," I said, then went back into prayer. "Drop a cancer net all over them, a net of cancer, cancer so strong. I've prayed to you a couple of times and you've always answered my prayers—even prayers that seemed unreasonable. Remember when I prayed for the end of communism in Russia, and you ended it? And I prayed that the Berlin Wall would come down, and it did. Now I pray for cancer for the FCC, my one last prayer, then I will forever be your servant.

"Please, Jesus, don't make me turn to Satan. Help me with this. I see you on the cross, I see you with nails in your hands and feet, and I know you can answer my prayer. Notice I'm not praying to Buddha, or any of the other jerks that people pray to—like Mohammed, or someone stupid like that. I've always stuck with you; you stick with me. We're together in this, Jesus H. Christ. Anything you want to add, Robin?"

"No, I think you covered it all," she said.

"That was a lot of groveling. That's not easy for me to do," I said. Just then, Gary came into the studio. It

Controversy followed me on television. The above scene never aired because my legs were spread so wide . . . and I was playing the Virgin Mary. They ran close-ups of my face instead. Cheech and Chong appeared as the Wise Men with bongs, and I as the Virgin Mother gave birth to . . . Baby Dan Forman, my producer, as the Holy Child (left).

**Another scene deemed too offensive was Handicapped Beat the Clock, where a paraplegic took on a one-legged man in an obstacle course.**

seemed that there were a couple of callers who were very angry about my cancer prayer.

My father called me that night. "Howard, you've gone too far."

My radio bosses were very upset over my comments. But I swear to you, I didn't mean anything by it. Many times in my life I've wished other people dead. This was just a more creative way to say it.

Besides, why wasn't I allowed to have a tantrum? Why couldn't I act like a two-year-old? You have to admire that I'm not a phony.

A lot of angry callers made their way onto the air:

"So you want people to suffer through cancer?"

"Yes," I said.

"Why don't you just vote 'em out of office?" the caller suggested.

"I can't vote the members of the FCC out of office," I explained.

"So then work through the laws."

"I can't pray to Jesus? You have never said, 'I hope someone dies'?" I asked him. "Do you think the guy's really gonna get cancer by me praying for it? Why don't you go cross the path of a black cat? See what happens. Walk under a ladder. Like Jesus is listening to my stupid prayer. *'Oh, I got to work on that right now. I'll forget about Somalia right now and I'll go over and take care of Howard's problem.'* Jesus is busy."

"You don't even have his number, do you?" Robin asked.

"Actually, I do, that's the funny thing. It's 1–500–52–STERN. It's the same number to order my tape, *Butt Bongo Fiesta*, as a matter of fact. But forget it. Who cares? It's so silly. It's like saying Casper the Ghost is real."

"I always love it when people get upset when you make those pleas," Robin said.

"I'm talking to Jesus privately and everyone's gotta comment on it. Do I comment on what they pray to Jesus for?" I asked. "Did anybody ever pray for a house to live in? Well, that's what I'm doing. I'm praying to Jesus that he gives cancer to the guy who's trying to end my career, so I can keep my house. That's all."

And you guys must think I'm pretty powerful, that

Jesus is gonna answer my wish. I don't think he's gonna pay attention, personally. Maybe I should read my Christmas list while I'm at it, in case Santa's listening, too.

Well, Jesus never listened to me.

Sikes recovered, retired, and is still running around blabbing about me. It's the only way anyone will interview him.

Now there's another FCC commissioner and he seems to have a real appreciation for my art:

Speaking to the Michigan Association of Broadcasters, FCC commissioner James Quello said, "I wouldn't be a bit surprised if someday a lightning bolt comes out of the sky and hits him right in the crotch." How dignified, how eloquent. How I would love it if anything hit my crotch at this point.

But this guy Quello is a bit confused. I believe he secretly loves me, too. He confessed to Jill Brooke from the *New York Post:* "I'm almost ashamed to say it, I find him tremendously funny. He's a very entertaining smart-ass." But that's just it. None of this makes any sense. He says he's ashamed to admit that he enjoys me. Why is there so much shame in this country? Why are we so afraid to say what we like and to talk about sex? What happens to a man when he hears the words *breasts* and *vagina?* Will it turn him into an ax murderer?

There are thousands of broadcasters talking about sex *every day.* In fact, there are thousands of people *having* sex, but out of all those people, when I talk about sex, people get nuts. No one in the history of broadcasting has ever been threatened with fines close

to a million dollars because he found Aunt Jemima sexy. No one, until me, that is.

But I do have my supporters, I must say. And I applaud their bravery. Because you've got to be brave to stick up for me. Ed Koch, the best mayor New York has ever had, a workaholic who tirelessly gave to this city, had this to say about me:

> For the FCC to try to limit and turn you off is an outrage. It is more than an abuse of power. It is hypocrisy at its worst.

One of my biggest supporters through all my tribulations with the FCC was our great U.S. senator from New York, Alfonse M. D'Amato:

> Dear Chairman Sikes:
> I am deeply concerned by the Commission's contemplated actions against radio personality Howard Stern.
> I therefore urge the Commission to reject these narrow-minded calls for punitive actions against Mr. Stern, to stand

up for common sense, and to preserve our constitutionally guaranteed freedoms.

> Sincerely,
> Alfonse M. D'Amato
> United States Senator

But very few people have come foward to defend me. The reason they don't is because most people don't think that this censorship thing is for real. The FCC is trying to scare radio stations away from working with me. They've put a chill in the air by making an example out of me. I had hoped Bill Clinton would see the lunacy in all this, but to date I've seen no letup in this ridiculous crusade against freedom of speech.

All the religious nuts and zealots will continue to talk about the corruption of our children and will continue to receive huge donations to help get me off the air—all the while knowing that this is a bullshit issue.

> "As a person, as a style, he's not the kind of thing I normally listen to. But the question of his right to speak and his right to say the things he's saying, I think I would have to defend that even if I didn't like what he was saying."
> —Mario Cuomo
> Governor,
> New York State

But they won't stop me. 'Cause I've been through it all. Major mental illness, limited IQ, a small penis, and the jungles of Vietnam.

It's funny, but sometimes I look back on my life and I remember the times I was a little kid, thrilled to have a holiday and to have a chance to drive to work with my dad. I remember him tuning the radio, going from station to station, trying to find a voice that could make that horrid commute a little more tolerable. And I remember how much I wished that someday one of those voices would be mine.

I've become one of those voices now, despite the fact that everyone said I'd never make it, that I needed something to fall back on, and that I should "shut up and sit down, you moron," as my father mercilessly said to me for most of my life.

All my life the thing that drove me the most was probably trying to find a way to please my father. He was very tough on me, and I really wanted him to think I was great.

A couple of years ago my father said, "Howard, I still go from station to station when I'm driving in the car and since you've been on the air, I've noticed a real change in the parameters of all those other guys. You've really opened some doors. Suddenly, you're hearing things you never heard, words that people never used. And it's good radio." Then out of the blue, he shockingly said, "Howard, you're a genius." He was right. Finally, he knew the truth. It took me thirty-some-odd years of saying stupid things on the radio to get my father to

"Howard Stern may play 'butt bongo' on the radio, but Washington regulators are ready to spank the syndicated radio personality for real. If they do, the Federal Communications Commission will only succeed in making Stern the nation's latest First Amendment poster boy. They should leave him alone."

—Emil Guillermo,
*USA Today,*
December 10, 1992

give me one big compliment. And I mean a BIG compliment. My father doesn't throw that word around easily.

I savored the moment.

"Hey, Dad. Let me clarify that. Next to the guy who invented the polio vaccine, how much of a genius am I?"

"Shut up and sit down, you moron," he said.

# AFTERWORD
# A PSYCHOLOGICAL PROFILE

Based on Howard Stern's *PRIVATE PARTS*

by Sheenah Hankin and Richard Wessler, Ph.D.
Cognitive Psychotherapy Associates
New York, New York

**Howard Stern's autobiographical book reveals
a clear clinical profile of his personality.**

---

**HE DESCRIBES HIMSELF AS AN *OBSESSIVE-
COMPULSIVE*, WHICH IS CONSISTENT WITH THE
FOLLOWING TRAITS:**

---

• He insists that others submit to his ways, using any and all tactics of verbal persuasion—from charm and ingratiation, to inducing sympathy, to persistent begging and complaining of unfair treatment. When these methods fail, he resorts to bullying tactics, including public humiliation and denigration.

• He demonstrates excessive devotion to work and productivity, to the point of excluding his family and forgoing leisure activities.

• His displays of affection are highly restricted. He claims to love his wife but cites no examples of open affection toward her. His standard description of their sex life consists of either complaints about its infrequency and her lack of interest or mentions of quick encounters in which foreplay that arouses her is deemed burdensome. He seems content simply to satisfy her with a vibrator, which saves him the time, energy, and effort of lovemaking.

• He constantly claims to be scrupulously conscientious about ethical values governing this subject, but he expresses these by observing the letter of the law rather than its spirit. He voyeuristically examines women as they strip naked for him, and comments on the size of their breasts and presence or absence of pubic hair. He'll use any number of questionable ruses as an excuse to proceed further and fondle the women. Hence, he adheres to standards of marital fidelity in a narrow technical sense, and therefore feels both above criticism and justified in criticizing less faithful persons, whom he demeans by way of congratulating himself and assuaging his guilt. At the same time he gratifies his own self-centered sexual urges. It is acceptable to be rubbed all over by sexy women and to caress naked bodies for his own satisfaction. This, he claims, is *not infidelity* simply because he says it isn't. After all, he doesn't actually penetrate the women.

### STERN IS ALSO PRONE TO STRONG *NARCISSISTIC* TENDENCIES:

• He views as unreasonable anyone who disagrees with his strongly self-defined perspectives on life, and these people become the targets of his scorn, including listeners who call in to his show or his wife.

• He is interpersonally exploitive, especially with women, taking advantage of them to achieve his own ends. He uses the power of his fame as a means to fulfill his predominantly adolescent, self-centered sexual fantasies, and feels no guilt about this.

• He requires constant attention and admiration. His radio team, his basic support system, provides these for him.

• He lacks a sense of empathy. Either he does not know how others feel, or if he does, he rarely demonstrates concern for their feelings.

• Sexually, he is self-sufficient; he seems to enjoy masturbation rather than intercourse, which requires attention to the needs of a partner. His preoccupation with lesbians allows him to receive a great deal of sexual stimulation without having any obligation to return sexual favors. This is an avenue that allows him to focus solely on his own gratification. He can speak about how effectively he can satisfy a woman and grandiosely praise his sexual skills without ever having to demonstrate them on anyone except himself.

---

### ANOTHER SET OF PROMINENT TRAITS MAY BE LABELED *HISTRIONIC*:

---

• He is self-centered and uncomfortable in situations in which he is not the center of attention.

• He is seductive in his behavior, interjecting sexual questions and references into nearly every conversation.

• He is overly concerned about physical appearance, and although he is self-deprecating about his large nose and small penis, he is vain about his hair and other matters of grooming. He frequently comments on the appearance of others, particularly women.

---

### *PASSIVE-AGGRESSIVE* TENDENCIES MAKE UP YET ANOTHER PART OF STERN'S PROFILE:

---

• He is argumentative and uncooperative when asked to do what he doesn't want to do.

• He protests that others make unreasonable demands on him.

• He unreasonably criticizes people in positions of authority, especially radio executives, members of the FCC, and others who attempt to set limits on him and regulate his behavior. It was this behavior pattern that got him fired from his "dream job" at WNBC. He seems genuinely baffled by this firing.

Popularity as a radio personality has led him to have feelings of invincibility. He feels that he can do no wrong, and no one can stop him from doing whatever he wishes. Too much success can prompt self-defeating tendencies, which is exactly what happened to Stern. He fell victim to a false sense of psychological security and in turn was overcome by a self-defeating maneuver motivated by factors he was not and is not aware of.

It isn't difficult to understand how he evolved into the person he is. His mother has always been obsessively clean, overly fastidious, and extremely eager to please. Howard became a health fanatic and germ phobic who frequently refers to *smells*, drinks only from paper cups, and engages in the kinds of sexual play with women (aside from his wife, whom he views as "safe") that preclude any risk of dirt and infections that could result from actual vaginal penetration.

His father has always engaged in verbal put-downs. He calls Howard a moron, and now Howard refers to others in the same manner. He learned from his father the sense of power that comes from demeaning and humiliating people. He enjoys having power over people, and is highly amused by the suffering of others, including the diseased and dying, and cruelly jokes about their misfortunes. His craving for power can also be seen through his interest in bondage and mild forms of torture.

His mother's obsessive-compulsive cleanliness and father's anger problem are patterns that promote feelings of shame and humiliation in children. Such feelings often trigger rage, one of his most noticeable feelings. He expresses rage in verbal as well as physical attempts to humiliate others. These sadistic tendencies are based on his own sense of shame and lack of self-respect. To compensate for his feelings of inadequacy and powerlessness, he makes himself seem powerful so that he can shame and mock others.

The element of control is at the core of his behavioral pattern. His desire and attempts to control others are overwhelming. What is more subtle is the control he exercises over his own eating habits.

### THERE IS AMPLE EVIDENCE THAT HE HAS AN EATING DISORDER:

• He refers constantly to his own weight, and he denigrates overweight people such as Roseanne Barr and Rush Limbaugh.

• He restricts what he eats to a few low-fat, low-calorie foods.

• He prefers to eat at home, where he can maintain better control over his food intake.

• He "balloons up" under pressure, which is character-istic of a binge eater.

• He makes frequent references to vomit (which may in-dicate a purge problem) and to bowel functions (another one of his mother's influences).

Finally, there are indications that he is socially anxious like his mother and prefers to avoid public appearances and socialization with persons who are not part of his inner circle. He admits that he hates to go out, which indicates agoraphobia. He also needs his routine.

Because Stern learned to get along in a shaming family environment by complying on the one hand and causing trouble on the other, he successfully re-creates this pattern on this show. He causes trouble on the air, where no one can talk back to him and he can control the microphone and telephone, but underneath he still fears the shame and humiliation of his childhood.

His safety and security are derived from staying away from everyone except the few people he knows well and trusts, such as his agent of many years and his immediate family.

## SUMMARY AND CONCLUSIONS

Does Howard Stern need therapy? Yes. He is anxious, but not depressed. Yet there is a strong possibility that his self-defeating and passive-aggressive tendencies will lead to his losing a "dream job" once more. For example, he could continue to provoke the FCC into censuring him just as he provoked his father into humiliating him. A loss of job would lead to a major loss of face and to a huge in-crease in his habit of feeling a lot of self-pity and shame. To overcome an intense sense of deprivation he could, as before, indulge himself by binge-eating and could develop a Marlon Brando type of physique. Increased anger and neediness could put pressure on his already very limited social relationships.

What kind of therapy? Certainly not psychoanalysis, during which he could lie on a couch for years, as Woody Allen has done, and be the sole center of attention. This would only increase his narcissistic, self-centered patterns. Instead, he needs an interactive relationship with a strong-minded specialist in personality disorders who could confront him easily and enable him to face criticism rather than avoid it. He could also learn to consider others' feelings and responses to his sometimes antisocial actions that involve patterns of ongoing conflict. He might want to avoid therapy, as people with self-defeating tendencies often do. He might incorrectly think that therapy will change the dramatic features of his personality that have contributed to his professional success, for his whole career is built on speaking the unspeakable and showing the unshowable. But therapy does not change the entire person, only the underlying destructive characteristics. If some change does not occur, he could become depressed and very isolated. Instead of "What do you think of Howard Stern?," people may ask, "Whatever happened to Howard Stern?" Ironically, he might join the list of formerly famous people whose weight gains and losses are reported in supermarket tabloids.

# Exclusive Special Bonus Chapter

*Or,
How I'll get you to buy the
paperback after you already
bought the hardcover*

I decided to add a couple of extra pages to the paperback because my editor convinced me that the people who bought the hardcover will rush out and buy this new edition if there are a few more pages. This sounds like a lot of bullshit to me, but I am always willing to go along with a good marketing scheme if it means a few extra bucks in my pocket. People want to know if I feel any great sense of accomplishment from having had a number-one bestseller, and the answer is, "Of course, you asshole!" I never could have imagined that my words would be such an inspiration to all of mankind. To be quite honest, I had the worst case of the shits during the writing of this record-breaking tome worrying about whether anyone would buy it or read it. . . . Wow! . . . A number-one bestseller! Well, fuck you. Fuck everyone. I did it. . . . No one thought this book would be big. To be quite honest, I never would have bet a dime on its chances. If I knew how successful it would be, I would have written it years ago and I would have run out and bought stock in Simon & Schuster.

My critics don't understand why, despite all their predictions of me being a flash in the pan, I continue to dominate radio, television, pay-per-view, and now the literary world. Ten years ago I began hearing that my fifteen minutes of fame were up. When I held a press conference to announce my book deal, there were those who said I would never complete the manuscript. Others merely smirked and said even if I completed it, no one would buy it. There is a built-in snobbery in the world of publishing that assumes that the average *shmendrick* in the street doesn't go near a bookstore and won't buy a book.

This book has once again taught all those asshole critics a lesson. What that lesson is, I don't know, but you must admit that for a guy who has read only three books, and has the reading level of a nine-year-old Appalachian, writing a masterpiece is a big deal. Do you know how many people were angry that this book rocketed to number one? First of all, English majors with Ph.D.'s in literature who have been submitting their Great American Novel to Simon & Schuster and getting rejection slips from the receptionist on a bian-nual basis; they got really pissed. Now they all teach high-school English somewhere and dream of being Howard Stern, the author.

Second, those newspaper reporters who thought I was too stupid to compete in their exclusive World of the Written Word were livid. Newspaper guys have been knocking me for years, and this has to be a major kick in the ass when you consider that most of them can't even get it together to *complete* their manuscript that would get rejected anyway by Simon & Schus-ter's receptionists. Wanna-bes. Fuck 'em. They will never know the joy of having their completed works bound between hard covers and worshipped by mil-lions. Oh, how they must have suffered when my genius sold quicker than *For Whom the Bell Tolls* and *A Farewell to Arms*. Those crap books. I laugh at that bastard Hemingway. Journalists—cocksucking hose monsters. They all wanted to see me fall flat on my ass but instead begrudgingly ended up writing great reviews of *Private Parts*.

Not only did I anger those simple-minded dopes, but I shocked a few geniuses as well. Even the preten-tious literary elite at the publishing company were awestruck by the success of the book. They were caught completely off guard by the rapid sales as we went into our nine-hundredth printing the first week of release. I must admit that there were many folks at my beloved publishing firm who figured that signing Howard Stern was a dog of an idea, but by now every-one has recognized me for the true literary hero that I am. In fact, they're pretty damned pleased with my success at Simon & Schuster because now they have a new star on their roster and they don't have to kowtow to that bloated pumpkin head Rush Limbaugh and that yakking hyena Kathie Lee Gifford.

But why the hell do I still sound so bitter when I'm supposed to be so happy? How should I know? I'm just a stupid disc jockey. Look, never mind all the gloating, let me tell you what's going on with this bonus chapter. I want to somehow give you an overview of everything that went on after the book was released. It shot to the top of the charts, then got banned by several book chains for no apparent reason other than that the book was written by me. Then I went to sign a few books and a near riot broke out. Did my life change? No, not really. I figure a guy who writes a magnum opus deserves a sexual encounter with a *Penthouse* pet, but it hasn't happened. My wife isn't really all that impressed and hasn't increased her sexual output. My kids want to read the book but I'm really not ready to have them learn about my daily masturbation. So the book doesn't sit proudly on my coffee table or anything. My parents were proud but my mother still constantly reminds me not to act like a big shot and to be a regular person. I'm in Hell! Save me!

Then Hollywood came knocking on my door and a major motion picture based on *Private Parts* is being prepared for a (hopefully) quick release. A lot of studios were hot to trot for a shot at producing this film, and I went with Rysher Films, which I pray knows what the fuck it's doing. But, Howard goes to Hollywood is a whole other story. I'll save that for another time. . . .

# MY PRIVATE PARTS ARE VERY HOT

**Simon & Schuster was caught off guard as stores quickly sold out of my important testament.**

## Stern's Private Parts Very Hot

BY TIMOTHY D. SMITH

Dave Markowitz, a manager at Borders Book Shop in Beachwood said the response to the book has been nothing short of tremendous. "We've already sold 250 copies of *Private Parts*, and every other call seems to be someone putting their name on our waiting list."

Markowitz said that in his five years of working at bookstores, only one other author had gotten as much attention as Stern.

"The only thing that even comes close is Salman Rushdie's *The Satanic Verses*," said Markowitz, "and when that came out, no one knew what they were buying."

• • •

## Howard Stern's Autobiography Is Instant Bestseller

BY MEG COX
*Staff Reporter of* THE WALL STREET JOURNAL

NEW YORK—Radio "shock jock" Howard Stern is shocking booksellers all over the country. They can't believe how fast his autobiography is selling.

Mr. Stern, whose profanity gets him in hot water with the Federal Communications Commission, writes as crudely as he talks in his book, "Private Parts." Though the book hit bookstores only a week ago, it already has jumped to the top of most bestseller lists. In many cities, bookstores sold out immediately, and the publisher had to order 500,000 more copies from printers. Some 850,000 copies will be in print by next week.

• • •

"This is the fastest-selling book and the biggest event we've ever had," crowed Robert Wietrak, director of merchandising for Barnes & Noble Inc.

The book appears to be selling fastest in the 14 markets where Mr. Stern's show airs, including New York, Los Angeles, Philadelphia and Cleveland. Joan Hulbert, owner of five Wit & Wisdom bookstores in Clevland said: "We pride ourselves on being an intellectual bookstore, but this is the fastest-selling book we've ever had."

• • •

# Exposing Himself

*He's a genius. He's also a jerk. And Howard Stern's new book,
'Private Parts,' is every bit as naughty, outrageous, and
smart as his radio show.* BY OWEN GLEIBERMAN

HOWARD STERN IS the most brilliant—and misunderstood—comic artist in America. In the years since he first launched his New York radio show (which is now syndicated to 14 major markets), he has made it all too easy for the media to dismiss him as a gross-out king, a "shock jock," a ringleader of sleaze who jacks up his rating points by getting beautiful young women to strip on the air. He has made it easy because, of course, Howard Stern is all these things.

He is also the Lenny Bruce of the information age: a kamikaze hipster with a machine-gun brain, a slash-and-burn rock & roll nihilist who, in his hostility and wit, his dazzlingly intuitive observational powers, his savage compulsion to smash every taboo that middle-class society places in his path, is probably the only professional entertainer in the country who answers to no one but himself. On the air, Stern creates a kind of manic free-associational theater, chainsawing through the pretensions of celebrities and politicians, of conformists and "rebels," and of the entertainment-media culture that binds them all together. What his fans cherish is his blessedly untamed hilarity, the rollicking *freedom* of his voice.

That voice comes through with buoyant abandon in **PRIVATE PARTS** *(Simon & Schuster, $23)*. Penned by Stern himself (though he might almost have talked it into a tape recorder), this blasphemously funny autobiography-scrapbook is, in essence, Howard's radio show jammed between two covers.

* * *

*Private Parts* is studded with amusing anecdotes, from Stern's one homosexual experience—an adolescent masturbation session—to his fumbling sexual encounters at Boston University, where he emerges as a kind of '70s-collegiate Holden Caulfield, to his beleaguered attempts to help Andrew Dice Clay shop for a ranch house. The book is most fascinating when it traces the development of his radio career.

* * *

The second half of the book is compulsively readable, like brain candy, and for anyone who has never actually heard Stern it may prove an irresistible introduction. For anyone else, though, it can't help but seem a substitute for the real, live thing. By the end, you long to hear the bad-boy jester in his own court. **B+**

Much to my surprise, the reviews for the book were exceptional, but I still found reason to complain. This first one says, among other things, that I'm the Lenny Bruce of the information age, and that I'm the most brilliant and misunderstood comic artist in America and that basically this might be one of the best books ever written, but then the reviewer gives me a B+. Who do I have to blow to get an A around here?

# WINNERS & LOSERS

**HOWARD STERN**
His book is an instant megahit, proving his fans can read

**ROBERT OAKLEY**
U.S.'s new Somalia envoy takes charge, gets hostages released

**CHURCH OF SCIENTOLOGY**
After 40-year struggle, the IRS finally agrees to treat it as a religion

**BRAVES PITCHER GREG MADDUX**
$28 million contract, a Cy Young—and he chokes in N.L. final

**WOOL & MOHAIR RANCHERS**
Their WW II-era subsidies to be phased out, saving $500 million

**JEFF GRALNICK**
NBC News exec calls Aidid and Somalians "jungle bunnies"

Gerardo Somoza

Ronald C. Modra

Excerpted from *Time*, October 25, 1993. Copyright © 1993 Time, Inc. Reprinted by permission.

MR OUTrageous

Excerpted from *The Buffalo News*

# Stern's Book Trashes All

Excerpted from *New York Newsday*, October 7, 1993

## Stern bares all in 'Private Parts'

**By Marshall Fine**
Staff Writer

The world can be divided into two groups: people who think Howard Stern is funny and people who have no sense of humor.

The odd thing is that I can't imagine either group not being seduced to laughter by Stern's wildly confessional, outrageously outspoken book, "Private Parts."

• • •

The book is more than 400 pages long. Yet it is fast, entertaining reading that never drags or gets repetitive. His feuds with stars, his career rollercoaster — Stern covers it all.

Reading the book is like listening to Stern on the radio — but a focused Stern who doesn't get distracted or sidetracked. With the help of collaborator Larry "Ratso" Sloman and his editors at Simon & Schuster, Stern finds his voice in print, in all its smart-alecky, profane, funny candor.

• • •

Howard Stern's "Private Parts" is raucous, riotous and undeniably funny.

Excerpted from Gannett Suburban Newspapers, October 10, 1993

# The King of All Media exposes his 'Private Parts'

By Rob Errera

• • •

*Private Parts,* his first book, can only be seen as a turning point in the entertainer's versatile career. It's the first book he's ever written and the fourth he's ever read, according to the author. Yet it debuted at number one on the New York Times Best Seller List, is the fastest selling title in Simon and Schuster's 70 year catalog and gave birth to what may have been the biggest book signing in the history of publishing. This book is making waves, and Howard Stern will never be the same again.

• • •

Excerpted from Today, October 27, 1993

# It's Stern Against the World

Excerpted from *New York Newsday*, October 7, 1993

# Howard Stern Makes My Day

## Stern chronicles career hilariously in 'Private Parts'

By Fred Shuster
*Daily News Staff Writer*

Forget "SeinLanguage." Put down that copy of "The Bridges of Madison County." Howard Stern's "Private Parts" is the most entertaining read to come down the pike since you discovered your sister's diary in her underwear drawer.

· · ·

There's a laugh on practically every page.

Excerpted from L.A. Daily News, October 9, 1963

**Stern**: Ready for therapy?

Excerpted from *The Buffalo News*, October 26, 1993

# Howard Stern—raw, funny and real

**By ROBERTO SANTIAGO**

Autobiographies of comedians and radio personalities often prove to be disappointing — essentially works of fiction where superficial reminiscences and ego are packaged in the guise of journalism.

Without a live audience, the neophyte authors are puzzled about how to understand, then chronicle the bizarre humor that comes out of their most intimate pain. Consequently, their books are nothing more than safe whitewashes of their public personas, never revealing precisely what makes them — as people and performers — loved, celebrated or condemned.

The most notable exception in the past quarter-century has been Lenny Bruce's "How To Talk Dirty And Influence People," up to now the *magnum opus* of comic autobiographies.

• • •

Who would have thought that decades after Bruce's death, and after countless attempts by personalities ranging from Joan Rivers to Larry King, that a much derided yet very accomplished syndicated radio satirist by the name of Howard Stern would find himself joining Bruce's literary spotlight?

Stern's autobiography, "Private Parts," written with the silent collaboration of Larry Sloman, is a hysterically funny exploration of Stern as human being and entertainer. Stunning in its raw honesty, the book is more engrossing and entertaining than his New York City-based radio show could ever be.

It's extraordinarily provocative writing. Only a reader totally lacking in a sense of humor — or offended by frank and graphic depictions of human sexuality and bizarre, emotional behavior — could possibly dislike this autobiography.

Like Bruce, Stern moves his narrative through his upbringing by seemingly dysfunctional parents, through a young adulthood wrought with sexual frustration and damaged self-esteem, to a recognition that his anxieties, shallowness, hypocrisies, cruelty, racism, sexism and infantile outlook on life and politics could prove successful only in the entertainment field. His language and depictions are borderline pornographic. His emotions are volatile.

Like Bruce, the popular Stern faces political condemnation by a select but powerful few. In the final chapter, he gives the last word to a psychotherapist who substantiates what Stern and fans and haters of his radio show have known all along — Stern is a man with a "personality disorder."

Mercifully, Stern differs from Bruce: The embracing of his personality disorder is a creative and life-saving redemption.

*Santiago is an entertainment writer for The Plain Dealer.*

Here's a review from the *Cleveland Plain Dealer* that meant a lot to me because the reviewer had been writing some pretty bad articles about me and then did a complete turnaround. Phrases like "raw honesty" and "Stern joining Lenny Bruce's literary spotlight" made me feel real good and had me seriously considering giving up radio and becoming a full-time author. I mean, this is all the shit I had been saying on the radio for years, but the man found it funnier in print.

FOLLOWING THE ANTICS OF AMERICA'S BEST SELLING AUTHOR SINCE 1989 #63

# THE KING OF ALL MEDIA NEWSLETTER
### AN INDEPENDENT PUBLICATION NOT AFFILIATED WITH THE HOWARD STERN SHOW
THE NATION'S AUTHORITY ON HOWARD STERN™ DEC.'93

# The "Wack Pack" Reacts To Howard's "Private Parts"

I recently caught up with some of the members of the "Wack Pack" at Howard's book party and asked them to share some of their thoughts on Howard's new book. Because of the limited space in this special issue, I unfortunately couldn't cover every member.

### King Of All Messengers: Chris Giglio

What do you think of Howard's new book?

*"I think it's great. It's the first book I've ever read in my life. I've read 300 pages.*

### Kenneth Keith Kallenbach

What was your favorite part of the book?

*"Ah...Page 263, the page I was on."*

If you could add or delete something about yourself from the book, what would it be?

*"Ah...I don't know. Um, I don't think I would have added or deleted anything. I like Chapter 10 because I was holding the sign, I think that looks pretty cool."*

### Melrose Larry Green

What effect did the book have on your life?

*"Positively... It certainly caused me to read more, I haven't read a book in a while. And negatively... It's cost me a fair amount of money because everyone wants a copy and I can't get free copies so I have to buy them."*

# MY PRIVATE PARTS GET MANGLED

It was Dan Klores, Publicist to the Stars, who warned me that after the great reviews came out, I could expect bad reviews to follow. I like this one a lot because the guy admits he doesn't need to read a book to try to ban it. This dude's logic is awesome. . . . He's for the First Amendment as long as bookstores decide what books we should read only by making certain books available. Give him a medal.

## *EDITORIAL*

### A Stern Rebuke—A Strong Commendation

The *United Methodist Relay* commends in strongest terms book stores around the country which have placed decency above profit by refusing to display and/or sell the recent book by shock-jock Howard Stern.

We are quick to defend the First Amendment right of free speech and press.

. . .

By the same token, we believe that the retailer should have the freedom to stock or to refuse any book they wish. This is not a censorship issue at all.

We have not read Mr. Stern's book. How then can we comment upon it? One does not need to wallow in filth in order to smell it. Anyone who has happened upon a Stern broadcast either by accident or intent knows that what passes for humor reveals the sophomoric mind of a middle-aged adolescent in an advanced stage of arrested development. For most of us humor requires more than a genital fixation of ethnic slurs. We choose not to indulge in scum and slime.

. . .

We wish Mr. Stern no ill will. Rather we pray that he be touched by grace, freeing him from his pathetic preoccupations, and enabling him to replace tasteless vulgarity with winsome style and good humor.

# MORE JEALOUS PEOPLE WRITE REVIEWS...

## Stern's 'Private Parts' proves anything can be a 'book' "Except the Stuff You Write!"

By Scott Shuger
SPECIAL TO THE GLOBE

**Book Review**

People in book publishing are always complaining about how much material they have to wade through and how little of it is any good. Well, guys, with the publication of this book—essentially a 446-page attack of verborrhea from morning radio man Howard Stern—it's going to get much worse. For anybody who still doubted, "Private Parts" proves that in America today, anything can be a "book" and anyone can be an "author." Indeed, it proves that anyone can be the nation's No. 1 best-selling "author." Yet another triumph of democracy over quality.

And based on Stern's effort, I have this advice for all the newly inspired who will soon be transom-bombing Manhattan with their manuscripts: Put in everything you ever thought of (Stern even included instructions on how to defecate), and be sure to have a chapter on lesbian sex (Stern has *two*).

* * *

The result is that "Private Parts" isn't about anything. Or to be a little more accurate, it's all about Howard Stern, and he isn't about anything. What's promising about Stern is that in this age of public relations, he's spontaneous, and in this age of pretense, he's plebeian. But as useful as these qualities are—as much as America could use more of them—they are form, not substance. By themselves, they are neither valuable nor interesting. Lincoln was spontaneous and plain-spoken, but so was Dillinger.

The conflation of form and substance is the modern mistake and, especially, the American mistake. What do you get when a culture is in its grip? The French philosopher Michel Foucault observed that in the transition from the pre-modern to the modern understanding of the self, "the child is more individualized than the adult, the patient more than the healthy man, the madman and the delinquent more than the normal and the non-delinquent." And the American social critic Paul Fussell notes that nowadays daily conversation "seldom touches on objective phenomena unrelated to the self. It dwells all but exclusively on personal desires and images." As if to drive these points home, we now have a best seller in which the writer prays for those disagreeing with him to die from cancer or AIDS or to be disfigured in car accidents, in which he asks his mother if she has anal sex with his father, in which he tells his young daughters a bedtime story about "a daddy who ripped out a cat's uterus." On the whole the book is a lot like one of Stern's favorite topics (and activities)—masturbation. Something best kept private, and purely self-referential.

* * *

If a publisher is content to profit from a book like this, it might as well just open a string of massage parlors.

# Of Best Sellers and Private Enterprise

### By Zel Levin

I thought at my age (I turn 80 this month) that I was shock-proof.

I'm not. I'm shocked. More than that, I'm disgusted and outraged. But I have a problem. Where or to whom do I direct my anger—at imbecilic TV talk host Howard Stern? At the giant book publisher, Simon & Schuster? Or at the First Amendment of the Constitution, guaranteeing free speech?

But, I'm ahead of my story.

* * *

I made a trip recently to New York. Barnes & Noble topped my itinerary. Since I write reviews for the Cape Codder and other publications, I'm always interested in the latest releases. The store has a section displaying the New York Times "best sellers" and there, staring me right in the face was "Private Parts," which for weeks has topped the list in the Times and the Boston Globe.

It is written by Howard Stern, a sleazebag broadcaster who earns a rich living, peddling schlock nationwide and who has been hit by the Federal Communications Commission for his on-the-air smut. How was it possible, I wondered, that a book he authored could attain "best seller" status?

So I picked up the book, sat in a far corner, and read "Private Parts," a title incidentally which says just what you think it says. I read the book in 55 minutes, every lewd, lousy, stupid, obscene, libidinous word.

It is horrible. It is insulting. AND IT'S NUMBER ONE!

* * *

What's the book about?

It's about nothing. It is inane. It's about Stern's sexual adventures with nothing left out. It's about Stern's "I'll do anything to get attention" attitude. It's about all the people that Stern doesn't like. It's about the size of women's breasts. It's about homosexuals who are a particular target of his venom. It's about what a great broadcaster and interviewer he is.

He berates Johnny Carson. He ridicules Oprah. He insults Arsenio Hall. He makes fun of comedian Bob Hope. He goes into excruciating detail, describing his pornographic dreams and suggests an illicit friendship with Billionaire Donald Trump.

* * *

Sure I'm outraged by Stern. He's offensive, gross and disgusting.

Sure I'm critical of Simon & Schuster for lowering its standards to publish such a ribald obscenity.

But remember this. "Private Parts" became a best seller only because thousands of thoughtless people rushed to buy it. Stern wrote it to make money. S & S published it to make money. However contemptible, that's private enterprise.

But for Heaven's sake, what excuse do book lovers have to spend good money on the worst collection of garbage ever printed? Think about it.

## IN DEFENSE OF HOWARD STERN

Chatham

To the Editor:

As a die-hard Howard Stern fan, I wish to take exception to Zel Levin's editorial.

In the first place, Barnes and Noble is a bookstore, not a library, and you are expected to pay for the merchandise. Mr. Levin purports to have read every word in 55 minutes at 80 years old. Give me a break, Zel, it took me four hours in my quiet living room and I'm 47.

Lastly, as Howard has said over and over, if you don't like the show turn the dial. Perhaps Mr. Levin should have picked up Rush Limbaugh's book instead, or better yet, stick to the Empire State Building.

Thomas F. Cronin

**I'm not an anti-Semite or anything (maybe half an anti-Semite), but it looks bad when Jewish guys sit in bookstores and read books for free.**

# It's Down And Dirty With Stern

**BOOKS** *Patricia Holt*

To give "shock jock" broadcaster Howard Stern every benefit of the doubt — and one has so *many* doubts while perusing his autobiography, "Private Parts" — there are occasions when the radio talk show host who makes a career out of insulting celebrities and describing bad sex on the air can be very funny.

* * *

Stern has childishly horrible things to say about Roseanne and Tom Arnold, Oprah Winfrey, Arsenio Hall, Dick Cavett, Richard Simmons, Yoko Ono, Bob Hope, Patti Davis and a number of rock stars. But his deliberate stupidity (on travel: "to tell the truth, I hate every f ---ing place in the world") finally allows a point of agreement when he says about gay sex, "I can't fathom the ass as a sex object. I mean, why don't I just go and put my d --- in a garbage pail?"

What a wonderful idea.

# Stern's book is great — to keep away from your private self
## Just ask Howard: You'll get the blame

**By Elizabeth Peryam**
FOR THE JOURNAL-CONSTITUTION

Men like Howard Stern used to hide under rocks. Now they hide behind the First Amendment. Howard Stern has no private parts, except perhaps his heart and cerebrum, if any. We know his reptilian brain works; it's the part of him that, when it senses danger, responds instinctively and immediately by attacking. Which is a summary of this book, come to think of it.

* * * He uses the First Amendment to fix his fangs into the nation's ankle, pumping his own poison into minds softened by too much TV.

Read his "book" if you want. But you can save $23 and get the same effect by flushing a dollar bill down the toilet and imagining, moment by moment, its journey through the sewer system all the way to West Point Lake.

If you do buy it, when you're finished see if there's not some friendly farmer who can use it for fertilizer. Or take it into a wooded area and hide it under a rock, with the other slimy, slithery creatures.

# BANNED IN

## *Now you see it (sort of) . . .*

**OH, HOWARD:** *This bare-babe-laden cover was rejected by Howard Stern's publishers.*

**OH, NO, HOWARD:** *As was this hands-strategically-placed solo pose by the popular shock jock.*

# At last, Stern is censored —

Not only was the book controversial, but the fucking cover shots were causing a problem. I considered the cover we chose to be very conservative by today's standards. Just take a look at Fabio on the covers of those romance novels; Demi Moore and Sylvester Stallone posing completely nude for *Vanity Fair;* and

# CONNECTICUT!

## *now you don't*

By BILL HOFFMANN

Howard Stern has finally been censored — but this time it wasn't the FCC that muzzled the shaggy-haired shock jock.

Simon & Schuster — publisher of Stern's autobiography "Private Parts" — refused to run an X-rated photo the dirty-mouthed morning man chose for the cover of his new book. It hits the stores Friday and is sure to be a best-seller.

**OK, HOWARD:** *Here's the cover — title over Stern's naughty bits — that passed muster.*

# by his own publisher

Janet Jackson with hands over her breasts on the cover of *Rolling Stone*. With only my torso and legs showing, you would see more skin with a guy wearing a bathing suit. The way some bookstores and distributors were reacting, you would have thought I had whipped out my minuscule cock.

# Supplier Kills Order for Stern Autobiography

By DANIEL CERONE
TIMES STAFF WRITER

Howard Stern, who routinely accuses others of trying to censor the spoken word on his nationally syndicated radio show, has received similar heat over his written words from a West Coast book distributor.

Sapak Inc., a Huntington Beach company that supplies books to such Southern California retail chains as Fedco, Gemco and Pace, has canceled an order for 20,000 copies of Stern's raw autobiography, "Private Parts," which is due in stores Friday.

Terry Millar, a buyer at Sapak, said she turned the order away after receiving sample pages of the book. "I don't believe that it would be appropriate for family-oriented stores, which is the type we supply," she said.

• • •

# DEPT. STORE CLOSES THE BOOK ON STERN

BY BILL HOFFMANN

A major department store chain has banned Howard Stern's raunchy best seller "Private Parts" from its bookshelves.

And, in a creative bit of editing, it also eliminated the book from The New York Times best-seller list—a feat that has the newspaper fuming.

The furor began when the Caldor chain decided the shock jock's tome was too outrageous for its mainstream image, and decided not to carry it in its 150 stores along the East Coast.

The chain also decided to obliterate the title from The Times' influential best-seller list, which it displays in every store.

Stern's book has been No. 1 in the Times' non-fiction hardcover category for three straight weeks, and will remain in that spot next week, officials of the newspaper said.

But Caldor executives have been editing the list, removing Stern's title from the No. 1 spot and moving all the books under it up one notch.

On the revised list, "Seinlanguage," by TV comic Jerry Seinfeld, which has been No. 2 in recent weeks, is now listed as No. 1.

The deception has the Times up in arms.

"We're very unhappy that Caldor has displayed an altered version of The New York Times best-seller list," Times spokeswoman Nancy Neilsen said.

• • •

# WMass residents have their say

• • •

Last week Caldor Corp. announced it would not sell Stern's new autobiography, "Private Parts."

• • •

People interviewed at Eastfield Mall in Springfield defended Stern's right to speak his mind and the public's right to read about it.

• • •

Most of the people interviewed had little positive to say about Stern.

• • •

"Personally I think he's a jerk and I wouldn't want to read his book, but the choice should be left up to the public," said Carol Davis of Springfield.

Barbara Giguere, 57, of Ludlow agreed.

"He's definitely a weirdo, but just because I don't want to read it doesn't mean others shouldn't be given the opportunity," she said.

Gary Lockwood, 64, of Springfield, was equally harsh.

"He's a bunch of garbage, but if someone wants to buy his book they should be able to," he said.

• • •

—KEITH J. O'CONNOR

Excerpted from *Union News*, Springfield, Massachusetts, November 12, 1993

It's nice to know that in a confused and angry world we all agree universally on two things—*Private Parts* should not be banned and Howard Stern is a jerk. Now I can sleep at night.

And now my favorite two articles in this chapter. A year later the controversy still rages on as a small town in Texas goes on a witch-hunt. One of these free thinkers believes you can tell that the book is pornographic just by looking at the cover. So what he's saying is you can judge a book by its cover. What the fuck is so pornographic about that photo? So they took a vote and threw me out but allowed a book about clit removal to stay on the shelves. Go figure that one out.

*VALLEY*
# MORNING STAR

## Weslaco city commissioners express displeasure at book choice for library
### By NOLENE HODGES

WESLACO — City commissioners were unanimous Tuesday in their opinion that sexually explicit and other so-called "dirty" books be kept off the shelves of the Weslaco Public Library.

The subject was brought up by Commissioner Charlie Krause at the end of a three and a half hour meeting.

Krause was armed with a copy of the Howard Stern book, *Private Parts,* which he described as "not very good" and "nasty." He said the book was purchased for the library.

Krause addressed Library Director Pam Antonelli in the audience, saying "I think we need to look at the way we're running the library."

Antonelli said to book was brought to her attention in December, but at that time was not on the Library Board's agenda and President Hank Page said it couldn't be discussed.

She said the book was taken off the shelves on recommendation of the board, but could be checked out if requested by an adult.

Antonelli said she bought the book without knowing it might be objectionable. Later, she said she learned about it on a TV program, "and if I had seen the TV show first, I wouldn't have bought it."

• • •

Krause showed newspaper reports about the book being objectionable.

"Frankly, I'm surprised you didn't know about it," Mayor Pro Tem Richard Vaughan told the librarian.

He said there was much publicity over a long period and he was "amazed" she had missed it. He described it as "disgusting" and said the cover alone should indicated it wasn't suitable.

"We don't want this to happen again," Vaughan said. "This is a conservative, small town with a limited amount of money to buy books ... It's nothing to do with you personally, but I do think you need guidance."

• • •

# MID-VALLEY

D Section        Wednesday, July 13, 1994        Valley Morning Star

## Weslaco library board removes Stern's 'Parts'

**By NOLENE HODGES**
*Star News Staff*

WESLACO — The controversial book, *Private Parts,* written by Howard Stern, has been removed officially from the Weslaco Public Library.

The action came during a Tuesday meeting by unanimous action of the library board.

Two other books up for consideration on the agenda — Alice Walker's *Warrior Marks* on female genital mutilation, and Alexandra Penney's *How to Make Love to a Man - Safely,* — remain.

The board voted 6-2 to keep the Walker book.

A decision on the Penney book was tabled.

There was little discussion on *Private Parts.* It came up last week at a meeting of the Weslaco City Commission, with those present agreeing it was pornography. Mayor Gene Braught was away on vacation, but the four commissioners said they were in agreement after it was brought up by Charlie Krause.

At the library board meeting, a visitor, Charles Warren, wanted to know if anyone had checked it out. Library Director Pam Antonelli said "about nine" had checked it out. She said as soon as it was brought to her attention, it was put on reserve, available for those requesting it, but not on the library shelves.

In answer to questions from Warren, a high school teacher, she said it was a joint decision on the part of the city and herself. Warren said books shouldn't be removed unless they were "out and out pornography."

He said it concerned him that a mayor and four commissioners "decide what we read."

Antonelli said she agreed "in theory." But she said she felt removal of *Private Parts* was "not censorship."

On the Alice Walker book, Board Member Irma Gonzalez moved it be kept, stating "Alice Walker is a fine author." Others in the room agreed.

• • •

Excerpted from *Valley Morning Star,* Harlingen, Texas, July 13, 1994

**The Thomas Paine Freedom of the Press Award goes to (drumroll, please) Weslaco Public Library director Pam Antonelli, who agreed "in theory" that a mayor and four commissioners should not be telling us what to read but felt removal of *Private Parts* was "not censorship."**

# KISSING, PLUGGING, AND PROMOTING

Now all the talk shows needed me as a guest. Initially, Phil Donahue was not interested in having me, but when the book hit number one in a week he demanded an immediate appearance. Most people would have told Phil to fuck off, but when they told me his program really sold books I rushed to his side. The show was fun but definitely not X-rated, and I was shocked when certain areas of the country were not allowed to see it. In the markets that it aired, Phil received record-breaking ratings. Phil's words on the First Amendment were greatly appreciated and I admire his program.

. . .

**DONAHUE:** Well, let me get it in before the show's over, Howard. You've come a long way without my defending you, but I want to say one— God bless Joan Rivers for her early and courageous and up-front support of you. I think the FCC's notion of fining stations that carry your show, as you might say, sucks. I don't think it's a good idea. I agree with you that the— I think you make it easier for other people to puncture the balloons of pretense. I do think we have a media that can be very reverent and passive and go-along, and I think guys like you make it easier for guys like me to be just a little more outrageous.

**Mr. STERN:** Thank you.

**DONAHUE:** So hurray for you, Howard. *[crosstalk]*.

**Mr. STERN:** Phil, let me say something. Phil.

**DONAHUE:** Sir—

**14th AUDIENCE MEMBER:** Yes.

**Mr. STERN:** Come down here, I'm going to kiss you on the lips. Come here.

. . .

"Donahue" excerpt and photograph, Multimedia Entertainment, Inc., 1993

**Kissing Phil and plugging my book
all at the same time.**

# Stern judgment

## Channel 8 pre-empts 'Donahue' appearance

### By Ed Bark

"Cruel and unkind racial comments" made during Howard Stern's appearance on *Donahue* led WFAA-TV (Channel 8) to pre-empt the program, vice president and general manager Cathy Creany said Monday.

The station in turn was deluged with phone calls from fans of the controversial radio personality, whose syndicated show airs weekday mornings on KEGL-FM radio (97.1). From 9 a.m. to 5 p.m. Monday, Channel 8 logged 1,900 calls, almost all of them protesting the pre-emption.

Ms. Creany said she made the decision on her own after viewing a tape of the program over the weekend. A *Donahue* rerun aired in the show's regular 9 a.m. time period Monday.

"I thought it was unacceptable based on our standards, and I thought it would be offensive to many of our viewers," Ms. Creany said.

She specifically objected to four "racial slurs" that host Phil Donahue orally excerpted from Mr. Stern's new No. 1 best-selling book, *Private Parts*.

Mr. Stern "confirmed" the excerpts, Ms. Creany said. They included references to masturbation, Aunt Jemima, Filipinos and Mr. Stern's description of sexual activities he would perform with actress Michelle Pfeiffer.

"I looked at it and I said, 'Nope,' and that was the end of it," Ms. Creany said. "I feel the content was inappropriate, and I don't regret the decision at all."

• • •

# STERN SIGN LANGUAGE

Street protesters condemn Channel 8 for pre-empting 'Donahue' featuring DJ

**VOCAL FANS:** The sign-waving scene got lively outside Channel 8 on Friday afternoon as protesters questioned the station's decision to pre-empt Howard Stern's appearance on Donahue

NO HOWARD PEACE

CHANNEL 8 IT?

*The Dallas Morning News: Michael Ainsworth*

Not only was the cover of the book banned, and the contents of the book banned, but now my TV appearances promoting the book were being banned.

AP/Wide World Photos

**Plugging Joan on the promotional trail.**

Bernard Fallon/HBO

**My favorite television program—HBO's "The Larry Sanders Show." Not only did I get to plug my book, but I was able to get my hand near Garry Shandling's girlfriend Linda's sphincter.**

*Top:* I'd kiss anyone to plug my book. You have no idea how much pleasure I received from that prickly moustache hair.

*Bottom:* I asked Alison, my wife, to help me plug my book on "Geraldo." Instead, she held up a bag of rice. Thank you, love of my life.

AP/Wide World Photos/Margaret Norton

**Promoting with Jay:** "C'mon, Jay, be a man and rip the heads off your enemies." "The Tonight Show" doubled its ratings that night.

# HOWIESTOCK—THE BIGGEST BOOK SIGNING IN HISTORY

Newsday/Oliver Morris

## Stern Causes Near-Riot at NYC Signing

■ **Radio:** The author of the best-selling 'Private Parts' becomes caught in traffic himself as thousands of fans jam the bookstore.

**By JANE HALL**
TIMES STAFF WRITER

NEW YORK—Radio talk-show comic Howard Stern caused a near-riot in mid-town Manhattan on Thursday with an appearance at a bookstore to sign his hot new tome, "Private Parts."

More than two hours before he was even scheduled to appear, about 2,000 people were in line waiting to get Stern's autograph, and police on the scene later estimated that there were 10,000 people in the crowd that peered into the windows of Barnes & Noble and spilled onto the streets in the blocks around the store, stopping noontime traffic along Fifth Avenue.

A marketing executive for Stern's publisher, Simon & Schuster, called it the biggest book signing ever, outdrawing the likes of Magic Johnson and retired Gen. Norman Schwarzkopf.

• • •

Excerpted from *Los Angeles Times*, October 15, 1993

A few thousand
close friends wait
for their pal
Howard to arrive.

Mike Gange

Mike Gange

My mom consoling an overwrought fan.

Swifty Lazar Power Frames grace my father's face
at the book signing.

Oscar Abolasian/GAMMA LIAISON

Barnes & Noble clocked me at more than
900 signatures an hour.

# REUTERS

## October 15, 1993

NEW YORK (Reuter) - Thousands of Howard Stern fans thronged a Fifth Avenue bookstore Thursday for a book signing event by the controversial radio talk show host.

Police estimated about 6,000 people, some of whom had camped out for the night, turned out for the event, forcing the temporary shutdown of the busy thoroughfare.

Stern's new book "Private Parts", his first, revels in the smutty mudslinging for which he has become famous.

One fan, Joe Dickinson, 27, said he arrived two hours before the doors were opened for the signing and was still half a block from the store five hours later.

"Sure it's worth it," he said grinning, "it's Howard Stern."

Inside the store Stern, looking fit and wearing his trademark dark sunglasses, signed books in a frenzy with a large black magic marker.

Officials at the Barnes and Noble store said it was by far the most-popular signing session at the outlet.

Stern's wife Alison also attended. She said the couple's three young children were not allowed to read the book.

"It's not the kind of book you want your kids to read," she said.

# The New York Times

### NEW YORK FRIDAY, OCTOBER 15, 1993

# The Metro Section

CITY

**Crowd Swamps Fifth Avenue to Meet a Radio Star**

Howard Stern, the New York talk radio host, was greeted by thousands of fans gathered outside the Barnes & Noble bookstore on Fifth Avenue and 48th Street yesterday waiting for him to autograph copies of his new book "Howard Stern, Private Parts." The book will be listed as the No. 1 hardcover nonfiction seller on Publishers Weekly list next week.

# *10,000* Maniacs

## Howard Stern fans jam 5th Ave. book-signing

Excerpted from *Newsday*, October 15, 1993

# A Holiday for 10,000 Maniacs

**Books:** If Howard Stern writes it, they will come

JERRY ADLER

THIS IS GREAT. WEDNESDAY NIGHT I get thrown out of the China Grill after one drink because Madonna has booked the place for a private party, and then Thursday morning I can't get across Fifth Avenue because something like 10,000 people are lined up outside Barnes & Noble to get books signed by Howard Stern. I haven't seen such a concentration of white men in one place in Manhattan since the hockey playoffs. You live in New York, you expect to spend a lot of time behind police barricades waiting for somebody like Idi Amin to go from his limousine into the Waldorf, but to be held up by Howard Stern is an insult. It's like getting stuck behind Kathie Lee Gifford's motorcade.

But, hey, maybe I was being unfair to him. Howard Stern IS NOT JUST ANOTHER RANTING LOWLIFE WITH A RADIO SHOW. He has a computer now,

too! And somebody showed him how to use it, because his new book, "Private Parts," has more capital letters, boldface and italics than an Italian soccer magazine!

• • •

Within a week of publication Simon & Schuster had printed more than a million copies, which means that in the time it takes Howard Stern to reach sexual climax (two minutes, he writes, including walking to the bedroom and getting undressed) 200 PEOPLE HAVE BOUGHT HIS BOOK! That's a claim you can't imagine Rush Limbaugh making.

• • •

**New York's Finest helping me inside.**

**SHOCK JOCK GRIDLOCK IN MIDTOWN**
Page 3

**ARISTIDE'S TOP AIDE SHOT DEAD**
Page 4

**MADONNA & HER RAUNCHY 'GIRLIE SHOW'**
Review: Page 8

# NEW YORK POST

### METRO EDITION

# SHOCK-JOCK GRIDLOCK!

## Howard Stern fans shut down 5th Ave. during book bash

By BILL HOFFMANN

Shock jock Howard Stern's book-signing bash turned Midtown into Gridlock City yesterday as more than 5,000 racuous, cheering fans turned out to meet their foul-mouthed hero.

Chanting, "Howard! Howard!" and "Stern Rules!" the wild mob closed Fifth Avenue to traffic for an hour.

Businessmen and tourists stared in disbelief as some women fans lifted their shirts to expose their breasts and suggestively shook their bodies to bawdy catcalls and cheers from the crowd.

• • •

Stern's mother, Rae, told The Post: "It's awesome. I figured it would be a nice little gathering with a a few people coming in and out — but nothing like this.

"His fans may call him the 'King of All Media,' but he's still just little Howard to me," she said.

• • •

**HORN HONK:** Hey, I understand why they love me, Howard Stern (above) seems to say at book signing, which attracted some 5,000 fans (inset).

**FOR THE RECORD** Mounted cop keeps thousands of avid Howard Stern fans in control during the radio bad boy's book signing gig at Barnes & Noble on Fifth Ave. yesterday. So many people were interested in the shock jock's "Private Parts" that Simon & Schuster has printed 850,000 copies, and the book is entering best-seller lists at No. 1.

*Daily News photo/Budd Williams, October 15, 1993*

# HOWIE SET TO SELL ON SHOCK EXCHANGE

**FIRST IN LINE:** *George Harvey, 36, staked out his spot in front of Waldenbooks two days before Stern's scheduled appearance.*

Michael Alexander

AP/Wide World Photos/Michael Albans

Steve Allen/GAMMA LIAISON

Always anxious to please, I spent extra time signing body parts for these poor under-privileged children.

AP/Wide World Photos/Mark Lennihan

**Fans of radio shock jock Howard Stern wait behind police barricades for a book signing in New York City, Monday, October 18, 1993.**

# Thousands flock to see the jock of shock

When radio star Howard Stern came to South Street to autograph copies of his bestseller, so did his fans. In droves.

**By Joe Logan**
INQUIRER STAFF WRITER

When most authors have a book signing, they set up a card table in the back of some bookstore and hope enough people show up so they're not embarrassed.

But most authors aren't Howard Stern.

Stern, the insanely popular radio and TV personality and author of the New York Times' current No. 1 bestseller *Private Parts*, held a signing on South Street yesterday, and thousands and thousands of people showed up.

It was a line that snaked out of Tower Books at 425 South St., then headed down Passyunk Avenue, turned left onto Bainbridge Street, then went down to and along Fourth Street for blocks. In some places, the line had those back-and-forth wraps

**Howard Stern had little time** to even turn his head yesterday. He was signing so many autographs the felt-tip markers kept running dry.

you see at Disney World to accommodate more people. WYSP-FM (94.1), Stern's local radio outlet, was claiming 25,000 people.

• • •

**It was important for me to go to Philly, the first city to carry my
show in syndication. Record-breaking crowds again. Half the fun
was fans meeting other fans and hooking up after the signing.**

Dear Mr. Stern,

I have an excellent lesbian story to tell you about what I witnessed
from the crowd in Philadelphia on Saturday, October 23, 1993 at
your book signing.

I was to the left of the stage and I looked behind me and saw this
dude with two girls yelling "We have nudity--let us to the front of
the stage!!" No one really looked too interested, I was shocked and
turned all my attention to the threesome. The dude looked at me
and said, "Can we get through?" I said, "Where's the nudity, pal?"
With that the girls smiled and looked at each other. They were two
pretty hot looking babes. One was 5'8", blonde, blue eyes, and built
like a brick shit house. She had a thong crammed neatly up her ass
and I could see a wet dot at her most intimate of areas. As soon as I
saw this I was instantly pitching a tent. The other girl was only
about 5'5" but had a kick-ass athletic body with perky little breasts.
She was a brunette with big cute brown eyes. Immediately after I
said, "Where's the nudity?," the little one nonchalantly moved the
blonde's  thong underpants or bathing suit bottom to the side and
began to gently finger her. I was out of my mind with lust when I
saw this, and I was surprised no one else was noticing this. Then the
blonde having felt the burn of passion jammed her tongue down the
brunette's throat. They pushed their tits together and I could see
their nipples were hard as rocks. At that point is when you came out
on the stage and made your appearance with Enuff-Z-Nuff and
fucked up my entire fantasy. I always dreamed of seeing two
women in a lustful embrace and maybe I could have seen more if it
wasn't for you.

However, the show was still great. I didn't get my book signed but I
understood that it was just too much. There were 25,000 or more
people there and you were clocked at signing about 800 an hour.
What more could anyone ask for? Besides the dick cops in Philly
wouldn't let you stay. But from a listener who is grateful to have
had the opportunity to at least witness a portion of a long desired
fantasy, I want to say thank you and don't ever change. And the
people should always remember that only at a Howard Stern
gathering is the untouchable touchable.

Thanks again--Eternally grateful,

Not only had the book cover been banned, followed by the book being banned, only to have the TV appearances promoting the book banned—now it was the book signings being banned!

# Angry Stern set for Hollywood showdown

### By ANGELA C. ALLEN and BILL HOFFMANN

A livid Howard Stern declared war on West Hollywood yesterday after the posh town blocked him from signing copies of his best-selling book.

The shaggy-haired shock jock was set to appear at a bookstore on the Sunset Strip tomorrow when town officials insisted the shop post a $25,000 bond to cover possible damages by Stern's fans *and* pay $18,000 for police overtime.

"I see it as an amateur attempt at a shakedown. I have a right to go sign books — I have a right to speak my mind," Stern said at a hastily-called midtown press conference at WXRK-FM, where he does his popular morning show.

**HOWARD'S END:** *Radio bad boy Howard Stern gives his side of the story at a Midtown press conference yesterday.*

New York Post: Bolivar Arellano

"This is just a bad attempt at taking away my civil rights."

Even more infuriating, Stern added, is that West Hollywood constantly welcomes other big stars and events to its streets.

"You have people like Demi Moore, Sylvester Stallone and Ar-nold Schwarzenegger walking around, and huge crowds with the Grammy and Emmy awards, the Gay Pride Parade — and yet there's a problem with me," the top-rated radio star griped to reporters.

He said he may file a civil-rights suit against the town.

---

**An Open Letter to the Readers of the Los Angeles Times:**

Our apologies to anyone who planned on attending the Howard Stern booksigning yesterday for any inconvenience you may have been caused.

By imposing punitive terms on us, the City of West Hollywood effectively squelched our opportunity of presenting this controversial author.

West Hollywood is a city with one of the highest per capita tax bases in the country, yet boasts no great parks, no great libraries, no school system of its own, almost no public parking, and no effective public transit system.

What it does have is a group of creative citizens and business people who define national trends in culture.

Isn't it time for the city to realize this and serve their needs?

**Glenn Goldman**
**Owner, Book Soup**

**Refusing to be intimidated, like Moses, I took the crowds to Pasadena.**

# Pasadena is Howard's town now

**By Gigi Hanna**
STAFF WRITER

PASADENA—"Stern town" was quiet last night, as an encampment of Howard Stern fans braved a cold night for a glimpse of their outspoken and controversial idol.

About 100 fans were camped in the parking lot of Vroman's Books & Stationery, 695 E. Colorado Blvd., 18 hours before the New York-based radio shock jock was scheduled to appear at the store to sign copies of his best-selling tome "Private Parts."

A handwritten sign on a fence near the campers marked the spot as "Stern town."

"He's a popular guy, he stands for the great unwashed," said Michael Shores, 40, of Sherman Oaks. "I'm raising my children on his new book."

• • •

Vroman's was open all night to accommodate fans wanting to buy the book, but Pasadena police were not concerned about the 5,000 to 10,000 people expected to turn out for the event.

• • •

# Stern draws 10,000 to book signing

**CULTURE:** The self-proclaimed 'king of all media' declares that West Hollywood is out and Pasadena is in.

**By JAMES ANDERSON**
*The Associated Press*

PASADENA—Thousands of Howard Stern fans waving "Private Parts" tomes descended on Vroman's book store Thursday for an encounter with the ribald radio personality.

Enthusiasts began lining up for Stern's appearance 18 hours early, many braving overnight temperatures in the 30s. Lt. Jack Robertson estimated 8,000 to 10,000 people queued up for signatures.

• • •

# Stern book-signing mobbed

## Pasadena store opposes censorship of his free speech

**Fans wave Howard Stern's book, *Private Parts*, while waiting for him to autograph them.**

## Jock's Flock

It's Sweet Talk, Not Shock, as Radio's Racy Howard Stern Greets Fans

**By CLAUDIA PUIG**
TIMES STAFF WRITER

He came to town and they came from far and wide to pay homage. They slept in the streets, braving near-freezing temperatures. Mothers kept their children out of school. Postal workers left overflowing sacks of Christmas mail undelivered. One surgeon abandoned his patients.

No, it wasn't President Clinton they had come to pay tribute to. Nor was it an early sighting of Santa Claus. It wasn't even a once-in-a-decade papal visit, although some would argue it was indeed a religious experience.

"Howard Is God," read a placard with huge, black lettering.

"Impeach Clinton, Howard for President," said another in Day-Glo green.

The event, which drew an estimated 10,000 people, was an appearance and book signing in Pasadena on Thursday by radio phenomenon—and deity to some—Howard Stern.

\* \* \*

"This is like a once-in-a-lifetime thing," said Sarah Tesser, who confessed she had gone AWOL from her supervisory position at United Parcel Service to meet Stern. It is the busiest time of the year for her company, but she had her priorities.

"I don't care," she said. "I need Howard."

\* \* \*

# Independent
### HOLLYWOOD

Tell us your news! Call (213) 932-NEWS

FREE! 61 Vol 78 No. 49 **Wednesday, December 22, 1993**

For classified advertising, call (213) 932-8100

## A city apologizes to Howard Stern

Despite what you may think, West Hollywood city officials want you to know, they do have a sense of humor.

Last Friday was declared "Howard Stern Day" in the Creative City, complete with a proclamation commending the radio personality, author and self-proclaimed "King of all Media" for "his vociferous commitment to freedom of expression as demonstrated through his broadcast confrontations with city officials" last week.

City Councilman John Heilman came up with the idea, and the rest of the council agreed, after thousands turned out last Thursday for Stern's "Private Parts" book signing in Pasadena.

Photo by Gary McCarthy

'Shock Jock' Howard Stern waves to fans at his Pasadena appearance. Meanwhile, the West Hollywood City Council proclaims its apology (inset).

**The city council offered this half-assed apology for its cowardly act of censorship.**

**It's a wonderful life:** Our favorite panhandler sighting of the holiday season was made in Santa (not Claus) Monica, where a street person was munching on a croissant and reading Howard Stern's "Private Parts" (in hard copy) outside the upscale supermarket Pavilions. While begging for money, of course.

# THE BOOK PARTY

Simon & Schuster invites you to celebrate the publication of
HOWARD STERN'S PRIVATE PARTS

You should have seen Simon & Schuster's original book-party invitation. It was a Xeroxed form letter. After a few embarrassing phone calls, we agreed on this snazzy invite.

Here's a list of all the celebrities who
were invited and didn't show up . . .

Arnold, Roseanne, and
Tom
Baldwin, Alec
Baldwin, Steve
Barbi Twins
Barkin, Ellen
Barkley, Charles
Berle, Milton
Bernhard, Sandra
Carver, Daniel/KKK
Chung, Connie
Clinton, Roger
Crawford, Cindy
Davis, Patti
Dinkins, David
Fabio
Flavor Flav

Franklin, Joe
Funny Gay Males
Gabel, Sukhreet
Gabor, Zsa Zsa
Gibson, Debbie
Gina/Lesbian
Giuliani, Rudy
Goldberg, Whoopi
Guns N' Roses
Hope, Bob
Jackson, LaToya, and
Jack Gordon
Jones, Chuck
Leno, Jay
Letterman, David
Madonna
Malika and Sabrina

Milli Vanilli (Rob and
Fab)
Orlando, Tony
Porizkova, Paulina
Povich, Maury
Schwarzenegger, Arnold
Seinfeld, Jerry
Sharpton, Al
Simmons, Richard
Spelling, Tori
Steinbrenner, George
Tiny Tim
Trump, Donald
Turner, Ike
Westheimer, Dr. Ruth

. . . and here's the one who did.

Actually, the party was packed with a lot of good friends
celebrating the success of *Private Parts*. Joan Rivers has always
been a great friend, Ed Koch was the best mayor New York City
ever had, and Senator Alfonse D'Amato was the first (and
only) public official to come out and blast the FCC for trampling
on the First Amendment when it fined me. He has never asked me
for a favor in return.

AP/Wide World Photos/Michael Albans

## Mothers & senator honor King Stern

**A party for shock-jock Howard Stern, now a best-selling author, attracts a diverse group of fans.**

### by ROBERT STRAUSS

NEW YORK — "He signed my breast. Howard signed my breast," the woman shrieked to the dozens of folks pressed up against the barricades that held them back from the goulash of celebrities and other nebulous invitees at last night's Party of the Night, the party for "Body Parts," the best-selling book by Howard Stern, self-proclaimed King of All Media.

"I want you to know these breasts nursed three children and now are nursing Howard's name," the woman bellowed to the crowd on the sidewalk in front of the new Harley Davidson Cafe at 58th Street and The Avenue of the Americas.

The woman, pulling down her chic white blouse only slightly to bare just the top half of her right breast, the part signed by Stern in rather shaky black-marker script, claimed she was Lauren Taylor, who plays Stacey on the ABC soap opera "Loving." ("She's the girl next door" the woman giggled.)

• • •

Midway through the bash, Stern ascended a small stage with a strange threesome of acolytes: Joan Rivers, former New York City Mayor Ed Koch and Sen. Al D'Amato, R-N.Y. Stern hugged Rivers more tightly than a linebacker in mid-sack and proclaimed of Koch, "As far as I'm concerned, he will always be the Mayor of New York."

D'Amato, clashing sartorially with Stern by wearing merely a conservative suit, grabbed the microphone to castigate the Federal Communications Commission for fining and harassing Stern for what the FCC claims is the Stern show's obscene material.

"The last thing they should do, those jackasses in Washington, is to censor him," said D'Amato, who occasionally trades jibes with Stern on the air. "I'm here because Howard Stern was a real friend when things didn't look so good. . . . Howard Stern is a real friend."

• • •

Excerpted from *The Asbury Park Press*, October 28, 1993

# IN the act

## BY DAVID HOCHMAN

## Book of the Mouth

**THE EVENT:** A book party-cum-mass media freak show at New York City's brand-new Harley-Davidson Cafe to whoop up *Private Parts*, Howard Stern's literary debut.

**THE BOOK:** Nearly 500 pages on the secret and should-have-been-kept-secret life of the 39-year-old nationally syndicated radio host, including his geeky early days when his overprotective mother chased after him with a rectal thermometer, the "flaming heterosexuality" of his adolescence and his achievements in radio and television, including Fartman, "The Lesbian Dating Game" and "Bobbing for Tampons." It is the best-selling book in America.

undertow of hangers-on. "If P.T. Barnum were alive today, he'd hire you at double the salary!" gushes "Amazing" TV psychic Kreskin before he, too, is pushed aside by women who want their breasts autographed by Stern. Mr. T muscles his way in for a longer audience. "He's pale, but he's a whale. He's white, but he's all right. He's a blue-eyed soul brother," raps the bejeweled poet.

**PARENTAL GUIDANCE:** Ray Stern, Howard's mom — the woman who, according to the book, raised Howard like "a veal" ("in a box with no lights on") — is never too far from her son's side at the party. "I'm very proud of him," she says, as she squeezes past Mary Jo

**America's most embarrassing celebs toast Howard Stern's chart-topping 'Private Parts'**

**HOWARD'S INFERNO:** At 6 p.m., VIPs and assorted human curiosities descend into a basement reeking of salty hors d'oeuvres and wet leather jackets — the party room dubbed Harleywood. It's a surreal commingling of slightly famous people, biker chicks, musclemen, psychics, politicians, fans, reporters and the simply strange. The piped-in thunder of engines roaring and hell-on-wheels rock nearly obliterates conversation, yet some intrepid souls still try. Ex-Mayor Ed Koch shouts to Mr. T; nearby, Rachel the Spanker, a frequent guest on Stern's program, describes her unique way of smoking cigarettes. To one side, Sen. Alfonse D'Amato nervously scrambles to avoid being photographed with a voluptuous woman in a hot-pink butt-thong. One by one, America's most embarrassing celebrities filter in, accompanied by a shower of raucous salutations: "Geraldo!" "Cheech!" "Grandpa Munster!" "Robin Leach!" "David Lee Roth!" And... "Oh my god! Joey Buttafuoco himself!" Disposable instamatics chronicle every move. "Anybody who can get me and Joey Buttafuoco in the same picture," says Geraldo, "is a great diplomat."

**THE EYE OF THE STORM:** Stern — six feet five, wearing a purple satin robe and combat boots and looking like a churlish Big Bird on a very bad-hair day — arrives at 6:30 on a leopard-skin litter, escorted by a train of perfectly proportioned bikini models. For the rest of the night, he will be floated upon a sweaty sea of bosoms and bustiers, spangles and spandex. Those who get near him are allowed just one or two words before they are swept away in an

_Private Parts_, "a self-hating megalomaniac who spends his days hiding from his family and his nights masturbating," obviously had some influence on his son. "What do you think of these women that are running around half-naked?" he asks.

**IN THE NIGHT KITCHEN:** Before long, Stern, flanked by Koch and D'Amato, is led up a back stairway through the sweltering kitchen to address a standing-room-only crowd on the main floor. But there is some confusion as the politicians are herded one way, Stern another. "Make way for Howard! Here comes King Howard!" yells the former mayor and Slim-Fast pitchman. "He takes big steps!" Pastry chefs hop for their lives, and Stern slips through the tumult to his awaiting fans. "I'm genuinely thrilled," he tells them.

**THE GOD COMPLEX:** By the end of the night, half-drunk pundits are offering their prophecies on the future of Howard Stern. "It's going to be the Marx Brothers meet the Beatles, and onward," says Jackie "The Joke Man" Martling, Stern's beer-bellied sidekick and gagman. "This guy is gonna score big," predicts Kreskin. "Two movies, I tell you!" Meanwhile, Stern, perfectly happy to share a few moments with even the most nutty-looking guests, maintains a Zen-like calm, as though enjoying the bash from on high. What's the difference tonight between Howard and God? "God," Stern says, in his best Charlton Heston voice, "is probably relaxing."

Buttafuoco. "But frankly, I've never seen anything like this." Howard's father, Ben, who turned his son into, as Howard puts it in

■

By David Hochman, from US magazine, January 1994, by US magazine Company, L.P. 1994. All rights reserved. Reprinted by permission. Photo by Gerardo Somoza.

# I GET FEEDBACK

## Putting Howard Stern's Audience on the Couch

*My fans . . . they're not idiots.*
—Howard Stern, on Tuesday's program

by DAVID KRONKE
SPECIAL TO THE TIMES

Radio surveys tell us that the typical listeners of Howard Stern are white and male. Psychologists add that they are also mad as hell.

Stern, of course, is best known for having transformed the act of slapping young women's exposed backsides to the beat of Led Zeppelin songs into a form of pubescent performance art, and for browbeating gays, women and ethnic minorities as gleefully as Pat Buchanan did at the 1992 Republican Convention.

•  •  •

Critics are violently divided on whether Stern himself is an inspired satirist leading a kicking-and-screaming America into necessary debates of difficult subjects or an ill-informed, politically rudderless buffoon hiding behind the First Amendment. But what about his fans, who are clearly numerous and extraordinarily loyal? A Nov. 1 Time magazine cover story described Stern's listeners as "people from the broad American middle-class—small-businessmen, taxi drivers, working stiffs who unapologetically enjoy action movies . . ."

Ann Panofsky, a psychologist in private practice, compared Stern's most empathetic audience members to those who likewise responded to "Falling Down," last spring's white-rage drama with Michael Douglas as the film's tragically befuddled protagonist, D-FENS.

"Both appeal to people who are feeling threatened right now," she said. "Like the character in that movie, [Stern's listeners] are feeling that women are taking over, that minorities are taking over. If they're suffering in this recession, white males enjoy hearing other groups getting knocked down when they're feeling vulnerable. Howard Stern says what they feel but feel they can't say."

Stuart Fischoff, media psychologist at Cal State Los Angeles, said that Stern himself can be compared to D-FENS, only with longer hair and cooler eyewear.

"The anger in society is similar in both characters," he said. "But it's safer to support Howard Stern than a real-life Michael Douglas character. Because it's presented with humor with Howard Stern, as opposed to the theatrical presentation in 'Falling Down,' it bypasses the usual sensibilities and social censors that society has. If I say that Mexicans are lazy cretins, you'd think, that's terrible to say something like that. But if Howard Stern tells a Mexican joke, you laugh, even if it's transmitting the same information. Humor subverts social consciousness.

"These are ugly times, and ugly times need ugly celebrities."

Linda Beal, a marriage-family-child therapist, is philosophical about Stern's anti-PC campaign. "Political correctness was something that was a long time in coming, but it tends to be terribly strident, so the reaction to it needs to be equally strident."

Fischoff said of the people he knows who listen to Stern's show, "They're all well-educated, highly paid—and they're all angry. Howard Stern taps into that anger. . . . He's tapped into a kind of moral cancer in our society, and he's working it well."

**This article says psychologists think that my fans are a bunch of frustrated angry white males. The following letters prove they're right. . . .**

DEAR HOWARD,

THE FIRST PAGE IN THE "STUTTERING JOHN" CHAPTER IN YOUR NEW BOOK IS FUNNIER THAN THAT ENTIRE RAG JERRY SEINFELD HAS RELEASED AND ALL OF HIS T.V. SHOWS COMBINED AS WELL.

THE FINEST BOOK I'VE HAD THE PLEASURE TO READ — AND PURCHASE.

---

Dear Howard,

I am a great fan—listening to your show certainly inspires a smile and at times near fatal car crashes when I can hardly drive because I am laughing so hard.

My favorite section of your book was when you were a little boy with gas pain in the city on Sundays. Nothing is worse than unexpelled gas, especially during a family outing (supposedly to have fun). I suffer from irritable bowel, lactose intolerance, and anal fissures. None of it is a picnic.

Do not ever call yourself UGLY. You may not be classically handsome but you are very cute and sensual. No need to try and hide that nose, it adds a certain charm to your face.

P.S. Since I know your need for specific facial and body characteristics:

Many people say I look like Princess Diana with dark hair and finer features. I have a model type figure, not voluptuous (36A) but elegant. I am long legged with a very pretty face.

Love you alot. Keep up the great work.

Bababooey—If you are screening this letter please be sure Howie reads it. Your are hilarious too.

I almost forgot to mention I work in Obstetrics and Gynecology (a canary factory) . . .

MR. DONALD CLARK, PRESIDENT
CALDOR DEPARTMENT STORES
20 GLOVER STREET
NORWALK, CT 06856

DEAR DONALD CLARK,

I AM SEVERING TIES WITH CALDOR DEPARTMENT STORES, AFTER MANY MANY YEARS, BY RETURNING MY CREDIT CARD TO YOU AND ASSURING YOU THAT I WILL NEVER BUY ANOTHER ARTICLE THERE AGAIN.

A SMALL PROTEST OF YOUR HEFTY ATTEMPT AT UPSETTING THE MORAL FOUNDATION OF THIS COUNTRY BY ILLEGALLY ALTERING THE NEW YORK TIMES BEST SELLER LIST. HOWARD STERN'S AUTOBIOGRAPHY HAS BEEN NUMBER ONE ON THAT LIST SINCE OCTOBER 24, 1993. I AM VERY MOVED BY HIS PLIGHT, TESTING THE LIKES OF MARKETS LIKE YOURS. CALDORS CARRIES VERY SEXUAL NOVELS WITH COVERS THAT DISPLAY WOMEN'S BREASTS BEING FONDLED BY MEN. YOU ARE ALLOWING CHILDREN TO SEE PART NAKED WOMEN BEING SWEPT AWAY BY BRUISING, HULKING MEN WHO SEEMINGLY WILL THEN TAKE ADVANTAGE OF THEM. BUT CALDORS WILL NOT CARRY A BOOK WITH A COVER OF A MAN WITHOUT A SHIRT.

I AM, AS A WOMAN, MOTHER OF A WOMAN, GRANDMOTHER OF A FUTURE WOMAN, AND DAUGHTER OF A WOMAN, DEEPLY OFFENDED BY YOUR DISREGARD FOR THE SANCTITY OF A WOMAN'S SEXUALITY. DISPLAYING SEXUALLY ACTIVE NAKED WOMEN IS NOT A PROBLEM FOR YOU. AND YOU DISPLAY THE NOVELS CARELESSLY AT EYE LEVEL FOR CHILDREN WHO WILL BE FOREVER SHAPED BY SEEING THESE WOMEN IN COMPROMISING POSITIONS.

MEN MUST NOT BE DISPLAYED IN IRREVERENT WAYS ON YOUR SHELVES. HOW VERY CONCERNED YOU ARE IN PROTECTING THE MALE MODESTY. IS AN HONEST LONE MAN WITHOUT A SHIRT SO MUCH OF AN OFFENSE TO YOU THAT YOU ARE WILLING TO COMMIT A CRIME BY CONVINCING YOUR CUSTOMERS THAT THIS MAN WITHOUT A SHIRT IS NOT THE NUMBER ONE AUTHOR IN AMERICA?

I WILL ENLIGHTEN EVERYONE ELSE I KNOW TO THIS HERESY!

*I WAS AT Barnes + Noble with my wife and daughter in Queens. The Book was sold out. But my daughter noticed a copy of it misplaced in the childrens section. She took the Book and was trying to find me in the store. And this mn took the Book away from her saying this Book is not For you. When my daughter pointed him out to me, He was on line to pay for the Book. I approached him grabbed the Book, A fight Broke out But I won...*

It's about time somebody restored life to literature. But who in their right mind would have thought it would have been you. I'm sure academia and literati have snubbed their noses at you. They better dissect Private Parts very carefully because they have served up so much slop that when I walk into a book store there's a foul stench permeating the air. The drains are clogged with genre novels taken from today's headlines. The consumers are desensitized, brainwashed and repressed. Don't get the wrong impression. I'm not saying you've got an intellectual masterpiece on your hands, but what you do have is a human document that pulsates with life, raw, naked, vulnerable, life. Add a dab of Howard Stern humor and you've got an explosion of art, a slap in the face to the world of literature, a wake up call if you will.

I can't help compare your situation to that of Henry Miller. Here's what Henry would have said about your book: "This then? This is not a book. This is libel, slander, defamation of character. This is not a book, in the ordinary sense of the word. No, this is a prolonged insult, a gob of spit in the face of Art, a kick in the pants to God, Man, Destiny, Time, Love, Beauty...." (Tropic of Cancer, Henry Miller)

# Of course, we also heard from Lesbians. . . .

Dear Howard,

I LOVE Private Parts! I read it in two nights... it was such a great read!

Howard, your lesbian stories have finally gotten to me; they have stirred up many a lesbian fantasy in my mind. My roommate was looking through the Gina chapter. She commented about how she couldn't believe she would let nude photos be published. I told her that I was glad they got published because the photos were HOT! My roommate casually said "Yeh, she's a turn on." One thing I know she's all over me. Neither my roommate nor I had ever had a lesbian experience, but our clothes were off in about 3 seconds. Her 36-Cs felt so good against my 34-Cs. I licked and kissed every inch of her body. It was the most fabulous sex in the world, and I've been with my boyfriend for over a year. THANK YOU HOWARD!

I just now finished reading your book.
It only made me more confused about why
I am a fan of yours. You are such a "man"
that its sickening - but yet I love it!
I've been listening to your show for about
2 years. I used to masturbate to it all
the time. Now that I've finished the book
I have alot of new fantasies that should
keep me occupied for a while!

My favorite part of the book was
your segment with ~~Path Davis~~ Reagan. I
absolutely loved how you explained your methods
of tying a woman up. I nearly creamed myself!
I would love for that to happen to me, only with
another woman. All of my fantasies revolve around
women. I've never actually been with one - but
they're everywhere in my fantasies! When I
close my eyes and start fingering myself - I
picture a gorgeous girl with huge tits
eating me out with her long soft tongue.

I like to look at women with big
tits. (That ~~gets~~ me hot.) Not too big though, I
wear a 38D and I think anything much bigger
than that looks sloppy.

I would just like to say that
before I listened to your show - I was
embarrassed that I fantasize about having
sex with other women. But now I know that
it's okay - and I'll bet every other woman does
it too whether they'll admit it or not!

So if you know any~~one~~ women who
want to tie me up so that I can experience
my first lesbian love affair - let me know.
I'd also love to be watched as it happened -
That puts more of a thrill into it!

God - I'm so horny now!

**Now here's a fun game you can try at home.**

Howard,

Read the book, it was great! The first picture I whacked off to was the picture of Allison's feet on page 101, twice!

Although I don't think you're into it, foot fetish is more popular than most people admit to, and is pretty harmless.

Please, more bare feet on your shows in the future. How about putting one of those models in a stock on New Years and playing her feet like a fiddle, with a feather. Or a milder, footworship segment.

**And from the "You Can't Please Everyone" department — a little negative feedback.**

$23.00 FOR THAT PIECE OF SHIT PHOTO ALBUM

NO WAY JEWBOY

**That's half Jewboy to you!**

DEAR HOWARD,

YOU SUCK! I WROTE A LETTER TO YOU AND YOUR GREEN-TOOTHED MONKEY OF AN ASSISTANT, ASKING IF I COULD BRING OR MAIL 3 COPIES OF YOUR BOOK TO BE SIGNED.

NEEDLESS TO SAY, I RECEIVED NO RESPONSE. WELL, LET ME TELL YOU SOMETHING

MY NEW YEAR'S WISH FOR YOU IS THAT YOU GO DOWN IN FLAMES BIG TIME. I HOPE YOU GO DOWN THE DRAIN WITH ALL THOSE DUMB MACHO LOWER MIDDLE CLASS PIGS WHOSE POCKETS YOU RELISH PICKING.

I WILL NEVER PURCHASE ANYTHING FROM YOU AGAIN. I WILL NOT SEE YOUR MOVIE (I'M SURE IT WILL STINK) NOR PATRONIZE YOUR SPONSORS.

YOU BURNED ME AND NOW I CAN'T STAND YOU. GOODBYE MR STERN. GOOD LUCK AND DROP. DEAD.

**Just 'cause I didn't sign his book, now I suck.**

I've been reading the lesbian stories in your book and they were so hot that I had to put the book down and do you know what. This is the most awesome book I've ever read. It is ten times better than what John Grisham or Anne Rice writes. This is something that is worth the $23.00. This has to be your crowning achievement.

You are truly the King of All Media and if anyone disagrees, then they can kiss your ass.

Howard,

I can't believe I'm even wasting a stamp on you, but your book got so boring, I had to put it down.

your a jerk. Do you know that?

You're so dam proud of your book; well did you have a professional or that dumb blond bimbo you mention in your book proofread your book?

Turn to page 250. Now, go down to the line where it says "Let's call Australia, boy Moron. well, where the hell are the closing Quotation marks? Do you have them on your copy? because I don't have ~~too~~ them on mine!! And you're book is on the best seller list?

~~And 1 more thing~~ You asshole The reason you don't cheat on your wife is not because you love her. ~~This is really~~ ~~and~~ You couldn't cheat on her - ~~you~~ because if you did you'd be screwed professionaly and financially. She'd get you for all you have. You're actually a horny prisoner. You'd know you'd like to be with 2 maybe 10 women at one time but you can't (your a prisoner) ~~Because~~ if you did you'd be ruined! Allison would write a book about the Real Howard - She'd tell every one how small your penis really is. And you know what - it would be an even bigger best seller than your stupid book. And it would probably have the proper punctuation marks you jerk!

~~Your newest fan~~

Dear Howard!

After reading your wonderful book "Private Parts", I am still very depressed. You never tell us if you piss straight in an arc or in circles. Do you hold your penis in your right or left hand or do you just open your fly and let him do his job without bothering him? How many buttons do you have to open in your pants to piss without inconvinience? What is the color of your kaka and what is its consistency and weight?

Howard--

I read your book (it was a Christmas present), laughing all the way. But you did leave an important question unanswered, namely:

Have you ever gotten a woodie while holding one of your daughters in your lap?

# HOWARD STERN—POP ICON

*"She's the muse for Howard Stern's new book."*

HOWARD STERN'S "Private Parts"
(3) Autographed. $500 Each.

LOST in a Drawer? Gathering Dust

accepted. Call PUTNAM COUNTY HUMANE SOCIETY IN CARMEL, XXX-XXX-XXXX

HOWARD STERN COLLECTORS BOOK " Private Parts" autographed by Howard
Stern, $700. XXX-XXX-XXXX

PENNYSAVER CLASSIFIED CUSTOMERS
TAKE ADVANTAGE OF OUR EXTENDED HOURS! Pennysaver doors and

## #1 ON THE CONGRESSIONAL LIST

From *The New York Times* crossword puzzle to police blotters, the book was everywhere . . . including *The National Enquirer.*

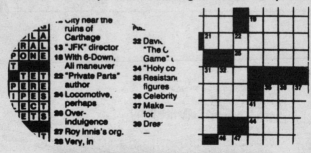

...City near the ruins of Carthage
13 "JFK" director
18 With 6-Down, Ali maneuver
22 "Private Parts" author
24 Locomotive, perhaps
26 Over-indulgence
27 Roy Innis's org.
29 Very, in

32 Davi...
"The ...
Game" ...
34 "Holy co...
35 Resistan...
figures
36 Celebrity...
37 Make —
for
39 Dres...
—

**POLICE BLOTTER**

**Tinton Falls**

Someone broke into a residence Oct.28 and stole and stole the book "Private Parts" by Howard Stern valued at $17.95.

# NATIONAL ENQUIRER

October 19, 1993

$1.25/$1.29 CANADA

**LARGEST CIRCULATION OF ANY PAPER IN AMERICA**

# Radio's raunchy wild man Howard Stern confesses: I'm really a henpecked husband

America's top shock-jock Howard Stern is the most outrageous personality on radio — but off the air he's a "henpecked" family man who gladly lets his wife rule the roost.

The syndicated radio host, who has 15 million listeners, even lets his wife dictate what he says on the show!

Stern's raunchy antics — which have included vivid descriptions of strippers peeling off their clothes in his studio — are so way out, he's triggered more than $1 million in FCC fines in the past five years.

But he's a real-life Jekyll and Hyde — when the show's over, Stern turns from wild man into mild-mannered homebody!

"I like to be a regular guy with my wife and kids, cooking burgers in the yard," Stern revealed in an exclusive ENQUIRER interview.

## 'I love to help out in the kitchen & read stories to the kids'

"I love to play games with the children, help out in the kitchen and read the kids stories."

Instead of all-night parties, the bad boy of broadcasting, prefers to spend quiet evenings watching TV.

"People visit and are surprised to find me so domesticated — they expect me to be shocking at home, too," he said. "I'm almost a hermit. I hate to go out."

Stern — who has a bigger audience than even Oprah Winfrey — admits his wife Alison "is the boss at home" and describes himself as a "henpecked husband."

His wife's say-so also carries a lot of weight when it comes to the radio show.

"When that phone rings at the studio and it's Alison on the line I know I've gone too far," he chuckled. "I have to back off.

"If I've been getting hot and

BAD BOY Howard Stern, who's just written a book about his life, lives up to his outrageous image by wearing the outfit above at a video awards show. At left: Howard on his wedding day 15 years ago. At right: Howard relaxing with wife Alison and one of their three children.

heavy with some girl in the studio, Alison picks up the phone and tells me to cool it. She tells me I'm embarrassing her in front of her friends who listen to the show."

Stern's on-air frolics with beautiful girls and his frank revelations about intimate details of his marriage sometimes infuriate his wife.

"There've been times when Alison started thumbing through the yellow pages looking for a divorce lawyer," admits the gangly, long-haired Stern, 39.

And no wonder! He once even joked on the air about a miscarriage Alison suffered — blaming it on his own drug use.

"I did a bit about God punishing me for doing LSD in the 60s.

"She went ballistic on me and

screamed, 'You're a moron!'"

The New York-based radio star is a vigilant dad. He won't let his three young daughters listen to his program — because it's too racy.

"I'm talking to adults," explains Stern, who also hosts an interview program on the cable entertainment channel E!

The master of shock — who's written a new book about his life, "Howard Stern: Private Parts" — is proud his

marriage has lasted 15 years.

"Alison puts up with all my craziness because she loves me," he explains.

"Where am I ever going to find another woman like that?" — STEVE COZ

## Me-owch! The high cost of owning a cat

It costs a whopping $475 per year to own a cat. That price includes $185 for foods and treats, $150 for litter, $35 for routine medical care, $30 for toys and $25 for grooming supplies, according to The New York Times.

## Quotes of the week

"I thought I'd come to the time of my life when I'd ease up a bit — but this business is so seductive." — Gene Hackman, 62

"Bruce and my children are my No. 1 priority. I work everything around them." — Mrs. Bruce Springsteen (Patti Scialfa)

"I've been through every-

thing that success breeds — from cars, to boats, to women, to money and to an entourage of hangers-on. I've gone through it all despite the fact that I swore I never would. Success is like a drug. Before I knew it, I was hooked." — Sylvester Stallone

"I certainly loved my

mother and my aunts and sisters . . . but I never had any intention of being like them when I grew up, living by those kind of rules. I never planned on staying home with kids, devoted to one man." — Dolly Parton

"I'm not so ready to punch people out as I used to be." — Mick Jagger

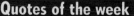

Copyright © 1993 National Enquirer Inc.

**People had to defend their books from theft . . .**

# Bx. man, 93, KOs intruder

**By JOSE LAMBIET**
Daily News Staff Writer

One minute, 93-year-old Ole Thorsen was relaxing in his rocking chair, slippers on his feet.

The next, he was using the same slippers and a broomstick to clobber an intruder who was duking it out with a neighbor.

"I don't fight usually," he said yesterday, just hours after he helped arrest a man who police said is also being questioned in a dozen burglaries in Thorsen's and neighboring buildings. "I kicked the guy in the head, but I was wearing soft slippers, so he barely felt it."

In all likelihood, Santiago Carosco, 36, of Livingston Ave., the Bronx, will remember Thorsen's four-story apartment building in the Woodlawn section of the Bronx.

Carosco allegedly entered the E. 237th St. building about 10 a.m. and walked to the top floor, residents said last night. There, he reportedly knocked on the door of John Kelly, 35, a Metro North Commuter Railroad electrician.

Kelly said he opened the door and saw a man who fit the description of a burglar

READY FOR ALL COMERS: 93-year-old Ole Thorsen shows the form that left intruder Santiago Carosco, 36, reportedly one of the hands on the spot.

police say may be responsible for a dozen burglaries in Woodlawn. Kelly confronted Carosco about it and the suspect allegedly lunged at Kelly.

"I was drinking coffee and reading the Howard Stern book," said Kelly. "I was having a good time and the next thing I know, I'm fighting with this guy. He just caught me at a bad time."

While fighting, the two men rolled down the stairs to the third floor and landed in front of Thorsen's door.

"I heard people in the hallway screaming bloody murder," explained Thorsen, who emigrated to America from Norway in 1922. "I open the door and I see my neighbor grappling with a man on the floor. So I grabbed the broomstick and hit the guy."

Hard enough to break the stick in half.

• • •

. . . and I even became a Trivial Pursuit answer! Now my life's complete.

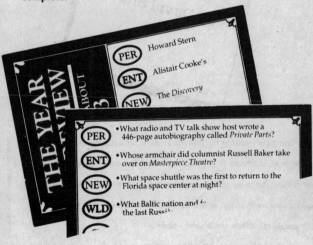

THE YEAR REVIEW 3 ABOUT

(PER) Howard Stern

(ENT) Alistair Cooke's

(NEW) The Discovery

(PER) • What radio and TV talk show host wrote a 446-page autobiography called *Private Parts*?

(ENT) • Whose armchair did columnist Russell Baker take over on *Masterpiece Theatre*?

(NEW) • What space shuttle was the first to return to the Florida space center at night?

(WLD) • What Baltic nation and f̶ the last Russi̶

**Students everywhere benefited from all of the important knowledge on these pages. I understand anal fissures are down 10 percent thanks to my tips on wiping.**

PRIVATE PARTS
Book Report
by David Shaw

This book, written by Howard Stern, is an autobiography describing his life from childhood to present day. He tells about his youth, which was difficult because of racial differences in his neighborhood. He worked very hard to get where he is today, a famous radio personality with excellent ratings and a vast audience.

In his earlier years, his father was somewhat abusive, and his mother was always worrying about her son, both which made his childhood an unpleasant one. In his teenage life, he was a loner that followed the crowd, but to no avail, as he was still unpopular. As he got older, he had many jobs in radio, small ones, with little pay. He was married to his wife Allison ~~inns~~ *later*. His first real job was with WNBC, which he enjoyed at first

but it became a struggle with executives trying to change his radio
format.

This book has many themes, and I will try to list them all. First, if
you work very hard, you will most likely be successful and find happiness.
Second, don't let other people get in your way. Third, most people are
reasonable, and if they give you a hard time, it isn't always your fault.
Fourth, don't get discouraged if you can't find a job you like. Eventually,
you will find something better, and if you don't just work hard at your job
no matter how much you hate it. Fifth, be creative. This characteristic
can impress people and help you gain respect. But mainly, his point is
don't take life too seriously. Have fun. Lighten up. It will make life much
more pleasant.

This book was a very rewarding experience. I thought it would be a book
that had no underlying meaning, and it was just a long joke. What I found
was just the opposite: interesting, serious, but it still kept the reader
laughing.

*IT'S HARD NOT TO LAUGH AT HOWARD, EVEN THOUGH HE GOES WAY TOO FAR FOR MY TASTES SOMETIMES.*

*THIS IS AN EXCELLENT REPORT. I LIKE YOUR ABILITY TO PICK UP AND COMMUNICATE THE THEMES IN THE BOOK.*

*FOR WHAT IT'S WORTH, I THINK HOWARD WOULD BE PROUD!*

## PICTURE CREDITS

Pages 333, 334, 336, 338: Jeff Kravitz

Page 349 (bottom): Courtesy of Melrose Larry Green

Page 368: Courtesy of Gary Dell'Abate

Pages 350 (left), 397, 404, 407, 436 (middle): Ralph Cirella

Page 422: Courtesy of Howard Stern and Fred Norris

Page 423: Courtesy of Jackie Martling and Gary Dell'Abate

Page 427: Courtesy of Stacy Galina

Page 435: Neil Drake

Page 443: Danny deBruin

Page 458: Reprinted with permission. Copyright 1988 NATIONAL EN-
QUIRER INC.

Page 497: E! Entertainment Television/Chris Haston

Page 501: Tom Vollick, Courtesy of Gold's Gym

Pages 519, 520, 521, 523: Courtesy of Gina Rose

Pages 538 (bottom), 544: Courtesy of John Melendez

Page 560: Jack Ohman. Reprinted by permission of Tribune Media Services

Page 569: Denise Sfraga

Page 572: David Miller, syndicated cartoonist and frequent listener

Pages 574, 581: Rex Babin, *Times-Union* (Albany, New York). Reprinted
with permission